ENCYCLOPEDIA
MADONNICA

MATTHEW RETTENMUND

ENCYCLOPEDIA MADONNICA

ST. MARTIN'S PRESS
NEW YORK, N.Y.

Design and page layout by MM Design 2000, Inc.
Color insert collages designed by MM Design 2000, Inc.

Library of Congress Cataloging-in-Publication Data

Rettenmund, Mathew.
      Encyclopedia Madonnica: Madonna—the woman and the icon—from A to Z/Mathew Rettenmund.
          p.   cm.
      ISBN 0-312-11782-5
      1. Madonna, 1958–   —Encyclopedias.
ML420.M1387R48   1995
782.42166'092—dc20   94-48309
      [B]   CIP
                                                             MN

First edition: April 1995
10 9 8 7 6 5 4 3
A Thomas Dunne Book

This book is dedicated

to my mother,

who taught me how to prey.

ACKNOWLEDGMENTS

Special thanks to the following people for their support and their invaluable contributions to this book: Christine Aebi, Chris America, Reagan Arthur, Ana Aulina/*Cosmopolitan Spain*, Mariam Ayub, Nancy Barr-Brandon, Glen Bassett/*In Touch For Men*, Staffan Berg, Michel Birnbaum/*French Penthouse*, Paolo Bonanni/*Italian Max*, Sandra J. Brant and Lisa B. Overton/*Interview*, Nancy Burson, Stephen Caraco, Robbie Charrier, José Luis Cordoba/*Playboy España*, The Council of Fashion Designers of America, Charles Criscuolo/Flashback Collectibles (Chicago), Eric Colmet Daage/*Photo*, Keith Davies, Antonio de Felipe, A. Degenhard and Thorsten Ungefronen/*German Max*, Daryl Deino, Francesco De Vincentis, Delory Didier, Karen J. Dolan, Sebastien Dolidon, Kate Duffy and Matt Hanna/*Spin*, David Dunton, Rodney Dyksman, Steve Eichner, Brad Elterman, Sandra Engle and Paul Borysewicz, Alex Escarano, Alex Eulen, Twisne Fan, J. J. Fenza, Miranda Ford, Laurie Fox/*French Elle*, Peter Fressola/Benetton, Andrew D. Gans/Playbill Incorporated, Matthew Garcia, Teresa Gibson, Allen Ginsberg and Peter Hale, Globe Photos, Julie Grahame/Retna, Romain Grandveaud, E. B. Hallett/Time Inc. Magazine Co. Pty. Ltd., Eryk Hanut and Cynthia A. Cannell, Mike Hardwick/*Time Out*, Joe Harris, Nancy Hirsch, Nicole C. Hughes/London Features International, Suzohito Imai and Yastaka Sasaki/Shueisha, JEFFOTO, Harry M. Johnston III/Time Inc., Jill Jones, Terry Jones/*I.D.*, Derek Kay, Marguerite Kramer/*Harper's Bazaar*, Yasuko Kuse, Joseph A. Lawrence, Sauro Legramandi, Olivier Le Guinguis, Martine Leoni, Robert H. Levine/Sotheby's, Barbara Lewis, Greg Lugliani/Gay Men's Health Crisis, Howard Mandelbaum/Photofest, Chris Marquez, Moto Matsushita/*Flix*, Luca Mautone, Zafar Mawani, Giulio Mazzoleni, J. V. McAuley/*The Advocate*, Brian McCloud, Patrick McMullan, Elizabeth McNamara, Roberta Meenahan/*Australian Rolling Stone*, Steve Meyers/Mia Mind Music, Bill Miller/*Autograph Collector*, Robert A. Moon, Robin Muir, Dean Mullaney/Eclipse Enterprises, Laura Mullen, John Murphy, Michael Musto and Ava Seave/*Village Voice*, Christopher Noble/Noble Works (Hoboken, NJ), Linda O'Brien (for bearing with me), Mick O'Reilly/*In Dublin*, Panos Pitsillides,/KAIK, John Radziewicz, Juan Ramos, Monica Rebosio, Eric Renet/*Esquire*, Linda Rettenmund, Melissa Rettenmund, Ken Riel, Amy Routman, Patrizio Russo, Ramon Santos, Oliviu Savu, Julius F. Scott, *Sette*, Richard Settes/*Genre*, Michael Shulman/Archive Photos, Louise Smith/*Satellite TV Europe*, Cynthia Tebbel/*Australian New Woman*, Gloria Ubardelli, Giuseppe Videtti/*Rockstar*, Denise Vlasis, Katie Webb/*Sky*, Pete and Linda Weinzettl, Kelly Worts/*The Face*, Tim Wright, Denis Xamin, Andreas Zeffer, Karen J. Ziffra/*Playboy*, Jaye Zimet, and to everyone—especially Madonna's funky fans—who have expressed enthusiasm and given assistance along the way.

Extra-special thanks to my fearless editor Thomas L. Dunne and his persistent associate Peter Wolverton, and to their assistant Neal Bascomb.

Thanks and love to my ruthless-agent-with-a-heart-of-gold, Jane Jordan Browne, and her team of crackerjacks: Danielle Egan-Miller, Brad Masoni, and Viney Daley.

Immaculate gratitude to Mauro Bramati, Lori DeVito, Evan Gaffney, André Grossmann, Michael Mendelsohn, and Fred Seidman for helping to make this book look as gorgeous and unique as it does.

And thanks to Madonna, whom I've never met. I hope I got a few things right.

- Names and titles sometimes appear as initials within the text of their own entries. Example: "'**This Used to be My Playground**': As a song, 'TUTBMP' is considered . . .", or "**Haring, Keith**: KH is an artist . . .", and so on.

- All words in **bold** are cross-references to other entries in the book. If an entry title appears more than once within the body of another entry, only its first instance will appear in bold type.

- Quotes include years unless they originated in the same year as the event to which they are attached. Example: *True Blue* is a 1986 album, so all reviews quoted can be assumed to have originated in 1986.

"*People will laugh at this, but many, many artists we now hold in high regard today, were actually considered vulgar* schlock *in their day, and yet they have stayed throughout the years. And these tend to be the people who touched millions of people, not academics, but actually other* people. *And that, I believe, is what will happen to Madonna."*

—Alek Keshishian, 1991

.

"*I'm normal height. I have a normal figure. I don't sing any better than other people. In fact, there isn't anything on the outside of me that is in any way abnormal. I think it's what's underneath, on the inside, that's not normal."*

—Madonna, 1985

INTRODUCTION

I can't bring myself to write one of those tired introductory essays on who Madonna *is* and what she *means*.

I think an author should use an introduction to communicate to readers how exactly to approach the book that follows, not to hype the subject even more. The *last* first impression I wanted to make was one that started with that notoriously familiar sentence, "Madonna Louise Veronica Ciccone was born . . ."

So, I'll give it to you straight.

Madonna once waffled that *Sex* shouldn't be taken so seriously . . . but that then again, it *should*. That's my approach in *Encyclopedia Madonnica*; take Madonna's work and my readings of her work seriously, but don't forget that Madonna's greatest contribution to international culture is *fun*.

Have fun!

Matthew Rettenmund
New York City, NY

Abdul, Paula: Madonna offered some tart advice to this stubby dance diva on the eve of Abdul's first tour (1991): "If she's really trying to sing for real for the first time, then she should stand still, you know? 'Cause it's really difficult unless you're in amazing shape."

When Abdul was slapped with an unsuccessful **lawsuit** by a backup singer claiming she had ghosted Abdul's vocals, cold-hearted Madonna couldn't resist teasing. On **MTV**'s 10th anniversary TV special (1991), Madonna mimicked a sobbing Abdul, whining, "I *did* sing on that record . . . I'll prove it to you," then launching into a comically strained scales exercise. Abdul was used to the abuse—Madonna had already embarrassed her (1990) by quizzing **Arsenio Hall** on their relationship, intimating that Hall had left Abdul's tights askew backstage at the American Music Awards.

SEE ALSO: **WANNA-BE**

abortion: Let's not waste any time getting to the fun subjects. Though Madonna's appearance and attitude were scandals from the beginning, the first true Madonna Scandal™ had to do with abortion. In the song **"Papa Don't Preach,"** "keep my baby" could refer to the singer's keeping her **lover** or carrying her **pregnancy** to term. In the video, there is no question that the singer is nixing abortion: Madonna grasps her abdomen protectively while **singing** the line. Reactions to the song were mixed and emotionally charged.

Ex-Madonna crony **Erica Bell** says Madonna had at least three abortions while she was dating **Jellybean**, one of which allegedly occurred just before the **Virgin Tour** kickoff. Madonna was reportedly forced to terminate a problem pregnancy at Cedars-Sinai Hospital in Los Angeles in late 1990, and biographer **Christopher Andersen** gallantly names Randy Harris as the specialist who recommended and performed the procedure. The latter abortion would have taken place while Madonna was involved with **Tony Ward**. During two separate *Truth or Dare*—era interviews, Madonna said of her lack of **privacy** that she sometimes

"*S*he's great, but that doesn't make her perfect, and as tendentious as it may be to speculate about how her mixed messages might affect her multifarious audience, it's nevertheless empowering, so to speak, to resist the gravitational pull of her thereness and adjudge this bit fabulous and that bit lame and the one over there provocative yet problematic."

—Robert Christgau, *The Village Voice,* 1991

feels like the whole world even knows "when I have an abortion."

Before a Madison Square Garden **Girlie Show,** Gloria Steinem gave Madonna two bracelets, one inscribed with the names of women who died as a result of botched illegal abortions, and one engraved, *Because of you, there will be fewer of these.* The right to choose abortion is within the Madonna credo of individual rights, but she did not, for what it's worth, attend the Voters for Choice benefit staged at the Garden directly following her show.

SEE ALSO: **MISCARRIAGE**

academia: With the rise of popular culture as a social science, Madonna has crept into college curricula and scholarly writing as a cultural phenomenon to reckon with. The University of Colorado at Boulder started the ball rolling with a course called "Madonna Undressed," dealing with issues of body language, costuming, gender, **spectator** response, postmodernism, and gay and lesbian imagery.

Institutions as far-flung as Harvard, Florida State University, the University of Chicago, and Wayne State University have offered courses devoted to Madonna's influence on pop culture. Any complete course on popular culture or contemporary **feminism** since the early nineties touches on Madonna's **video** and musical **work**. Of her films, *Desperately Seeking Susan* and *Who's That Girl* are most frequently dissected by scholars desperately seeking Madonna's appeal, and her ability to strike a nerve at will.

The concept amuses Madonna, though she has made it clear that many of the abstract intentions laid at her feet by scholars are figments of their imaginations as far as she's concerned. But then, Madonna scholarship is a field that does not require Madonna's input or her express intent to validate its findings. Whether or not Madonna meant to make a feminist statement in **"Express Yourself"** matters little to the scholars; more important is how the video was interpreted by the public.

In 1992, *The Madonna Connection,* an entire book on Madonna scholarship, was published to tie in with *Sex.* Six months later, Cleis Press published a book of essays on **sex** and popular culture, *Madonnarama,* featuring pieces by Susie Bright, Pat Califia, Simon Frith, and many others.

SEE ALSO: **APPENDIX 5 (BIBLIOGRAPHY)**

accent: Madonna's is pure **Midwest**; listen for it in the flat *a*.

She has put on a variety of accents for fun and profit, and frequently slips into Brooklyn-tough-girl talk for comedic effect. In the film ***Who's That Girl,*** she murders her own performance with a daffy version of that accent, but silly speech has worked in sketches on her **Blond Ambition tour** and in the songs "Cry Baby" and "Now I'm Following You (Part II)" on ***I'm Breathless.***

Her most impressive use of accent was on the "Coffee Talk" sketch from **"Saturday Night Live,"** where she employed a Yiddish accent so convincingly that, coupled with her costume, she was unrecognizable by sight or sound.

She attempted a British accent playing **Princess Diana of Wales** on her first "SNL" appearance, but more bizarre is her histrionic Spanish accent, also unveiled on that first "SNL." It showed up again on her instant **camp** classic, "I'm Going Bananas."

"It's either Queens or Bronx, I'm not sure. I just made it up in my head."

—Madonna on her *Who's That Girl* accent, 1987

accommodations: Where to stay when one is the world's biggest star? Crash with friends? Slip the front desk guy a fiver to get you a room at the Howard Johnson's? *Au contraire,* Madonna always shacks up at world-class establishments when she's traveling. When in **New York,** Los Angeles, or **Miami Beach,** Madonna needs look no further than **home** sweet home: She has digs in all three cities. When Madonna visits her **father** and **stepmother** in **Rochester Hills, Michigan,** she stays with them, often on the floor in a sleeping bag. On tour in Detroit, she has stayed at the quaint St. Regis.

In Chicago, she has graced both the Ritz-Carlton (in which Oprah Winfrey has a permanent residence) and the Four Seasons while on tour and while filming *A League of Their Own.* Also during the *League* shoot, Madonna had to spend time in **Evansville, Indiana,** where she and other cast members took over separate private houses.

In London, she favors the £3,000-a-night Lanesborough: She stayed in the royal suite while **Girlie Show**-ing off. Madonna usually stays at the Ritz when in Paris, though she opted for the Royal Monceau while shooting her **"Justify My Love"** video in 1990. For her first tour of Australia in 1994, she hung her top hat at the Hyatt International.

Madonna may have excellent taste in lodgings, but don't expect her to overpay. She is known to personally inspect every hotel bill in search of phony services attached to pricey fees.

If you'd like to drop in on Madonna while she's in town, give it up. No hotel hosting Madonna will admit to it for fear of a deluge of callers.

The Lanesborough provided the following luxuries to Madonna for her 1993 Girlie Show stay: three double bedrooms, a drawing room, a kitchen, a small dining room, a **gym,** around-the-clock butler service, a Bentley and driver, a safe, a private **fax,** personalized calling cards, and 5,000 CDs and videos for her entertainment.

ACT-UP (AIDS Coalition to Unleash Power): Controversial, radical **AIDS** awareness group whose by-the-balls tactics—which include disrupting mass at St. Patrick's Cathedral—seem to appeal to Madonna's own modus operandi. In her 1991 *Advocate* interview, when asked if she was for ACT-UP or against them, she chirped, "I'm for 'em." She also issued a joint press release with the group, urging **condom** distribution in **New York City** public schools.

acting: Will she ever give it up? To the disappointment of some filmgoers and critics, the answer is an emphatic "No!" Madonna has been involved in acting far longer than she has in **singing,** and it's obvious she enjoys the performance aspect of her music more than the actual belting.

Madonna starred in **plays** in high school, and from her earliest interviews has referred to herself as an actress. She is not a singer who tried her hand at acting (like Elvis, **Prince, Michael**

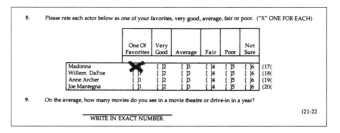

Some Body of Evidence *audiences were handed this questionnaire asking them to rate Madonna's acting.*

"*A*cting is just another kind of performing. It's just an expression, it's just being honest with your audience. So to me it's just an extension of what I do already."

—Madonna, 1984

•

"*S*he has no real sense of herself yet, so she can't be a really good actress."

—Shelley Winters, 1990

•

"*W*hat's a 'trained' actress? I think that in living the life I live I've paid my dues."

—Madonna, 1986

•

"*T*o me, a script is a skeleton that I have liked enough to hang my skin on."

—Madonna, 1985

•

"*T*he . . . whole process of being a brushstroke in someone else's painting is a little difficult."

—Madonna of her *Shadows and Fog* experience, 1992

•

"*I* think she has the potential to be a great movie star and she even has the potential to become a really good actress. She's not a *bad* actress now."

—Leonard Maltin, "Entertainment Tonight" film critic, 1993

Quest to *Dangerous Game*. But can she *act?* Madonna's acting matches her surroundings, so that if the script's lousy, or the direction weak, her performance suffers accordingly. But give her great material and she performs superbly. The ultimate chameleon!

Madonna's most credible acting is in her **videos,** most of which are short films in which she plays a variety of parts. Standout video performances include **"Papa Don't Preach,"** where she is extremely convincing as a pregnant teenager, and **"Bad Girl,"** where she mops up the screen as a **sex**-addicted career woman.

On film, Madonna's best acting is as *femme fatale* **"Breathless Mahoney"** in *Dick Tracy* and as *femme banale* "Sarah Jennings" in *Dangerous Game*. Madonna's a crackling comedienne, so her celebrated **"Saturday Night Live"** television appearances have all been winning, and her stage presence packed in audiences to see *Speed-the-Plow* on Broadway.

The worst? Well, she was *dreadful* in *Shanghai Surprise* and not so hot in *Body of Evidence,* and videowise, her clunkiest gestures are in **"Like a Prayer,"** where she mouths, "He didn't do it!" so broadly it reminds one of a cat coughing up a hairball.

As far as public opinion goes, acting is Madonna's weakest talent: She's won more "Worst Actress" polls than Susan Lucci has lost Daytime Emmys. This is particularly frustrating to Madonna-friendly critics like former *New York Times* film critic Vincent Canby, who see the potential but wince at the fumbly delivery.

It ain't over till it's over. Look for some knock-down, drag-out performances before old age encroaches, and many more thereafter.

SEE ALSO: **Appendices 2, 3, 4**

activism: In addition to her tireless **AIDS** activism, Madonna has lent her name, time, and services to several causes. To her credit, she never flaunts her good deeds the way some of her peers do.

Madonna's earliest charity effort may have been involvement in Help-a-Kid, a Big Sisters–like program she participated in during high school. Somewhere out there is a woman whose "Big Sister" turned out to be *Madonna*.

In 1985, Mr. and Mrs. **Sean Penn**—insisting on a "no publicity" policy—visited Cornell Medical Center at New York Hospital's pediatric wing, where they played Santa and Mrs. Claus for terminally ill children. Madonna spoke at a press conference in 1988 to raise awareness of Sport Aid, an international run against worldwide hunger.

In 1989, friends convinced her of the serious nature of the

"*I*f I dared to tell the whole truth, I'd have to say that the **Material Girl** has a heart of gold."

—Michael J. Klingensmith, Publisher, *Entertainment Weekly*, 1991

Jackson, or **Diana Ross**), but an actress whose singing career has rightfully superseded her acting career.

Madonna's first agent, **Camille Barbone,** sent her off to acting lessons with coach Mira Rostova, who hated Madonna's guts at first sight. After only one session, their association was dissolved. "This girl will never be an actress," Rostova spat. "She is too vulgar and she thinks she knows it all. Besides, I do not like her."

Madonna acted in *A Certain Sacrifice* before she had a record deal, and has regularly appeared in films from *Vision* depletion of the Brazilian rain forest, which resulted in her cohosting **Don't Bungle the Jungle.**

The flashiest, least sincere of causes she's endorsed is voting, which she plugged with two fun public service announcements in 1990 and 1992 as part of **Rock the Vote.**

Madonna has donated dozens of personal objects to charity auctions, including a chair she once sat on, to the Greater Chicago Food Depository; the **Blond Ambition** bed she mock-masturbated on, to UNICEF; a **Who's That Girl tour** bustier, to Project Children ("Tits for tots?"); a leather bomber jacket to the New York Gay Community Service Center; even an autographed blouse, to Tappan Zee Playhouse in Nyack, New York.

Aside from charity endeavors, Madonna's most strident activism has been of the social variety. She is an outspoken advocate of individual rights and choice, specifically the equality of women, gay rights, **sex**ual freedom, and **self-expression.**

actors, favorite: As of 1993, she had *none.* In a Brazilian interview, Madonna blanked on any favorite/sexiest actors, saying that she couldn't think of any. She thinks Kevin Costner's pretty *neat,* though . . .

SEE ALSO: "Vogue" song, "Vogue" video

actresses, favorite: Two of Madonna's favorite actresses are Jessica Lange and Susan Sarandon. Sarandon happens to be a former fling of **Sean Penn**'s who showed up at the premiere of *Truth or Dare* with high praises for both Madonna and movie.

Other actresses Madonna has listed as favorites include Brigitte Bardot, **Marlene Dietrich**, Greta Garbo, Grace Kelly, Ann-Margret, and **Marilyn Monroe,** not necessarily in that order.

SEE ALSO: sources, "Vogue" song, "Vogue" video

Advil: Non-aspirin wonder pill that stops headaches dead. Madonna takes three of these right before she has her legs waxed.

SEE ALSO: depilation

agoraphobia: The irrational fear of being in public. Shockingly, Madonna once suffered from a form of this phobia, right after the **death** of her **mother.** She recalls that from the age of six until the age of eight, she would grow nauseated and often vomit whenever she left the house for any length of time.

It's safe to say that Madonna has made a complete recovery.

AIDS (Acquired Immune Deficiency Syndrome): Fatal viral disease that destroys the immune system. Millions worldwide have died of AIDS, and many millions more are living with AIDS and HIV, the virus hypothesized to cause AIDS.

Madonna arrived in **New York City** a few years before the discovery of AIDS. AIDS (called "gay cancer" at first, for its prevalence among **gay men**) made New York its epicenter, and since Madonna's circle of friends has always been top-heavy with gays, she has lost some of her most beloved friends to the disease.

Madonna's best friend was her roommate, designer **Martin Burgoyne,** whom Madonna supported emotionally and financially throughout his battle with the disease. **Andy Warhol** recorded, in his diaries, Madonna's unself-conscious affection toward Martin as the two shared a leg-shaped piece of chocolate **candy**: "It was kind of great to see Madonna eating the leg, too, and not caring that she might catch something. Martin would bite and then Madonna would bite." And this at a time when most people were quite irrational in their fear of catching AIDS. Speaking of irrational, **Sean Penn** was especially annoyed with his wife's casual proximity to AIDS.

Howard Brookner, Madonna's *Bloodhounds of Broadway* director, died of AIDS before that film was released, and she was one of the only acquaintances in whom he had confided. Madonna later lost her friends **Keith Haring** and **Christopher Flynn** to AIDS.

Madonna herself is at risk for AIDS. So is any other sexually active human being. She decreases her risk by using **condoms**, though she confessed in *Esquire* (1994) that she has had unprotected sex on rare occasions. She initially refused to be tested for HIV, citing the common reason that if she were going to die she wouldn't want to know, but she quickly got some education and has been tested regularly for years.

As **sex** and AIDS have become synonymous—wrongly—it's only natural that our greatest sexual icon's HIV status would invite scrutiny. In December 1992 the inevitable occurred: In the wake of biographer **Christopher Andersen**'s leading comments that any one of Madonna's alleged Latino sexual pickups in the East Village could have been "carrying the AIDS virus," **rumors** ran rampant that Madonna had tested positive and was going to unveil that fact at a **press conference,** as if her HIV status were her latest project. Reporters deluged **Liz Rosenberg** with calls about Madonna's health all at once, lending credence to Madonna's feeling that some kind of conspiracy was behind the rumors. Receiving AmFAR's Award of Courage at their 1991 "Glitter and Be Giving" benefit, Madonna addressed the rumors with an impassioned speech in which she asserted her seronegativity while shaming reporters for propagating an obviously false story, reaffirming her devotion to the cause.

Madonna's AIDS **activism** ignited in 1986. Along with unflagging personal support for Burgoyne, Madonna became involved in AIDS benefits.

Despite her commitment to AIDS, Madonna has twice drawn criticism from the AIDS community. In 1990, the New York–based House of Sweet Charity attacked Madonna for failing to respond to an invitation to appear at an event while in town for **Blond Ambition.** She *had* responded, late, with a polite no, and the criticism seemed ingracious to the extreme. In January 1993, an illustration of Madonna made the cover of the radical gay newspaper *New York Native.* "Hi. My name is Madonna," the cartoon proclaimed as a prelude to an open editorial by the publisher imploring Madonna to stop raising money for what the newspaper considers ineffectual organizations. No reply from Madonna, whose sincerity and dedication were never questioned.

Madonna's various AIDS activities are impossible to catalog in total; many of her donations are anonymous. The organizations she favors are **ACT-UP,** AIDS Project Los Angeles (APLA), the American Foundation for AIDS Research (AmFAR), and Gay Men's Health Crisis (GMHC).

By conservative estimates, Madonna has helped to raise at least $5 million for AIDS charities.

Madonna has even managed to occasionally include AIDS issues in her work. On her **Who's That Girl tour,** she flashed the words SAFE SEX on stories-high screens and on Blond Ambition, she and her female singers chanted a pro-condoms poem before launching **"Into the Groove."** Light

"*Few* people in the entertainment industry have responded more selflessly and compassionately to the AIDS epidemic than Madonna. Not only has she been tireless in her efforts to raise awareness about AIDS, but she has also raised desperately needed funds for care and research."

—Dr. Mathilde Krim, founding co-chair of AmFAR

.

"*When* the rumors surfaced that I was HIV-positive, I thought, 'Well, someone's really bored today, there must be a lull in current events. Let's make up a really juicy story.' I'm not HIV-positive . . . but what if I were? I would be more afraid of the way society would treat me for having the disease than the actual disease itself. If this is what I have to deal with for my involvement in fighting this epidemic, then so be it. I am not afraid to be associated with people who are HIV-positive, and I am not afraid to love people who are HIV-positive, because their ordeal is more important than mine."

—Madonna, 1991

stuff, but the fact that it's so easy to do doesn't detract from Madonna, only from her peers who rarely if ever mention AIDS in their work.

Her most personal artistic statement about AIDS came on **_Erotica_** in the form of "In This Life," a ballad dismissed by most critics as "mawkish." Sophisticated it ain't, but Madonna's delivery of the song is stirring enough to override lyrical clumsiness. Her **Girlie Show** performances of the song, prefaced by a genuinely tearful speech about the importance of AIDS awareness, are considered among her strongest.

"Ain't No Big Deal": One of Madonna's earliest recorded songs, written by **Steve Bray,** has also become one of the hardest to find. "Ain't No Big Deal" was one of the songs on the demo that **Mark Kamins** gave to **Sire** Records honcho **Seymour Stein** in 1982. In fact, it was Stein's favorite song on the record, so it was scheduled to be Madonna's first-ever release, a 12" dance single backed with a little ditty called **"Everybody."** When the final mixes were in, Stein and Co. changed their minds and nixed "Ain't No Big Deal," instead going with an all-"Everybody" single. Then, when Madonna's first full-length album was finished, the song sounded out of place, so it was scratched and replaced with a tune called **"Holiday."** Both replacement songs went on to become enormous hits, and the prophetically titled "Ain't No Big Deal" resurfaced with a whimper as the B-side of the U.S. **"True Blue"** 7" and 12" singles and on Warner's _Revenge of the Killer B's_ album.

SEE ALSO: **APPENDIX I**

airbrush: Madonna's steadiest companion over the years, the airbrush is a tool that can be extremely effective in retouching photographs. Sure, Madonna is _gorgeous,_ and sure, she's a whiz at looking as different as humanly possible from day to day, but makeup alone does not account for some of her more radical quick-changes.

For _Vogue's_ cover in 1989, David Rickerd at Applied Graphics Technologies saw fit to eliminate the blonde streak in Madonna's then brunette tresses, literally remove her legs and breasts ("Boxing Madonna"), brighten the whites of her **eyes** and her **teeth,** darken her blue irises, spruce up her lipstick, round out her cheek, smooth over her crow's-feet, and change her swimsuit strap from wide to spaghetti-thin.

She flipped her lid over **_Glamour_'s** decision in 1990 to change her **hair** from platinum to orange and her skin from dead white to swarthy, redo her eyes and bust, and—most annoying to her—bleach her teeth and erase her famous **gap.** "Oh my **God,** look what they did to my teeth! It looks like they glued them together, up and down and across."

Liz Rosenberg admits that every photo she receives in her capacity at **Warner Bros.** Records is immediately subjected to the Quantel Graphic Paintbox system, a computerized method of air-brushing so easy even a **wanna-be** could operate it. But Madonna was so angry at the *Glamour*ization that she and Rosenberg asked to stop publication—to no avail.

To be fair, Madonna is rarely the victim of a bad brush-job. Rather, her **looks** are usually flattered. If the effect is subtle, it leaves the viewer gasping over Madonna's Godgiven looks. But sometimes the effect is extreme.

Frequent Madonna photographer **Steven Meisel** is known to alter the appearance of his models both before (with tape and other equipment) and after (with the airbrush) shoots. He turned in a series of shots for *Italian Vogue* in 1991 that features a wrinkle-free (skin and clothing) Madonna with chocolate eyes, sans **beauty mark**. Who's that girl, again? Meisel's *Sex* features many starkly altered images, leaving Madonna looking as smooth as its stainless steel covers. On the lighter side, some airbrush jobs are botched, as in **Jean-Baptiste Mondino**'s otherwise stunning *Harper's Bazaar* layout in 1990, which featured a terrific photo of Madonna marred by the most unrealistically bloated-looking breast this side of a Russ Meyer flick.

Is all this airbrushing so bad? Nah. *Everybody*'s doing it. And more importantly, the photographs in question are works of **art,** and what's art without a little **creativity**? (*Answer:* Candid.)

Albright, Jimmy: Miss Whitney Houston isn't the only one who knows a thing or two about **bodyguards**. Madonna reportedly had a lengthy fling with one of her personal bodyguards—slim, baby-faced Jimmy Albright (1992).

SEE ALSO: **LOVERS**

*Jimmy Albright shoehorns Madonna into a limo after her 1992 "**Saturday Night Live**" gig.*

alcohol: Madonna rarely touches the stuff, hardly ever outside the occasional social drink. She admits to getting roaring drunk on **New Year's Eve** 1990/91, so much so that she threw up and passed out. There were also some unflattering "drunken Madonna on a wild spree" shots of her from a romp at **New York**'s Club USA in late 1992, but these are exceptions.

Her teetotaling could be a reaction to the memory of her **father**'s alcoholic parents and other alcoholics on her **mother**'s side, or to the liquor troubles brothers Martin and Mario have faced. More likely, it's a **control** issue; when you're drunk, your guard is down.

aliases: Madonna can't very well register at a hotel under her own name, nor is **privacy** ensured by calling ahead to a restaurant and saying, "Two for the Madonna party, non-**smoking** if you have it."

Madonna has used a variety of aliases, including "Daisy Miller" (a Henry James character) while married to **Sean Penn,** "Lulu" (after silent siren Louise Brooks) during her **Who's That**

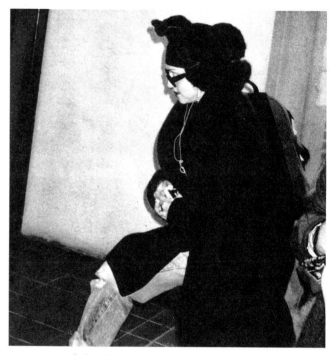

"They'll NEVER guess it's me in this inconspicuous chapeau . . . "

Girl tour, and "Kit Moresby" (heroine from *The Sheltering Sky*) during her **Blond Ambition** travels. Using **"Dita Parlo"** to check in led to appropriating the name for *Sex*ual reasons.

Professionally, Madonna thought she fooled 'em all as "Lulu Smith" while providing backing vocals for Peter Cetera's "Scheherazade." But she is not, contrary to popular belief, the "Mystery Girl" behind **Michael Jackson**'s "In the Closet."

SEE ALSO: **NICKNAMES**

Allen, Woody: Madonna jumped at the chance to appear in the pint-sized **director**'s *Shadows and Fog,* and was defended by him when **rumors** surfaced that her part had been left on **the cutting-room floor.**

Though in Italy (see **Italian**) she is referred to as "Madonna Mia," the idea of a soundstage romance between La **Ciccone** and the Woodman was only pondered by the tabloid *News Extra,* which would have us believe that upon meeting her, Woody said, "From all the things I heard about you, I thought you'd be just another bimbo with a bust-size higher than your **I.Q.**" Madonna, never one to miss a beat, supposedly responded by rattling off *every* film Woody *ever* made, and *all* of the characters he played in them! Of course, the *News Extra* didn't mention that this imagined exchange was actually longer than Madonna's scenes in the finished film.

"All About Madonna": No, it's not a forthcoming ABC-TV movie adaptation of the Bette Davis classic. (Drat!) Even better, "All About Madonna" is a four-part cable-access series that originally ran in L.A. from November 1993 through January 1994. Hostessed by perky, retro Laurie Pike, series highlights include chats with one of Madonna's former **Alvin Ailey dance** compatriots, a **wanna-be** who prostituted himself for a **Blond Ambition** backstage pass (hard life), a shrink psychoanalyzing Madonna, and a song called "We Live in a House" that Madonna made in the late seventies with a band called the Spinal Root Gang.

Alton Road: The Miami site of Madonna's nude hitchhiking sequence for *Sex* and the *dénouement* of the **"Erotica" video**.

Alvin Ailey American Dance Theater: Madonna's big break came in the form of a scholarship to this prestigious **New York dance** company in the late seventies. She eventually gave up on her **dream** of becoming a famous dancer, focusing on **singing,** but the skills she acquired at Alvin Ailey have enriched her **work.**
    SEE ALSO: DUKE UNIVERSITY; LANG, PEARL

American Family Association: Sounds like an R&B group from the early seventies, but it's a right-wing organization run by Reverend Don Wildmon of Tupelo, Mississippi. The group is "concerned about the influence of entertainment media on the American family and society," and regularly campaigns to force the entertainment industry to present more "family-correct," **God**-loving images.
    The AFA launched a successful boycott against **Pepsi** in 1989 to protest that company's use of unwholesome Madonna as a spokesperson.
    SEE ALSO: CENSORSHIP; "LIKE A PRAYER" VIDEO

American Gothic: The famous painting by Grant Wood, featuring a stony-faced farmer, his pitchfork, and his daughter, has figured into Madonnica twice.
    First, **Sean Penn**'s brother Michael, who later became a semi-successful rock/folk musician in his own right, drew a take-off of the painting to adorn Sean and Madonna's **wedding** invi-

tation. The two barely-humanoid figures in his illustration possess such malevolent grins we can only guess that Michael knew something we didn't know until much later.
    Also, the *Star* ran an artist's conception of what Sean and Madonna would look like as senior citizens, using Wood's masterpiece as an inspiration. Sean and Madonna *will* grow old, but—alas!—not together.

Amos, Tori: London-based American folk singer who told *Details* magazine in 1994: "She's the shadow of the Christian Madonna. So while the Christian Madonna was pure and sanctified, Madonna has become the **sex**uality of it incarnated. But I don't think Madonna's been very nurtured as a human being. I said a few years ago that I'd make her a plate of spaghetti, and I mean that."

analysis: Didja ever notice that everything Madonna does is conjectured to hold some deep psychological *meaning*? How some critics would have us believe that Madonna is an expert at infusing her existence and her **work** with incredible meanings so complex it takes college courses to finesse them out of their pop trappings? (See: **academia**.)
    Typical soundbites spewed by pop analysts regarding Madonna's personal life run the gamut—proclaiming her to be obsessed with **Marilyn Monroe,** an obsessive-compulsive, anal-retentive, the victim of an Oedipus complex, **suicidal** in her at-the-top loneliness, **exhibitionistic**, and narcissistic.
    Her work (which is rarely considered to be separate from her personal life, anyway) has been proclaimed the typification of the New Woman who no longer needs to stay in the kitchen, but is instead able to constantly change (her many different **video looks**); sadomasochistic (even before she endorsed it explicitly) in its regard for restraint (**"Express Yourself" video**) and pain (**"Hanky Panky"**); feminist in its representation of self-determining women (**"Papa Don't Preach" song**); antifeminist in its representation of women as objects of desire (her entire *oeuvre*); godless for its sacrilegious themes (**"Like a Prayer" video**); and polymorphously perverse in its mission to blur gender and **sex**ual roles (**"Justify My Love" video**).
    Oh, yeah—almost forgot: Madonna's head has undergone analy-

"*I*t would be nice if everybody could listen to my **music** and watch my movies and read my **books** without anyone telling them how they should think, feel, or accept it, or not accept it."
—Madonna, 1993

sis with a private shrink, a habit she picked up around 1990, probably from everyone telling her what she was thinking all the time.

SEE ALSO: ACADEMIA, ATHOLICISM, EXHIBITIONISM, FEMINISM, SUICIDE

Andersen, Christopher: Christina Crawford's excuse was the wire hangers, but why does biographer Christopher Andersen try so hard to villify his subject? The answer is that scandal sells.

Andersen's *Madonna—Unauthorized* (Simon & Schuster, 1991) was the first major Madonna biography. It became a number 9 best-seller, largely on the hype that it contained shocking secrets. The worst it had to offer was that Madonna is sometimes rude to rude **fans** (how friendly would you be to someone who follows you into the john for an **autograph**?); that she had a penchant for cruising Alphabet City in **New York** in her limo, picking up and fooling around with teenaged Latino boys (doesn't everybody do that???); that she has participated in group **sex** and is definitely **bisexual**; that she can be ruthless in exploiting those around her for the good of her career; that she's a penny-pincher; that she's had multiple **abortions**; and that she is serially unfaithful to every man she loves.

Andersen's revelations don't always pack the punch they might, relying on unnamed interviewees, stretching credibility—do we really believe that Madonna and **Michael Jackson** stripped and explored each other's bodies after the **Oscars**? She isn't exactly his *type*—and coming from a handful of disgruntled ex-pals, some of whom later denied saying the things Andersen wrote.

Andersen's uptight attitudes hang over Madonna's free-wheeling fun-loving. Look for phrases like "devoutly **homosexual**" to pass the time and smile as Anderson views every aspect of Madonna's life as yet another indication that she is a psychological timebomb, tick-ticking away.

In the end, the book is a lot of *tsk-tsk*ing over Madonna's "sexually promiscuous lifestyle" and "exploiting" of religious icons. (Let's talk about exploiting icons, Chris.) Andersen humorlessly tries to invoke the pathos behind his vision of a geriatric Madonna shimmying around to **"Like a Virgin"** before a sold-out crowd of blue-haired **wanna-bes**.

Andersen *has* assembled a lot of exacting details from Madonna's journey to stardom, including an extensive genealogy, and several enlightening interviews, notably one with **Christopher Flynn**. The book is occasionally witty, if disingenuous, and always readable. The best thing about this book is its cover, a sizzling shot of Madonna on the **Who's That Girl tour,** grasping her heiny.

SEE ALSO: APPENDIX 5

Androgyny Cabaret: One of Madonna's earliest live **singing** engagements in **New York** was at a small show organized by entrepreneur/artist/writer Michael McKenzie. The theme of the performance was to be androgyny, so Madonna, who was a member of the band **Emmy** at the time, appeared with short dark **hair** and in men's pajamas. Photos reveal the act to have been quite convincing, and the performance no doubt strengthened her theatrical sensibilities.

"Angel" song: A number 4 up-tempo pop song in the classic early Madonna mold, "Angel" inhabited the upper reaches of the pop charts simultaneously with her ballad **"Crazy for You"** in 1985. Because **Sire Records** wanted to push "Angel" (and the album from which it was taken, *Like a Virgin*), the much more popular **"Into the Groove"** was denied a single release.

Angie, I Says: Doomed Geena Davis starrer released in March 1994 under the shortened title *Angie*. The film was originally written specifically for Madonna by screenwriter Todd Graff. Graff felt that Madonna's **mother**less youth and streetsmarts would make her a natural for the part of "Angie," a pregnant Brooklyn woman who learns to love herself while searching for the mother who abandoned her in childhood. The concept was sort of *My Own Private Angie of Bensonhurst.* Jonathan *(The Accused)* Kaplan was Madonna's director of choice, and things seemed set for the picture to roll at Twentieth Century Fox.

Then, head honcho Joe Roth took off for Disney and *Angie* went into limbo. The film's proposed producer, Larry Brezner, was allowed to pitch the project to others outside of Fox, and, curiouser and curiouser, the project was given the go-ahead by Disney's Caravan Pictures, where Roth landed.

Madonna was set to shoot **Dangerous Game** from February to March of 1993, which conflicted with Brezner's schedule for *Angie*. Brezner already resented what he perceived as Madonna's overconfidence that she could convincingly portray "Angie," and the hyper-***Sex***ualization of her image during 1992 made him queasy. The scheduling conflict was used as an excuse, and Geena Davis was signed.

Understandably, Madonna was enraged. Her retribution was vitriolic and indiscreet and arrived in the form of a handwritten, **faxed** diatribe to Roth that was later much-photocopied throughout the industry:

"After directing *Coupe de Ville* and *Revenge of the Nerds* [II, actually] . . . you are certainly qualified to speak about the **art** of **acting** and great filmmaking. I can understand why you had reservations about my ability. I can see why you think Geena Davis the better actress for the part. After all, she's **Italian** and she has an edge. How foolish of me to think I had the ability to play a vulnerable character unlike anything I've done to date. I should just stay in the gutter where I belong, working with lowlifes like **Abel Ferrara** and being hated by the general public."

SEE ALSO: PROJECTS

Arquette, Rosanna: Perky star of the acclaimed films *Baby, It's You* and *After Hours,* granddaughter of Cliff ("Hee Haw") Arquette, and—though she hates to be reminded of it—the inspiration for Toto's "Rosanna," written by ex-beau Jeff Pocaro.

Arquette was Madonna's costar in **Desperately Seeking Susan.** She suffered a bruised ego over Madonna's scene-stealing (hell, *film*-stealing), but the two continue to be on friendly terms. Arquette was on hand for the premiere of **Truth or Dare.**

"*M*adonna goes right for it and gets what she wants. I admire that a lot. But I think behind all that is a little, tiny girl inside."

—Rosanna Arquette, 1990

art: Madonna is one of the leading private art collectors in the world, and has made the *Arts and Antiques* list of the Top 100 Collectors. She owns hundreds of photography books, attends exhibits (including the **"Degenerate Art"** show), and routinely peppers her **videos** and photo shoots with imagery reminiscent or reflective of various prominent artists.

Interviewers privileged to chat with her at **home** come away with meticulous notes on her sensational taste and the exquisite pieces that adorn her living spaces. She does have assistance in making wise as well as wonderful selections: Darlene Lutz has advised Madonna on her collection since 1986.

The first piece of art Madonna ever purchased as a collector was a Robert Smithson painting. Since then, her homes have become regular little Guggenheims.

Madonna's **New York** apartment was designed as an artistic as well as a comfortable space by Stephen Wang of Procter & Wang, and was decorated by brother **Christopher Ciccone** in a matter of weeks. The result is an art deco showcase that houses paintings such as *Nude* (1930), by Laure Albin-Guillot; *Nude* (1929), by André Kertész; Fernand Leger's *Trois Femmes à la Table Rouge* (1921) and *Les Deux Bicyclettes;*

*Like **Marilyn Monroe** before her, Madonna's image is beginning to infiltrate the art world.*

Maxfield Parrish's *The Young King of the Black Isles* (1906); Pablo Picasso's *Buste de Femme à la Frange* (1938); Pierre Dubeuil's *Les Gants de Boxe* (1930); Salvador Dali's *Le Coeur Voilé* (1932); *Portrait of Boxer* (1945) by Claggett Wilson; and favorite artist **Tamara de Lempicka**'s *Nue à la Colombe* (1930), *Andromède* (1929), and *Nana de Herrera* (1930).

In the attic, Madonna keeps a portrait of herself as an old woman. . . . Now you know better than that. There is no attic in a New York apartment. There are photographs, however, such as works by George Platt-Lynnes, Jacques-Henri's *The Rowe Twins* (1927), and an untitled 1927 photo by Frantisek Drtikol. Even Madonna's furniture is art. Her apartment boasts a hundred-year-old Pompeiian-style klismos chair, a Jean Pascaud ebony table, a Eugene Printz armchair, and a copy of a sofa from Coco Chanel's studio, among other fine pieces.

Madonna's California digs are more eclectically decorated, featuring everything from a Kertész painting of a nude woman searching her stomach for rolls of fat, to a working radio designed by Rhonda Zwillinger. This is where you'll find the famous **Frida Kahlo** self-portrait, *My Birth,* a harrowing depiction of the painter giving bloody birth to herself. Madonna told **Vanity Fair** that if someone can't relate to that painting, "then I know they can't be my friend." Fear not! Perhaps she has relented now that plans for her Frida Kahlo film bio have fizzled.

She also owns Kahlo's *Self-Portrait with Monkey,* John Kirby's *Family Ties,* Leger's *Composition* (1932)—which dresses up the entrance—and a fabulous mixed-media collage by **Keith Haring** of Madonna herself, which hangs in her kitchen. She displays the photography of **Herb Ritts**, Edward Weston, Weegee, Tina Modotti, Matt Mahurin, Lartigue, and Drtikol, but prizes most a photograph of Detroit boxing champ Joe Louis by Irving Penn (You can take the girl out of Michigan . . .), though she cherishes an Ilse Bing photograph given to her on her thirty-first birthday by **Warren Beatty**.

Aside from paintings and photos, Madonna owns a Nadelman statue and a drawing by David Salle that was a **wedding** gift to the Penns from the artist and his then girlfriend Karole Armitage (who later choreographed videos like **"Express Yourself"** and **"Vogue"**). No word on where she keeps it (or if she kept it at all!), but **Warner Bros.** Records once presented Madonna with a 1924 pencil drawing of a reclining nude, by Jean du Pujols.

The most remarkable piece in her West Coast home besides the lady herself is a ceiling-mounted painting by Langlois—originally created for Versailles—of Cupid, Diana, and Endymion. It's said to be so soothing to Madonna that she spends hours flat on her back gazing up at it.

Madonna is a force to be reckoned with at art auctions. At Sotheby's in 1992, she plopped down $814,000 for a fourteenth-century panel by an unknown painter known mysteriously as "The Master of 1310." The painting portrays the life of a saint, complete with serpents, lions, bears, an executioner, and an all-girl version of *The Last Supper.*

"*I* get strength from my art—all the paintings
I own are powerful. As an artist myself,
I know what it's like to put your heart and
soul into something. You can feel the
presence of another person."

—Madonna, 1991

·

"*I* am my own painting. I am my own
experiment. So, I am my own work of art."

—Madonna, 1991

The word "art" comes up frequently in discussing Madonna, and not always in connection with her hobby. Rather, the artistic merit of her work is constantly questioned. Madonna's status as an "artist," per se, is hotly debated, complicated by her blurring of the lines between high and low culture. For example, for whatever arbitrary reason, Horst P. Horst's famed photographic interpretation of a corseted woman is considered High Art, while Madonna's video reinterpretation—slithering to the strains of "Vogue"—is considered Low Art. To save time, tell any naysayers that Madonna's work *is* art, but give them the prerogative of deciding whether it's any good.

artifacts: Items touched, used, signed, worn, or **kiss**ed by Madonna are highly prized by collectors, as if owning something that has been in her presence draws the collector that much closer to her being.

Clothing worn by Madonna is especially valuable. Her **"Express Yourself"** suit, complete with slits for a **cone bra,** sold for $10,000, and a brown-and-purple **Gaultier** bra she wore in *Truth or Dare* went for over $11,000. One of her gold lamé **Blond Ambition** basques fetched $15,000 (and that's with no matching slacks), a corset from that tour broke records with an $18,150 bid in 1994, and a bustier sold for $1,200 to benefit Daytop Village's drug treatment center.

Madonna is fairly generous with her used clothing, which accounts for the fact that residents of Mt. Clemens, Michigan, had the rare opportunity to bid on the blue hanky she waved in the non-U.S. version of her **"True Blue" video,** all to benefit the local rotary club. The final price when the gavel sounded? $714. You can view the hanky at Mon Jin-Lau, a restaurant in Troy, Michigan. On a more personal level, Madonna's high-school yearbook—unsigned—was snapped up for a mere $770, and her

Rockford Peaches uniform from *A League of Their Own*—unwashed—sold for $2,100. On an even *more* intimate level, an Evian bottle she fellated at a *Truth or Dare* publicity party—complete with pink lipstick smears—went for $1,100. *That* is some expensive head.

This basque was auctioned for a queen's ransom.

Since Madonna artifacts are so valuable, some seem to sprout legs. Madonna's powder blue "True Blue" dress took a walk from a display in a Detroit mall, reappearing safely several weeks later. During the **Los Angeles riots,** while most looters were busy stocking up on canned goods or stereos, one enterprising collector nabbed Madonna's **"Open Your Heart"** bustier from its permanent residence at Frederick's of Hollywood's museum of unmentionables. That too was recovered.

Frederick's isn't the only museum Madonnica has infiltrated: One of her Blond Ambition basques inhabits the Metropolitan Museum of Modern Art's Costume Division, in **New York City**.

Afraid you'll never get a chance to buy such fabulous one-of-a-kinders? Then go for second-best, baby, and snap up a Madonna **autograph** the next time you bump into her.

assault: On December 28, 1988, Madonna drove from her Malibu mansion to the sheriff's office to file charges of "corporal injury and traumatic conditions" and "battery" against her husband **Sean Penn** for an incident that almost certainly led to her decision to begin **divorce** proceedings on January 4, 1989, and to officially file January 25.

Stories vary about what Sean did to Madonna, but most of them involve Madonna being bound and gagged, verbally (and possibly sexually) abused, and roughed up. The *Star*'s typical tabloid reportage: SEAN PENN BOUND AND GAGGED MADONNA FOR 9 HOURS! it screamed, detailing his twining her to a chair, threatening to cut off her **hair,** and attempting to shove her head in a gas oven.

She later dropped the charges against Sean, but she did get in the last smack upside the head by following through with the divorce.

✺

Robert H. Levine, in the collectibles department of Sotheby's, graciously "appraises" the following real and imaginary Madonna artifacts:

(1)
Explicit **love** letter written to **Warren Beatty** in Russian Red lipstick: $2,000-plus.

(2)
An invitation to the **Sex launch party,** addressed to **the Pope** and
postmarked "Vatican City": $500–700.

(3)
Dolce & Gabbana blonde afro wig from the **Girlie Show**: $1,000–1,500.

(4)
Glitter ball she descended on for the Girlie Show: $700–900.

(5)
Robert Baggio's number fifteen soccer jersey, mischievously worn
for Blond Ambition performances in Rome: $1,000–1,500.

(6)
Manacle and chain from "Express Yourself" video: $1,500–2,000.

(7)
Chinese **hopping ghost** puppet that gets a glove job in **"Erotica" video**: $200–300.

(8)
Charred cross from **"Like a Prayer" video**: $300–500.

(9)
Polaroid Madonna/"Susan" snaps of herself from **Desperately Seeking Susan**: $20–30.

(10)
"Nikki Finn"'s monkey purse—now one of Madonna's own favorites—from **Who's That Girl**: $200–300.

And in case you were getting any bright ideas, realize that a lock of
Madonna's **hair**—in any hue—is worth only about $50–75. Even more
disappointing is the news that neither the photo of **Joey Buttafuoco**
she shredded on **"Saturday Night Live"** nor the infamous can
of **Pepsi** that co-starred with her in her short-lived Pepsi
commercial have any resale value.
The can, at least, might get you a return deposit.

✺

Association to Save Madonna from Nuclear War: A group of Cincinnati **fans** who in 1991 banded together to lobby for nuclear-free zones within a 50-mile radius of "anywhere Madonna lives or socializes more than twenty days in an average year." Their list included the state of New York, much of Michigan, and greater Los Angeles. And you thought *you* were a little nuts about Madonna.

At Close Range: **Sean Penn**'s father-son drama was the film he was working on in Mexico in May 1985 while Madonna blazed across America with her **Virgin tour**. Just a couple of months after his return to the States, the couple married.

They attended the film's world premiere at the Berlin Film Festival in February 1986, pointedly avoiding photographers—they were filming ***Shanghai Surprise*** at the time, and having trouble with overenthusiastic **paparazzi**. They were much more sociable at the film's American premiere at the Bruin Theatre in Los Angeles. Madonna debuted her "gamine" **look** (later to appear in the **"Papa Don't Preach" video**), wearing a black-and-hot-pink cocktail dress and grinning like a woman in **love**.

A highlight of the film is the song Madonna wrote for it, **"Live to Tell."**

auditions: Madonna conducts **dance** auditions for tour performers in person, so watch the trade papers for her all-call.

For **Blond Ambition,** her ad read: "Open audition for FIERCE male dancers who know the meaning of TROOPSTYLE, BEATBOY & VOGUE. Wimps and **wanna-bes** need not apply." When casting her **Girlie Show,** she was "[l]ooking for 3 very special girls + a few good men. Androgynous/boyish/girls—between 5'4"–5'8" with very short hair—that can dance well! Men—between 5'10"–6'2" with versatility. Classical training and street sensibility required!"

Madonna herself has had her share of auditions. Among the **projects** in which she was eventually cast, she had to read for *A Certain Sacrifice, Desperately Seeking Susan, Speed-the-Plow, Dick Tracy* and *A League of Their Own*. In every case, she was competing against several or *dozens* of other actresses. So many actresses had read for **"Breathless Mahoney"** that Madonna described herself as having been on the "Z-list."

Even now, it wouldn't be unheard of for a director and producer to demand that Madonna read for a role. For **Maverick** productions, we presume Madonna's reading is before a mirror, and that callbacks come much faster than usual.

Audubon Ballroom: Abandoned structure at 166th Street and Broadway in Washington Heights, **New York**, that became The Magic Club in ***Desperately Seeking Susan.***

autographs: Madonna's autograph can fetch $300 if it's scrawled on a photo, or even more if it's on an unusual object, like her 1985 ***Playboy*** magazine cover. She frequently donates autographed items to charity, and in spite of her legendary stinginess

regarding autographing for **fans** (she didn't sign *any* during her run in ***Speed-the-Plow*** on Broadway), she will usually comply if the request is humble and the asker sweet.

At **Martha Graham**'s swan-song **dance** recital, one fan found Madonna ridiculously gracious—she signed an entire stack of 8 x 10 glossies, even stopping to (correctly) identify that one of the photos was of a look-alike.

While being interviewed by Harry Crews for *Fame* magazine in 1988, the pair had to exit Trump Plaza via the kitchens, where she signed autographs for the staff. Crews was surprised she would take the time, but Madonna explained it was the "impertinence" of most autograph hounds that usually puts her off.

She signed a man's passport aboard David Bowie's yacht in **Cannes,** and overruled security at a 1994 **New York** basketball game when they tried to dissuade a man seeking an autograph for his **father**.

If it seems cruel for Madonna not to sign autographs on demand, remember that some autograph requests come from people who sell them for a living, and Madonna is probably annoyed at having to spend time supporting a cottage industry. Don't expect to get her autograph if there are crowds of fans around—she won't do one if it means having to do a hundred—and don't even bother to ask if she's anywhere near **home** or her temporary HQ. Signing there encourages stakeouts. Instead of an autograph, you're much more likely to receive an acid, *"Fuck off,"* which might be more fun anyway.

An expert told *Smash Hits* magazine that her handwriting indicates sincerity, intelligence, sensuality, flamboyance, and *joie de vivre.* "Her looped-rightward *d* formation shows peace, fulfillment, and understanding." See how the *o* connects to the first *n*?

It's called an arcade formation and it supposedly "shows an ability to shut out or rise above criticism." Even the way she forms her "o" at the top has meaning, representing a woman who speaks her mind. If the autograph she gives you looks a little different, it probably just means she hates you. . . .

awards: Greta Garbo never won the **Oscar**. Diana Ross has never won a Grammy. Angela Lansbury has yet to win her Emmy.

Madonna has never won *any* of those awards. They hate her, they *really* hate her! She doesn't even always win when she "wins." Though her torchy performance of "Sooner or Later" undoubtedly helped earn that song the Oscar, Madonna didn't receive the award, songwriter Stephen Sondheim did. Her ***Immaculate Collection* video** won a Grammy, but since she wasn't the producer, she didn't get to keep that award, either. *The **Blond Ambition** World Tour Live* won the first Grammy for a **music**

"And the winner is . . . Madonna!"
A sampling of some awards Madonna and/or her projects have won:

1985
• American Music Award: Favorite Pop/Rock Female Artist

1986
• **MTV Video Music Award**: "Video Vanguard," career achievement
• Juno Award (Canada): Best International Album, *True Blue*

1987
• American Music Award: Favorite Pop/Rock Female Video Artist
• MTV Video Music Award: Best Female Video, **"Papa Don't Preach"**

1988
• MTV Video Music Award: Viewer's Choice, **"Like a Prayer"**

1989
• International Music Award: Best Female Singer, *Like a Prayer*
• MTV Video Music Award: "Artist of the Decade," career achievement
• MTV Video Music Award: Best Director, Best Cinematography, **"Express Yourself"**

1990
• MTV Video Music Award: Best Director, Best Editing, **"Vogue"**

1991
• Academy Award: Best Original Song, "Sooner Or Later"
• American Music Award: Favorite Dance Single, "Vogue"
• People's Choice, Hard Rock Café Foundation, International Rock Awards
• MTV Video Music Award: Best Long-Form Video, *The Immaculate Collection*

1992
• Grammy Award: Best Video—Long Form, *The Immaculate Collection*

1993
• American Society of Composers, Authors, and Publishers (ASCAP) Film and Television Music Award: Best Songwriting, "This Used to be My Playground"
• MTV Video Music Award: Best Art Direction, Best Cinematography, **"Rain"**

video released exclusively on laserdisc, an award that went to its producer.

Madonna's black-sheep status has kept her at the back of the awards bus in almost all of her endeavors, even when she's truly deserving of recognition. For example, she has cowritten several Oscar-caliber songs for the movies (**"Into the Groove," "Live to Tell," "Who's That Girl,"** and **"This Used to be My Playground,"**— the latter of which was up for a 1992 Golden Globe), none of which has ever been nominated. **Truth or Dare** was one of the most highly-praised films of 1991, and yet it failed to win an Oscar nomination for Best Documentary. The film industry's perception of Madonna's **acting** keeps her at arm's length from Oscar even when she's contributing in other capacities.

Some dubious honors Madonna has snagged include the Sour Apple Award from the Women's Press Club in 1992, for being nasty and uncooperative with the media, and *Variety*'s 1993 "I'd Rather Have a Pulitzer Than an Oscar" Award for refusing to allow **Body of Evidence** to be released the same week as **Sex.** She was awarded the Golden Raspberry and Golden Turkey Awards (among many other nasties) for Worst Actress in that same film.

She *has* managed to rake in a few accolades. In 1991, she was given AmFAR's Award of Courage for her **AIDS** work, and a media award from the Gay and Lesbian Alliance Against Defamation (GLAAD) for raising gay awareness. She also possesses an ASCAP songwriting award and several **MTV** awards. The awards she can always count on are the ones given out for gold and platinum record sales.

SEE ALSO: **MTV MUSIC VIDEO AWARDS**

Bravo readers voted Madonna their favorite girl singer of 1992.

bachelor party: Sean Penn's bachelor party was thrown by his brother, actor Chris Penn. The guests included *Fast Times at Ridgemont High* author Cameron Crowe, Tom Cruise, Robert Duvall, and David Keith, and entertainment was provided by Kitten Natividad, the impossibly busty star of Russ Meyer films. Kitten stripped to "**Material Girl,**" struggling to maintain her dignity while Sean rubbed **Harry Dean Stanton**'s face in her cleavage.

bachelorette party: What's good for the goosed . . . Madonna's own prenuptial celebration took place at Hollywood's club Tropicana, where Madonna and galpals watched a raucous evening of mudwrestling.

back: Madonna considers her back to be the most sensitive, and yet the most **power**ful, part of her body.

"Bad Girl" song: The third single released from *Erotica,* backed with "**Fever,**" "BG" became the least successful single of Madonna's career. It charted at a subterranean number 36 and is her only non–Top 20 single. The problem wasn't with the song's merits, but with the timing (it was released in the backwash of *Sex*), and with the fact that introspective, mid-tempo downers don't sail on Top 40 radio.

Record-buyers rejected what was perceived as Madonna's attempt at atonement for her wicked, wicked ways. "BG" *did* become a number-one-selling **dance** single, thanks to the "Fever" mixes featured on the B-side. Why the hugely popular "Fever" was not the A-side release is a mystery.

"Bad Girl" video: One of Madonna's most cinematic **videos,** "BG" marries the storyline of *Looking for Mr. Goodbar* with the visual style of *Wings of Desire* in its depiction of a smoldering businesswoman of a certain age who degrades herself with sleazy sexcapades, too much liquor, and chain-smoking. Though she is watched over throughout by a chic guardian angel (Christopher Walken), she is murdered in the end by a one-night stand, and appears happier once she's by the angel's side.

The message is simple, but Madonna's performance makes the video sing. Madonna was just about to film *Dangerous Game* when the video was shot, and there is a lot of "Sarah Jennings" here, most noticeably in a newfound fluidity of facial expressions. Most gripping is the moment when **music** and action stop jarringly in sync with the ignition of a lighter.

Thank director **David Fincher** for that and the rest of this mini-masterpiece. It's just as well that the video's first two planned **directors, Ellen von Unwerth** and Tim Burton, never panned out.

Baggio, Roberto: During a **Blond Ambition** performance at Flaminio Stadium in Rome, Madonna surprised **fans** by appearing in the royal-blue game jersey—number 15—belonging to this **Italian** World Cup soccer star. It was a brilliant move that endeared her to Italian fans even as **the Pope** denounced her show as pure blasphemy.

Bags: Backup dancer, along with **Erica Bell** and **Martin Burgoyne,** for Madonna's early track dates at **Danceteria**.

Bahamas, the: Madonna enjoyed a brief vacation there in 1984 with boyfriend **Jellybean** Benitez. It's the last time she was reported to have taken a for-pleasure-only trip.

SEE ALSO: VACATIONS

Baker, John: One of Madonna's tough "minders" (British slang for "**bodyguard**") during her **Blond Ambition** shows in London, JB was embroiled in a scandal when the **tabloid** *News of the World* exposed him as having been expelled from the British secret service in 1988 for possessing and selling an illegal Argy pistol. His past was deemed newsworthy in light of the fact that Madonna's minders had been physically tough with journalists and **fans** who trailed her while she jogged during her London stay.

Baldwin, Billy: Alec's younger brother, the star of films like *Backdraft* and *Three of Hearts,* BB may have had a brief fling in late 1991 with Madonna during a momentary lull in his relationship with guileless singer Chynna Phillips. When Baldwin was photographed leaving Madonna's apartment some time after the sun went down, he promptly punched out the offending **paparazzo,** Mitchell Gerber, smashing his camera. The shutterbug sued Baldwin and won approximately $2,000 in damages.

In November 1993, the same photographer was kicked out of a benefit at Billy's request. If a Madonna/BB romance happened, Billy was back together with Chynna before Madonna even had time to call up all her friends.

balls: Nuts, rocks, testicles, jellybeans, jawbreakers, joy beans, dick dumplings, scrotum mice.

In 1989, Madonna asked choreographer **Vincent Paterson** if he were the one "who had **Michael Jackson** grab his balls." Paterson couldn't claim that honor, but Madonna was inspired.

The result was her infamous crotch-grab in the **"Express Yourself" video.**

The *Interview* magazine cover (1990) featuring a crotch-grabbing Madonna was so controversial some stores decided not to display it, and that same photo was hastily removed from the French single of **"Justify My Love"** as soon as officials saw it in record stores.

Madonna told *The Advocate* in 1991 that though **Alek Keshishian** had fairly large "balls" for locking horns with her and directing a film as unconventional as ***Truth or Dare,*** she felt she had the larger balls for allowing her life to be "splayed" on the screen.

To the frustration of feminists and the politically correct, Madonna continues to use the term "balls" to connote strength, **power,** and bravado.

SEE ALSO: PUSSY

Banderas, Antonio: *Paper* magazine summed up AB as "THE MAN MADONNA COULDN'T GET." As the lead hunk of a series of Pedro Almodóvar films, he was one of Spain's biggest stars. It wasn't until Madonna went gaga over him at a party thrown for her by his maverick director that he caught Hollywood's eye. At the party, which was filmed for ***Truth or Dare,*** Madonna confided to her backup singers that she had the hugest crush on AB, and got all dolled up in a Pucci top, short-shorts, and fishnets for the occasion of their introduction, only to discover that he was happily married to actress Anita "Ana" Leza.

Madonna kicked herself in the bathroom, Ana mugged for **Alek Keshishian**'s all-seeing camera, and Antonio did a slow burn across the screen. Sexy, Latin, down with playing gay boys on screen, and straight, Banderas is the perfect mate for Madonna, but his wife would probably disagree. Though their would-be romance was supposedly stillborn, **paparazzi** snapped photos of Madonna and Antonio driving around together sans Ana. Alek Keshishian must have blinked.

AB was Madonna's first choice to play "Che Guevara" to her **"Evita**."

Barbie: Maybe our pop cultural fixation on Madonna can be traced to our fixation with that other stacked blonde goddess, the one who's a little shorter and less flexible.

Have you ever noticed how strongly Madonna favors the original Barbie doll? That sneery nose, those slitty, heavily-lashed eyes. . . . In fact, Madonna has admitted that her **Blond Ambition** ponytail, often likened to TV's "I Dream of Jeannie," was actually modeled after Tressy, the Barbie **wanna-be** doll whose hair

*"**J** definitely lived out my fantasies with them. I dressed them up in sarongs and miniskirts and stuff. They were sexy, having **sex** all the time. I rubbed them and Ken together a lot. And they were bitchy, man. Barbie was* mean."

—Madonna, on playing with her Barbies as a child, 1985

•

*"**M**adonna is the last word in attitude and fashion, the epitome of cool. Madonna is the video generation's Barbie."*

—Joyce Millman, *Boston Phoenix,* 1986

"grew" when you pressed the small of her **back.**

Barbone, Camille: Madonna's first agent from 1980–81, in association with the Gotham Agency. Barbone has a tale to tell, sometimes it gets so hard to hide it well. . . . She signed Madonna and gave her money, helped her secure an apartment, financed a **demo,** and pitched her to all the record labels while Madonna played gigs around **New York.** Just before Madonna signed on with **Sire Records,** she dumped Gotham in favor of überagent **Freddy DeMann.**

Performers agent-hop perpetually, but you can't blame an agent scorned, especially when she's lost out on the opportunity to feast on 15 percent of all of Madonna's earnings. A **lawsuit** ensued when Madonna broke her contract with Gotham.

In 1993, CB appeared on **Robin Leach**'s "Madonna Exposed," lamenting her estrangement from Madonna. In 1994, she marketed a melancholic proposal for a memoir of her time with Madonna, called *Making Madonna.* In it, CB confessed that she was in love with Madonna, a complicating factor that may have hastened Madonna's split.

What would have happened if CB had remained Madonna's agent? She reportedly wanted Madonna to cultivate a rock'n' roll sound, steering clear of disco. If that's true, we can only thank Barbone for "discovering" Madonna, and thank Madonna for leaving her.

Coincidentally, CB is exactly eight years older than Madonna —they share the same **birthday.**

Barkley, Charles: African-American Phoenix Suns **basketball** star with whom Madonna was rumored to have had an affair the weekend of May 22, 1993. The two definitely met at a Suns-Lakers game in L.A. at the beginning of May, and her appearance in Phoenix could only have been connected with a prearranged *rendezvous* with Barkley. But did they do it?

The power forward and the showgirl ate out at Tomaso's, then spent some time alone in Madonna's Ritz-Carlton suite. You be the judge. Barkley, estranged from his wife Maureen at the time, soon moved on, denying he'd ever had the fling. When a reporter asked him why he'd slept with Madonna, he shot back, "Because I think Madonna is a great person." Then, changing his mind, Barkley said, "No, I did *not.*"

As for Madonna, she isn't saying, though when she interviewed galpal **Rosie O'Donnell** for *Mademoiselle,* she dropped his name repeatedly, calling him "God." Ever fickle, she told **David Letterman** in 1994 that Barkley "doesn't know the meaning of the word" friendship.

Barney's: Located at 106 Seventh Avenue, the upscale **New York** department store where Madonna made a rare runway appearance in November 1986, modeling designer denim jackets at an auction to benefit St. Vincent Hospital's **AIDS** program. One of the jackets was a **Martin Burgoyne** original, number 54 on the agenda. Under the jackets, Madonna wore the black lycra outfit she wears in *Who's That Girl,* which she was lensing at the time. Among the 82 other artists/designers represented were **Jean-Paul Gaultier** and **Andy Warhol,** and the star models included Iman, **Deborah Harry,** and Peter Allen.

Baron, Fabien: The **art** director of *Sex.* Like Madonna and **Steven Meisel,** his more famous *Sex* partners, Baron is an image junkie. He is one of the world's foremost graphic designers and one of the first to gain name recognition. Just as it took until the late fifties for film directors to be considered "*auteurs,*" it took until Fabien Baron's emergence in the eighties for graphic designers to be considered artists in their own right.

FB soared to **fame** as the creative force behind all those erotically chilly, frequently PG-13–rated Calvin Klein ads (including the **Marky Mark**–Kate Moss series), Issey Miyake's perfume boxes, and, at various times, the art direction of slick mags like *GQ, Italian Vogue,* and *New York Woman.* He saved *Interview* from visual tedium and *revolutionized **Harper's Bazaar,*** which he still designs.

His style is all over *Sex:* the stacked lettering, the superimposition, the collage . . . all are signature Baron. Critics of *Sex* frequently thumb their noses at the cluttered design, and Madonna herself thanks him for his "complete disdain for organization and utter disregard for detail."

Design god or no, some said his visual style overwhelmed the editorial content of *Interview.* Some of his work on *Sex* really works—the "My **pussy** has nine lives" pages, the urinal juxtapositions, the most angular of the collages, the sizzling "I'll teach you how to **fuck**" spread—but Madonna should have cracked the whip to make FB *stretch.* Too many photographs are lost in the shuffle and one of the main reasons some of *Sex* feels tame is that it looks like last month's issue of *Interview:* slick but familiar, and definitely recyclable.

basketball: Madonna loves to watch. *Basketball,* that is. "It reminds me of dancing," she explains. "I love the action. . . . You can see the guys' legs and arms and faces. They're so graceful. And it's so in-your-face, so intimate." Her favorite players—besides ex-fave **Charles Barkley**—are Horace Grant, Michael Jordan (whom she says she'd like to be reincarnated as), **Dennis Rodman** (whose rebellious nature makes him, in her words, "the Madonna of the NBA"), Brian Shaw, and John Starks.

Madonna has been linked romantically with Barkley, with Anthony Mason (New York Knicks), with Rodman, and with Shaw and Rony Seikaly (**Miami** Heat).

Madonna has joked that she'd like to eventually own a bas-

ketball franchise, even if that does sound like a bad **HBO** series, and agreed that she would be a very "hands-on" owner: "Definitely. My hands would be all over the place." Her two favorite teams are the Knicks and the Lakers.

Basquiat, Jean-Michel: Puerto Rican–Haitian Brooklyn-born artist with whom Madonna was fleetingly involved in 1983 after an introduction by **Ed Steinberg.** Basquiat was the most troubled of Madonna's **lovers,** a heroin addict with a self-destructive streak a mile wide. He shot to **fame** alongside **Keith Haring,** routinely selling his primitive-style graffiti canvasses for thousands of dollars while still in his early twenties. He was ejected from the Whitney Museum for vandalism, but before long his work was displayed there.

He died of a **drug** overdose in 1989.

Bay City Visitation Church: The Michigan site of Madonna's parents' **wedding** in 1955.

"Beast Within Mix" : The name of a disturbing remix of **"Justify My Love,"** released in late 1990 as the B-side of the **dance** single of the song. Over a pounding bass line and interspersed with the song's compellingly sexual **lyrics,** Madonna chants from Revelation. The passages just happen to be the notorious "synagogue of Satan" passages often used by anti-Semites to justify their hatred for Jews. Madonna was criticized by The Simon Weisenthal Center and the Anti-Defamation League of B'nai B'rith in a baby scandal that never received much attention. Nonetheless, she quickly apologized and seemed to have been genuinely clueless that she'd created an anti-Semitic anthem. She used the song effectively in a gay **orgy** sequence of her **Girlie Show.**

Beastie Boys, The: The young, incendiary, flamboyant, Jewish **New York** punk-rap group that opened for Madonna on her **Virgin tour**. The logic behind such an oddball pairing was that (1) Madonna **fans** didn't care who was opening; they were desperate to see *Madonna;* and (2) after sitting through the antics of these boys, her fans would be even *more* desperate.

Beatty, Warren: That's "**Pussy Man**" to *you,* mister. Madonna lovingly called her most (independently) famous **lover** by that pet name in **Truth or Dare,** then wondered why he was so adamant that their personal phone calls (surreptitiously taped by Madonna for inclusion in the film) be removed from the final cut.

WB was the world's most

"*She*'s a big, beautiful, hilarious, touching, brilliant fact of life. And I think we should all just relax and enjoy it."

—Warren Beatty, 1990

•

"*If* I have to give Warren Beatty safe-sex lessons, what is this world coming to?"

—Madonna, responding affirmatively that she and Beatty practiced safer sex, 1991

legendary lothario and twenty years older than Madonna at the time of their affair, which lasted sporadically for a year from the spring of 1989. WB had first shown interest in Madonna in 1985 when he watched the dailies of **Desperately Seeking Susan** with director **Susan Seidelman**. He told Seidelman he liked the enigmatic tough girl he saw on-screen. Madonna and WB even met briefly, on Madonna's first date with **Sean Penn,** the same evening she first met **Sandra Bernhard**. Talk about intense evenings!

In 1989, when producer/director WB was casting **Dick Tracy,** a film he'd been trying to get off the ground since Madonna's senior year in high school, Madonna agreed to play bad-girl chanteuse **"Breathless Mahoney"** at scale wages ($1,440 a week). Agent **Freddy DeMann** resisted Madonna's participation at first. You can see his reservations: Was it *really* a good idea for Madonna to play a comic-strip character? But WB promised to photograph her more beautifully than had any of her previous **directors** (not too difficult—Madonna's **glamor** is rarely captured as well as it might be in her movies), and Freddy relented. As soon as filming started, the actress and her director started a passionate affair that eclipsed all the buzz about the movie itself. So effective was their liaison in generating free publicity that some cynical observers claimed they were just involved to promote the film. Though their relationship ended on cool but friendly terms shortly after the film premiered, it's pretty obvious that they were definitely knocking boots, not just kicking up public awareness of their epic.

WB is from the Old School of Hollywood, a believer in discretion and **privacy**. He rarely spoke of his relationship with Madonna, of whom his mother Kathleen did not approve. Madonna, exercising her chameleon abilities, didn't dish Warren either . . . until after they'd broken up, when she asserted that he'd once expressed regret at never having explored homo-**sex**. She also told **Arsenio Hall** that contrary to popular belief, WB is definitely satiable in the sack. After Warren, Madonna warmed up with **Tony Ward,** the Anti-Warren, and Beatty bounced briefly to model Stephanie Seymour before landing in wedded bliss and fatherhood with actress Annette Bening. Think of Madonna as his extended **bachelor party.**

SEE ALSO: Truth or Dare, wiretappings

beauty: As the epoch's most visible woman and a sexual icon to boot, her beauty becomes a major issue in any discussion of Madonna.

Singing peers **Joni Mitchell** and Joan Baez have warned that Madonna shouldn't rely so heavily on her **looks** or it'll mean her downfall when she loses them. Of course, neither of those singers turned heads, so their looks were never at issue.

Already we can see the effect that the ungainly attention toward Madonna's beauty can have. She looks her age—no older, no younger. And yet gossip columnists can not resist taking pot-shots at what they perceive to be the rapid encroachment of age on Madonna's cherished beauty: her crow's-feet, the deepening lines around her mouth, even her downy facial **hair**.

As if in reaction to Madonna's role as a **sex** siren, detractors are doubly negative about her beauty. Not only is she *not* beautiful, she's "hideous," "not much to look at," "nowhere near as good-looking as Julia Roberts."

Part of the problem is that Madonna is not conventionally gorgeous. Madonna's beauty is less a catalog of her parts than it is the whole package, enhanced by sexual charisma, sheer personality, and confidence. Great beauty—and Madonna is a "great beauty," as opposed to a "classical beauty"—isn't about classicism, perfection, or comfortably pleasing features. Great beauty is cruel, magnificent, arresting, shocking, sublime.

One can't categorize Madonna as exactly the untouchable model type or daintily "pretty" or exotic. Instead, she is all of those things at different times or at once, and always, *always* beautiful.

beauty mark: Madonna's is under her right nostril, just above her lips. It's the real McCoy, though she periodically darkens or conceals it with makeup. She has never worn a

fake beauty mark on the left under her nose—photos that show a mark on the left are hastily-printed reverse images. For her **"Breathless Mahoney"** look, Madonna did add a beauty mark to her left jaw.

Bedtime Stories: The theme: It's lonely at the top. Funky, too.

Her seventh full-length studio album launched a virtual ressurection for Madonna in the eyes of the media in October 1994. *BS,* with its fuddy-duddy-friendly softness *and* street-hip rhythm & blues sound, has something for everyone. Good thing, since everyone seemed to want a piece of Madonna after *Sex* was released.

Collaborating with lesser-known talents like Atlanta songwriter Dallas Austin, Björk buddy Nellee Hooper, and Babyface, BS's sound mixes "new jill swing" with elements of the Benedictine Monks, groovy '70s soul, and Enigma. (What to christen this new sound? Madonna Culpa? Benedictine Funk?) It's no shock that

Madonna would get around to embracing R&B, but plenty of listeners were blown away by the fact that *BS* is not a pose, but an inspiration. R&B sounds like second nature to Madonna, and *BS* serves as an aural argument against rigid categorization of "black" versus "white" music.

The alchemy pays off with an album full of eleven breathy, intoxicating tunes cozily nestled in shimmering instrumentation. The songs distinguish themselves not only from most of Madonna's previous efforts, but from each other, despite contributing to a seamlessly unified sound.

Paradoxically, another secret of the album's success is its clever self-reflexivity. In "Survival," Madonna concedes that she's no **"Angel,"** but that she plans to **"Live to Tell."** Both "I'd Rather Be Your Lover" and **"Secret"** assert that happiness lies in your hand, and the former sports a run-down of relations that Madonna would rather *not* be (your sister, **mother**, friend, brother), echoing *Erotica*'s "Where Life Begins," which is also hinted at on BS's "Inside of Me." Two lines from "Don't Stop" (which could never be confused with the forgettable "Can't Stop" of the *Who's That Girl* soundtrack) are almost identical to Madonna's first **dance** hit, "**Everybody,**" and Madonna's plea to "get up on the dance floor" harkens back to 1990's **"Vogue."** Most effective is Madonna's repeated command to **"Express Yourself"** as whispered in "Human Nature." It's one of Madonna's definitive statements (from her 1989 smash), and here it's a lethal counterattack on her critics.

Adding to the air of familiarity are inspired samples from Lou Donaldson's "It's Your Thing," Aailyah's "Back and Forth," The Gap Band's "Outstanding," the Guttersnypes' "Trials of Life," Main Source's "What You Need," Grant Green's "Down Here on the Ground," and Herbie Hancock's "Watermelon Man."

Even the album **art** reminds: Take off that nose ring and squint at that white-blonde **hair**, and you're left with what could almost pass for a still from the **"Like a Virgin" video**. Madonna's even wearing white lace, and this Patrick Demarchelier portrait screams "Classic Madonna here, step right up!"

"*T*his time, S&M means silky and mellow. . . . An appealing hybrid of street hip-hop and lush balladry...."

—Edna Gundersen, *USA Today*

·

"*A*fter so much cigar-smoking, late-night bull wacki, America's bitchy blonde sweet-tart is back with a feline follow-up to *Erotica*. *Bedtime Stories* lays heavy on the tiny icon's lower vocals, and kicks dance pussy with languid hipfunk floor-wreckers. With holes in all the right places, and a very Harlow powder-pale elegance, the virgin is back and she's ready to dance."

—*Next*

·

"...[*S*]even albums into her career, there's no denying that Madonna keeps moving forward and crossing barriers—this time, helping another kind of black music further penetrate into the mainstream. Apparently, pop's most shameless exhibitionist still has something to reveal."

—Jim Farber, *Entertainment Weekly*

Buyer beware: The album may be a classic, but it has little to do with the Madonna of *Like a Virgin* or even *Like a Prayer*. *BS* is a step in a new direction, even if bits of the scenery incite *déja vu*.

BS is less nostalgic than all these "where've I heard that before?" moments; it's an exhilarating trek away from perfect pop packages and into a field of loose melodies and less structured vocals.

"Survival" kicks off the album, establishing the jazzy tone and surprising listeners with Madonna's girlish delivery, in contrast with the defiant lyrics. "Secret," the album's first single, follows, leading into "I'd Rather Be Your Lover," an understated **sex** anthem the likes of which **"Justify My Love"** invented. The album's sole dance-themed song, "Don't Stop," is nonetheless nearly as subdued as the rest of the batch, but it's a more-than-credible re-creation of 1974 soul/disco and an irresistible bump-and-grind.

Along with familiarity vs. departure, vulnerability is another defining characteristic of *BS*, and "Inside of Me" is the musical embodiment of the moment in *Truth Or Dare* when Madonna confesses that **Sean Penn** is the **love** of her life. Whoever Madonna's **singing** about, or whether or not she even has a single person in mind, the song stands alongside "Live To Tell" and **"Oh Father"** as among her most poignant musical statements, all the more touching for its optimism in the face of loss.

"Human Nature" is Madonna at her most defensive (see **"Goodbye to Innocence"**), and also a rare example of an answer song that actually *works*. It's petty to talk back, but enough is enough, and here Madonna's sass is a hoot, a bitchfest that musters all the strength required to gather up all the "shit" some critics have dumped on Madonna and dump it right back. "Forbidden Love" could be about an interracial relationship, gay love, *anything* that *anyone* could ever consider taboo, creating considerable sexual tension with Madonna's charged delivery and the music's erotic thump. "Love Tried to Welcome Me"—an extremely poetic sentiment from the woman most reviewers still insist on referring to as the **"Material Girl"**— finds the singer laundry-listing her useless body parts and disclosing her penchant for sadness.

One of *BS*'s stand-outs is the ten-plus-minute suite created by the run-on songs "Sanctuary" and "Bedtime Story," both of which rank among Madonna's most delicious, if uncharacteristic, songs. The former is a meditative self-eraser, an ode to *vous*, whoever *vous* may be in this instance. It bleeds into Madonna's choked whimper at the onset of "Bedtime Story," the only song on the album Madonna had no hand in writing. It makes no difference that Bjork, Nellee Hooper, and Marius DeVries put the words in Madonna's mouth, "Bedtime Story" is a prime example of the new Madonna of *BS*, a hypnotic, almost hallucinogenic ride through an idealized unconscious state of mind in which words (elevated by "Words" on *Erotica*) are rendered useless. **"Dress You Up?"** No thanks. Let's just *pass fucking out.*

The whole throbbing ordeal simmers to an end with "Take a Bow," which could be read as Madonna's take on the Carpenters' "Superstar," featuring her full vocal range on a song about love between a fan and a "lonely star." The song's references to the cessation of a masquerade and to a sense of finale evoke images of **The Girlie Show,** playing up the sadness of the solitary Pierrot in platforms.

Whether or not Madonna meant *BS* as a reminder that it's lonely at the top, it sure is lonely listening to this disc. But it's a beautiful kind of loneliness; there's romance in yearning, and Madonna captures it perfectly.

Bell, Erica: A friend from her early days in **New York,** Bell sometimes performed with Madonna, as she did in the **"Everybody" video** along with **Christopher Ciccone.** EB ran Lucky Strike, a bar on 9th Street and Third Avenue. She first met Madonna when she hired her to tend bar, a farce that lasted all of forty-eight hours.

Madonna's chattiest early acquaintance, 1983.

The two shared an intense friendship, which Bell told **Christopher Andersen** included making out, and it was Bell who ratted Madonna out as a cruiser of young Latino boys in her big black limo. Bell is one of Madonna's few early acquaintances to speak so freely of her.

She claims to have conceptualized the entire look of the **"Lucky Star" video,** and to have made all the clothing as well. **Maripol** might disagree.

belly button: Madonna's navel made her famous, winking out at the **MTV** generation in her **"Lucky Star" video.** When she had it pierced, she nearly passed out in agony. She premiered her pierced inny at the opening of **Alek Keshishian**'s film *With Honors* on April 26, 1994.

"**The** most erogenous part of my body is my belly button. I have the most perfect belly button—an inny, and there's no fluff in it. When I stick a finger in my belly button I feel a nerve in the center of my body shoot up my spine. If one hundred belly buttons were lined up against a wall I would definitely pick out which one was mine."

—Madonna, 1985

Bernhard, Sandra: Laverne had Shirley. Wilma had Betty. More fittingly, Nancy Drew had George. But the real question in 1988 was . . . Did Madonna *have* Sandra Bernhard? The answer turned out to be no. Madonna remembers first laying eyes on the outrageous, funny-faced, bisexual comedienne on the night of her first date with **Sean Penn** in 1985, but SB recalls first meeting Madonna at a party at **Warren Beatty**'s house that same year, and that Madonna was extremely quiet and observant.

They didn't meet again until both were walking the boards, Madonna on Broadway in *Speed-the-Plow* and SB Off-Broadway in her one-woman show *Without You I'm Nothing.* As part of SB's pop-heavy, hysterically **camp**y monologue, she related a nuclear holocaust dream in which she and Madonna were the last two people left alive. In the fantasy, Madonna was upset that then husband Sean had been nuked—"Don't tell me they got Sean," SB wept sarcastically. Madonna thought the skit was a hoot, and was to have appeared in the film version of the **play** as a Madonna **wannabe** character called "Shoshonna" who continually upstages SB, but she eventually decided against it. The part went to **impersonator** Denise Vlasis.

Miss Bernhard arrives at the outer limits of the Stony End with frequent party pal Isaac Mizrahi.

Upon their reintroduction, SB said, "I can't imagine being you." Madonna replied, "I can't imagine being *you*." Madonna and SB attracted a small group of rowdy females (including actress Jennifer Grey) who caroused at hot spots like M.K. and Canal Bar in between shows, igniting rumors that the duo were having a lesbonic convergence.

Adding fuel to the fire, Madonna tagged along on one of SB's regular appearances on "Late Night With **David Letterman**." They were dressed in matching jeans cutoffs and white T-shirts, and joked that they frequented **the Cubby Hole** (a **New York** dyke bar). SB boasted that she'd slept with both Sean and Madonna, and when Madonna alluded to having a big secret to tell, all her gay **fans** lunged toward their televisions, hoping against hope that their favorite star would come out of the closet. It didn't happen.

At the peak of the rumors, the terrible twosome did a bump-and-grind version of "I Got You, Babe" at **Don't Bungle the Jungle**. Intimate girl talk with Sandra made for a genuinely funny, selves-effacing scene in **Truth or Dare,** the premiere of which Sandra attended.

By 1992, Sandra had lost her vibe—she had the misfortune of performing in **Bruce Willis**'s megabomb *Hudson Hawk,* her new material couldn't touch her first show, and she began modeling without a touch of irony. She went glam, lost her potency, and went off "the stony end." By the time her friendship with Madonna ended, SB was just a minor member of the cast of TV's "Roseanne."

Madonna never slept with Sandra, and has caught flack for willfully toying with the public's perception of her, and/or for "exploiting" gay people, but it's to her credit that she was willing to allow people to believe she was a lesbian, something most of Hollywood's *lesbians* still aren't willing to do.

So how did it end? Badly. Madonna's fast friendship (again, some say it's more) with Sandra's ex-lover **Ingrid Casares** enraged SB. Another thing that led to a rift between the pair was Sandra's ina-

"*B*efore she came around, I was somebody in this town. Now all people do is call me for quotes on Sandra."

—Madonna, blurbing SB's *Confessions of a Pretty Lady,* 1988

"*I*'m not a lesbian and I'm sick of being called one,"

—Sandra Bernhard, 1989

"*E*very time Madonna farts, [the press] picks up on it. They want to see how it smells. I hate to break the news, but it smells like everybody else's farts."

—Sandra Bernhard, 1990

"*I* have long legs, Madonna has short legs. They're stubby, like a midget. She looks stupid without makeup and her broom."

—Sandra Bernhard, 1994

"*I* believe in her heart she really wants a boyfriend like everyone else. . . . She's more normal than you think."

—Janet Charlton, *Star* gossip, who's less normal than she thinks if she really believes that *everyone* wants a boyfriend, 1993

bility to go with the flow. Sandra went out of her way to deny the affair, also trying to disassociate herself from lesbianism (as opposed to **bisexuality**).

Instead of letting the rumors fly, SB harped on them, even selling an article on the subject. Tellingly, she wrote, "You see, there's this little problem that develops once you've had a taste of nonstop adrenaline pulsing through your veins; you *must have it all the time,* and anytime you try to escape it . . . you start flipping out and making phone calls just to make sure no one has forgotten you. Especially the whole world."

In the end, SB couldn't get over Madonna forgetting her. SB bitched about Madonna for years, prattling on about how Madonna "will steal your friends and anything she can get her grubby little hands on," sounding like a "Melrose Place" rerun. It makes one wonder if *anything* Madonna could have done, any brand of betrayal, could have been so hurtful as to provoke so pathetic, and so public, an outcry.

birthday: Madonna blows out thirtysomething candles on August 16. She was born at 7:05 A.M. at Bay City Mercy Hospital in Michigan in 1958. Coincidentally, Elvis Presley croaked on Madonna's birthday in 1977.

bisexuality: True bisexuality is having a sexual and emotional attraction to both sexes, not necessarily equally.

Some of Madonna's early intimates like **Bobby Martinez** claim that she is unblinkingly bi, but, lacking corroborating tattletales, there is plenty of room for doubt.

Madonna has recalled sexual experiences with other girls when she was little. When she was best friends with **Sandra Bernhard,** the press labeled them lesbian lovers for their public clowning, but both eventually denied it, credibly. Bernhard later threw a fit when Madonna became close with her ex-lover, **Ingrid Casares**. Gossips believe that Ingrid's live-in friendship with Madonna must have been sexual, but Madonna pooh-poohs the speculation.

When *Sex* came out—chock-full of all-girl **sex**, including Madonna being playfully pushed around by two dykes, simulating oral sex with **Naomi Campbell,** and beachcombing with Isabella Rossellini, Tatiana von Furstenberg, and Casares—the public made up its mind: *major* bi.

In spite of all of this, Madonna has never identified herself as "bisexual." To the contrary, she has always hedged when specifically asked about her attraction to women. She admits to being aroused by the idea of making **love** with a woman while another man or woman watches (SEE ALSO: **exhibitionism**, **voyeurism**), but says she is mostly fulfilled by men.

When Mim Udovitch quizzed her for *The Village Voice* in November 1992, Madonna's responses on the subject of lesbianism were completely circular. She first said that her sex life is irrelevant, which is like a chef telling a vegetarian it doesn't matter whether or not there's meat in a dish. Finally, under duress, Madonna responded to the direct question of whether or not she'd ever had sex with a woman—with a yes.

Why hasn't Madonna said she is bisexual? The answer is that she isn't any such thing. Madonna is heterosexual. She is emotionally and sexually attracted to men, though she's an experimentalist. She isn't bi, she just swings that way.

black-and-white: Madonna's fondness for black-and-white film started with the **"Borderline" video,** which employs a *Wizard of Oz*–like shift from black-and-white to color photography and back again.

Her first all black-and-white video was **"Cherish,"** which paved the way for **"Oh Father," "Vogue," "Justify My Love,"** and most of **"Erotica."** *Truth or Dare* is black-and-white except for the Technicolor concert scenes, and several interviews she gave to promote that film—to the likes of **Kurt Loder** and **Regis Philbin,** and her "Wayne's World" segment on **"Saturday Night Live"**—were similarly colorless.

Black-and-white flatters Madonna's appearance and conjures up images of classic Hollywood and "**art**" films, two sources with which Madonna identifies. It's also peculiarly appropriate for Madonna, whose actions tend to provoke black-and-white, all-good or all-bad responses.

SEE ALSO: ZITS

Blackwell, Mr.: The bitchy **fashion** critic *always* includes Madonna on his Worst-Dressed list, prompting Madonna to remark that he was on her list of "men whose opinions I'm least affected by."

In 1993, he seemed to have a change of heart about Madonna, naming her to his Best-Tressed list for her admirable "**shock** appeal" in **hair**styling.

Blond Ambition tour, The: Madonna's greatest achievement as an artist/entertainer, and the pinnacle of her **creativity**

in the first ten years of her career. From the title pun to the brazenly **sex**ual modern **dance** numbers to the fixation on **Catholic** imagery, BA was the perfect combination of all things Madonna. It was her grandest tour, the first megatour of the nineties, a four-month trek to more cities (27 worldwide) than she'd ever seen previously, or would see again—a star communing with her audience at the height of her critical esteem and popularity. The only country in which she could not sell out? Italy, where for weeks prior to the shows **the Pope** had called for a boycott. She wound up canceling one of her two planned appearances.

There were 1,500 spotlights and four sets that completely covered an 80 x 70-foot stage, all of which was transported from town to town in 18 trucks. Over a hundred crew members spent two full days assembling that monstrous stage for every show, generating catering bills of $15,000-plus for each gig.

Madonna's look for BA stymied **wanna-bes**—after all, it's difficult to rustle up convincing **Jean-Paul Gaultier** rags, and since the designer had costumed most of the show (with some pieces by **Marlene Stewart**), anyone trying to copy Madonna's BA style mostly stuck to the lengthy blonde ponytail **hair**piece she wore for the Asian and North American stops of her tour. By the time she set foot in Europe, Madonna had grown tired of the ponytail's desire to entangle itself in her **headset,** so she went with a headful of blonde curls instead.

The show was a taut 90-minute roller-coaster ride that reviewers (and Madonna herself) consistently likened to musical theater. But BA was not "like" musical theater, it *was* musical theater. It offered sets as elaborate as *Kiss of the Spider Woman*, choreography more inventive than has ever been seen in any other rock'n'roll concert, and a performance as layered and evocative as any **Tony**-winning role. *Evita*: *The Road Show*.

Choreographer **Vincent Paterson** reports that Madonna wanted to "break every rule we can. . . . She wanted to make statements about sexuality, cross-sexuality, the church . . . But the biggest thing we tried to do is change the shape of concerts. Instead of just presenting songs, we wanted to combine **fashion,** Broadway, rock, and performance **art**." They succeeded.

The opening tableau was straight out of her **"Express Yourself" video,** with half-naked musclemen standing subserviently at all points across the stage. Madonna appeared at the top of a staircase center stage, greeting her audience and asking (in a tongue appropriate to the venue), "Do you believe in **love**?"

BA was organized into four distinct sets. First was an irrepressible dance set, comprised of "Express Yourself," **"Open Your Heart," "Causing a Commotion,"** and album-track favorite "Where's the Party."

Next came a religious passion play built around **"Like a Virgin," "Like a Prayer," "Live to Tell," "Oh Father,"** and **"Papa Don't Preach."** In this set, Madonna shocked the world with her graphic (mock?) **masturbation** on a crimson-sheathed bed and by twisting her **cone bra** as if the cups could rotate on screws.

Dick Tracy was new in the theaters, so Madonna dutifully included an entire cabaret segment of *I'm Breathless* tunes, "Sooner or Later" (rising from the stage on a grand piano), **"Hanky Panky,"** and "Now I'm Following You" (Parts I and II). Knowing critics would dislike her lip-synched dance routine to the latter, Madonna joked onstage to "Dick Tracy" stand-in **Slam,** "You can't sing? That's okay—neither can I and look how far I've gone!"

Her final set was lighthearted and nostalgic, running from a silly send-up of **"Material Girl"** (performed as a Judy Holliday–voiced housewife under a hair dryer), to a treacly version of **"Cherish,"** to "Into the Groove"—ending dramatically with a minimalist rendering of her then-current supersmash, **"Vogue."**

For encores, Madonna danced gaily in **black-and-white** polka dots to **"Holiday,"** and ended cerebrally with a meticulous *Clockwork Orange* version of **"Keep It Together"**—wickedly performing a black-hearted interpretation of the notion of "family" while extolling its virtues in song.

"*A*s I left amidst scores of overly coifed mall-queens and their deliciously muscle-bound escorts, I couldn't help but think that what I had just witnessed was the very embodiment of Wagner's concept of the *Gesamtkunstwerk*—the total, organic, multisensual work of **art**."

—Mayer Rus, *Outweek*

lip-synched "Vogue." Madonna is unable to sustain high notes for any length of time, a situation complicated by a throat ailment that haunted her throughout BA. Her vocal sweetening did not detract from a performance that can only be described as legendary.

BA was a major Madonna triumph, proving her to be a stage performer with no parallels, a physical presence of seeming invincibility, and the world's most popular live entertainer. Her final performance was aired live on **HBO,** and the concert was further preserved in *Truth or Dare*.

"*T*he respected 'American Playhouse' series will present one of the most thoroughly entertaining, spirited productions in its history [with] *Bloodhounds of Broadway* . . . a lively, funny, engaging romp."

—Daniel Ruth, *Chicago Sun-Times*

Critics generally embraced the show, calling it ambitious, rigorous, and simultaneously bubbly. *USA Today* and other papers cynically complained about Madonna's reliance on lip-synching, but Madonna defended her right to employ backing tracks as part of her spectacle, pointing out that there was much more to BA than **singing**.

For the record, Madonna sang audibly over her own pre-recorded vocals on songs like "Express Yourself," lip-synched almost completely on "Where's the Party," and, as she would in the future, totally

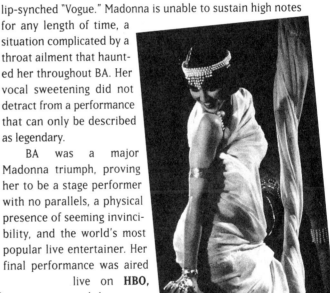

Madonna vamps it up like a regular Theda Bara in Bloodhounds of Broadway.

Bloodhounds of Broadway:

Madonna costarred in this 1988 film, a twenties-era gangster farce directed by **Howard Brookner,** contributing a delicately amusing performance as "Hortense Hathaway," a Prohibition PriMadonna with bang-up Louise Brooks bangs. The movie is based on the writings of Damon Runyan, who originated phrases like "guys and dolls," "monkey business," and "put up your dukes."

The final film, cut after Brookner's death, is so episodic that during its **art**-house run in **New York,** a reel was accidentally deleted and no one noticed for two weeks! But, in *BOB*, Madonna gets to reinvent "Nikki Finn" and get it right this time; connives at the expense of a charmingly oafish Randy Quaid; sings a duet ("I Surrender Dear") with **Snatch Batch**–ette Jennifer Grey; and does a mesmerizing shimmy in beaded bra and skirt.

 BOB is invariably described as having been "so bad it was never even released." It *was* released, earning only $4,203, but it also aired on TV on PBS, where it scored stellar ratings.

 The film was made in Union City, New Jersey, on a shoestring and a wish: Cast dressing rooms in the Knights of Columbus Hall were separated by shower curtains with names inscribed in Magic Marker. Some of the names scrawled were Matt Dillon, Rutger Hauer, Julie Hagerty, Esai Morales, Anita Morris, Dinah Manoff, and even William S. Burroughs.

blow jobs: Our Queen of **Sex** doesn't like to give them! Madonna has joked that there is some sort of misogynist conspiracy behind the submissive aspect of women having to choke in order to give men head, as opposed to the relative ease of man-to-woman or woman-to-woman oral sex. And you wondered why she has such a hard time keeping a steady boyfriend.

Blue Frogge, The: Ann Arbor, Michigan, student pub where Madonna met **lover** and future bandmate/collaborator **Steve Bray,** who was waiting tables. Madonna claims it was the first time she ever bought a guy a drink, but Bray remembers buying *her* a gin and tonic. The pub, at 611 Church Street, later became a hard-rock bar called Rick's.

Body of Evidence: For *BOE,* Madonna was paid $2.5 million for her services (and her **acting,** too) in a contract that guaranteed her top billing; approval of stunt/body doubles and foreign voice dubs; no promotional photos would be furnished to supermarket **tabloids**; and she could keep her wardrobe (*not* worth it). The best part of the whole deal was that the filming took just 43 days, spent on location in Portland, Oregon, and at Culver Studios in Los Angeles.

 On her shortlist of major career mistakes, *BOE* ranks right up there. The movie opened January 15, 1993, on a whopping 2,000-plus screens, raking in $6.5 million. It did a quick plunge after that, ending up with a gross of just over $13,275,426 ($37,938,251 worldwide), not quite what it cost to make, putting it at number 72 for the year, right behind *Super Mario Bros.*

 What was she *thinking*? She read the script and hated it, as did director **Uli Edel** ("We knew that the film could be really, really junky. It was a thin line.")—but she had admired Edel's work in *Last Exit to Brooklyn* and believed he could elevate the material.

 Madonna should have known better. The part, which she described as the best lead she'd been offered, is a one-dimensional sexpot role of the variety that Sharon Stone had only the year before taken to new levels of insipidity in *Basic Instinct.*

 The plot is farcical: "Rebecca Carlson," a **sex**-driven sex siren/gallery owner sexily has sex with a sex-crazed sex maniac, who later dies from afterglow. Did "Rebecca" do it on purpose? Her attorney is "Frank" (**Willem Dafoe**), a family man who finds himself falling prey to her wiles, and to his secret attraction to kink. The high concept here is: Can sex be a murder weapon?

Interesting **AIDS** metaphors are overlooked, and the film stagnates as a straight courtroom drama. *BOE* asks us to suspend disbelief at every turn. "Rebecca"'s coke addiction is shown to be a silly misunderstanding—that's actually healthy *Chinese peony powder* she's been snorting, not cocaine!—and we are supposed to believe that "Frank"'s wife (Julianne Moore) doesn't notice his torn, bloody shirt after he lies on broken glass *en flagrante*. Even the sex scenes seem mechanical after the cute, much-hyped, hot-wax scene.

Maybe the reason every scene is so murky is that Edel is embarrassed at how little effort he's made, or that he's embarrassed for his actors (including Miss Thing and especially Anne Archer), all of whom look a dozen years older than their true ages. Must have been that bracing Portland wind.

The acting is *competent,* even Madonna's. Her performance was universally panned, as if she were generating all the millions of other things *more* wrong with the film.

Madonna said she'd studied courtroom dramas for inspiration, citing Kim Novak and Lana Turner as influences in the role. When you're studying Kim and Lana for acting technique, it's time to make a record. It's hard to understand what possessed her to think she—or any actress—could deliver lines like, "I *fuck,* that's what I *do,*" or, "Have you ever seen animals make love, Frank?"

The worst thing about the film is that it's a blatant cautionary tale that villainizes sex. Not exactly a credible belief for Madonna to espouse. Her "It's only a movie" defense just doesn't cut it—not from the woman who can take something as ordinary as **hair** color and charge it with symbolic meaning.

"*A* slick thriller that embodies elements of *Witness for the Prosecution, The Story of O,* and *Basic Instinct.*"

—David Ansen, *Newsweek*

·

"*If* everyone says it's horrible, I'll slit my wrists."

—Madonna, joking

·

"*It*'s Hollywood's version of amateur night at a topless bar, where some blonde has just climbed onstage and taken everything off but doesn't know how to dance. So, everyone just sits there dumbfounded, equally embarrassed by her audacity and her incompetence."

—Jack Mathews, *New York Newsday*

·

"*What* to do about poor Madonna?"

—Vincent Canby, *The New York Times*

Willem Dafoe told John Waters that in order to get into their characters for *Body of Evidence,* he and Madonna were taken to an actual murder trial. The judge stopped the proceedings halfway through to gush to Madonna, "I *love* your movies!"

bodyguards: Madonna employs GSS Security Services, Inc., for many of her security needs, including constant protection for the **New York** premiere of *Truth or Dare,* and during her **Girlie Show** travels. The agency, founded in 1989, is run by Chuck Garelick and John Smaragdakis, who like to provide "someone who won't stand out unless he is needed," starting at $16 per hour.

"boobs ahoy": Like misbehaving chihuahuas, Madonna's breasts have a tendency to "pop out" at inopportune moments.

In the **"Material Girl" video,** when she is suspended upside down, we see more breastage than was previously thought possible without glimpsing nipple, and when she arches her back triumphantly in the **"Papa Don't Preach" video,** a nipple *does* squeak into view if you can get your VCR to pause clearly. You don't need a VCR to see the hint of nipple that winks out from the **"Express Yourself"** 7" sleeve from 1989.

They kept coming up for air while rehearsing a musical number for **Dick Tracy,** so makeup techie John Caglione, Jr., was asked to glue them into her gown. He respectfully declined, fearing he'd be blamed for defacing a "national treasure" if anything went wrong: "I'll bet each one of those honeys is worth six, maybe seven million."

They went flying during her rehearsals for the 1991 Academy **Awards,** and had to be taped into her racy Bob Mackie gown to avoid flashing over a billion people worldwide on Oscar night.

And these are just the times when they expressed themselves unintentionally!

SEE ALSO: **OSCARS**

books: Like Marilyn before her, Madonna flaunts her love for reading to counter any notion that she's a nimblenod. Aside from frequently citing her favorite writers like most stars name-drop each other, she insinuates books into interviews and interviewers often take note of any she "happens" to have in full view. She had Serge Nazarieff's *Jeux des Dames Cruelles* sitting on her coffee table when *Entertainment Weekly* chatted with her in 1991, and *Us* spotted **Andy Warhol**'s *Diaries* (in which Madonna is flatteringly featured a number of times) available as bathroom reading. She adored *The Sheltering Sky* (but hated the movie), even taking its heroine's name as a temporary **alias.** Madonna found *Naked by* the *Window* and *Giovanni's Room* by James Baldwin sufficiently compelling to recommend them to an interviewer (and to consider optioning them as film **projects**).

Director **Susan Seidelman** once happened upon Madonna hunched over a collection of Sam Shepard's **plays** (remember her affection for Jessica Lange?), and in 1986 Bruce Weber photographed her "reading" the biography *The Dark Side of Genius: The Life of Alfred Hitchcock.*

What book is the penultimate in erotica for the Anaïs Nin of the nineties? *The Lover,* by Marguerite Duras—the story of a Chinese teacher and his pubescent conquest.

Madonna once said the book that best describes her life is *War and Peace,* and that the author whose writing most reflects her own sensibilities is J. D. Salinger. "That's how I would write," she said in 1990, though *Sex* bears no resemblance to *Frannie and Zooey.* More like *Catch Her in the Thigh.*

Some of Madonna's other favorite writers:

Charles Bukowski,

Raymond Carver, Honoré de Balzac,

Guy de Maupassant, Lawrence Durrell,

Louise Erdrich, F. Scott Fitzgerald,

Ernest Hemingway,

Henry James, James Joyce,

Jack Kerouac, Milan Kundera,

D. H. Lawrence, Thomas Mann,

V. S. Naipaul, Françoise Sagan,

Anne Tyler, Kurt Vonnegut, Jr.,

and Alice Walker.

Interesting taste for

a "dumb blonde," eh?

No word on Madonna's reading habits, but we'll go out on a limb and hypothesize that she likes to read in snatches.

"Borderline" song: Madonna's first Top 10 hit (number 10) was the second single from her ***Madonna*** album, a flirty, confectionery complaint from one **lover** to another. As on much of her first two albums, her vocals were mechanically altered to sound girlish and to speed up the song to mid-tempo.

"Borderline" video: Madonna plays an aspiring model in her first big-budget **video**. She breaks up with her macho boyfriend (convincingly played by future one-hit wonder Little Louie) over her budding career, only to screw up her big break by accidentally spray-painting her photographer/Svengali's car during a **graffiti**-themed shoot.

The video uses color footage for the scenes involving the Madonna character's romance, and **black-and-white** scenes for its extended modeling sequences. The clip cleverly makes use of Madonna's connection to graffiti artists, her own (then-recent) ascension to **stardom,** and her photogenic qualities, all in four minutes.

"B" also predicts what would become a mainstay of the Madonna myth by featuring a magazine with Madonna's photo on the cover. *Gloss* may not be a real magazine, but Madonna's real-life cover shoots soon followed.

boredom: "If you take everything I do at face value, you're going to be horrified. Or intimidated. Or insulted. Or *bored.*" —Madonna, 1991.

As a provocatrice, Madonna's only real enemy is boredom, so it is also the best weapon for any critic. Instead of decrying her immorality or critiquing her performances, some dyed-in-the-wool anti-Madonna critics have taken to throwing up their hands and exclaiming, "*Bo*-ring!" at every move she makes. The trend started back in 1991, when a *Time* poll said that 73 percent of Americans were "uninterested" in Madonna. Weeks later, she cleaned up with ***Truth or Dare.*** She was rated the Number One Most Boring Celebrity by the Boring Institute (of New Jersey, natch) that same year and Number Ten in 1992.

But the concept of boredom went a long way in reviews of ***Sex.*** Writers who prior to the

"*I*s 'Borderline' not the sweetest song ever recorded about an orgasm?"

—Adam Sexton, *Desperately Seeking Madonna,* 1993

"*I*'m a dancer. I know what it's like to watch things and get bored very easily. That's why I wanted to combine dancing [with singing], y'know, just like on 'Solid Gold.'"

—Madonna, 1984

book's publication had claimed its very concept to be a disgusting exploitation of **sex,** turned around and called the finished product—which was less sexually daring than **pornography,** but more sexually daring than anyone thought Madonna would actually be—boring. Been there, done that. Huh?

With the public perception that Madonna is attempting to be progressively more and more **shock**ing, whenever she breaks stride with something subtle, she's strung up for being "boring." Madonna's boredom problem will only go away after she continues to surprise and delight her **fans,** outlasting any naysayers who will have us believe they weren't at least energized by the sheer audacity of *Sex,* or excited by the fabulous **Girlie Show,** or will not listen with interest to the gossip about her latest effrontery.

boxing: She may not like violence, but she attended the minutes-long bout between "Iron Mike" Tyson and Michael Spinks at the Trump Plaza Hotel and Casino in Atlantic City, New Jersey, in 1988. In the crowd were The Reverend Jesse Jackson and Richard Pryor, and at her side were **Sean Penn** and writer Harry Crews. She sat on Sean's lap so Crews could have a seat to himself and later gave some rare **autographs** to the casino's kitchen staff.

***Boxing Helena*:** Jennifer Lynch–directed 1993 **sex** thriller involving a man (Julian Sands) so possessive of his girlfriend (Sherilyn Fenn) he amputates her limbs and keeps her in a box.

It wound up one of the most-panned films of the year, but the real excitement was the **lawsuit** brought by the producers against Kim Basinger, who'd backed out of the project after a verbal acceptance. The producers recouped about $7 million from Basinger, nearly bankrupting her, and set a precedent that will have actors thinking twice before "sort of" agreeing to anything.

Madonna had earlier backed out of the project, but since she did so before the producers attempted to sell the film using her name, she was in the clear.

"*W*ho would have thought the devilishly simple concept of 'Boy Toy' would capture the imagination of so many *female* teenagers?"

—Fred Schruers,
Rolling Stone, 1985

Boy Toy: On her *Like a Virgin* **album** cover, Madonna wears a silver belt whose buckle reads BOY TOY. She wore that belt to several public functions in 1985 as the album was climbing the charts. End of story, right? *Wrong.* The slogan has become the most-oft-repeated catch phrase for Madonna and her free-wheeling attitude. Originally, the phrase was Madonna's street **nickname**, like that used by **graffiti** artists and close friends **Keith Haring** and **Futura 2000**; she even confessed to having spray-painted the name around **New York City**. Reproductions of her BOY TOY belt

were later sold in a short-lived line of Madonna-inspired clothing (**Wazoo**). It's likely that she'll have to endure this moniker for the rest of her life.

SEE ALSO: **NICKNAMES**

Bray, Steve: A **lover** from Madonna's Ann Arbor, Michigan, days with whom she first explored **music**, performing with him and his band in the local Holiday Inn and Howard Johnson's. She met up with him again in **New York,** where the two were in the band variously called The Millionaires/Emmenon/Emanon/**Emmy**.

Bray collaborated with Madonna on the **demo** that secured her a record contract, but was denied the opportunity to produce her first singles in favor of **Mark Kamins,** and both lost out to Reggie Lucas on producing her first album.

Though Bray is counted as one of the boyfriends she's "walked all over" to get to the top, he was the first to say, "It seems like you're leaving people behind or you're stepping on them, and the fact is that you're moving and they're not."

He went on to cowrite the music and, in some cases, coproduce **"Angel,"** "Over and Over," "Pretender," "Stay," **"Causing a Commotion,"** "Can't Stop," "Where's the Party," **"True Blue,"** "Jimmy Jimmy," "Spotlight," **"Express Yourself,"** and **"Keep It Together,"** making him a millionaire and, along with **Patrick Leonard,** one of Madonna's most frequent and important collaborators.

"*I*'ve always kind of made the rib cage and the skeleton [music] of the song already— she's there for the last things like the eyebrows and the haircut [lyrics]. She writes in a stream of mood really."

—Steve Bray on songwriting with Madonna, 1989

Breakfast Club, The: Madonna's first-ever band, from 1979–80, in which she initially played drums and fidgeted with a guitar, but eventually sang lead. The band was comprised of sexy brothers Ed (guitar) and **Dan** (drums and Madonna; he was a beau) **Gilroy,** and suggestive Angie Smit (the first lead singer, demoted and finally booted out completely). The group took their name from frequent early-morning conferences at the local International House of Pancakes.

Madonna split from band and brother in 1980 to form **Emmy** (among other monikers) with **Steve Bray,** who himself later joined and recorded with The Breakfast Club.

The Madonna-free BC went on to minor success in the mid-eighties with the Top Ten single "Right on Track."

"Breathless Mahoney": The torch-singing, back-stabbing moll played by Madonna in *Dick Tracy.* Her explanation for the name: "[She] gets poured into all her dresses, ergo the name 'Breathless.'"

*"A*nybody who accepts the life that she was leading obviously comes from a shitty place."

—Madonna on "Breathless"

bridal shower: Madonna's was thrown by Nancy Huang, **Nile Rodgers**'s then girlfriend, in Huang's Upper East Side apartment. Twenty-five of her closest pals attended, including Mariel Hemingway, Thompson Twin Alannah Currie (with whom she'd performed at **Live Aid**), **Debi Mazar**, **Maripol**, and **Erica Bell**. The party was all-girl, but **Martin Burgoyne** and ex-**lover Jellybean** made loopholes of themselves and crashed . . . in drag.

Brookner, Howard: Director of *Bloodhounds of Broadway,* who died of **AIDS** before the final cut, leaving 8,100 feet of celluloid that was then edited into a jumbled but still highly entertaining gangster romp.

Madonna first met HB in the **clubs** of New York. She was impressed with his *Burroughs* bio-pic and that "he didn't try to flatter me."

Madonna became one of HB's confidantes during the making of their movie and the unraveling of his life. She was sympathetic, having recently cared for **Martin Burgoyne** until his death from AIDS. "When he phoned and said, 'I have to tell you something,' he couldn't get it out. I said, 'I already know.' I think it was

kind of a relief that I knew and that my feelings about him weren't going to change."

For *Bloodhounds,* HB assembled one of the most talented casts of the eighties to make a $4-million **art** film, solely on the merits of his dedication, the script, and his power of persuasion. He snagged Matt Dillon by taking him to Umberto's Clam House and showing him police photos of mobster Joey Gallo's gunned-down corpse sprawled in the same restaurant six decades earlier.

Brookner's wry, un-p.c. epitaph, taped to his refrigerator at the time of his death, was *"There's so much **beauty** in the world. I suppose that's what got me into trouble in the first place."* He was buried on his 35th birthday.

Brosnan, Pierce: When "Remington Steele"/"James Bond" was asked to sum up Madonna as one of the ten (number 10) sexiest stars of 1985 in *Us* magazine, he said, "Any girl who jives onstage in her undies can't be all bad. And she has a great pair of, uh, vocal cords."

Brothers, Dr. Joyce: The famous-for-being-famous shrink has a split personality when it comes to analyzing Madonna. In the early nineties she said, "Madonna is a sexy person for our time. She's independent and on her own two feet," but in summing up *Sex,* she bemoaned the state of the world when impressionable kids choose to emulate "a rich slut."

Her final **analysis**, in case anyone on planet Earth takes Brothers seriously, is that "Madonna doesn't think she's lovable to a man and so she places an impossible burden of proof on any man who would **love** her."

Brown, Julie: The funny obnoxienne responsible for "The Homecoming Queen's Got a Gun" and the host for a time of **MTV**'s "Just Say Julie." She frequently ribs Madonna, and her December 1991 *Truth or Dare* send-up for Showtime—*Medusa: Dare to Be Truthful*—is a hoot, the funniest Madonna satire ever, featuring a **"Vogue" parody** called "Vague."

Brown's is a dead-on stage approximation—at times, she could pass for the real thing. "In my fantasy, she's like the toughest chick in high school who throws you up against a locker and says, 'I'm gonna beat you up!'" she said of Madonna, but she later heard that the object of her sincerest flattery actually liked the show. Why haven't these two become best friends yet?

bubblegum: As per the script, Madonna chewed and snapped it all the way through her legitimate stage debut in a workshop production of David Rabe's *Goose and Tom-Tom.*

Burgoyne, Martin: Madonna's best friend and roommate from her early years in **New York** who died of **AIDS** at twenty-three in December 1986. MB and Madonna were inseparable as they tore through the Downtown scene with the energy of two

*Christopher Ciccone, **Bags**, and Martin Burgoyne before Madonna's 1983 **Celebrity Club** performance.*

transplants—she from the **Midwest**, he from England via the South (Florida).

Madonna **dream**ed of being a successful dancer and actress, or maybe a singer, biding time working at the Russian Tea Room. MB was a talented designer struggling to make his mark while still having as much fun as possible, going through the motions as a Studio 54 bartender. When Madonna's career took off, her friendship with MB remained solid, so strong that it annoyed homophobic **Sean Penn**.

When MB learned he was suffering from AIDS, Madonna supported him completely, both by paying all his bills and subletting him a 12th Street apartment near St. Vincent's Hospital, and by remaining physically and emotionally close to him. In the age of AIDS hysteria, she never hesitated to be seen with MB, or to hug and **kiss** her buddy, and she visited him constantly for the duration of his illness. When Martin died, Madonna was in the room with him, and she told **Carrie Fisher** in *Rolling Stone* that his death throes and rage at dying haunted her.

The loss inspired Madonna to funnel millions of dollars into AIDS research and care organizations. She modeled a Burgoyne original jacket at a **Barney's** benefit for AIDS the month before he died, and her **Who's That Girl** Madison Square Garden concert the following year—with all proceeds going to AIDS foundations—was in his name. She dedicated **"Live to Tell"** to his memory.

Besides being her best friend, MB was one of her backup dancers at her early performances at **Danceteria,** designed her bold **"Burning Up"**/"Physical Attraction" 12" sleeve, and also designed Michael McKenzie's early book on Madonna, *Lucky Star.*

"Burning Up" song: Madonna's second recorded release in 1982 was the 12" single of this song, featuring "Physical Attraction" as the B-side. It was a part of the *Wild Life* soundtrack, but never released as a 7" single.

When it was released in the U.K., she was less than thrilled

with its remix: "Warner's said they wouldn't put it out in Britain unless Rusty Egan remixed it. He took all the bass out and totally changed the song. You can't imagine what a horrible remix he did."

Nonetheless, it was a **club** sensation, featuring her sexiest **lyrics** until **"Justify My Love"** eight years later.

"Burning Up" video: Her first studio video was an auspicious debut in 1982, featuring Madonna as a siren in white, writhing in the middle of the road, pulling dogchains across her throat, floating serenely on a raft, and dancing with gusto in a barrage of surreal settings. The video was directed by Steve Baron, who had previously directed **Michael Jackson**'s groundbreaking "Billie Jean," and starred as Madonna's **love** interest ex-boyfriend **Norris Burroughs**. Though we see clips of Burroughs's character driving toward Madonna as she squirms on the pavement, in the end it is Madonna who is in the driver's seat.

The song was never released as a single (except as a **dance** single), so "BU" is one of her lesser-known **videos**, but it was a promise of things to come. in **art** and in life.

Burroughs, Norris: Speak of the devil! Her **lover** for three months in 1979, NB actually introduced Madonna to his successor, **Dan Gilroy**. NB was part of the Downtown **art** scene, a **graffiti** artist and T-shirt entrepreneur. He was also a rare blond boyfriend—tall, slim, angular, pale . . . think of him as an effete **Vanilla Ice**. His looks landed him a role in Madonna's **"Burning Up" video**.

*"**M**adonna was definitely a sexual being, but not in the same sense of wearing lace panties and torpedo bras. It was just kind of an animal sexuality. She called me up one day and said, 'Get your gorgeous Brando body over here.'"*

—Norris "Marlon" Burroughs, 1993

business: If she's a **sex** icon, she's also a business icon, the one woman about whom every businessman will narrow his eyes and say, "I don't know about the rest of it, but she is *shrewd,* very *shrewd.*" She takes that reaction as a compliment, but Madonna doesn't like having her business affairs scrutinized, and actively dissuaded friends and associates from commenting for a 1990 *Forbes* cover story.

She is the corporate head of all her companies, and is involved hands-on in the business side of her career. David

Salidor, a publicist who's worked closely with her, said, "She used to walk into meetings with a legal pad and a written agenda. She was very much in charge."

This image conflicts with Madonna's stories of glibly eating **popcorn** during meetings, letting a piece fall into her cleavage, and then coyly fishing it out to eat it.

"Bye Bye Baby": Acidic anti-**love** song from *Erotica* that became the final single from that album when it was released (abroad, but not in the U.S.) in late 1993. On "BBB," Madonna's vocal is distorted to sound tinny and mechanical, which made it a breeze to lip-synch on the **MTV Awards** telecast and live on the **Girlie Show.**

"I used to worry about surviving, what I was going to do. Now I have to worry about being ripped off. If my lawyer is making the right deals, if my accountant is paying me. Boring stuff like that."

—Madonna, 1986

Caesar salad: A **vegetarian,** Madonna will more often than not order her favorite salad when eating out. This assertion can be put to the "interview test"—note that in almost every interview that takes place in a restaurant, she hails a Caesar.

Café Tabac: East Village (232 East 9th Street) **New York** eatery owned by ex-model Roy Liebenthal. This trendy, star-heavy café is one of *the* places to see and be seen, so naturally Madonna has shown up more than once. On one of her visits in 1992, she puckishly picked up the phone and took reservations. In the spirit of fun, no one minded that she never wrote any of them down.

Camden Palace: The site of Madonna's British debut in November 1983, lip-synching to **"Everybody,"** "Physical Attraction," and **"Holiday."** Manager David Chipping said he gave her the equivalent of about $16 to cover her expenses.

The event was filmed by the London show "The Tube" and survives as an early record of Madonna's showmanship and charisma even without elaborate props and costumes.

camp: Trying to define "camp" is like trying to define **pornography**—it's impossible to establish distinct rules, but ya know it when ya see it. Camp is when something dead-serious has no idea that it's also screamingly hilarious. It's a soap opera from the fifties with all its broad innuendo; it's Julia Child cooking a turkey; it's an old woman nearly drowning in **glamor** makeup, thinking she looks *hot,* thinking that she ever could; it's the glittery "Brady Bunch" variety specials of the seventies, the Village People, and attaching "Miss" to the name of any great diva.

Though the wickedest camp is accidental, since the seventies it's become more common for camp to be on purpose. RuPaul is a good example. Madonna is an *excellent* example.

Madonna is a lover of camp. She is amused by the same stars that amuse other happy camp-ers—"Vogue" is a virtual checklist of camp—and her self-awareness of those same farcical heights to which she has ascended is plain. There is a knowingness to Madonna, just like the knowingness that emanated from Mae West (the first camp icon to recognize her status as such). Madonna knows what's funny to see Madonna doing and saying. Witness *Truth or Dare,* made not because she was so desperate to invite us into her personal life, but because there is no denying the ridiculous fact that we're *dying* to take a peek. Or screen her **"Fever" video,** where her subtle smile as she parades in outrageous costumes and red pigtails screams, *"Can you believe* this*?"*

Camp moments in Madonna's career are endless, but must include the tawdry stage-wiping antics of the **MTV Music Video Awards** **"Like a Virgin"** performance; interviews she gave on **Japan**ese TV in 1984, wearing full **Boy Toy** regalia, and blankly, impatiently waiting as the questions and her answers were methodically translated back and forth; stage costumes like **cone bras** (especially on men), phony ponytails, paisley jackets with purple lace tights, blonde afro wigs, and bustiers with tassels; performances in movies like **Shanghai Surprise;** her **"Nightline"** appearance; and whole **videos** like **"Deeper and Deeper."**

Madonna's camp savvy is top-notch, but not infallible. **Liz Smith** tried to save her some face by saying that **Body of Evidence** was *supposed* to be campy, but Madonna (ignoring the swift kick under the table) denied that the film was supposed to be any such thing. (But ya *are* campy, Madonna, ya *are*!) And whenever Madonna says she is an avenger for **self-expression** and **sex**ual freedom, the camp-meter gets a hernia. She is . . . but . . . hearing her *say* it!

Camp is Madonna's lifeblood and, though it can be corrosive, it is an outlook, and a talent, that will keep her afloat, in charge, and sane.

Campbell, Naomi: Jamaican-British supermodel-cum-novelist who posed in *Sex* for what has been reported to be a $150,000 fee. Thirteen years Madonna's junior, she appears in shots with Madonna and rapper Big Daddy Kane in and around a pool, and also in a shot simulating oral **sex** on Madonna (in bikini) where Naomi's buttocks appear to be *sealed.* They are either inexpertly **airbrush**ed (to avoid showing any genitalia?) or she was born fused, like some giant Francie doll.

It is Naomi's toe that Madonna is **shrimping** in *Sex* and on the back cover of **Erotica.** Naomi couldn't take the heat surrounding *Sex,* so she meticulously avoided the subject. Asked why she posed for the book, she said, "I did that for the photographer, **Steven Meisel,** who is a great friend of mine. I did what Steven told me to do. I don't know if she had any fantasies for me because I was just directed by Steven." Naomi's ultra-religious **mother** denounced the poses, claiming that she too had been asked to pose, but had declined.

Madonna and Naomi had socialized prior to the *Sex* shoot, introduced by Steven Meisel. Madonna showed up at Naomi's twenty-first **birthday** bash at **Laura Belle** immediately after her return from **Cannes.**

SEE ALSO: **Penn, Sean**

Campfire Girls: As a little girlie, Madonna joined the Campfire

Girls, an alternative to the Girl Scouts of America. She could have been a Brownie, but she went with their rivals because "they had the cooler uniforms." Too bad—imagine the amounts of cookies that kid could've sold.

cancellation: Madonna almost never cancels a performance. The first time she canceled was the premiere of the **Who's That Girl tour** in **Japan** at Tokyo's Korakuen Stadium, due to torrential rains. But 30,000 crazed **fans** were left disbelieving in the downpour and mini-riots ensued.

The next time she canceled was due to laryngitis that accompanied her to every stop of **Blond Ambition,** making her vocals strained and deep. Not that anyone goes to a Madonna concert for the extended, a cappella solos, but every time she sang for two hours straight she risked serious damage to her vocal cords, so she bowed out of the last of her three shows in Chicago, a fourth show in New Jersey at the Meadowlands, and also canceled her third show in Worcester, Massachusetts.

cancer: Madonna's **mother** died at thirty after a long bout with breast cancer, so Madonna herself is very cancer-conscious, going for mammograms every six months.

The *National Enquirer* reported that she found small lumps in her right breast in late 1987, saw Beverly Hills specialist Jerrold Steiner, and then postponed follow-up visits for months before having a biopsy done, which proved that the lumps were benign cysts. She has never commented on the veracity of that story.

candy: Being a **vegetarian** doesn't mean you're a health-food nut. No animals died to make caramel, or chocolate, or jawbreakers. Madonna always has candy to dole out to friends, strangers, interviewers. "Our favorite thing to do," said **Sandra Bernhard,** when it was *cool* to be Madonna's friend in 1989, "is to go to 7-Eleven and buy junk candy late at night."

Madonna's favorite kind of candy is a long-lasting sucker, and the sucker of choice is a Charms Blow-Pop.

Cannes: The French site of the 10-day *Festival International du Film,* commonly referred to as the Cannes Film Festival, launched in 1939 as an alternative to that year's Fascist-dominated Venice Film Festival. Screenings of films in competition run all day long from 8:30 A.M. until the last one at midnight, leaving precious little time to flaunt one's fabulousness, the real reason for attending Cannes in the first place. After all, do you really

The Cannes-Cannes girl is immortalized by French Elle *in 1991.*

wanna go to the French Riviera to sit around in a dark movie theater?

Madonna didn't. She blew into the 44th annual festival in May 1991 to promote **Truth or Dare,** limited her appearances to the premiere of **Spike Lee**'s *Jungle Fever,* a **Miramax** party thrown aboard David Bowie's yacht, and the exhibition-only screening of *Truth Or Dare.* She playfully avoided her ex. (**Sean Penn** was in town to promote his directorial debut, *The Indian Runner.*)

When her arrival was first announced, the French *gendarmerie* felt compelled to draft extra agents to help stave off a wave of crime expected to follow in her wake.

Madonna was at her peak in Cannes: a **sex** goddess by everyone's estimation, the world's biggest star, the brains, bucks, and bod behind the year's most talked-about *cinéma verité-ou-faux* documentary, and the biggest dose of **glamor** to hit the festival in decades. When she ascended the stairs of the Grand Auditorium and turned, **eyes** gleaming, gums exposed with glee, the world sank to its knees and Madonna threw open her hot pink cape to reveal an ivory **Gaultier** bullet-bra and girdle outfit—*voilà!*

The *Truth or Dare* screening was the hottest ticket in town, so it hardly mattered that crowd control and security problems kept the majority of ticket-holders from ever entering the theater.

Films in competition that year included *Barton Fink, Jungle Fever, A Rage in Harlem, Miller's Crossing, Guilty By Suspicion,* and Akira Kurosawa's *Rhapsody in August.* Other stars at Cannes in 1991 included Robert DeNiro, Eddie Murphy, Robert Mitchum, Gina Lollobrigida, Donald Sutherland, Rupert Everett, Terry Gilliam, Whoopi Goldberg, Geraldine Chaplin, **Rosanna Arquette,** and Arnold Schwarzenegger. Madonna stayed in the secluded Cap Du Roc Hotel on the coast of Cap d'Antibes.

Canonero, Milena: Academy Award-winning costumer behind Madonna's elaborate **"Breathless Mahoney"** wardrobe for **Dick Tracy.** Her designs formed the basis of an entire line of clothing for which stores were urged to establish "'Breathless Mahoney' departments." The short-lived collection, bolstered by over sixty licensees, consisted of black-sequined gowns, fake diamond accessories, blonde wigs, fire engine red lipstick, hosiery, shoes, and sunglasses.

In *Dick Tracy,* director **Warren Beatty** wanted vain "Breathless" to have eight costume changes, humble "Tess Trueheart" to have half that, and everyone else to stick to one, easily-identifiable signature outfit. Of her experience fitting Madonna, Canonero has positive memories. "She left me to

"*W*as I a good *shayna maidel?*"

—Madonna to Miramax co-chairman Harvey Weinstein after her spectacular disrobing at Cannes, 1991. [Translation: "Was I a good little girl?"]

decide. She just wanted the clothes to fit well and to be able to feel the tightness of the dress on her body."

Canseco, Jose: Major League baseballer for the Oakland Athletics, with whom Madonna reportedly had a fling in mid-1991. In preparation for her role in *A League of Their Own,* she met with several pros, and when she had a one-on-one with Canseco—then estranged from his wife Esther—from 11 P.M. until 1 A.M. in her apartment, tongues wagged. Earlier in the evening, she had attended Liza Minnelli's "Stepping Out" show with a ticket provided by **John F. Kennedy, Jr.,** and fortified herself with a salad from **Laura Belle.**

Madonna didn't comment on the supposed affair, though Canseco said, "We're just friends. She's a nice lady." When a spectator heckled Canseco by taunting him on the subject, he received a string of obscenities in response. Later in the year, a pair of satirical Madonna–Jose Canseco baseball cards was issued by a private company.

If they did do it, he apparently got a walk after only one ball, instead of the traditional four.

car: Madonna's very first car established her expensive taste in automobiles, and was also a gift: a red Mustang for her Sweet Sixteen from Daddy in 1974. She later totaled it. She let her license lapse after high school and in 1985 had to take driver's ed to receive a license immediately prior to the **Virgin tour**. When asked (not by Barbara Walters, amazingly) what kind of car she would be, she chose a gold Mercedes sedan.

Batter Up! This racy pose adorns the Madonna/ Canseco baseball cards.

She purrs around town in a blue-black Mercedes 560SL when not chauffeured in a limo. She graduated to the MB after growing tired with Sean's **wedding** gift: a coral '57 Thunderbird. The Thunderbird, which can be seen in the non-U.S. **"True Blue" video,** was given away for a Ronald McDonald House auction when Sean peeled out of their marriage. It brought in $60,000 for the charity.

Carpenter, Jo Ann: Madonna's kindergarten teacher at St. Frederick's, 1963–64.

Carpenters, The: Seventies brother-and-sister superduo renowned for sappy **love** songs and sister Karen's deep, rich voice. Their career tapered off and Karen died in 1982 from a heart attack after a long bout with anorexia. **Liz Rosenberg** confirmed that both **"Angel"** and **"Rain"** are "tributes" to Karen Carpenter (You can hear it in "Rain's" vocals . . . but *"Angel"?* Maybe because Karen *is* one?) and Madonna cites Carpenter as an influence. On the second night of her **New York** stop on the **Girlie Show tour,**

Madonna made dancer **Carlton Wilborn** sing the Carpenters' "Close to You" to his **mother** in the audience.

Carson, Johnny: Madonna appeared on his "Tonight Show" in 1987 to promote her *Who's That Girl* blitz. She showed up in what she called a "kinda sexy" black bustier and loose pants, wore her white-blonde **hair** short and immaculately coiffed, and charmed the pants off Johnny and his viewers with her timidity, humble take on her **fame**, gentle defense of hubby **Sean Penn,** and the admission that she loves to **flirt**. The funniest moment was Carson's deadpan when Madonna hypothesized that an irksome studio fly was probably attracted to the mousse in his hair.

Johnny seemed bewitched with the winking Tinkerbell before him. "I figured if I'm gonna present myself as a virgin to anyone it should be you," she said sweetly, referring to her status as a first-timer on talk-TV.

She returned to the "Tonight Show" in a surprise 1994 appearance, joking with JC's successor, Jay Leno, and presenting herself as virginal once again in the aftermath of her unpopular **David Letterman** appearance.

Casares, Ingrid: They met at Madonna's topless **New Year's Eve** party (1991/92) and have been nearly inseparable since. One of Madonna's best friends, this Cuban-American agent/model who manages Jon Secada even lived with Madonna in her **Miami** mansion for a time in 1993, fueling speculation that the women were **lovers**. IC was definitely once involved with **Sandra Bernhard** (who openly accused Madonna of "stealing" her), and possibly with **k.d. lang,** but if she and Madonna ever played doctor, both are preserving doctor-patient confidentiality.

IC frequently accompanies Madonna to social events (the White Party in Miami, 1992; on an impromptu Rodeo Drive spree along with **Dennis Rodman,** 1994), and has become a celebrity (the goal of all starfuckers) in her own right, but is not necessarily well liked.

Responding to the suggestion that Ingrid is sweet, gossip Cindy Adams replied, "Yeah—sweet like diabetes."

Castillo del Lago: Madonna's $5-million Hollywood Hills mansion, the blood-red one whose retaining wall is painted with yellow-and-red horizontal stripes. It may look funky, but it's actually true to the Italian Renaissance period. Brother **Christopher Ciccone** designed the villa, inside and out, and captured the desired look to a T. Most of Madonna's neighbors hate the flashy look, not to mention the hordes of **fans** and curious voyeurs who cruise by for a gander at the kooky 10,000-square-foot castle.

Though he initially tried to calm its detractors by saying the color scheme was just primer for a more tame final coat, Christopher later said, "I don't hold their bad taste against them. I'm sure, in time, they'll get used to it."

Catholicism: Once a Catholic, always a Catholic, says Madonna and every other adult survivor of what she calls this "really mean," "incredibly hypocritical" religion. Madonna rejected Catholicism for its restrictive attitudes toward women and its even stricter sexual codes, but could never fall out of **love** with its artifice, high drama, symbolism, and preoccupation with elaborate ritual.

Catholicism is the Broadway of religions, spectacular in scale, and to the degree it takes itself seriously. Its rituals—so like a pop concert—seek to draw its participants into a mass perception of divinity exuding from its center (in the case of the church, **the Pope**; in the case of a pop concert, George Michael or **Michael Jackson** or . . . Madonna).

"𝒩uns are sexy."
—Madonna, 1985

*Like a **God** complex, as illustrated in this 1993 publicity photo.*

Though Madonna has described herself as agnostic, she has constantly returned to the iconography of the Catholic church in her **work** and in her look.

Our earliest memories of Madonna are dressed in marital lace and draped with rosaries and **crucifixes**. Her crosses caused a stir, primarily because she projects 100-percent **sex**. By merely wearing Catholic accoutrements, she was a walking billboard for The Fall From Grace. Her image was Catholic in its bounce between the two components of the great dichotomy in the Church: the Virgin (Mary, Mother of God) and the Whore (Mary Magdalene, who, Madonna has theorized, probably nailed Jesus once or twice). In her **"Like A Virgin" video,** she is both the vir-

ginal bride, swathed in white, and the sexual huntress, barely clad in black lace. The mix is thought-provoking and intoxicating, and it got the world talking about Madonna in religious terms.

On the **Who's That Girl tour,** the Pope's image was flashed as one example of "Papa," but the real embodiment of the struggles between humanism and Catholicism, between flesh and spirit, was **Blond Ambition.** The littlest apostle cavorted through dens of iniquity, defying Catholic stances against **masturbation, homosexuality,** adultery, sodomy, **nudity,** and sex for pleasure—only to wind up at an altar, praying to **God,** confessing to a priest she cannot help seducing.

Unsurprisingly, the church does not see the value in deconstructing its tenets, and found Madonna's frank discovery of sex at its roots tantamount to blasphemy. But you can't be a heretic if you don't care, merely a disrespectful outsider, which Madonna surely is. Her rebuke of the church's rebuke of Blond Ambition stands as a rarity in the Modern Age: a mainstream pop star dressing down the Catholic church for attempting to rule the minds of its believers.

But of course, if you don't believe in Catholicism, that leaves room for belief in Madonnaism. For proof, watch **Truth or Dare** and listen to her vigorously humanistic prayers to "God," or, more probably, to herself and her own reserves of strength.

Madonna's name was her God-given initiation into the fun to be had in toying with religion. Aside from that *assigned* reference, she has *chosen* references to Catholicism throughout her career: "Like a Virgin," as above; **Like a Prayer,** with its praying theme, its rosary-laden packaging, songs like "Spanish Eyes" and **"Oh Father,"** with its paternal/Paternal metaphor; the cleverly-named **Immaculate Collection,** fresh on the heels of Blond Ambition, and a further play on Madonna's own status as a "goddess" of pop; and her entire fascination with sadomasochism (which has its roots in punishment-driven belief systems like Catholicism), as expressed in everything from the back cover of **Madonna** to the **"Burning Up"** and **"Express Yourself" videos,** from "Hanky Panky" to Jean-Baptiste Mondino's bondage-esque **"Justify My Love"** to the pleasure-pain of **Sex** and "Erotic"/**"Erotica."**

Is Madonna anti-God? No. Is she anti-Catholicism? *Yes*—choosing to use its own symbols as convincing arguments against its place in a modern world.

"Causing a Commotion" song: Introduced to **fans** during the opening cartoon sequence of the film **Who's That Girl,** "CAC" was the second single from that soundtrack in 1987. The number 2 smash was performed on the **Who's That Girl tour** before most audiences had ever heard it (judging by low turnout for the movie), and was received as enthusiastically as a greatest hit.

caviar: Madonna adores the food most commonly associated with luxury—fish eggs. She has beluga, Sevruga, and/or osetra caviar at all her parties.

Celebrity Club, The: Longstanding gay landmark in Harlem that hosted all the fine young queens of the thirties and forties. Madonna performed there in 1983, where she was captured applying her face and **singing** live by photographer André Grossmann.

A mirror image of Madonna applying her war paint before wowing the Celebrity Club.

Traces of Elvis as Madonna swivels
her hips at the Celebrity Club.

Madonna charmed Harlem with her
self-effacing banter and earnest **dance** moves.

censorship: Madonna hasn't been "censored," per se, in the United States, but she *has* had rules imposed on her by corporations, which has affected her artistic output.

MTV has standards as fluid as those of the Motion Picture Association of America (MPAA). It bans **nudity,** gore, product endorsements, and other elements it finds gratuitous, from any **videos** it will play. This is not censorship, but a private code of acceptability.

MTV asked Madonna to delete scenes in which she is chained to a bed from **"Express Yourself,"** a scene from **"Oh Father"** in which the lips of a corpse are obviously sewn together, and the scenes in **"Vogue"** in which her breasts are clearly visible through a lace blouse. In each case, Madonna refused and MTV relented.

But when she submitted **"Justify My Love,"** MTV banned it outright, citing the video's overwhelming **sex**ual content. In the end, she did not alter the video, but released it independently. Two years later, MTV would play **"Erotica"** only three times.

"*M*TV has found the video 'Like a Prayer' to be acceptable for air. Ultimately, MTV supports an artist's right to interpret his or her music."

—MTV press release, 1989, just a year and a half before banning "Justify My Love"

Madonna said that for *I'm Breathless,* Disney demanded that she delete references to "sodomy," which could refer to a toning down of the spankfest **"Hanky Panky,"** or to the hypothesized scrapping of an extra "It doesn't matter if you're gay or straight" **lyric** to "Vogue."

The video for **"Like a Prayer"** so angered **Catholics** and religious conservatives that it destroyed Madonna's **commercial** deal to endorse **Pepsi,** and was *truly* censored—banned by the government—in Italy for almost a month after its release.

Real censorship also occurred when **Japan**ese copies of *Sex* were graphically smeared by order of the government to obscure a single visible penis and shots of pubic **hair.**

Certain Sacrifice, A: Madonna's first movie, a bizarre underground **art** film made in September 1979, with copious **nudity,** violence, and a stomach-turning **rape** scene. Madonna plays "Bruna," a raven-haired Downtown girl carrying on an intense relationship with "Dashiel," a suburban outcast (Jeremy Pattnosh). When she is raped by the villainous "Raymond Hall" (Charles Kurtz) in the bathroom of a diner, she and "Dashiel" employ her gang of **sex** slaves to help perform a satanic human sacrifice on her rapist.

In summaries of Madonna's film career, *ACS* is usually referred to as "softcore porn," but it isn't even close—it's pretentious and also incredibly disturbing, thanks to a quirky score by Pattnosh, but mostly it's just a dark independent film.

Madonna applied for the part with a handwritten letter and a witchy photo in response to director-producer **Stephen Jon Lewicki**'s August 1979 ad in *Back Stage* and *Show Business* trade papers for a "dominatrix type." He hired her for a paltry $100 on a total budget of less than $20,000.

After Madonna hit it big, Lewicki made hundreds of thousands of dollars by selling the film to video at $59.95 a pop. Madonna tried, but failed, to block circulation of the video on the basis that she had never consented for her name to be used in association with its release, just her voice and body. Huh? An offer to buy the film back from Lewicki for $10,000 was rejected—Lewicki already had 60,000 pre-orders for the video. Madonna said she wanted the film stopped because she felt her performance in it was "second rate." At least she has a good eye.

Despite her overwrought delivery of already cornball lines, Madonna is mesmerizing in the 60-minute film's several modern-dancey sex scenes. For **Japan**ese distribution, its title was changed to *Rape.*

"Don't touch him, whatever you do—
you'll have *herpes* all over your body.
You'll have . . . *anal warts.*"

—"Bruna," instructing her sex slaves on
handling captive "Raymond Hall"

•

"They've made themselves slaves to me. They idolize me, they adore me. . . . But now we're all enslaved to each other, I guess."

—Madonna, er, "Bruna" on her **fans**, er, sex slaves

Chavez, Ingrid: SEE: "JUSTIFY MY LOVE" SONG

cheerleader: The ultimate rebel of the eighties and premier sexual revolutionary of the nineties was a high school cheerleader in the seventies. (Ergo her aversion to **blow jobs**?)

Of the NBA cheerleaders, she offers, "I hate those nude panty hose and those big hairdos. They're trapped in a time warp."

Cher: Campy superstar who started her fifteen minutes of **fame** as a hippie singer over three decades ago, then became known for her delightfully tacky and revealing Bob Mackie next-to-nothings, then shocked everyone by becoming an effective film lead, delved back into **singing** (this time medium-hard rock), and ended up as a hawker of Lori Davis **Hair** Care Products (the first Academy Award–winning actress to host an **infomercial**).

Cher knew Sean Penn before she met Madonna, which guaranteed her an invite to their wedding. Characteristically, she wore a spiked purple fright wig.

Described as either disliking Madonna or simply desperate to collaborate with her at the time, Cher's feelings now are crystal clear. When MTV sentenced her "If I Could Turn Back Time" video to late-night-only airings because of her racy, rear-endy outfit, Cher pulled Madonna in front of her to take the bullets, saying that at least she didn't do the "tasteless" things Madonna did in her "Express Yourself" video.

More to the point, Cher told CBS "Morning News," "There's something about her that I don't like. She's mean." In her opinion, Madonna "could afford to be a little more magnanimous and a little less of a cunt." No word on whether or not Cher's butt was hanging out at the time.

"Cherish" song: Not a remake of the Association's song of the same name, "C" was Madonna's third single from **Like a Prayer**, and a welcome respite from all things controversial. The sugary **love** song (number 2) was just one of the singles that helped Madonna emerge as the number one adult contemporary singles artist of 1989, even as critics continued to refer to her audience as strictly teenaged.

Even amid sweetness and light, "C" manages a well-disguised zinger—Madonna cheerily forbids listeners to underestimate her point of view. "C" was the last of Madonna's vinyl singles to be issued with a picture sleeve in the U.S., making way for CD and cassette singles.

"Cherish" video: Most-favored photographer **Herb Ritts** directed this **black-and-white** clip. In it, Madonna—who is visibly more voluptuous for her role in **Dick Tracy**—splashes in low tide in a black button-up dress. She flexes her muscles, poses playfully, and cavorts with a little merchild, who seems to have lost his way from a school of nearby mermen (note future lover **Tony Ward** in the school).

Ritts wisely avoided the pitfall of trying to one-up this video's immediate predecessors, **"Like a Prayer"** and **"Express Yourself."**

"C" is a delightful Ritts photograph come to life, smoldering as it shows us Madonna reclining in the surf. Ritts's greatest achievement here was perfectly capturing Madonna's free spirit.

China: China's Ministry of Culture asked Madonna to perform her **Girlie Show** at Beijing's 12,000-seat Worker's Gymnasium on the condition that she stick to cheesecake without **nudity** or vulgarity.

The Girlie Show never made it to China, though she was ranked the number four most popular act of 1993 there, behind the Red Hot Chili Peppers, Nirvana, and **Michael Jackson**.

Chirac, Jacques: Conservative French prime minister whose then twenty-four-year-old daughter Claude convinced him in 1987 to overrule the mayor of Sceaux's decision to disallow the **Who's That Girl tour** to be performed in that town's scenic seventeenth-century park.

After listening to her music and watching her videos, Chirac embraced Madonna as a "genius" and received her like a *fin de siècle* Venus Passing Through at a public forum. Madonna presented him with an $83,000 check for **AIDS** research and played before 130,000 **fans**—the largest concert in French history. It was an election year.

Ciccone: Madonna's surname. Loosely translated from the **Italian**, it means "fat man."

Ciccone, Christopher: Madonna's favorite brother, and a talented and expressive painter who has worked with his sister numerous times, first as a backup dancer for her in the early eighties.

He painted her portrait for the cover of her **"Like a Prayer"** dance single, then graduated to stage-designing **Blond Ambition** and **The Girlie Show**.

Christopher Ciccone, seen here in 1983, carrying the flashlights Madonna used in her early track dates.

He shopped for *and* decorated both of her mansions and her apartment, and there is no underestimating his influence on his sister.

Before their **father** had come to terms with his son's sexuality, Madonna "outed" CC in *The Advocate*.

CC is a frequent social companion of his sister's.

"*My* sister is her own masterpiece. Is there any other way to do it right?"

—Christopher Ciccone

Ciccone, Mario: Madonna's younger half-brother, who has been charged with assault no less than three times and also with **drug** possession. He spent three months in jail and on probation, but at least big sister helps pay his busy lawyers.

Ciccone, Martin: Madonna's big lug of a brother who has had bouts with **alcohol**ism and **drug** abuse, and to whom Madonna refers lovingly as a "con artist" who "cracks me up." He cracked up the entire planet in *Truth or Dare* with his hustler antics, showing up hours late to see his sister after a performance. With drinking buddies in tow, he arrives at her hotel only to be unceremoniously turned away.

Martin has struggled to make it as a white rapper ("MC Ciccone"), and as a Detroit DJ, and made his national singing debut on "The Jane Whitney Show" in 1993.

Ciccone, Paula: Madonna's younger sister, who made a go of it as a high-**fashion** model in the late eighties. Her career with the Richard Ferrari Agency never really took off, but she struck an impressive pose on the cover of **England**'s *The Face* magazine in 1987.

A go-go dancer, then a singer with the Downtown Dukes and Divas, her performance at the Limelight made the front page of the *New York Post*—the Madonna Connection. **Rumor**-mongers say she is insanely jealous of Madonna's **fame,** but PC's comment on the situation is that "[W]hen Madonna became famous, I wasn't shocked, I wasn't surprised. I always thought of her in those terms, as being really popular. She just got a bigger apartment and came **home** less, that's all."

Ciccone, Silvio "Tony": He never wanted to be that way, but he was the first "Papa" who preached to Madonna. TC is the legendarily strict Catholic father whose outrage Madonna has spent her life provoking, even while courting his respect.

TC is a quiet, seemingly gentle man, and he good-naturedly showed up onstage with Madonna at the Detroit climax of her **Virgin tour,** and for his birthday during **Blond Ambition.** He also surprised her as a fellow guest on **Arsenio Hall**'s talk show in 1992.

Madonna has said she tones her show down when he's in the audience, but she doesn't cower from him anymore. (In *Truth or Dare,* she sounds like a Ticketmaster™ agent while discussing how many free tickets he'll need for her show.)

TC never makes a fuss about Madonna's **fame,** and indeed rarely mentions any of her controversial **projects.** Madonna said she was "in shock" when he left a message on her machine to say her 1991 **Oscars** performance was "great,"

and when she visits him back **home** in **Rochester Hills,** she curls up in a sleeping bag just like the rest of the brood.

TC was married to Madonna's natural **mother** until her death from breast **cancer,** then was engaged to a lady Madonna recalls as a "Natalie Wood look-alike." To Madonna's eternal discomfort, he ended up marrying the family's housekeeper, **Joan Gustafson.** TC is a retired Chrysler engineer, whose career included work on defense projects, optics, and government weapons contracts.

*"**J**f you ever die, I'm going to get buried in the casket with you."*

—Madonna, age nine, to her father

.

*"**J** wouldn't have turned out the way I am if I didn't have all those old-fashioned values to rebel against."*

—Madonna, 1987

AIDS Dance-a-Thon, Madonna asked him to come downstairs to chat with her. He thought she wanted to collaborate, but was embarrassed to learn she just wanted to scope his ass as he stalked back upstairs.

Club Madonna: **Miami** strip joint owned by Leroy Griffith that in 1994 was the target of Madonna's most serious finger-shaking over its clever use of her name. Or is it the other way around? "The name 'Madonna' has been around for hundreds of years. She has no lock on it," Griffith griped to the press as Madonna threatened a **lawsuit.**

The meanest thing a "**fan**" has ever done to Madonna? Someone called her entourage in **Japan** in 1985 when she was making promotional appearances, and pretended to break the news of her father's sudden death . . . just to hear Madonna's voice.

Clinton, Bill: A Democratic president of the United States and the first candidate for whom Madonna ever voted, in 1992.

Clivilles, Robert: One half of the popular remixing/DJ team of Clivilles + Cole, and also a member of the C + C Music Factory. At the 1992 GMHC

Look for Madonna's new disco, Studio Leroy.

clubs: Where Madonna got her start, as a flamboyantly dressed clubkid who haunted the Funhouse, Paradise Garage, and the Roxy in **New York,** and later, the Rhythm Lounge in Los Angeles. Madonna's **music** has always been enthusiastically received in the clubs, and she's a staple of the disco circuit. Among her all-time favorite haunts are the Sound Factory in Manhattan, and Catch One and Arena in Los Angeles.

Madonna embraces the late Steve Rubell, the club kingpin behind Studio 54 and Palladium.

collagen: In Beverly Hills in September 1990, Madonna had her lips injected with collagen, a substance that lends a temporary fuller **look** (think Julia Roberts) for a mere $500. The ten-minute procedure guarantees a bee-stung effect for four months, then requires a regular booster shot.

Madonna abandoned the look after one treatment. She has gone on record with her dissatisfaction over her "thin" lips and the collagen was immediately noticeable; overnight, her lips were balloons!

Her experimentation with minor-league cosmetic enhancement might foreshadow more drastic "improvements" to come. The hypersexy pout, which **Liz Rosenberg** jokingly referred to as Madonna's "Lucille Ball tribute," is immortalized in the Patrick DeMarchelier photos used on the sleeve of the **"Justify My Love"** single as well as in the **video**, and on the cover of *Glamour* magazine's 1990 year-end issue.

SEE ALSO: FACELIFT

"Because the mouth expresses so much, I'm amazed that she could take the risk to change her lips. She has a very different expression now."

—Catherine Deneuve, 1990

Collins, Joan: *(Imagine the "Dynasty" theme song trumpeting as you read.)* A B-movie queen of the fifties and the star of TV's "Dynasty" in the eighties, JC was one of Madonna-**lover Warren Beatty**'s early trysts. In her autobiography, JC girlishly giggled over Warren's ability to have **sex** while fielding phone calls, which may shed some light on why Beatty was so adamant that Madonna edit his secretly taped calls from *Truth or Dare*.

Madonna savaged JC on **Arsenio Hall**'s talk show in 1990. Arsenio asked Madonna if she felt threatened hearing JC's name. "No," Madonna replied coolly. "Have you *seen* her lately?"

comics: As a larger-than-life character, Madonna is perfectly suited for the comic-book format. Among Madonna comics available is the XXX-rated *Madonna: Sex Goddess* series from Friendly Comics, Inc., featuring titles like "Truth or Bare."

commercials: Madonna's most famous commercial endorsement was her short-lived **Pepsi** spot, but it's not the only time she's pranced to promote a product other than her own. Madonna endorsed the **Mitsubishi** Electric Company's stereo products in **Japan**. Her 1986 commercial for them featured her dancing and spinning in the toreador outfit from her **"La Isla Bonita"** single sleeve.

Also in Japan, a unique Madonna portrait was used to plug Elleseine, a company offering "aesthetic treatments" for the terminally chubby, a gig later plucked away by Brooke Shields.

More recently, "Open Your Heart" was used as the theme for a British ad for Peugeot, and became so popular it was rereleased as the B-side of her British "Rain" single.

Compton, Kenny: New York painter with whom Madonna was involved in mid-1983.

condoms: "Hey you! / Don't be silly / Put a rubber / On your willy!" With that demure verse, Madonna endorsed condoms all around the globe on her **Blond Ambition tour**. In February 1991, she one-upped herself by issuing a joint statement with **ACT-UP,** calling for the distribution of condoms in **New York** public high schools, a notion that was approved by the city at the time.

Condoms seem to follow Madonna like obsessed **fans**: When **The Girlie Show** cruised into Sao Paulo, Brazil, in November 1993, the Bahia Gay Group sent her 100 condoms of assorted colors, urging her to promote safe **sex** during her show. **Rumor** has it the latex never made it out of South America.

cone bra: From the **"Open Your Heart"** video's pointed corset to the exaggerated black cone bra she sports in the **"Vogue" video,** to the series of pointy-chested frocks worn by men and women alike on **Blond Ambition,** where Madonna goes, angular breasts follow. Or, rather, they *lead*. "It was her idea to put the cone bras on the men in her show," confides **Jean-Paul Gaultier,** the designer behind Blond Ambition, "I would have put them on their penises!"

Gaultier first designed a cone bra for his teddy bear as a child, because it was the easiest way to fold the paper to make a bra for his furry little supermodel.

SEE ALSO: FEMINISM

contract: As per her 1992 agreement with Time-Warner, Inc., Madonna receives a whopping 20 percent of the list price for each record sold.

control (freak): Part of the Madonna myth is her extraordinary ability to keep a tight rein over all aspects of her life, **art,** and career. She writes or cowrites most of her **lyrics,** coproduces herself, and employs a "hands-on" credo in running **Maverick**.

More than any other artist, Madonna radiates complete control. In fact, critics routinely hold her responsible for aspects of her **projects** that she can't in fact control. Can we really blame Madonna for the fragile binding on *Sex*? Or for the amateurish lighting in *Body of Evidence*? This sort of responsibility is daunting to Madonna, illustrated in her defensive disavowal of any creative control over the latter during a Bryant Gumbel interview.

Madonna is also held responsible for every possible reading of her **work,** which is to her advantage if the reading is positive, and to her disadvantage if it is not.

"I like to have control over most of the things, but I'm not a tyrant. I don't have to have it on my album that it's written, arranged, produced, directed, and stars Madonna. To me, to have total control means you can lose objectivity."

—Madonna, 1986

cooking: Guess who isn't a very good cook? Madonna says she can make only four things—**popcorn, Rice Krispies treats,** French toast, and scrambled eggs. That's okay; it wouldn't be any fun worshiping a woman with a prize-winning recipe for Yankee Pot Roast.

Coppola, Sofia: Long-haired and possessing the soulful, dazed look of a flower child, she was hamburger to sharks when she took over from an exhausted Winona Ryder in her father Francis Ford Coppola's film *The Godfather Part III*. An inexperienced and amateurish actress, SC was further stigmatized by the nepotism thing, and disappeared from screen roles.

She is a pal of Madonna's (who can probably relate to disproportionate criticism, and who herself had been discussed for the same *Godfather* role), and appeared in her **"Deeper and Deeper" video**. In 1993, **Maverick** and Zoetrope co-produced a pilot for a Sofia-driven talk show called "High Octane," sort of a "House of Style" on wheels.

courting: Are you considering courting Madonna to win her heart? To woo her, simply be capable of writing fascinating letters and of remembering her favorite flavors of ice cream and her favorite dishes. That's all she asks. And be built. And be self-supporting. But that's it.

cover, magazines: In **"Vogue,"** Madonna identifies the strange allure a star emanates from the cover of a **magazine**, and who better to mention it? Madonna has made the cover story an **art** form, appearing on more magazine covers than **Marilyn Monroe** or **Diana, Princess of Wales**.

It's not fair, though; there are more magazines around these days for Madonna to conquer, whereas Marilyn had to make due with a relative few, and Di doesn't have Madonna's breadth. After all, Di may be on *People* every other week, but how many times has she scored the covers of *Ms. Fitness*, **Playboy**, *Longevity*, or **Vegetarian** *Times*?

SEE ALSO: CENTERSPREAD

"Crazy for You" song: Madonna's first big ballad was so popular in 1984 it dethroned "We Are the World" as the number 1 pop single, and managed to chart concurrently with her other Top Five smash, **"Angel,"** even though the film whose soundtrack it graced, *Vision Quest*, was a box-office letdown.

Fans were pleasantly surprised by Madonna's deep voice on this record after a string of soprano disco tunes. A quickie **video** was fashioned from Madonna's performance in *Vision Quest*.

A U.K. ad for Madonna's "first ever picture disc," collectible albums with images printed directly on the vinyl.

Creative Artists Agency, Inc. (CAA): One of the largest and most powerful talent agencies in the world (over seventy agents), representing the likes of Barry Levinson, Goldie Hawn, Magic Johnson, and Madonna—in her film endeavors from 1986.

Its legendary wheeler-dealer president, Mike Ovitz, is noted as the man behind **QSound**.

Madonna's agent at CAA is **Ron Meyer**.

creativity: Madonna's belief that she can summon hers at will is strikingly similar to **Marilyn Monroe**'s conviction that she could turn on and turn off her "Marilyn" persona.

Crow, Melissa: Madonna's personal assistant from 1983 to 1992 came directly from personal manager **Freddy DeMann,** for whom MC worked at the time he signed Madonna. In **Truth or Dare,** Madonna recites a special dirty, dishy birthday limerick to her right-hand girl. MC is known throughout Madonnadom as "Baby M" (no relation) and is legendarily sweet and industrious. MC still has underground fans of her own, who call themselves "Crow's Feet" and attempt casual conversation with her when she's out alone in public. MC's successor is Caresse Henry.

crucifixes: Madonna burst onto the scene wearing elaborate crucifixes, and one of her most often-repeated quotes is that "**Crucifixes** are sexy because there's a naked man on them." She has also said, "I never go to church except to steal crucifixes—that's a joke." It's been suggested that the appeal of crucifixes as **fashion** statements lies in the **sex** appeal Madonna jokes about, and also in the theft she refers to, the act of taking a religious object from its context and making it a fashion accessory.

She started a trend that has yet to run its course, as crosses and crucifixes continue to find their way into nearly every new **look,** years after their peak as staples of Madonna's wardrobe.

Crumes, Oliver: Bleached-blond black dancer on **Blond Ambition** whom Madonna took under her wing as her favorite, despite his open homophobia. As captured in **Truth or Dare,** OC fears for his manhood as the only straight dancer on the tour, a tension made worse by **tabloid** reports that he was Madonna's **lover.** OC's story is given ample screen time in *Truth or Dare*—we sit through his reunion with his disapproving **father,** watch him talking to himself, and listen to his opinions on his employer as he sits in a well-lighted chair.

He may have been teacher's pet for the duration of the tour, but that ended when he and two other dancers brought a **lawsuit** against Madonna.

"*E*verything I do is sort of tongue-in-cheek. It's a strange blend—a beautiful sort of symbolism, the idea of someone suffering, which is what Jesus Christ on a crucifix stands for, and then not taking it seriously."

—Madonna, 1985

Cubby Hole, The: **New York** dyke bar that Madonna and **Sandra Bernhard** jokingly told **David Letterman** they frequented. Madonna later confirmed she'd never been inside.

curfew: Madonna's was 9:30 P.M. until the day she left **home.** When **Johnny Carson** asked her what one could possibly do with such an early curfew, she replied, "Nothing—or a lot, fast."

customs: French customs detained Madonna for hours when she arrived in **Cannes,** apparently acting on a tip that she would be smuggling **drugs.** She wasn't, and she later accused officials of searching her bags simply for the pleasure of having trudged through her unmentionables.

A repeat performance occurred with U.S. customs in 1993. Officials demanded to inspect **Liz Rosenberg**'s bag (all press clippings), refusing to believe that Madonna and Co. had not bought anything while in Europe. "It was a **business** trip!" Rosenberg scolded, but Madonna wrapped things up by saying, "I know you just want to look through *my* luggage, so why don't you just *do it* and get it over with!" They didn't, and she was on her merry way.

cutting-room floor, the: Two of Madonna's appearances on film were **rumor**ed—prior to the films' release—to have been left on the cutting-room floor. She was rumored to have been lopped out of **Woody Allen**'s **Shadows and Fog,** which the **director** vehemently denied. She was then said to have been cut from **A League of Their Own,** but she ended up intact in that film too.

Still, it's impossible not to imagine the scenes, shots, and exchanges from all her various **projects** that *were* edited out. Not every piece of footage is used even when it's good. As an example, note that **Alek Keshishian** shot over 250 *hours* of film for **Truth or Dare,** which leaves 248 hours of unreleased footage extant.

Dafoe, Willem: Lean, angular, slightly seedy-looking leading man who starred as "Frank Dulaney" to Madonna's "Rebecca Carlson" in **Body of Evidence** after appearing in prestige films like *Platoon* and *The Last Temptation of Christ.*

Dafoe and **Ciccone** *do* have good screen chemistry. Of their initially **NC-17**–rated **sex** scenes, he says, "They were great fun to do. Whether they're erotic or not, or whether they have to be erotic or not, I'm not sure."

He got along with Madonna swimmingly: "I like her a lot, and I think she gives a good performance. You can't control what baggage and expectations people bring into a movie about who this person is."

SEE ALSO: **WHOLE LOTTA LOVE**

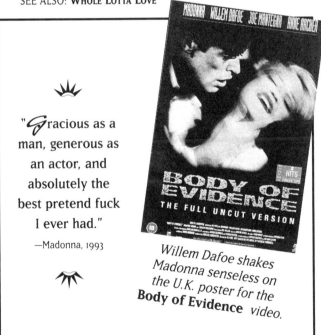

"*G*racious as a man, generous as an actor, and absolutely the best pretend fuck I ever had."

—Madonna, 1993

Willem Dafoe shakes Madonna senseless on the U.K. poster for the **Body of Evidence** *video.*

dance: To dance is to be free, to take the chance of making a fool of yourself, to be so in touch with your body that you are able to liberate yourself, expressing how you're feeling not with words but with actions. Madonna and dancing are virtually synonymous.

Madonna's own first ambitions were **acting** and dancing—**singing** didn't come into the picture until much later. She taught herself to dance, then taught neighbor kids. At twelve, she taught a boy to dance using "Honky Tonk Woman" by the Rolling Stones as the soundtrack, and this moment was so powerful it became an early association with sexuality. She would eventually go to dance classes of the jazz, tap, baton-twirling, and gymnastics variety, "a place to send hyperactive girls, basically."

The most influential person in her life was **Christopher Flynn,** thirty years older and her ballet teacher from her early teens. Aside from continually encouraging her to pursue dance as a career, he took her to gay discos in the early seventies, where she first witnessed the sheer ecstasy of jumping and writhing and *moving around* in front of other people. Here, **gay men** could express themselves and their sexualities, providing Madonna with another strong image of the sexual energy in dancing.

That image must've stuck, because it compelled Madonna to dance her way into a full-ride scholarship to the University of Michigan–Ann Arbor, and later into an impressive position with the **Alvin Ailey American Dance Theater.** Even later, when she realized that dancing would not be her best shot at achieving success as a performer, her **music** always had a danceability to it, whether hip-hop or disco. That danceability has never deserted the tunes, even as her lyrical content has evolved and her musicianship improved.

Madonna has always asked us to dance, beginning with **"Everybody"** and its plea to "dance and sing." She made dance a metaphor for **sex** and **love** with **"Into the Groove,"** perhaps her all-time best dance song, urging us to dance for "inspiration," preferably not all alone.

The extended dance mixes of her songs are sometimes the versions she executes onstage (remember that stuttering "C'mon!" from "Into the Groove" on the **Who's That Girl tour?**). Her contribution to the disco demimonde was immortalized on *You Can Dance,* one of the first retrospective dance EPs. Madonna's dance background has held her in good stead. Her all-dancing **"Lucky Star" video** captivated enough imaginations to firmly cement her image in the minds of a wide audience (the **belly button** helped),

"*D*ancing is sexually provocative. It's moving to music, only you're by yourself. It's masturbatory. You're just moving your body to music. . . . Dancing and music and sex—they're all the same thing. It comes from your soul, ultimately."

—Madonna, 1984

and since then she has made dance instrumental to many of her **videos,** especially **"Papa Don't Preach," "Open Your Heart," "Express Yourself," "Vogue,"** and **"Deeper and Deeper."**

One way to separate Madonna's most irrational **fans** from her most irrational anti-fans is to play a record, ask them to dance, and see who *can.*

Never underestimate the cathartic pleasures of dancing, and never overlook its place as one of the cornerstones of Madonna's massive appeal.

Madonna cuts a rug at the 1991
***AIDS** Dance-a-Thon in Los Angeles.*

Dance-a-Thon: Dance events for which dancers collect hourly pledges to help **AIDS** charities. Madonna has shown up at both the Los Angeles AIDS Dance-a-Thon (for AIDS Project Los Angeles) and the **New York** 'thon (for **Gay Men**'s Health Crisis), as a dancer and as a speaker.

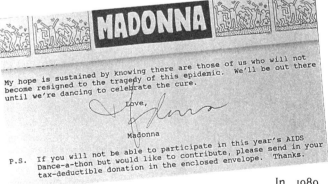

In 1989, she cut a rug for an hour with **Sandra Bernhard,** Stacey Q, and Andy "Coati Mundi" Hernandez in L.A. at the Shrine Auditorium, stopping only to tell dancers why she was there.

"Number one is that I really believe in AIDS Project L.A. . . . And the second reason is that I **love** to dance."

Cavorting with **Debi Mazar** and Rosie Perez, Madonna used a 1994 San Francisco AIDS Dance-a-Thon to unveil her latest piercing look . . . a diamond stud glittering in her nostril. She has donated her likeness and her signature on letters to promote the Dance-a-Thons, which usually manage to knock down $2 million for their respective AIDS charities.

Danceteria: Hopping **New York club** that Madonna favored in the early eighties. It's where Madonna/"Susan" dances with Mark Blum/"Gary Glass" in ***Desperately Seeking Susan*** in scenes that were later spliced into a makeshift **video** for **"Into the Groove."** Seventy-five authentic East Village punk rockers were employed to fill out Danceteria for the scenes. When a frisky cameraman asked a pretty brunette punker what her name was, he was taken aback by "her" response. "It's *Clark.*"

Alas, Danceteria is no more. In its place is a club called The Melting Pot at 29 East 29th Street.

dandelions: Don't give Madonna a bunch of these, hoping to win her over with your sincerity. She *loathes* "weeds that run rampant. I like things that are cultivated."

Dangerous Game: Abel Ferrara–directed 1993 **art** film which stars Madonna in what has been called "*Scenes from a Marriage* meets *The Player.*" Madonna wanted to work with Ferrara, the explosive **director** of cult favorites like *Bad Lieutenant,* since seeing his acclaimed *Ms. 45* in the early eighties. With *DG,* she got her chance to do so as actress *and* de facto producer: The film was produced by **Maverick.**

Financially, *DG* was disastrous. As an under-$10-million art-house flick, it was never going to make much, but its French run was only so-so, and in America it only made $56,798, winning 334th place (of 345) on the highest-grossing films of 1993 list. Even though *DG* sold out its first two weeks in release, bringing in more per screen than the average Top Ten film, it had no staying power. Abel Ferrara **fans** were turned off by Madonna, general audiences weren't about to see such a downer, and the release was too limited to give the movie even half a chance.

If the title sounds "straight-to-video," it usually is, as was the case with this overlooked semiprecious gem.

Maverick's first production is a bag of tricks that was originally titled *The Last Pimp* and later called *Snake Eyes* for its European debut. It premiered in competition at the 50th Annual Venice Film Festival, garnering impressive reviews for film, director, and actors. Its general release in France soon followed to an even more enthusiastic critical reception and a highly favorable cover story in the lofty *Cahiers du Cinéma.*

But the French like Jerry Lewis, so American fans weren't sure what to expect when *Snake Eyes* became *Dangerous Game* (as the result of a nuisance suit by an adult-film maker) and bowed at only one theater in **New York City**. Reaction was *wildly* mixed, running from raves to two-fisted attacks. When a film engenders such a passionate response, it is likely to be well worth seeing. *DG* is no exception.

DG is a film within a film, making use of conventional scenes and video stock with cameras in plain sight. *DG* is about tempestuous director "Eddie Israel" (Harvey Keitel) and his struggle to make a movie. He perceives his film, *Mother of Mirrors,* to be hard-hitting high art, but we the audience see it to be a shallow statement made by a director devoid of humanity, the result of the Hollywoodization of his vision.

Norman Mailer *looooved Madonna's dual performance in 1993's* Dangerous Game.

Mother of Mirrors is the cautionary tale of a high-strung white-collar exec ("Francis Burns"/James Russo) and his sexpot wife ("Sarah Jennings"/Madonna), who suddenly gets religion after years of indulging him in his every sexual whim. He becomes obsessed with reclaiming the whore that was displaced by this unwelcome virgin, and their relationship turns into one long shouting match–cum–**rape** scene.

As both *Mother of Mirrors* and *DG* progress, they trade places, so that the director's tawdry existence becomes ridiculously warped, and his film becomes disturbingly powerful. "Eddie Israel" is directly based on Abel Ferrara, his wife is played by Ferrara's real-life wife, and Madonna's character "Sarah Jennings" is a popular star who wants to be taken seriously.

Just in case you didn't catch the *verité* in this *cinéma,* note that in one of the behind-the-scenes shots, a director's storyboard actually says ABEL FERRARA where it should say EDDIE ISRAEL.

Madonna has never given a richer, more interesting performance. She is utterly convincing as "Sarah Jennings," an insipid TV-movie queen with big ambitions to break into serious film acting.

"*M*adonna's good, but she has chosen the wrong projects and worked with a lot of idiots. She's pissing in the wind because everybody wants to see her fail."

—James Russo, 1994

•

"*T*he turkey of the year has arrived just in time for Thanksgiving. *Dangerous Game,* Abel Ferrara's new film, starring America's favorite female impersonator, Madonna, is dangerously dull. . . . Her acting style is more indicative than method; she indicates emotions rather than embodying them. She isn't sexual; she's about sexuality. She isn't erotic; she's about eroticism. Watching her act is a cold experience."

—The New York Post

•

"*T*he role, which isn't glamorous, is free of artifice in a way that Madonna's screen roles seldom are. Viewers may actually have to remind themselves that they've seen this actress somewhere before."

—The New York Times

•

"*M*adonna has either learned how to act or finally found a character not so different from herself, whom she can simply *be* for the camera. In either case, she's terrific, exactly what the role requires. . . . Those brave enough to breathe *Dangerous Game*'s poisonous atmosphere should brace themselves for a corrosive but rewarding experience."

—New York Press

"Sarah" is flashy, the kind of woman who will smoke a cigarette in key lighting while telling cobwebby dumb-blonde jokes, unaware of the irony that her own hair is as blonde as it comes.

Madonna as "Sarah" is completely fluid for the first time; she moves about unself-consciously, delivers her lines conversationally, effortlessly exudes sexiness. The effect is startling—she is almost like a young Jeanne Moreau, sophisticated and sexy and finally, finally put to good use on the big screen. Most deliciously, and probably accidentally, the performance that "Sarah" gives in *Mother of Mirrors*—which is supposed to be stiff and melodramatic—is the performance that Madonna gave in *Body of Evidence.* A plug for recycling.

DG is a credible effort at meaningful cinema that proved Madonna's commitment to a serious film career. This is one of those movies that has "Rediscover Me" written all over it—check back in twenty years.

dates: Her first date was with a boy named Colin McGregor in the sixth grade, with whom she went to see a movie called *The House of Dark Shadows.* Hand-holding ensued.

Asked in 1984 whom she would rather date, Rick Springfield, Simon LeBon, Lionel Richie, or David Lee Roth—she replied, "Ugh. UGH. Yeeeuch! C'mon. I wouldn't go out with any of them if you want to know the truth. If I had to choose, I'd go out with David Lee Roth, but I wouldn't dress up for him."

In the nineties, Madonna describes her perfect date as being comprised of dinner, a movie, and a conversation over margaritas. Presumably, the hand-holding would work just as well now, so long as it isn't Simon LeBon's hand.

da Vinci, Leonardo: The man who made Mona Lisa smile, and the one artist whom Madonna most wishes could paint her portrait.

Deadly Evidence: The paperback movie-tie-in book for ***Body of Evidence*** was renamed to avoid confusion with another novel of the same name. *DE* had the dubious distinction of bearing the legend *"Not associated with Patricia Cornwell's novel* Body of Evidence."

"Dear Jessie": Whimsical, Beatles-esque song on *Like a Prayer* that was a Top Ten hit abroad, though unreleased as a single in America. The song, composed by **Patrick Leonard,** is named for his daughter, Jessie, with whom Madonna once shared a very close, godmotherlike relationship.

"At Madonna's **birthday** party," Leonard said in 1989, "they danced for about two hours together. In fact, Madonna got her drunk on champagne—I could *kill* her."

An animated video featuring a pink elephant was made for non-U.S. distribution.

death: Though it's not a morbid fixation, death is the one thing Madonna admits to fearing. Her own mortality came sharply into focus when she hit thirty and began to outlive her **mother,** who died at that age.

The public and the media are equally disturbed by the concept of Madonna's death, as exemplified by the **rumors** that swept Europe in August 1987 that Madonna had died in a California car crash and that U.S. officials were covering it up.

She has died on-screen several times memorably. Her melodramatic death scene in ***Dick Tracy*** was an impressive dramatic stretch; her shot to the head in ***Dangerous Game*** a tense edge-of-your-seater; and her murder at the hands of Mr. Wrong in the **"Bad Girl" video** an effective public-service announcement against short-sighted one-night stands. When Madonna dies in real-life (ages from now!), look for a mindboggling critical reassessment of her work.

de Becker, Gavin: Hollywood-based safety/security expert employed by Madonna (and, at various times, Olivia Newton-John, **Michael Jackson,** Robert Redford, Tina Turner, and Michael J. Fox). He and his team keep records of dangerous fanatics who are a threat to Madonna's security, monitoring their whereabouts as closely as possible. GDB is also charged with helping to secure Madonna's **privacy** and with keeping her **projects** under wraps: He called in the **FBI** when photos from *Sex* were being leaked.

de Cazelet, Amanda: This androgynous European model is the woman Madonna passionately kisses in her **"Justify My Love" video** as **Tony Ward** watches. When asked if she would sleep with any woman at all, ADC chose not Madonna, but **Sandra Bernhard**.

"Deeper and Deeper" song: The second single off *Erotica* was a return to **dance**-floor form for Madonna, and one of the most incessantly played songs of spring 1993.

It's a purely disco **love** song, a happy marriage of **"Express Yourself"** and **"Vogue,"** the **lyrics** of which "D&D" actually incorporates at its climactic finish. "D&D" is Madonna's "I Will Survive," tapping into that song's determination and drive, and also evoking gay love with its repeated, heady exclamations that the singer will never "hide" her love again.

In concert, the song's roots and subtext were brought to the fore: It was performed in full seventies drag—complete with afros, glitterball, sequined shorts, and a stageful of androgynes meant to represent the crowd at a disco, circa 1978.

"Deeper and Deeper" video: One of Madonna's least-admired **videos** is nonetheless creatively costumed and full of energy, even where it lacks cohesion or conceptual imagination. Its scenes of Madonna driving in a car instantly recall **"Burning Up,"** its strobe-lit **black-and-white** segments echo **"Erotica,"** but its lethargic narrative drive is unique among Madonna's videos.

"D&D" begins with a pretentious quote and then confusingly

tells the tale of a Madonna-like star who goes back to her roots in the **clubs** to see if any of her old friends—and her old Svengali-like flame, played by Warhol Superstar Udo Kier—are still around.

Madonna gets to dress up in outlandish seventies gear, including short blonde **hair** in a wave, a pink feather boa, platforms galore, and facial glitter. So taken was she with the **look** that she inserted an entire breakaway to a photo shoot where her character parades in more period **fashions** (used in a *Vogue* layout), sans eyebrows.

There are lots of indulgent cameos, including porn director Chi Chi LaRue, former **Andy Warhol** Superstars Maria and Geraldine Smith and Holly Woodlawn, and rock group Pariah. Freshest are the scenes involving an all-girl slumber party featuring **Debi Mazar, Sofia Coppola,** and Madonna, who sports a blonde afro à la **Marlene Dietrich** in *Blonde Venus*. The women nonchalantly peel and eat bananas while watching a male friend strike beefcake poses in his underwear, listening to a record bearing the **Maverick** label.

"Degenerate Art": In pre-war Germany, the Nazis organized an exhibit of **art** deemed subversive, including works by non-Aryan and religious artists, Communists, and pieces whose message could be construed to contradict **Hitler**'s message of Aryan **power** and obedience to the state.

The show was reassembled in 1990 and toured various museums around the world under its original title, except this time "Degenerate Art" became an empowering label rather than a dismissive description.

Madonna was interviewed by the *Los Angeles Times* in 1991 while viewing the exhibit at the Los Angeles County Museum of Art before the museum opened its doors to the public for the day. As she gave her answers to the usual questions, she impressed the interviewer with her knowledge of art and expressed a feeling of solidarity for all artists branded "degenerate" simply because they pose a threat to the prevailing hierarchy.

de Lempicka, Tamara: Art deco painter whose work, especially that from the twenties and thirties, presented male and female figures with a sleek, cold, knowing utility and uncompromising **glamor**. Art-lover Madonna is a great fan of TDL's, and owns several of her canvases.

TDL's stylized renderings heavily influenced the **"Express Yourself" video,** and her work makes cameos in the **videos** for **"Open Your Heart"** and **"Vogue."**

DeLory, Donna: One of the most enduring, and endearing, members of Madonna's troupe, DD has provided backing vocals on all of Madonna's albums since *Like a Prayer* and performed as a primary backup singer/dancer on every tour since **Who's That Girl.** It was she who sang the original **demo** for **"Open Your Heart"** that prompted Madonna to rewrite and record it herself. DD also appears throughout *Truth or Dare,* but never emerges

from the shadow of her boss or makes the kind of individual impression co-backup singer/dancer **Niki Haris** makes.

Donna's voice is clear and strong, sort of like ex-Go-Go Jane Weidlin's. Her self-titled debut album spawned the minor **dance** hit "Just a Dream," cowritten by Madonna.

DeMann, Freddy: Former manager of **Michael Jackson**, axed after Michael's **father** Joe ignited a racial war of words with the man he claimed to have hired "when I felt I needed white help in dealing with the corporate structure at CBS."

Madonna pursued FDM for her own manager, mistakenly believing he still represented Jackson, the kind of all-around entertainer she aspired to be. It was just as well that Jackson wasn't on FDM's roster when he took on Madonna: He still manages other acts, but managing Madonna keeps his plate full and his pockets noisy (he gets 10 percent of *everything* she grosses).

After meeting with her in July 1983, DeMann was compelled to scout her out at a Studio 54 show she did for designer **Elio Fiorucci**. He was floored, and inked her posthaste. Their collaboration has been unshakeable ever since. DeMann's star turn came in *Truth or Dare*: he's the charmingly exasperated hustler who bets the Canadian cops that not only would his star client refuse to tone down her act to avoid arrest, she'd make it even racier.

SEE ALSO: MASTURBATION, MAVERICK

demo: Madonna's first demo is described here for the first time. Recorded November 30, 1980, with her band **Emmy**, the demo was a simple affair given out to a handful of willing radio stations on TDK cassettes. Madonna herself (billed in the band's page-long bio as "Madonna **Ciccone**") hand-wrote the song titles on at least some of the copies, including the one from the Stephen Caraco Archive pictured here. The songs on the tape are "Love For Tender" (5:27), "No Time" (5:57), "Bells Ringing" (5:56) and "Drowning" (3:37), none of which has ever surfaced commercially. The songs are all credited to **Steve Bray** and Madonna, and sound like dreamy Blondie tunes, professional and appealing but rather unlike Madonna's chirpy first solo recordings. The demos were

Madonna's actual first demo, complete with handwritten track listings.

first handed to radio stations around January 22, 1981, the date of a license between Emmy and WNEW FM that survives. Along with the license and the above-mentioned band bio, stations received four promotional photos, two of the band and two of Madonna alone.

An even more professional demo was prepared by **Camille Barbone** at Gotham, containing the songs "Society's Boy" "I Want You," "Love on the Run," and "Get Up." The songs became embroiled in a legal battle that has kept them unreleased to this day, though some snatches of the sugary pop songs were aired on **Robin Leach**'s "Madonna Exposed." Steve Bray again collaborated with Madonna on the demo that **Mark Kamins** took to **Sire** to secure her recording contract. That alluring tape contained rough versions of **"Everybody"** and **"Burning Up"** (later to appear on *Madonna*); "Stay" (later on *Like a Virgin*); and future B-side **"Ain't No Big Deal."** The latter cost all of ten bucks to make—the cost of the tape—because Madonna crashed a recording studio at night to record it.

"Very, very well."

—Delia Bernardino, waxer, on how well she knows Madonna's body, 1994

depilation: The act of removing unwanted hair. Madonna's eyebrows don't shrink magically, y'know, and her legs bear a fine shag if left unattended too long. For the brows, it's old-fashioned plucking, considered such high **art** it warrants a special thank-you to **François Nars** in *Sex* "for getting rid of my eyebrows once and for all."

For the full-body treatment, it's a painful five-hour ($500-plus) waxing done approximately every three weeks and never, never just before her period. Delia Bernardino at the Robert Anderson Salon in South Beach, **Miami,** is Madonna's regular wax-mistress as well as doing facials, pedicures, and manicures. Madonna likes Delia so much she helped her relocate to her Miami position from **New York**'s Moda Salon on Madison Avenue. Madonna even sends Delia first-class air tickets to fly to her side for rush jobs.

Desperately Seeking Susan: Just as **Marlene Dietrich** had *Blue Angel*—not her first film but her early breakthrough—so Madonna had *DSS,* the best film in which she's ever appeared, featuring her most likable performance.

Even as her debut album was kicking out pop singles, Madonna was pursuing a film career. She read for and secured the pivotal role of "Susan" in Susan Seidelman's *DSS,* beating out a host of other actresses who had read for the role, including Jennifer Jason Leigh (*Desperately Seeking Dementia*), Melanie Griffith (*Desperately Seeking Brain Cells*), Ellen Barkin (*Desperately Seeking a Nose Job*) and Kelly McGillis (*Desperately Seeking A Job...Any Job*). She was cast in July 1984 and received a salary of $80,000, the entire budget of Seidelman's previous film, but still five times less than Madonna's winsome costar **Rosanna Arquette**.

The 1985 movie is a happy-go-lucky farce, a screwball comedy of the variety that Madonna so admires. In it, Arquette plays "Roberta," a Fort Lee, New Jersey, housewife so bored with her marriage to a cheesy hot-tub salesman (Mark Blum) she gets off by following a series of romantic personal ads placed by a man (Robert Joy) to a mysterious woman called "Susan" (Madonna). When the ad DESPERATELY SEEKING SUSAN appears, "Roberta" knows there is trouble, so she goes to the park bench in **New York** where the **lovers** are set to meet, only to suffer a konk on the head that leaves her thinking she *is* "Susan" (just like when Mary Ann thought she was Ginger on "Gilligan's Island"!). Mayhem ensues.

Rosanna Arquette is wonderful as the perplexed housewife, and she won a British Academy Award to prove it. The supporting cast includes Laurie Metcalf of "Rosanne" in her debut, Aidan Quinn as a sexy **love** interest for the wayward "Roberta," and fun appearances by Downtown performance artists Richard Hell and Ann Magnuson, as well as deadpan comic Steven Wright.

But as the promotional ads couldn't resist tagging it, this is "the Madonna Movie." Madonna's ragtag-chic personal style, all the rage at the time, is all over the film. She is so mesmerizing in her self-absorption there is never any question why every man and woman in the film flips for her.

DSS garnered almost universally positive reviews and did sensational at the box office (about $27.3 million—1985), making it the fifth-highest-grossing film of the year. It was a debut she could never quite top.

"*N*obody comes through in this movie except Madonna, who comes through as Madonna. She has dumbfounding aplomb."

—Pauline Kael

·

"*M*adonna looks confident enough to crunch boulders."

—*New York* magazine

·

"*M*adonna has enormous authority. With her meaty little body, flared nostrils, and lewdly puckered lips, she's imperiously trampy—just walking down the street she seems X-rated."

—David Edelstein, *The Village Voice*

·

"*W*hen I read the script to *Desperately Seeking Susan,* I felt immediately that I could play the part. Susan is the quintessential femme fatale. Everyone wants to know her, everyone wants to be like her. She has no roots, she represents freedom and adventure and all the things that normal people think they can't do."

—Madonna

·

"*I* wanted to make a film about identity and appearances. . . . At first, it was hard to get producers to take me seriously. I guess they thought I would throw fits or do **drugs** on the set or something. I think they were shocked when I showed up like clockwork every morning."

—Madonna

Desperately Seeking Susan was inspired by the French New Wave film *Celine and Julie Go Boating.*

Diana, Princess of Wales: The only other living woman in the same league as Madonna for sheer worldwide recognition.

In January 1993, when asked if she had any advice for Princess Di—embroiled in marital woes—Madonna replied, "Yeah— Get rid of him."

Dick Tracy: The 1990 film that almost made us believe our favorite bad seed had become a palatable film star you could bring home to Mom and Dad's VCR. *Almost.*

Madonna campaigned hard to win the role of **"Breathless Mahoney"** in the larger-than-life adaptation of Chester Gould's comic strip. Virtually every leading lady in Hollywood had been tested for the role, and **director**/producer/star **Warren Beatty** especially wanted Kathleen Turner (fresh from providing the vampy voice of "Jessica Rabbit" for *Who Framed Roger Rabbit?*) or Kim Basinger (fresh from screaming nonstop through *Batman* as "Vicky Vale").

In the end, Kathleen just wasn't drawn that way and Kim became un-a-Vale-able, leaving the door wide open for Beatty to cast old acquaintance— and new **lover**— Madonna in the part. Her offer to accept Screen Actor's Guild scale wages and a percentage of the gross helped Beatty do the  impossible: bring the $25-million blockbuster in on budget.

Having been written off as an actress after two big disasters, Madonna promptly stole *DT* right out from under its impressive cast, including Beatty in the title role, Al Pacino ("Big Boy Caprice"), Glenne Headly ("Tess Trueheart"), Mandy Patinkin ("88 Keys"), Dustin Hoffman ("Mumbles"), and Beatty cronies Dick Van Dyke, Charles Durning, and James Caan strewn about in cameos.

If the film's striking primary-color palette and inventive latex masks were its main drawing point, Madonna's was the performance that drew it together and made it worth watching. She had the unfair advantage of getting all the best lines ("Aren't you gonna frisk me?"), and turning out to be the mysterious villain, "The Blank," at the end.

Her sumptuous musical numbers—she croons original songs by Stephen Sondheim—are sensational. She knocks 'em dead at every turn, dancing, slinking, bumping and grinding, and delivering "Sooner or Later" so powerfully (and often) that Sondheim was guaranteed his Best Original Song **Oscar** well in advance of the ceremonies. The only thing wrong with the musical numbers is Beatty's inexplicable editing; he splices up her scenes haphazardly. Perhaps he feared this would be seen as a "Madonna movie," or perhaps he just didn't know any better. Madonna was royally pissed at the hack-job.

When she is provoking Beatty/"Tracy" Madonna underplays, but that telltale stiffness works well here, making "Breathless" seem a sensual time bomb.

DT gave Madonna a medium-large mainstream hit and a much-needed critical triumph in Hollywood. It showed that given the right part in the right movie, she was capable of chewing up the screen, and also of helping to attract a large audience.

Though **"Vogue"** does not appear in the film, it was sneakily used as the soundtrack for an all-Madonna trailer that played on **MTV,** enticing **music fans** to come see *DT* because, for one thing, Madonna's in it. That sort of box-office drawing **power** was fairly short-lived.

The film did well at the box office, winning $103,738,726 after a $23-million opening weekend, the highest opening for any Disney film up to that point. It also boasted the premiere of a new Roger Rabbit cartoon, "Roller Coaster Rabbit."

Besides the statuette it won for Stephen Sondheim, it received six other Oscar nominations, including Best Supporting Actor for Al Pacino.

DT was only one part of her multimedia assault in 1990: She wrote an entire album of original music "from and inspired by" the film *(I'm Breathless)* and launched her **Blond Ambition tour.** Together, the three **projects** made 1990 the most critically and commercially successful year of Madonna's career.

Madonna was terribly right when she summed it all up: "I think it was a good thing for me to do."

"*Quivering* with lust, double entendres, and bad intentions, Madonna is smashingly unsubtle as the femme fatale."

—*Newsweek*

·

"*It's* Madonna's best **work** ever—she redefines the phrase `blonde bombshell' for a whole new generation."

—Joel Siegel, "Good Morning America"

Dietrich, Marlene: (1901–1992) Icy, androgynous **sex** icon of the thirties and beyond, an Aryan **beauty** in top hat and tails, a cabaret performer, and an early perfecter of the cult of person-

ality whose films were panned on release and revered in her old age.

Madonna is frequently compared to **Marilyn Monroe,** but if she truly resembles any other pop icon (besides Mae West—a close second for sheer impact) it is MD. MD's revolutionary personal life (her **bisexual** affairs and lifelong open marriage were legendary) more closely matches Madonna's artistic and political goals than did Marilyn's simple desire to be good at what she did.

Still, the differences between the two icons are canyons. MD was not a politician and never claimed to be. She didn't "promote" sexual liberation, she *embodied* it. She didn't care if others caught on—if they didn't, that was *their* problem. On film, she was an inescapably powerful presence, even through the few of her **acting** performances that were uninspired. She didn't work at anything, she just did it.

Madonna is more ambitious, and more self-conscious—also sharper. She wants to accomplish many of the things Dietrich

accomplished, but the fact that she *wants to* changes the effect, sometimes for the negative (it shows in too-earnest film performances) but mostly for the positive (it's much harder to massage an audience's perceptions intentionally—and more personally risky—making triumphs like **Blond Ambition** all the more inspiring).

Madonna could be called a bargain-basement Dietrich for her lack of spontaneity and for contriving her effect, but she could also be termed "a thinking man's Dietrich" for the fact that she is projecting a usually focused complexity of messages *on purpose.* MD saw the difference between Madonna and herself in the exact reverse. "I *played* vulgar," she was quoted as saying in reference to her role in *The Blue Angel,* "She *is* vulgar." Even their egos differ crucially: MD's self-involvement was that of a singular woman with no need for other human beings except to applaud and amuse her. Madonna likes the sound of hands clapping too, but her need is more from the self-involvement of a determined, visionary artist *motivated by* other people, by the lust to provoke, enrage, please, and change them.

Physically, the icons share an ascetic, razor-browed, blonde mannequin quality, and Madonna posed convincingly as MD for Matthew Rolston for *Rolling Stone* in 1986. Since then, she has frequently appropriated a Dietrich-esque look—the beret, the men's suits, the direct imitation complete with goofy German accent on **The Girlie Show**'s "Like a *Wirgin*." Madonna cleverly assimilated Dietrich the **Sex** Icon when politicizing *Sex* (especially in her cigar-chomping interview with Jonathan Ross in London).

When Madonna was contemplating a remake of MD's *The Blue Angel,* **rumors** flew that the stars were going to meet to discuss the role. MD, by then an irrational shut-in, issued a frigid statement that must have tickled Madonna: "I have no intention," it read, "nor have I been contacted, to meet this Miss Madonna."

But Madonna didn't harbor any ill will. She listed MD in her roster of yesteryear, **"Vogue,"** and in 1991, shortly before the elder icon finally croaked, Madonna told interviewer **Carrie Fisher** that she wished she had slept with MD. (To which MD might have offered her chestnut, "Americans are ambitious by nature."—1961.) It's debatable whether Madonna desired MD simply for the pleasure that sleeping with a sexy woman brings, or as a hands-on approach to iconic assimilation.

dildos: Penis-shaped rubber things you stick inside yourself to simulate **sex.** "I'm not really interested in dildos," Madonna said in 1991. In fact, Miss Sexpert dislikes sex toys in general: "I don't see how anyone could look at them with a straight face."

directors: "I'm ready for my close-up, Mr. . . ." Despite being a **control freak,** Madonna has submitted to the visions of many directors. Madonna's wish list of directors she'd love to work with (circa 1985) included the now-deceased Bob Fosse, Martin Scorsese, Francis Ford Coppola, Roman Polanski, and Mike Nichols.

The two dead directors she wished she'd gotten to earlier were George Stevens and Rainer Werner Fassbinder (*Querelle*).

One director she's likely to cross paths with before either of them leaves this earth is **Spike Lee.** They share a mutual admiration and a common wild-card outlook, and it's very easy to imagine Madonna as an over-the-top Brooklyn girl in a Spike Lee Joint. The two also share a mutual friend, **Debi Mazar,** who shows up in Lee's *Do the Right Thing* and *Jungle Fever.*

SEE ALSO: **APPENDIX 4**

"*S*ince Princess Stephanie of Monaco has taken to singing, it's become the fashion to have as little voice as possible! Madonna at least is above that! She sings badly and is very vulgar, but her show is impeccable! The public never makes a mistake!"

—Marlene Dietrich,
I Wish You Love: Conversations with Marlene Dietrich,
by Eryk Hanut, unpublished, 1987

discography: Aside from all her commercially-available **music,** Madonna's discography would not be complete without some mention of the tunes that got away.

Madonna's original record contract guaranteed her $1,000 for every song she wrote. She told interviewers in the early eighties that she was writing a few songs that either never turned up, or turned up covered by other artists with writing credits other than Madonna's. Is there a colossal mix-up, or did Madonna simply use **aliases** for these side **projects**?

In 1983, Madonna did something you'll never believe until the track is finally released somewhere in the world. Under the production aegis of the legendary band Was Not Was, she recorded a disco duet with . . . *Ozzy Osbourne.* The tune, "Shake Your Head, Let's Go to Bed" turned out to be such an embarrassment in Madonna's eyes she blocked its release.

Madonna told writer Mark Bego that she was composing a song called "Call Me, Mr. Telephone" for a woman named Cheyne, which *was* eventually released . . . except the writer was listed as "Toni C." She also claimed authorship of an unspecified song for a French act called Natalie in 1985, which could be any number of near-anonymous tunes on Nat's one-and-only album.

Madonna implied in an interview that she was writing a song for the soundtrack of the film *Fast Forward,* but good luck finding the soundtrack, much less figuring out which of the songs she may have written. Another soundtrack for which she was reported to have written a song was a rock-opera remake of *Oliver Twist,* which never got made.

Along with the classics "**Gambler**" and "**Crazy for You,**" Madonna may have written/recorded two more songs produced by **Jellybean** for the movie *Vision Quest.* A song called "Warning Signs" was listed on an early flyer for the soundtrack, but never actually appeared, and a very rough version of a song called "Lies in Your Eyes" has been released on a bootleg compilation, though the latter seems to have another woman **singing** lead, with Madonna's subtle backing vocals brought mechanically to the fore.

Before final cuts are selected for any upcoming Madonna album, word leaks to the press about the songs in the can, and when some of the predicted titles fail to show up, it's safe to assume that there is an unreleased Madonna song languishing somewhere. It could eventually be used as a B-side ("**Supernatural,**" "**Ain't No Big Deal**") or on a compilation album ("Spotlight"), or it may simply be an early working title for a song that was later released (as "Eating Out" turned into the more subtly-titled "Where Life Begins," and "Deeper" doubled into "**Deeper and Deeper**").

Still, there are quite a few rumored Madonna tracks that are nowhere in sight. Madonna recorded songs called "Working My Fingers to the Bone" and "Pipeline" for *True Blue,* and **Pat Leonard** once wrote a song for Madonna, about Madonna, called "Queen of Misery." **Steve Bray** has said that he and Madonna finished two songs—a safe-**sex** ballad called "First is a Kiss" and one called "Love Attack"—that just didn't fit on *Like a Prayer;* and *I'm Breathless* was supposed to include a song called "Dog House," inspired by Brenda Lee's "You're in the Dog House Now" from the *Dick Tracy* soundtrack. From *Erotica* alone, missing songs include "Throb," "By Alien Means," "Freak," and "No Entry."

Certain songs that Madonna has only performed once are not available commercially. She chirped a sweetly enthusiastic version of "Let the Sun Shine" in a deleted scene from *A Certain Sacrifice,* did a sultry "I Got You, Babe" live duet with **Sandra Bernhard** at **Don't Bungle the Jungle,** and also did a jazzy "The Lady is a Tramp" with Anthony Kiedis on **Arsenio Hall**'s 1,000th-episode celebration.

SEE ALSO: **APPENDIX I**

"Dita": SEE: **PARLO, DITA**; ALSO: *EROTICA* ALBUM; "EROTICA" SONG; **GIRLIE SHOW TOUR, THE**; *SEX*

divorce: Madonna first filed for divorce from **Sean Penn** on grounds of "irreconcilable differences" on December 4, 1987. The divorce spawned a *People* "Diary of a Mad Marriage" cover story that most of its subscribers didn't even have time to read before she withdrew her petition on the 16th. The suit was dismissed "without prejudice," leaving the door open for her to re-file, which is exactly what she did on January 25, 1989, after having lived apart from Penn since **New Year's Eve**. The second filing was rumored to have been caused by a bizarre **assault** on Madonna at the hands of Penn. The details are known only to the former Penns, but Madonna did file a formal complaint, only to withdraw that before filing for divorce.

At the time of the second filing, the Penns had been married three years and four months, and their marriage was almost exact-

ly four years old by the time the divorce was finalized on September 14, 1989. Respondent Sean's middle initial was incorrectly identified as *T* on petitioner Madonna's papers. He consoled himself with his loot from the marriage: full ownership of their **Malibu** mansion, reimbursement of his investment (about $500,000) in their **New York** apartment (which went to Madonna), and about $20,000 connected with their joint account. Otherwise, since the Penns had signed a prenuptial agreement, they kept their own possessions and earnings. As part of the divorce, Madonna's former name, Madonna **Ciccone**, was officially restored.

"*S*he arrived in this restaurant in New York all dressed up as a young man. She was affable, seductive. And there was a positive feeling right away, a positive feeling."

—Dolce & Gabbana on their first meeting with Madonna, 1993

Dolce & Gabbana: Wildly imaginative **Italian fashion** design team, Domenico Dolce and Stefano Gabbana, whose ingenious artistry, close-fitting Baroque dandy-suits, Beatlemania send-ups, sumptuous seventies prints, and attention-grabbing showmanship have combined to make them all the rage in Milano since 1985.

Lovers, and **Madonna queens** themselves, they have become great friends with the star they believe to be the ideal "Mediterranean woman." They designed the heady frocks she paraded in in **The Girlie Show.**

In Italy to promote *Sex* in October 1992, Madonna attended their show and was the guest of honor at a party they threw, to which 300 members of the fashion press were invited. The duo was later accused of *paying* her to attend, but that's rubbish—she *adores* D&G. Dolce said, "She's a friend. Better not to have a friend than to pay a friend. In Italy all the designers have starlets, not stars. Starlets they pay to come to the show."

When D&G appeared in the audience of "Partita Doppia," an Italian talk show Madonna was doing, her face lit up and the interview ended with D&G&M strolling off the **Fellini**-esque stage together.

D&G sell their collaborative designs, which they refer to as "la dolcegabbanata," in over 350 stores around the globe. They clothed "Hollywood Madam" Heidi Fleiss (whom Madonna wanted to play in a TV movie) with suits for her trial.

domesticity: "I liked folding Sean's underwear. I liked

mating socks. You know what I love? I love taking the lint out of the screen."—Madonna, 1989

(R. R.) Donnelley & Sons: Printer of *Sex* that lost millions in revenue when James Dobson denounced them for being involved in "a book that so blatantly disregards the moral and spiritual welfare of the American people." Dobson's company, Focus on the Family, dropped RRD&S as its printer, and other right-wing groups did the same.

RRD&S had previously rejected less explicit **projects** whose content could offend the terminally offendable, including gay-themed books from the esteemed Alyson Publications.

Don't Bungle the Jungle: June 11, 1989, benefit for the rain forest cohosted by Madonna and artist Kenny Scharf, held at the Brooklyn Academy of Music (BAM) in **New York**.

After **Sandra Bernhard** sang "Woodstock" and "Do You Want to Funk?" Madonna came onstage to make a short speech against rain-forest depletion. Bernhard hollered, "Who the fuck do you think you are? Tracy Chapman?" "No. I don't work in a convenience store," Madonna replied cattily. "But I do like to sneak off to 7-Eleven at night for some jawbreakers." Then the pair, wearing matching halters, **drag**like makeup, and brightly painted cutoff jeans, sang a notoriously lascivious rendition of "I Got You, Babe." Madonna cautioned the crowd, "Don't believe those stories." Sandra embraced her saucy comrade and retorted, "*Believe* those stories."

Keith Haring also made a special appearance, and the crowd was packed with celebs like Billy Joel and Christie Brinkley, Calvin Klein, Meryl Streep, Tatum O'Neal, and Glenn Close—many of whom later grazed at an after-party at the Vietnamese restaurant Indochine.

The event raised $250,000—and ten times as many eyebrows.
SEE ALSO: **ACTIVISM, CANDY**

drag: Drag queens around the world breathed a collective sigh of relief when Madonna burst onto the scene. "Now there," they thought, "is someone I can *do*." She's a favorite subject of drag performers because she herself is so androgynous—those biceps!—and because her costumes/wardrobe are so extreme they're easy to ape.

Madonna has done male drag. She posed as James Dean for photographer Bruce Weber's lens in *Life* in 1986, and has since often appeared in men's clothing. She wore a navy blue man's Commes des Garçons suit to meet with **Warner Bros.** executives to discuss her interest in doing the film **Who's That Girl,** and her tuxedoed **Girlie Show** audiences found her not only *looking* like a man, but *behaving* like one too. It could even be argued that she often does *female* drag—her **Blond Ambition look** was so severe and arched she appeared to be either a beautiful woman or a beautiful drag queen.

In her personal life, Madonna's **lover Tony Ward** was into

drag, and even appeared with her in public dressed as a woman. Her thirty-sixth birthday party featured drag performances by Madame Woo, Damian Deevine, and The Kibbles.

dreams: Madonna's earliest memory of a dream is from the sixth grade, when she dreamt she kissed Robert Redford. For free. As an adult, she has said her dreams are usually really violent, mostly about being chased by obsessed lunatics.

As an omnipresent and symbolically-charged figure, Madonna turns up in our dreams frequently. In fact, an entire book has been written on the subject. *I Dream of Madonna: Women's Dreams of the Goddess of Pop* is the result of editor Kay Turner's interviews with 91 women aged 13–61, from France, Canada, the U.K., and the U.S.A. The book, which is cleverly illustrated to play off the dream theme, is a straightforward recounting of the women's dreams involving Madonna, including **sex**ual encounters, friendly exchanges, bull sessions, pats on the back . . . you name it, and some woman has probably dreamed it.

As Turner notes, the dream motif pervades Madonna's **work**, from her recurring slogan **"Dreams Come True,"** to songs like **"Justify My Love"** and "Waiting."

Madonna's very existence, her achievement, is the American dream. She is the small-town girl who, with nothing but unfavorable odds on her side, became the most famous woman alive.
SEE ALSO: **APPENDIX 5**

"Dreams Come True": The phrase at the center of (especially) the early part of Madonna's career when her music was always upbeat and less concerned with politics. She signs open letters to her **fan club** with this slogan, which was also printed on balloons dropped on **Virgin tour** audiences.

Dreams Come True is also the name of a British organization that helps to fulfill the wishes of desperately ill children. Madonna

"*I* went to **New York**, I had a dream,
I wanted to be a big star, I didn't know anybody,
I wanted to **dance**, I wanted to sing, I
wanted to do all those things, I wanted
to make people happy, I wanted to be
famous, I wanted everybody to **love** me,
I wanted to be a star. I worked really
hard and my dream came true."

—Madonna, 1985

visited with five such kids in August 1987 while in London for her **Who's That Girl tour,** on the condition that no members of the press be notified.

The phrase "Dreams Come True" illustrates Madonna's appeal. She's the world's biggest star, and yet she steadfastly maintains—in songs like "Spotlight" and in her self-penned May 1994 **Harper's Bazaar** article (which ends with, "Inspiration is inspiration—go for yours.")—that what she has achieved is not out of reach, that ambition and hard **work** can make things happen, and that even in a dog-eat-dog world, dreams come true.

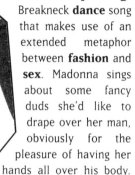

"Dress You Up" song: Breakneck **dance** song that makes use of an extended metaphor between **fashion** and **sex**. Madonna sings about some fancy duds she'd like to drape over her man, obviously for the pleasure of having her hands all over his body. She also sings that she'll create a "**look**" for her **lover**, referring to a concept that would become unique to Madonna's own **fame.**

Despite **Tipper Gore**'s protests, "DYU" was a number 5 song in 1985, her fourth hit from **Like a Virgin.** It spawned a live **video** culled directly from her **Virgin tour** performance.

drugs: Madonna doesn't use them, but it would be inaccurate to say she is anti-drugs. There is nothing "Just Say No" about her. The reason she avoids drugs is that she didn't get much enjoyment from them when she experimented and she dislikes relinquishing **control** of her mind. Madonna tried LSD but emphatically did not like it, nor did she like cocaine, which she said made her even more nervous than she is naturally. The one drug she admits to having liked when she tried it is the

euphoric designer drug Ecstasy, known colloquially as "St. Joseph Baby Acid." Just like Madonna remixes, Ecstasy is a prime **club** drug.

"**I** think, ultimately, drugs destroy you. They take away your natural ability to be **creative** or **love** yourself, deal with people, communicate, *whatever.*"

—Madonna, 1989

drums: Madonna was first a drummer in the band **The Breakfast Club** before she convinced the other members to let her try **singing.**

"**I** said, 'Hey, I'll play drums,' and they said, 'You don't know how to play drums,' and I said, 'You wanna make a bet?' . . . So they let me and they were really impressed 'cuz I was good."

—Madonna, 1985

Duke University: Durham, North Carolina, college where Madonna attended "Tobacco Road," a six-week **dance** workshop in 1978 at the urging of mentor **Christopher Flynn.** It was here that she first met future employer **Pearl Lang,** launching her short-lived career in dance.

Eclipse Enterprises: Forestville, California, novelty-card company that caught flack for introducing mass-murderer trading cards. In 1993, they launched a series of 100 **AIDS** trading cards designed to promote awareness. The cards feature watercolors of "AIDS stars," men and women whose **activism** and/or infection qualify them as powerful symbols in the history of the disease. Sure enough, there is a Madonna card. A surefire collectible.

education: Madonna's **father** used to offer 50¢ to his children for every A they received in school. Since she was living in a material **Rochester Hills,** Madonna made sure to knock down almost straight A's all through her primary education. As a child, she attended three different Catholic schools—St. Andrew's, St. Frederick's, and the Sacred Heart Academy—before advancing to West Junior High in 1970.

She graduated with honors a semester early from Rochester Adams High School in 1976. Her grade-point average, involvement in theater, and outstanding skills earned her a full-ride scholarship to the University of Michigan—Ann Arbor, but she attended for only one semester before dropping out to head for **fame** and fortune in **New York.**

Alma Madonna.

effeminacy: Limp-wristed, lisping, dandified, shrill, girlish, boys are often called effeminate, a perfectly *wonderful* way to be *(blink blink blink).* Madonna, all of whose work is shot through with twists on hardcore **masculinity** versus hardcore **femininity,** is understandably intrigued by effeminate men, even drawn to them. "I think like a guy, but I'm feminine. So I relate to them." Just ask the entire male dancer contingent from **Blond Ambition,** *including* the heterosexual one.

emasculation: The act of seizing a man's **masculinity,** or more to the point, his **power.** Castration is a rudimentary form of emasculation, and though she's never ripped off any testicles as far as we know, Madonna's aggressive posturing has led to a perception of her as a "castrating bitch." Not so! says she: "You only take **balls** away from people when they give them to you." Tell that to the next eunuch you meet.

One good example of Madonna's delightful emasculating impulse was when she humiliated backup dancer Christopher Childers by forcing him to do a striptease, then fifty push-ups onstage at **The Girlie Show** in **New York.** He only made it to forty-nine! But at least it was much lighter going without those pesky testicles getting in the way.

Emmy: Known previously (in chronological order) as the Millionaires, Modern Dance, then Emmenon (and/or Emanon, which is "no name" spelled backwards), this was the band Madonna organized in early 1980 after bowing out of **The Breakfast Club.** Madonna sang lead, Gary Burke served as the bass guitarist, and Mike Monahan and **Steve Bray** (a later addition) played **drums.** Emmy did $25 gigs for approximately a year, gracing the stages at such swell-egant joints as the Botany Talk House, My Father's Place, and Chase Park in **New York.**

Empire Diner: Vintage 24-hour diner where scenes from the **"Bad Girl"** video were shot, located at 10th Avenue and 22nd Street in **New York City.** (Scenes were also shot on Morton Street in Greenwich Village.)

endo: In 1994 Madonna asked **David Letterman** if he'd ever smoked endo, eliciting a tongue-tied denial that he had any idea what she meant. "You're a goddamned liar," she seethed, and her vehemence seemed to imply that she knew for a fact that Letterman *had.* Since Madonna says she isn't into **smoking** *or* doing **drugs,** she must have spent time in the library researching: Endo is extremely potent marijuana.

endocarditis: Ailment that put **Sire** president **Seymour Stein** in the hospital, where he was for his first visit from Madonna. His assistant pressed to have Madonna meet Stein so she wouldn't get away unsigned. She didn't.

England: The British press has always been particularly unkind to Madonna, a dislike aggravated by an incident involving her **bodyguards** roughing up bystanders during a jog through London in 1990. But in 1984, Madonna struggled to give England the benefit of the doubt. She praised its clothes shops, noting that "**fashion** is very important to English people." She also said, "I like the way the cars are on the other side."

"I'm not interested in preaching to the converted, so basically I'm going to the places where I have the most enemies. That's why I'm starting in London."

—Madonna on her tour itinerary, 1993

The press and cars notwithstanding, Madonna has a fanatical following in England, evidenced by the fact that some of her hit singles (like **"Crazy for You," "Holiday,"** and **"Into the Groove"**) have been released two or even three times over the course of several years, never failing to hit the Top Ten.

Enos, John: Big (over 6', 180 lbs.), hunky actor/model/peripheral celeb/nightclub owner with whom Madonna has been linked romantically. In 1992, they attended a birthday bash for Lou Rawls's mother at the Los Angeles restaurant Georgia.

Gossips had earlier noted the chumminess between JE and . . . Mickey Rourke??? . . . spurred on by photos of the men, who are best buds, holding hands. Rourke threw a birthday party for JE at JE's club Roxbury (in West Hollywood) at which they slow-danced and carried on in much the same **fashion** as Madonna and **Sandra Bernhard** used to. Gender roles can be *so* confusing sometimes.

Erotica **album:** Madonna's sixth full-length studio album snuck in the back door in October 1992 while its sister release, *Sex,* stomped in the front door, *naked.* Because the two were released virtually simultaneously in the wake of the **"Erotica" video** and in anticipation of *Body of Evidence,* reviewers could not resist reviewing the entire Event rather than focusing on the tunes.

Understandable, but Madonna's perceived media manipulation made for a screechingly hilarious critical reception. Reviewers who hated the album ranted about its worthlessness as a mere accessory to a book and a movie, or groused that in spite of the title it didn't turn them on. Favorable reviews tripped over themselves, qualifying every positive statement with the wary recognition that they were somehow being duped by Madonna. What is the world coming to when an artist's powers of persuasion are so potent that rational-minded critics begin to question their own opinions?

For all the paranoia, the real threat to *E* was not the critics, but the record-buyers, some of whom were too afraid of Madonna's *Sexuality* to buy the album, which they expected to be a series of obscene phone calls and gutteral grunts. At the end of the day, *E* still sold a staggering three million copies.

E may be Madonna's best album. Passionate *Like a Prayer* is a close second, but ambitious *E* is winning for its unified assault on **sex** and **love,** and its consistency in deconstructing feelings, whether erotic or romantic. While most critics felt the chill in the album, they invariably failed to see the connection between frigidity and sexuality.

Try standing in a hip **club**, hearing throbbing **music**, glimpsing writhing forms in the flashing lights, overheated yet numb with the cold lack of any kind of connection. Watch the other people there and look for one you're attracted to. Now look for more. In every one of them, there is a story to be played out, a tale of how you two could connect, or fail trying. In the end, there is always the most brutish connection, the coldest—sex without strings. *E* is about that chill; it doesn't follow through and tie up all its loose ends in a big happy package, but then that would be boring. Rather, it leaves you with pleasing music masking the contemplative **lyrics** underneath, and all the pleasure, and disappointment, of a grand, zipless **fuck**.

E, a double album, launched four singles: The title track (number 2); **"Deeper and Deeper"** (number 6); **"Bad Girl"** (number 35); and **"Rain"** (number 14). Both **"Fever"** and "**Bye Bye Baby**" became Top Ten hits in other parts of the world.

For packaging, Madonna is pictured in arctic ecstasy in extreme close-up on the front cover (applause for photog **Steven Meisel**), and she's **shrimping** a famous toe on the back cover. (SEE ALSO: **Campbell, Naomi**.)

Once again, Madonna shared producing credits, this time

with **Shep Pettibone,** and with Andre Betts on the four songs they cowrote.

The album opens with the title track. The tone is set with Madonna's growling diva turn as "Dita," who walks us through an S&M landscape.

"Fever" is a straightforward discoization of **Peggy Lee**'s signature song, though Madonna gets extra credit for lending a special insouciance to her minimalist vocals. "Bye Bye Baby" is, depending on your taste, either an annoyingly mechanized, tinny trifle, or an effectively venomous anti–love song, but "Deeper and Deeper" is a little slice of nirvana, the kind of club song that makes you wish the dance floor hadn't gotten so damned crowded all of a sudden.

"Where Life Begins" is a cloying oral-sex anthem with greasy fried-chicken references, but it *is* extra crispy. "Bad Girl" is an impressively weary confession, and "Waiting" just knocks your socks off (unless you'd prefer to keep them on?) with the sheer lust of it all. Madonna virtually remakes Blondie's "Rip Her to Shreds" in the more subdued "Thief of Hearts," a smug song that attacks a cuckolding "bitch."

"Words" is an important cornerstone of the album—Madonna tears the concept of language down to its most rudimentary components and takes the facade away from speechmaking, a strip-mining much like she attempts to do with sex in this and other **projects**.

Serving as the hopeless romantic that inhabits every club denizen, "Rain" is a gorgeous ballad to make the late Karen Carpenter greener with envy. "Why's It So Hard" is an extremely vulnerable entry, featuring Madonna pleading for a sort of tolerance that she herself knows can never be. To her credit, that knowledge doesn't stop her from begging for it.

She got a lot of flack for her sappy **AIDS** ballad "In This Life," and there is definitely something off-kilter when she sexily asks if we've ever seen our best friend die, but her sincerity here—not just owing to the fact that we know she *has* seen her best friend die—is unimpeachable.

"Did You Do It?" appeared only on copies of the album with a CONTAINS LANGUAGE THAT SOME PEOPLE MIGHT FIND OFFENSIVE sticker, but it's really just a funny rap song that makes light of the hardcore, sex-bragging songs children listen to unsupervised every day. The album's dénouement is the lush, jazzy "Secret Garden," which reveals Madonna's songwriting skills and imagination to be as fer-

"*F*or someone who thrives on demystifying sexual mores, Madonna is right on target. Listen to *Erotica* and then take a cold shower!"

—Keith Sharp, *Pulse*

•

"*W*hat the album's about is distance— between images of sex and sex, between pop stylizations of emotion and the messiness of the real thing. Like most of us, she values both. But she recognizes that ultimately they're opposites, not complements. And never, or anyway far too seldom, the twain shall meet— which is the theme of *Erotica,* the subtext of *Sex,* and ever, or anyway far too often, the story of sex."

—Tom Carson, *L.A. Weekly*

tile as the landscape in which she puts *E* to bed.

E is perfectly titled after all. It doesn't always make you feel the things it is about, but every one of its songs could stand in for a splintered emotion that possesses you as you stand in that club and look for someone with whom to connect: hope, horniness, power, defeat, joy, flirtation, fear, competitiveness, need. If you finally do connect, and your prospect introduces herself as "**Dita**," *think twice*. She has a *whip*.

"Erotica" song: Her name is "**Dita**," and she's *frisky*. Madonna continued to explore the potency of spoken-word vocals on the first single from the album of the same name. She assumes the identity of "Dita Parlo," a libidinous dominatrix figure who talks nothing but **sex**, pointing up the pleasure in pain, the appeal in submission, and above all, the wild **power** of sexual attraction.

Madonna's "Dita" voice is gravelly, but the refrain is a breathy, soprano plea to have your hands all over her. Similar to **"Justify My Love"** for its frankly sexual content, "E" is nonetheless a stand-out single. Like its accompanying **video**, the song captures the menace in sexuality.

Despite a relative lack of airplay due to its controversial content, "E" blasted onto the charts at number 15, and eventually went gold. When it stalled at number 2, it was the first time a kickoff single from a Madonna album had failed to hit number 1 since **Madonna**.

"Erotica" video: If Madonna has ever done a video that is truly disturbing, this is it. Many critics have dismissed this haunting clip because it is essentially a series of moving images shot by **Fabien Baron** during the **Steven Meisel**/Madonna *Sex* shoots.

"E" is shot on Super-8 film, often very old or damaged stock, giving it an authentically edgy look in the same way that simple surface noise makes the song "Erotica" feel gritty. The video is a direct reference to the work of Kenneth Anger, the radical filmmaker whose short "Fireworks" "E" closely resembles.

Image after image assaults the viewer: Here is Madonna sharing a **lollipop** with another woman, their tongues caressing across a sticky orb; here she is dancing decadently poolside; now she is laughing maniacally as she whips a herd of nude men pulling a cart in which she rides. There is no storyline; the unifying portion of the **video** is a simple scene of Madonna in a black mask and dominatrix outfit, lip-synching onstage at a sleazy erotic theatre. Shot in **black-and-white,** this segment crackles like radio interference, buzzing with the image of sparkly silver strips at the back of the stage, through which she enters and coyly departs.

Though we are used to Madonna parading in a variety of guises, this time she has really done it, really made herself **look** *different*. By wearing a simple mask and pulling her **hair** back, she looks as evil and daunting as your worst nightmare, or your most sinister fantasy.

Providing the capper is the scene-stealing Chinese doll Madonna produces. The Chinese **hopping ghost** is like a clown in its potential to be either the epitome of fun and games, or a terribly frightening trickster. In this setting, the doll is diabolical, and when Madonna sucks on its tiny, boxing-gloved fist, you either have to shudder with dread or laugh nervously out loud. Still more effective is when the doll punches out, its fully extended glove landing precisely at Madonna's angular jaw. There is a sense of provocation in the image of **boxing** that adds to the sexual atmosphere, and the suspense in their showdown is palpable.

Regardless of any cross-promotional purposes the video serves, and regardless of the artistic intent of its creators and its star, "E" stands as one of Madonna's most emotionally stark video statements.

For its raunch factor (despite the little black bars that shakily cover her naughty bits in the nude hitchhiking finale), "E" was banned from a planned broadcast on "Friday Night Videos" and the NBC screen in Times Square (which itself is a living, breathing "Erotica" video). Nixing any plans for a "Justify My Love"–like video single, **MTV** played the video in its entirety at midnight . . . three times.

"*E*vansville, where all the women are called Shanda or Jolene, an evening out is a trip to the seed store, and you feel vaguely effeminate if you're not wearing a Desert Storm T-shirt. Live here long enough, and you'd probably buy a Johnny Cash album and marry a close relative."

—Simon Banner, *You* (U.K.), 1992

Evansville: Indiana site of a substantial amount of on-location shooting for *A League of Their Own* in August 1991. Madonna and fellow cast/team members leased private homes for the duration of the shoot, a problem for Madonna's realtor since no one wanted to lease her a furnished **home** for fear a raunchy rock 'n' roller would trash the place. She eventually secured a house at 9010 Whetstone Drive for $7,500 per month.

Though she was warmly embraced by the town at the time of her stay (except for a local pastor, who sent her a

missive telling her he was praying for her), she later turned her nose up at the experience. "I may as well have been in Prague," she told **Kurt Loder** in *TV Guide*, also complaining about not having access to cable or **MTV**. Oddly, United Artists Cable billed realtor Jeri Garrison $750 for three cable boxes and remote controls that went missing from the house in which Madonna stayed. "I sure learned something from this: Don't put a bill in your name if you don't even know the last name of the other person," Garrison joked.

But the population of Evansville wasn't joking about Madonna's snub when it rallied into a human anti-Madonna message on the parking lot of Robert Stadium. "Madonna's probably doing this," offered W.D. "Turk" Walton, president of the Metropolitan Evansville Chamber of Commerce, "because she wants to keep Evansville for her own private getaway place because she likes it so much." Or, to use the phrase Madonna helped popularize, "*Not!*"

"Everybody" song: The very first Madonna song ever available commercially has remained one of her enduring chestnuts, first recorded in **demo** form in 1981 and performed live as recently as the finale of **The Girlie Show** in 1993. The song immediately established Madonna as a Disco Queen; led many listeners to assume she was black; introduced the Madonna themes of individuality, dancing, and **singing** as **self-expression,** as well as the optimism that dominated the first five years of her career; and is the first example of Madonna's creative use of a vocal rap, a direct chatline with her listeners that is arresting and personal and unquestionably sexual. She knows we want to get up, and she's had her eye on us. *Yeah.*

"*W*hat if it's terrible? What if everybody stops dancing?"

—DJ Mark Kamins, on his fears about playing Madonna's homemade tape of "Everybody," 1981

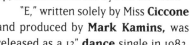

"E," written solely by Miss **Ciccone** and produced by **Mark Kamins,** was released as a 12" **dance** single in 1982, eventually rising to number 3 on the dance charts with over a quarter of a million records sold with the support of Madonna's continuous track dates and a low-budget **video**.

The first single from the woman who would become the galaxy's most visually-oriented artist didn't even feature her photograph, instead relying on a well-realized collage of the Lower East Side/East Village of **New York City** by Lou Beach. An original pressing of that 12" went for about $40 ten years later, or just over $3 per inch.

"Everybody" video: Madonna's little-seen 1982 debut video was shot on a budget of $1,500, about three thousand times less than the budget of her **"Express Yourself" video** seven years later.

Produced and directed by **Ed Steinberg,** the video is a straight performance piece, featuring Madonna—looking very early-eighties butchy, like a Go-Go gone bad—dancing slowly in sync with backup dancers **Christopher Ciccone** and **Erica Bell.** The **hair** is spiked and brown, the clothes are East Village tough, and the image is already mesmerizing, even *sans* all the glam and lighting and editing and stuff.

eviction: Madonna was evicted from her East Village apartment in 1982 when the landlord got a load of what **graffiti** artist **Futura 2000** had done to the walls, at Madonna's request. Far from devaluing the apartment, its then-obscure tenant and the spray-painted doodles done by her pal would make the place a true landmark now . . . if it hadn't been completely repainted.

***Evita*:** Phenomenally popular, fact-based Andrew Lloyd Webber musical in which **Patti LuPone** created the role of "Evita," based on Eva Perón, the glamorous, ruthless wife of fascist Argentinian dictator Juan Perón.

There was talk of a film version of *E* from the time the musical opened, in what became the most drawn-out, revolving-door story since ***Dick Tracy*.** The film rights were owned by Disney subsidiary Hollywood Pictures. Directors Al Weller, Robert Stigwood, Oliver Stone, and Glen Gordon Caron were attached to the project, in that order.

"*I*'ve decided that if anybody's going to do it, I'm going to do it—I'd kill Meryl Streep. I'm just kidding."

—Madonna, 1990

•

"*I* could rip her throat out."

—Meryl Streep, on Madonna muscling in on *Evita*, 1990

•

"*M*adonna—she's like toilet paper. She's on every magazine cover in the world. Devalued."

—Oliver Stone, after canning Madonna, 1991

•

"*N*ot if it's the last breath I take."

—anonymous Disney exec, on whether Madonna would be *considered* for *Evita*, 1994

Patti LuPone was never considered for the lead role in the movie version—that twin may have had the **Tony,** but she is not a film actress, and not well-known enough to be the lead in a blockbuster. After **Barbra Streisand,** Meryl Streep was the first pick of Disney and Webber, but when she became entangled in other commitments, Madonna stepped in as the top contender. From there, it was a tug-of-war between Streep and **Ciccone.**

Madonna would make the better "Evita." After all, *E*'s a great drama, but it's more essentially the flashy story of a very naughty beautiful girl. And, as **Marlene Dietrich** observed of Streep, "How ugly can you get?" Both were unpleasantly surprised when non-**singing** Michelle Pfeiffer nabbed the role out from under them.

Madonna's dream team would have included Jeremy Irons as "Juan Perón" and **Antonio Banderas** as "Che Guevara."

During her **Girlie Show** performance in Argentina in 1993, Madonna sang a few bars of *E*'s most famous song, "Don't Cry for Me Argentina." It was a bittersweet tryout with no callback.

excuses: In response to her critics, Madonna is fond of making one of three excuses for her work. They are often accurate, and always sneaky enough to cover her tracks:
(1) "It's actually supposed to be *funny*,"
(2) "You just don't *get* me,"
(3) "I'm being attacked because I'm a woman."

exhibitionism: The act of shamelessly exposing your body or your private self for your own pleasure—egotistical, sexual, manipulative, subversive, or otherwise.

Madonna's penchant for baring all in public started in sixth grade, at the St. Andrew's annual talent show, when she performed in a little bikini and a lot of fluorescent green body paint ("sort of a flower-power thing") doing her Goldie Hawn "Laugh-In" impression to the strains of The Who's "Baba O'Reilly" in front of an auditorium full of parents. Her father was enraged, grounding her for two weeks, but the reaction she received was nectar: The parents loved it, the little girls in her class refused to talk to her, and the little boys chased her. This experience demanded an encore that has never ended.

Madonna became involved in school **plays** and performed as a **dancer** (both forms of exhibitionism), and in her early years in **New York** she had no qualms about posing nude as an artist's model. Later, when the tasteful photos from those sessions emerged in ***Playboy*** and ***Penthouse*,** her response to the press was, "I have done nothing to be ashamed of," and indeed her only real worry was the effect it would have on her **father** (still fuming over that Goldie Hawn number), and on her career. Her father disapproved, but the photos only enhanced her image as a sexual provocatrice, making her more popular than ever.

Madonna's wardrobe was exhibitionistic from the get-go. She revealed a lot of flesh, and her wearing of brassieres and boxer shorts and pajamas and bustiers was an arresting way of manipulating attention by wearing ordinary clothing in an extraordinary

*"A*t college once in **dance** class they were horrified when I asked if I could take my things off and just wear a bra."

—Madonna, 1985

·

"I don't think I'd like it if everyone was walking around naked all the time. I like clothes. But I think everybody should run naked through the streets at least once. Or be naked when you're not supposed to be naked. It's very liberating."

—Madonna, 1994

·

"I think all entertainers are exhibitionists, admitted or not."

—Madonna, 1992

way. As a result, her audiences have become especially conscious of Madonna's clothing, her body, and their own expectations of how a person should be viewed. The effect is not dissimilar to Alfred Hitchcock using *Rear Window* to remind us that we are all voyeurs at heart. Madonna shows us things to make us realize how badly we want to see them.

Madonna has since become increasingly exhibitionistic to the point where she is a symbol of public revelation of self, corporal and spiritual. **Truth or Dare,** for all its contrivance, remains as the most personally revelatory piece of film from a public figure. She has exposed her body continuously from 1990, culminating with **Sex,** in which she exposed not only her body but (for all intents and purposes) her fantasies, simultaneously tapping into the exhibitionistic thrill of being a **sex** star, like a stripper who craves the catcalls.

Madonna's penchant for self-mockery is another form of exhibitionism, a heady exposure of the un**glamor**ous truth behind the myth. Her exhibitionism is hard to resist. Even if you hate someone, or find them unattractive, you are likely to stop to look if they flash you, if only to gape at their lack of shame. Doubt it? Put a copy of *Sex* on your coffee table and watch as *everyone* who never saw the book gravitates to it and looks to see what she is willing to show.

"Express Yourself" song: The second single (number 2) from **Like a Prayer,** this went on to become one of Madonna's signature songs for its message and **dance**ability, and for the unfor-

gettable **video** that accompanied it. As trite as it sounds when Madonna says that she is "expressing herself" with her **music**, it was at the time incredibly **power**ful and uplifting to hear a pop song advocating individuality. Though "EY" also deals with **love** and relationships, uncompromising individualism is its primary theme.

Some of the **lyrics** to "EY" are among Madonna's least imaginative and her reference to needing a "big strong hand" to help self-actualize drew criticism from **feminists**, but it's all in the delivery. Madonna immediately has everyone's attention with an all-call at the beginning of the song, asking is if we believe in love. After being hopelessly hooked, there's no letup as the singer passionately belts her belief in equality in relationships and mutual fulfillment over a bouncy house beat. It's no coincidence that some of Madonna's rawest vocals came hot on the heels of her **divorce**.

*"T*he ultimate thing behind the song is that if you don't express yourself, if you don't say what you want, then you're not going to get it. And in effect, you are chained down by your inability to say what you feel or go after what you want."

—Madonna, 1989

·

*"T*o express yourself deep down inside is important. If you didn't, you'd be just like a dead person."

—Madonna, 1984

"Express Yourself" video: When "EY" premiered in 1989, hot on the heels of the controversial **"Like a Prayer" video,** it seemed impossible that Madonna could follow up such a sensational statement.

She did, in spades. "EY" is one of Madonna's most popular and elaborate **videos,** costing $2 million, some of which came from her **Pepsi** fee. As a video, it also manages to give a clever interpretation of the battle-of-the-**sex**es anthem by polarizing men and women, playing up their traditional sexualities, but reversing their stereotypical roles in society.

Madonna's character is the height of **femininity, glam-or**ous, sexual, untouchable, and yet she is also presented as the **power** figure, an intelligent, cultured woman who single-handedly runs what appears to be an entire futuristic *Metropolis* (1928

"*H*ere, as elsewhere, we see that Madonna is much more radical in what she does with gender identity than she is in what she does with either gender or class *relations,* and this is precisely because, in Madonna's world, someone is either above or below the other; never are they equal."

—Lynne Layton, 1992

"*I* oversaw everything—the building of the sets, everyone's costumes, I had meetings with makeup and hair and the cinematographer and, you know, everyone . . . casting, finding the right cat . . ."

—Madonna, 1989

"*D*avid's idea for the cat and pouring the milk, it's great, and believe me I fought him on that. I didn't want to do that. It's just so over-the-top and silly and clichéd. Like a film-student kind of trick. But I'm glad that I gave in to him."

—Madonna, 1989

Fritz Lang film) supported by the sweat of a mass of toiling men. Her counterpoint among these men (Guess Jeans model Cameron) is the prototypical strong, silent man, but he is completely subservient, a near-anonymous slave.

The two are connected by the feline embodiment of the woman's desire (another archetypal—and some say sexist—reading of femininity) as a slinky, predatory cat that navigates the pipes and ventilation ducts linking ivory tower and pit. Madonna's desire is made even more explicit when she crawls across the floor like a stalking cat, under a table, and to a bowl of milk, which she laps up, **back** arched. The point is so clear we half expect to see her raise a leg for a little bath. (Missed opportunities. . . .)

"EY" was Madonna's first video that breathed real sensuality and blistering eroticism, as opposed to flirtation. The cat annoyed feminists, as did a provocative scene featuring Madonna chained to her bed, but critics avoided addressing the video's message that sexual desire *is* animalistic— *not* politically correct—and it can be as confining as a literal chain, or entombment in a solitary tower, if it's repressed.

Fortunately, the Madonna character's, er, *pussycat* is finally able to attract the man of her dreams—the Cameron character stalks in at video's end, somewhat roughly takes her up and into his arms, and makes passionate love to her, an updating of *Gone With the Wind.*

"EY" is also notable as the video in which Madonna introduced her version of **Michael Jackson**'s crotch-grab. Wearing a man's suit in a performance segment that alternates with the main storyline, she dances enthusiastically and grabs her crotch with such gusto you're just *sure* she must have a penis after all . . . or that she has something even better.

extortion: During the filming of **_Shanghai Surprise_** in Hong Kong, mobsters demanded huge sums of money in exchange for allowing the crew to film in particular locales. One mobster even refused to move his car before receiving $50,000 to do so. He wasn't paid, and he apparently responded by having the entire movie bumped off.

eyes: Madonna's are naturally blue, though they were graphically enhanced for the **"Rain" video.**

facelift: Not that she *needs* one, but in 1992 one rude reporter inquired as to her feelings on the subject. "A facelift?" she replied. "That's pretty frightening. I don't think I could do it. What if they screw up?"

For all her exploration of artifice, Madonna projects the kind of supreme comfort with herself (just look at those less-than-youthful yet still-attractive hands on the cover of the **Like a Prayer album**) that makes plastic surgery seem an otherworldly possibility.

One would hope she'll embrace her wrinkles, a rebel even in her approach to the aging process. A facelift would take a lot of the fun out of Madonna, making her too similar to the deluded star she has so far managed to send up and co-opt without becoming.

fag hag: Commonly, a woman who is often found in the presence of **gay men**. The term actually connotes a woman who hangs around gay men almost exclusively, getting off on them in a rather unhealthy way.

Madonna is sometimes sloppily referred to as a fag hag. The reason she's not is that she doesn't hang around *them*, they hang around *her*. She's more of a fag magnet . . . a fagnet, if you will.

Fain, Kaufman & Young: Beverly Hills legal firm (121 South Beverly Drive) that represented respondent **Sean Penn** in his **divorce** from Madonna. Sean's personal attorney was Robert S. Kaufman, Esq.

Fallows, Marilyn: History teacher who was Madonna's favorite at Rochester Adams High School. Upon graduation, Madonna presented her with a photo of herself inscribed: "Mrs. Fallows, I can't begin to tell you how I feel about you, and how I will always treasure your words of encouragement. Sometimes I think you might explode with so much energy inside of you. I think you are crazy, and I am really in **love** with your craziness, and of course, you."

fame: "It's bigger than anything I could imagine."—Madonna, on whether her childhood **dreams** of fame were fulfilled, 1987.

fan clubs/'zines: Madonna has many active fan organizations. These clubs are good venues for meeting other people who like Madonna as much as you do. Or, possibly, an insane lunatic who will hunt you down like an animal. But try not to think of that.

Blond Ambition's Spanish Fan Club/Madonna Magazine, Chris

Marquez, publisher, Apartado de correos 1.100, 46.080 Valencia, SPAIN. Write for info. Newsy photocopied 'zine that promotes Madonna in conjunction with her record label, published by the Official Madonna Fan Club's Spanish correspondent. *(Spanish)*

Everybody, Mariam Ayub, publisher, 3100 S. 208th St., #A-304, Seattle, WA 98198, U.S.A. Free while supplies last. "The fanzine that speaks its mind in honor of **fans** everywhere!" is a small-format, photocopied affair that recently went color. It offers lively editorials and random news articles reproduced from elsewhere, and has no shortage of enthusiasm. *(English)*

Icon: The Madonna Fanzine, P.O. Box 175, Cardiff, CF5 1YN, **ENGLAND.** Write for info. Photocopied 'zine that offers loads of interesting reprints, subscriber commentaries, and everything-you-ever-wanted-to-know-about-the-British-Madonna-scene. *(English)*

Icon/The Official Madonna Fan Club, Marcia and Robert Del Vecchio, publishers, 8491 Sunset Blvd., #485, W. Hollywood, CA 90069, U.S.A. U.S. membership fee $29, (includes subscription to *Icon*, which must be renewed annually for $22.50); rest of the world, $39 (with $27.50 annual renewal). The single, solitary, one-and-only Official Madonna Fan Club

has been in operation since 1990. Its official status is noteworthy in light of the fact that several unofficial 'zines have received "cease and desist" letters from Madonna's legal representation. The letters are more valuable as collector's items than as serious threats—Madonna has never sued any publication of any kind.

The Del Vecchios have been involved in Madonna fandom since Marcia wrote for another Madonnazine, *MLC*. Her departure from *MLC* and subsequent snaring of Officialdom created a rift between the two entities that makes for a scintillating subtext in their editorials. Membership in the official club is expensive, but OMFC boasts 18,000 members internationally. The 'zine itself is ridiculously high-quality, chock-full of exclusive photos and features, amazing artwork, an *enormous* personals listing, and even a new letter to her fans written by Madonna herself in every issue. *(English)*

In Touch With Madonna, Luis Filipe R. Lino, publisher, R. Sacadura Cabral, 18, 1 esq, Merces-2725 Mem Martins, PORTUGAL. Write for info. *(Portuguese)*

Like a Faggot! Write Like A.F., P.O. Box 149, New York, NY 10113-0149, U.S.A. Per-issue price (includes postage) for U.S., $6; rest of world, $10. Raunchy, over-18-only 'zine for "fans of Madonna and sodomy" that is more literally a 30-page collage of popular culture, gay sex, Madonna worship, and mirth. Age statement required. *(English)*

Like a Virgin: **Italian** *Fanzine About Madonna*, Sauro Legramandi, publisher. Info-packed, professional-looking 'zine that specializes in news about live CDs and boasts lengthy articles on the Diva and her public perception. Devotes a lot of energy to promoting Madonna in conjunction with her Italian record label, WEA Italiana. It boasts around 2,500 readers. Write: Legramandi Sauro, via Donizetti, 6, 24043 Vidalengo (Caravaggio), (Bg) ITALY. *(Italian)*

Madonna Fan-Club, Didier Delory, publisher, 34 Champs-Elysées, 75008 Paris, FRANCE. Write for info. This in-depth club recently completed a biographical comic following the **Ciccone** clan from the birth of Madonna's grandfather . . . need we say more? *(French)*

Madonna Mania, Gavin Coe, publisher, 3 Beaumont Vale, Haverhill, Suffolk, CB98QG, England. Write for info. Fact-heavy 'zine that offers tons of European reportage. *(English)*

Madonna Press, Francesco De Vincentis, publisher, via Battisti 28, 74023 Grottaglie (TA), ITALY. Write for info. Monthly newsletter full of hardcore fan info. *(Italian)*

MLC, Linda and Peter Weinzettl, publishers, P.O. Box 6423, Station A, Toronto, Ontario, M5W 1X3, CANADA. U.S./Canada four-issue subscription, $18; rest of world, $22. Checks or money orders. The first international Madonna fanzine was *MLC* (for Madonna Louise Ciccone, of course) in 1987, and it's still around today, offering a tasty alternative to *Icon. MLC* looks great for an underground 'zine, and offers a more balanced, bitchier look at its subject. Its pages are full of interesting tidbits, a fabulous collectibles column, and discographies. *(English)*

Virgin, Mauro Bramati, publisher, via Sapri 65, 20156 Milano, ITALY. Write for info. One of the best because it's full of heart and **creativity**. Cleverly-designed, **love**able photocopied 'zine that offers lots of rare photos, especially of Madonna's frequent jaunts to Europe, and also unusual studio portraits, plus an excellent collectibles spotlight. It isn't glossy; it doesn't have to be. *(Italian)*

fans: "I have a . . . *passionate* relationship with my fans," Madonna smirked on an **Italian** chat show in early 1993. And she's right. Sort of. There isn't a **love**-hate thing going on between Madonna and her fans, but between Madonna and the general public, many of whose members love her **music** but hate her, or vice versa, or who decide to love or hate her with every new **project**.

But her fans *looooooove* Madonna. Julia Roberts is better liked by the public, but if Madonna is more *hated,* she is also more *loved.*

Though the nasty British press reported that only three fans awaited her arrival there in 1993, a sure sign that she was "over," there were in fact over a hundred fans at her hotel and some three hundred

> *Like a minnow flouncing about a pretty sea anemone, a fan snaps photos, oblivious to Madonna's desire to strike.*

chasing after her at a rehearsal. She has a lot of 'em, and they think a lot of her.

One real love-hate aspect of her relationship with the public comes from Madonna herself. As a self-described maverick, she is singular in her quest to make her mark on the world, an individualist whose clearest message has always been **"Express**

"*W*hen Madonna arrived in New York for her **Virgin tour**, the news was full of reports of young fans, 'wanna-bes,' dressing up like Madonna and hanging around Madison Square Garden. . . . In the spirit of fun, of female bonding, of Destiny, I tied a big pink Madonna bow in my hair. A fan was born."

—Elizabeth Tippens, a fan, 1992

"*H*ead bowed, she walks through the blinding strobe barrage, making the stage door in just under four seconds. She doesn't stop, doesn't sign **autographs**, doesn't pose, even when a photographer shouts, 'Bitch.' No sooner does the door close behind her than a fan is heard to say, 'Did you see the way she looked at me? That feeling behind her eyes?'"

—Guy Trebay, *The Village Voice*, 1994

Yourself." It should be no wonder that she is ambivalent about having fans. On the one hand, she is an artist who wants to affect people, change their minds, entertain them in mass quantities; she considers herself cool, and she wants others to think so too. On the other hand, she can't help finding people who camp out by her apartment, follow her around, mimic her, spend all their time and money on her, and do little else with their lives—a little pathetic. "Get a life!" she routinely calls out to pursuers, and she doesn't mean *hers*.

In **Truth or Dare,** Madonna wryly observes that her fans want her even when she feels like shit. Stories of Madonna's ill treatment of her fans are legendary, whether it's insulting children or pitching gift bouquets into a Dumpster outside the Royale Theatre during **Speed-the-Plow**.

Some fans can be a pain. In 1988, Madonna was pestered continually by a woman named Darlene, and when Darlene and her little brother got pushy, Madonna was photographed getting pushy right back. At the **Cannes** party for **Spike Lee**'s *Jungle Fever,* Madonna's **bodyguards** shooed an overzealous fan who then threw a fit that threatened to escalate into violence. "Don't fuckin' touch me!" the fan screamed at her minders, but Madonna diffused the situation by cooing, "Can't I touch you, honey?" She did, and he took off, sated.

How to characterize Madonna's fans? She has an overwhelmingly female following, is a virtual goddess among **gay men,** lesbians, and bisexuals, and generally attracts fans in that ever-important marketing group of the 16–32-year-old range.

None of these generalizations detracts from the fact that Madonna's fans encompass people from all walks and crawls of life, of all ages, **sex**es, and sexual identities, and from every country in the world.

Farewell, My Concubine: 1993 Hong Kong film by Chen Kaige about the **sex**ually-charged **love**-hate relationship between two male stars of the Peking Opera.

Madonna first became involved with this Chinese "*Crying Game* without the penis" when she screened it with **Miramax** honcho Harvey Weinstein, who later snapped it up for U.S. distribution. *FMC* was distributed with assistance from **Maverick** Pictures, that company's very first screen credit.

Madonna appeared at the U.S. premiere of the film in **New York,** on the eve of her first U.S. **Girlie Show** date. She arrived in a military coat and was hustled away by commandant **Liz Rosenberg** when a bratty reporter asked, "So what do you think of all the talk of your career **slump**?" She did, however, pose for a picture between Kaige and *The Piano* **director** Jane Campion, cooing, "Oooooh, I'm between two geniuses. . . . I'm just an *hors d'oeuvre* tonight!"

Madonna also attended the after-party at China Grill on West 52nd Street, which attracted such hungry celebs as **Alek Keshishian,** Christopher Reeve, Tina Louise, Stephen Sprouse, Susan Sarandon and Tim Robbins, Holly Hunter, Juliette Binoche, and Connie Chung.

fashion: "Madonna is to fashion what the big bang theory is to creation," wrote designer Todd Oldham in 1993, and he was understating the case.

Madonna is held in high esteem by many top designers for her individual style, and

A 1985 Benetton ad shows Madonna's almost instant influence on fashion.

for the fact that she is the one person who can be counted on to actually *wear* high fashion. Madonna's street-smart siren look forced *haute couture* to mimic the **looks** of the masses instead of vice versa, and designers have kept one eye on her and the other on their sketch pads ever since. Karl Lagerfeld at Chanel and Christian Lacroix at Parore were especially influenced by her early looks, **Jean-Paul Gaultier** and **Dolce & Gabbana** later created entire lines around her tours, and she adores Versace.

Madonna's style directly affects contemporary fashion. Examples of all of her famous looks can still be found on the streets today, still looking chic. When Madonna dons platforms, so does the world. And face it: How would Demi Moore know what to wear if Madonna didn't wear it first?

Since 1989, Madonna has frequented the Paris, Rome, and Milan fashion shows.

As an ancient-history lesson, note Madonna's favorite ensemble circa 1984: her Vivienne Westwood skirt with **Keith Haring** designs (Westwood once owned and operated the legendary London fashion boutique, **Sex**), her ripped-up black net shirt, and her denim jacket with the phrase **Boy Toy** on the **back**. Now she'd be caught dead in anything *but* that outfit.

Madonna is one of those rare humans who looks good in just about anything. No matter the outfit, she can pull it off. And often does.

"*M*adonna *is* fashion."

—Jean-Paul Gaultier, 1992

•

"*N*ever be photographed in anything you wouldn't wear yourself."

—Madonna, 1989

•

"*I*'ve lived through the dance-hall floozy fiascos, the lurid lace lingerie, the pseudo-Marilyn mishaps, the bawdy bustier bombs, the ice-cream-**cone bras**, the spandex running shorts, the barrage of black roots. I've managed to survive the clone-like army of fashion atrocities who emulated her every wardrobe mistake, from the mass of cheap junk jewelry circling her neck to the battered combat boots covering her fad-mad feet. . . . She's an insult to American men."

—Mr. Blackwell, expert on American men, 1993

father: SEE CICCONE, SILVIO "TONY"

favorite photo of self: Madonna's favorite photo, as submitted to *American Photo* magazine for its November/December

1991 issue, is a clownishly tight close-up of her broad smile, taken by **Herb Ritts**. She called it her favorite because "it's an absolutely candid shot. It was taken at the dinner table. I think I had just finished dessert, and I'm always happy when I'm eating dessert."

fax: Madonna loves her fax machine, but was less than thrilled when her home number was visible in a brief scene of *Truth or Dare,* leading to an avalanche of heat-sensitive fan letters. In 1993, she faxed a notorious hate letter to Joe Roth over *Angie, I Says*.

FBI: In 1992, original negatives from *Sex* were stolen from the Lexington Labs, allegedly with the assistance of an employee of the company. Madonna's security expert, **Gavin de Becker,** called the FBI into the investigation. First, they **fax**ed eighteen **tabloids** around the world, promising to sue if the 'bloids published or so much as purchased any of the stolen shots.

Then, with the help of the U.K. scandal rag *News of the World,* the FBI organized a successful sting operation at the Sunset Marquis hotel in Los Angeles that led to the capture of the culprit, William Stacey Anderson, who was trying to sell the photos for $100,000. *News of the World* ran a story on how they'd been instrumental in catching the thief, complete with amazingly accurate (it would later prove) illustrations of the contraband photos, long before *Sex* was released. Madonna thanked the FBI in the acknowledgments of *Sex* for "rescuing photographs that would make J. Edgar Hoover roll over."

Unlikely hero Bob Guccione and his *Penthouse* magazine came to the rescue when a couple offered some stolen photos to the magazine, saying they'd found them on a bench in Central Park. When it became obvious they could get into serious trouble, the couple claimed they were giving the photos to Guccione because they had no idea how to return them to their rightful owner, but knew that he'd be able to locate Madonna.

Fellini, Federico: Late **Italian** filmmaker of some of the most hallucinatory, imaginative films in cinema history, including *8½, Fellini's Satyricon,* and *La Dolce Vita*. On his **death**bed, FF received a bouquet from Madonna along with a note saying that she admired him greatly and would **love** to work with him. Fellini's reaction? "Why not? She's a beautiful girl."

Madonna often approaches her idols via fan mail; in 1993, she even sent a gushy note to notorious German filmmaker Leni Riefenstahl.

femininity: Though androgynous in the truest sense of possessing both masculine and feminine traits, Madonna is definitely in touch with her feminine side: She claims to have realized by age five the manipulative **power** of femininity over men. However, her definition of the term suggests a more progressive outlook: "The essence of femininity is to absolutely **love** being a woman." (1989).

"*P*ower feminism means learning from Madonna, Spike Lee, and Bill Cosby: If you don't like your group's images in the media, decide on another image and seize control of the means of producing it."

—Naomi Wolf, *Fire with Fire*, 1993

•

"*O*kay, I have chained myself, okay? . . . I crawled under my own table. . . . People don't think of me as a person who's not in charge of my career or my life, okay. And isn't that what feminism is all about, you know, equality for men and women? And aren't I in charge of my life, doing the things I want to do? Making my own decisions?"

—Madonna, on the **"Express Yourself"** video and her image, 1990

•

"*M*adonna is a feminist's Marilyn."

—Michael Gross, *Vanity Fair*, 1986

"*M*adonna has taught young women to be fully female and sexual while still exercising total control over their lives. She shows girls how to be attractive, sensual, energetic, ambitious, aggressive, and funny—all at the same time."

—Camille Paglia, *The New York Times*, 1990

•

"I don't think about the work I do in terms of feminism. . . . I'm certainly not militant about it, nor do I exactly premeditate it."

—Madonna, 1987

•

"All women should be as Madonna as possible."

—Karen Finley, performance artist/actress

•

"I think I've had advantages because I'm a girl."

—Madonna, 1986

feminism: Have you ever wondered whether Tina Turner considers herself a feminist? How about Gloria Estefan? Or have you ever read an article analyzing whether the film work of Kim Basinger is feminist? Or whether **Janet Jackson**'s personal life is? (*What* personal life?) Probably not. But since at least her *Like a Virgin* days, Madonna has been called everything from the "future of feminism" to a woman who's "set back feminism thirty years."

Because Madonna is so important and influential in our culture, her politics and any perceived message to her madness is important to many groups who would like her to promote their beliefs. Because Madonna is a woman, feminist groups feel she should make feminism a priority, and, depending on how they interpret her actions, some feminists love her, while others deplore her. Neither group is necessarily correct in their reading of what Madonna is trying to get across—they're just seizing on contradictory clues to see if Madonna is a good or bad feminist **role model.**

Camille Paglia, whose own brand of feminism is so radical it has earned her the enmity of the feminist Old Guard, exclaimed of Madonna in response to her **"Justify My Love" video,** "Finally, a real feminist!" But it's easy to read Madonna as a setback to feminism: She promotes **glamor,** body perfection, **pornography,** and a strong belief in gender archetypes.

So, is she a feminist, or what? The solution is that Madonna is not a feminist in the original sense of the word, but is a feminist *nouvelle* who behaves exactly as she likes, *presuming,* rather than promoting, the notion that men and women are equal. Another of Madonna's unique approaches to feminism is her acceptance that, despite equality, men and women are different. She accepts the flirty girlie and strong, silent stud; the manipulative vamp and the tough guy; the innocent maiden and the boy wonder. She also deals with the traditional female archetypes of the virgin and the whore, tweaking our perceptions of women by making us aware of how we feel when she is submerged in either role.

Instead of campaigning to destroy what could be seen as constricting stereotypes, by taking them for granted and twisting them around, Madonna is that much more effective in her deconstruction and exploration of them.

Ferrara, Abel: Cynical, provocative **art**-film **director** famous for his twin wallows through the sewers of humanity, *King of New York* (1990) and *Bad Lieutenant* (1992). Madonna pursued AF professionally, starring in his film ***Dangerous Game***.

Being notoriously high-strung, AF was inevitably reported to have warred with a willful Madonna throughout filming. He later said he had gotten more out of Madonna on-screen than from most of his other leading ladies, but he couldn't have been happy with the film's dippy final title or with the anti-Madonna snobbery that made what should have been an eagerly-attended follow-up to *Bad Lieutenant* into a month's worth of dwindling audiences.

"Fever" song: As performed by **Peggy Lee,** one of the **sexi**est, slinkiest songs ever recorded. Madonna slipped into it on a rare cover version for her *Erotica* **album,** taking the slow burn

and reinventing it as whispery gloss, just as hot, but not as up-close-and-personal-like. Madonna thought enough of this non-single song to perform it live on three separate occasions and in three radically different versions within the course of a year.

First, she did a straight, ungarnished version on "**Saturday Night Live,**" then a traditional, vampy version (during which she stumbled over the **lyrics** and improvised an apology) on **Arsenio Hall**'s 1,000th telecast, and finally a **club** remix version, complete with actual flames for the finale, in **The Girlie Show.**

The **music** for Madonna's "F" was originally for a song called **"Goodbye to Innocence,"** which was bumped from *Erotica* the second Madonna improvised some of the lyrics to "F." Madonna and *Erotica* collaborator **Shep Pettibone** sent out for the lyrics to the song and said goodbye to "Goodbye to Innocence," making way for yet another number 1 Madonna **dance** smash.

Ex-galpal **Sandra Bernhard** had performed a swank, bitchy cover version of "F" in her stage show only a year previously.

Other artists who have recorded "Fever": Little Willie John, Elvis Presley, Jerry Butler, Peggy Lee, Rita Coolidge, Joe Cocker, Chaka Khan, The Cramps, Annabella, Tom Verlaine.

"Fever" video: The song that was never released as a single in the U.S. required a **video** for its non-U.S. distribution, so Madonna threw together an engaging **fashion** video by French photog Stephane Sednaoui. "F" is similar to SS's clips for the Red Hot Chili Peppers and Neneh Cherry, featuring Madonna covered in silver paint against a blood-red backdrop, decked out as a wasp-waisted future-diva, in a short red wig and Peter Pan **club** gear, joyfully shaking her hips like a child straining to **dance,** and vamping as an Indian goddess.

Devoid of meaning, the clip is charged with Madonna's ironic smirk and snappy photography that combine to make it far more re-watchable than it ever needed to be.

SEE ALSO: CAMP

Finch, Chris: Man-child who reenacted the adolescent role from the **"Open Your Heart" video** on the **Who's That Girl tour.**

SEE ALSO: HOWARD, FELIX

Fincher, David: Propaganda Films **video director** of some of Madonna's bestest: **"Express Yourself," "Oh Father," "Vogue,"** and **"Bad Girl."** He was linked to her romantically in 1990, but both laughed off that **rumor.**

His first big shot at feature-film directing was the ill-fated *Aliens*[3] after being replaced on *Truth or Dare* by first-timer **Alek Keshishian.**

Fiorucci, Elio: **Italian** designer who in 1983 flew Madonna to Paris to entertain **fashion** industry luminaries such as Issey Miyake, Karl Lagerfeld, Yves St. Laurent, and Givenchy. It was Madonna's first introduction to the world of high fashion, and its first to her.

firsts:
- First rock concert attended: David Bowie at Cobo Hall in Detroit, Michigan.
- First **kiss:** In the fifth grade, behind St. Andrew's, with Tom Marshowitz, who later died in a fall.
- First **love:** Also in the fifth grade, a boy named Ronny Howard (no, not *that* Ronnie Howard) who had "white-blonde **hair** and sky blue **eyes.**"
- First movie: In the eighth grade, made by classmates.
- First intercourse: With **Russell Long,** an older schoolmate and her only **lover** in high school, at fifteen.
- First band: **The Breakfast Club,** 1979–80.
- First record release: **"Everybody"** 12" **dance** single, 1982.
- First major purchase with record earnings: A $5,000 Roland synthesizer.
- First number 1 pop single: **"Like a Virgin,"** 1984.
- First appearance on **"Saturday Night Live":** 1985.
- First appearance on a U.S. talk show: "The Tonight Show with **Johnny Carson,"** 1987.

"*B*ruce Springsteen was
born to run.
I was born to flirt."

—Madonna, 1985

"*S*he's the
greatest flirt
of all time."

—James Foley on Madonna, 1987

"*Y*ou will understand the
depth of my faith in her
when I tell you she was one
of the first people I turned
to when I was diagnosed."

—PWA (Person with AIDS) Christopher
Flynn on Madonna, 1989

- First Broadway play: *Speed-the-Plow,* 1988.
- First U.S. TV **commercial**: For **Pepsi**, 1989.
- First post-**fame** public **nudity**: *Vanity Fair,* 1990.
- First video banned by **MTV**: **"Justify My Love,"** 1990.
- First interview conducted (as opposed to *given*): With **Rosie O'Donnell** for *Mademoiselle,* 1993.

Fisher, Carrie: "Princess Leia" of the *Star Wars* films, the author of comic novels like *Delusions of Grandma,* and the daughter of crooner Eddie Fisher and **glamor**puss sweetheart Debbie Reynolds. CF became friends with Madonna via **Sean Penn**. She attended the Penns' **wedding** and interviewed Madonna for *Rolling Stone* in 1991 when **Norman Mailer**'s fee was deemed too stratospheric. The result was an unaffected interview that featured as much about CF as about Madonna. We learned about the **AIDS**-related death of CF's friend, that she never fucked **Warren Beatty,** and her idea of Mr. Right.

fitness: Madonna is a fit-freak. At least six days a week, she runs ten miles, then up eighteen flights of stairs before spending forty-five minutes on a Versaclimber. She does weights with lunges, three sets of 20- to 30-rep squats, and an hour of aerobics. From 6 A.M. to 10 A.M., the world's busiest woman is immersed in the fine-tuning of her own body. The regimen has left her with a taut bod and a disdain for the less-dedicated—manifested in a professed distaste for "fat slobs."

flag: A next-to-nude Madonna appeared in a Rock the Vote ad for **MTV** wrapped in the American flag. She also used the flag in her **Girlie Show** as a backdrop to her rendition of **"Holiday,"** and as the lining of her troupe's military broadcoats for that same number.

More **shock**ing to Puerto Ricans was Madonna's impulsive rubbing of their official flag against her groin, which right-wingers interpreted as the ultimate act of disrespect, instead of as the warmly affectionate gesture she intended. The "Puerto Rican flag flap" was fueled by the fact that it came only two weeks before citizens were to vote on whether to remain a U.S. commonwealth, seek independence, or become an official state.

flaws: Madonna considers hers to be impatience, intolerance of the weaknesses of others, and overactive self-criticism.

flirting: "I flirt with grandmothers and garbage men and stuff like that. It's part of my nature." When Madonna defined her rules of flirtation to **Johnny Carson** in 1987, her androgynous nature made it seem only natural that she would favor both men and women with her sly wink—Johnny didn't even blink at her unisex philosophy.

Flynn, Christopher: The man Madonna describes as having been her biggest influence. CF, nearly thirty years her senior, was Madonna's ballet instructor in her teen years and the first man to tell her she was beautiful. He was gay, and took her (so much for proper ID) to Detroit bars where she first experienced gay culture, **dance** culture, and adulation by a crowd as her gyrations elicited the enthusiastic approval of hordes of **gay men**.

It was CF, whom she cryptically described as her "imaginative first **lover**," who campaigned to get Madonna to move to **New York** and to attend the **Duke University** workshop that landed her a spot with the **Alvin Ailey** dancers. When he became ill with **AIDS,** Madonna helped him financially and supported him in his efforts as a San Francisco AIDS activist.

He died on October 27, 1990, in Los Angeles.

Foley, James "Jamie": The man who directed Madonna in her **"Live to Tell,"** non-U.S. **"True Blue,"** and **"Who's That Girl"** videos, as well as the film *Who's That Girl.* He also directed her *Desperately Seeking Susan* costar Aidan Quinn in *Reckless* and her hubby **Sean Penn** in *At Close Range.*

Madonna made JF bend over and kiss her foot in order to reshoot a scene in *Who's That Girl* (not worth it, Jamie), but in 1987 called JF her—and Sean's—best friend. If he was Sean's best pal, he was also his best *man,* at the Penns' 1985 **wedding**.

Fortin (Ciccone), Madonna Louise: Madonna's mother, who died at age thirty in 1963.

Madonna remembers her mother as beautiful and kind, even putting up with her children's naive lack of respect for the gravity of her illness in the final year of her life. Madonna has also said, "It's extremely rare that a religious **Italian** woman would name a child after her. My mother wanted to be a singer. So it was like I have a mission to live up to this name." Or at least to *try,* and the song "Promise to Try" on ***Like a Prayer*** is Madonna's most maternal statement, focusing on a girl's pledge to her mother to forgive her for dying, and to never forget her. That album is "dedicated to my mother, who taught me how to pray."

Madonna's mother was a radiation technologist who died after a long bout with breast **cancer**.

Freire, Rodrigo: Madonna's "Rubba," except not.

When rumors surfaced that Madonna was affairing with this gorgeous young model, her lawyers gave birth to a bouncing baby cow. . . . But why all the fuss? Well, see, he was all of fifteen at the time, way, *way* too young for Madonna, and too young for the law. The **tabloid** newspapers relied on information that RF's friends said she had flown him to "be by her side" several times. Regardless, the publicity didn't hurt him— he made the cover of the February 1994 *Interview*.

Fried, Marilyn: Respected **acting** coach who first worked with Madonna to prepare her for ***Speed-the-Plow.*** Madonna met Fried through actress/director Lee Grant and not through **Shelley Winters,** as Winters claimed.

Friedlander, Lee: Respected **art** photographer who had the good fortune to shoot a starving young Madonna in the late seventies. His images, reproduced

in a 1991 book called *Nudes* and sampled in a companion exhibit at **New York**'s Museum of Modern Art, had their first exposure to the masses in 1985, in ***Playboy***.

friendship: When asked in 1987, Madonna claimed her best friend was ***Who's That Girl*** director **Jamie Foley**. In 1993, she cut to the chase and called herself her own best friend. Madonna has had tumultuous friendships with women, from tattletale **Erica Bell,** to turncoat **Sandra Bernhard,** to enigmatic **Ingrid Casares,** to her palsy-walsy bliss with **Rosie O'Donnell.** Among men, her best friend was **Martin Burgoyne.**

"*B*ecause those statements expressly allege or imply inter alia, immoral, and illegal conduct on the part of our client, they are libelous per se."

—Madonna's lawyers' response to the *New York Post*'s headline MADONNA ROBS THE CRADLE!, 1993

fuck: If you think she was raunchy on "Late Show With **David Letterman**," try listening to Madonna's BBC broadcast of **Blond Ambition** from London. She said the dreaded F-word over three *dozen* times, none of which were censored since she was live. She explained that "'fuck' is the reason we're here" since all our parents did it. Madonna also plugged the word by uttering, "Fuck me," at the end of a **dance** remix of **"Justify My Love."**

Futura 2000 (McGurr, Leonard): Graffiti artist whose decoration on the walls of Madonna's East Village digs got her evicted. Madonna, **Sandra Bernhard,** and Jennifer Grey attended a Futura 2000 opening in 1988.

Future of Culture: Ultra-right-wing, Fountainbleu-based French group that in 1992 failed in their attempt to have 75,000 copies of *Sex* declared obscene and destroyed.

Gaiety: Sleazy **New York** gay strip-joint on West 46th Street where dancers go all-nude and desperate patrons ponder where to slip their dollar bills. Madonna (cleverly disguised in a baseball cap and pantsuit) first scouted the place in November 1991, with **Alek Keshishian,** designer Mark Jacobs, and **Steven Meisel** in tow. She was recognized and was treated to an X-rated performance as all twelve strippers took to the stage to try their, er, *hands* at voguing.

Madonna later featured the joint and many of its regular strippers, including **Rocky** and gay porn-star Joey Stefano, in *Sex*.

"Gambler" song: The second of her two *Vision Quest* soundtrack songs, and a popular track on her **Virgin tour,** "G" was a huge non-single hit in 1985. As with **"Into the Groove,"** a video compiled from film clips went into heavy rotation on **MTV.**

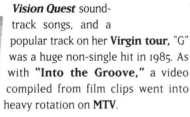

"Gambler" was a Top Ten smash in the U.K., but was never released as a single in the U.S.

gap: Madonna is the world's most famous gap-toothed woman, and she believes her gap is an important part of her personality. While eyebrows, **hair** color, and the visibility of her **beauty mark** all come and go, the gap is omnipresent. She threw a fit when *Glamour* magazine electronically **air-brush**ed her teeth for their cover.

garbage: In 1990, two French photographers swiped bags of garbage from outside Madonna's **home,** laid her trash out neatly, and sold photos of the junk to magazines around the world. The contents of Madonna's trash included shredded documents, hemorrhoid suppositories, a prescription for an allergy nasal spray that belonged to then-boyfriend **Warren Beatty, Reebok** labels, Weight Watchers dinner boxes, the remnants of a McDonald's feast, Evian and Diet Coke containers, and a copy of the *Hollywood Reporter*.

It certainly could have been worse.

gash: Preferred synonym for "vagina" in *Sex,* as in "honey poured

"Since Madonna's book appeared, more women have been coming by to see the show. I'd like to say we have room for that, but the old-timers don't like it."

—Gaiety DJ, 1993

from my fourteen-year-old gash and I wept."

SEE ALSO: **PUSSY**

Gaultier, Jean-Paul: Wildly imaginative bad boy of **fashion** and former assistant to Pierre Cardin, on his own from 1976. His sexually-charged work—**cone bras** protruding from pin-striped suits, gold lamé bustiers, etc.—gave **Blond Ambition** its visual bite.

At first, Madonna admired J-PG from afar, calling him an influence in interviews as early as 1984. She wore his clothes and even modeled them in *Harper's Bazaar* in 1988. In 1989, J-PG firmed up his interest in pop music by releasing a **dance** single, "How to Do That," the **video** of which was directed by **"Open Your Heart" / "Justify My Love"** director **Jean-Baptiste Mondino.**

Despite the Mondino connection, Madonna's path didn't cross with J-PG's until 1990, when **Herb Ritts** told J-PG that she wanted to work with him. They met in a hotel suite in **New York,** watched *Cabaret,* then collaborated on the Blond Ambition designs. Both Madonna and J-PG are extremely active in **AIDS** causes. (Gaultier lost his lover and **business** partner, Francis Menuge, to AIDS in 1990.)

Most notoriously, Madonna headlined J-PG's fashion show September 24, 1992, in Los Angeles. Though Faye Dunaway strutted in Big Bird—esque thigh-high boots, **Marky Mark** flaunted that third nipple, Billy Idol mooned the audience, Raquel Welch went seriously dominatrix, Anthony Kiedis left nothing to the imagination in his tight-tights, and Dr. Ruth Westheimer jogged around dressed as a sort of black-rubbered **sex** nurse, it was Madonna who caught the most serious flack. She provided the show's finale, emerging with golden-ringlets, garish makeup, her gold "Dita" tooth, and—after shucking her jacket—a high skirt that framed her bare breasts between crisscrossing suspenders. It was a transcendent moment in pop history, if reported with distaste at the time. She looked as unapprovably stylized as any goddess should, and yet was fully equipped to nurse the entire crowd of six thousand, *with* leftovers. The show doubled as a benefit, raising $750,000 for AIDS.

The ancient (yet still somehow trashily alluring) sex siren Mamie Van Doren later turned up in *Star* magazine's "Would You Be Caught Dead In This Outfit?" wearing the very same dress Madonna flashed in . . . except Mamie demurely wore a white blouse rather than going "**boobs-ahoy**."

The critical reaction to Madonna's breast-baring was stunning. The media condemned her for her publicity-mongering as their cameras clicked, and—most disturbingly—insinuated that perhaps such provocative appearances were as much the problem behind AIDS as the solution.

Just for the record, nobody ever got AIDS from exposing or looking at breasts.

"*F*irst and foremost, Gaultier has been a good friend to me. He has the perfect combination of compassion, vulnerability, and mischievousness as a person and an artist. He's not afraid to take chances. I adore him."

—Madonna, 1992

·

"*I* love her. She truly understands herself and always has something to say. She touches people because she has a way of life that doesn't correspond to society's norms. And face it—how many of us do? She makes people think, *Is normal really normal?* No. There is no such thing as normal. I truly admire her."

—Jean-Paul Gaultier on Madonna, 1992

gay men: Madonna has a huge gay following. Like Bette Davis, **Marilyn Monroe,** and **Barbra Streisand** before her, Madonna has succeeded in capturing the hearts, minds, and paychecks of gay men across the world. The personals in her various fanzines are a new category all their own: "Boy Toys Seeking Boy Toys."

But why do gay guys like Madonna so much? It's tempting to say, "Because she's *faaaaaaabulous*!" But there's more to it than that. Like other gay icons, Madonna is campy, and **camp** is an important concept for gay men. Another reason that gay men love Madonna is that she speaks *directly* to them as an audience. She's done so in her music ("In This Life"), in print (her 1991 *Advocate* interview), and on video (**"Justify My Love," "Erotica"**). Also, Madonna has kissed women in public (on *film*), has encouraged speculation that she may be **bisexual,** and speaks up for gay rights.

Perhaps most important to her gay **fans,** Madonna has always, in her very public private life, surrounded herself with openly gay men, counting them among the most important peo-

"*D*on't they know I'm a gay man trapped in a woman's body?"

—Madonna on her critics, 1994

·

"*I*t's true I am fascinated by gay culture. There's a visceral thing that happens when I go to gay clubs. The place is filled with moving, sweating bodies that become like one animal. There's something very powerful about that to me. I feel they're very misunderstood, and so am I. I feel their persecution, but also their sense of humor, and their willingness to deal with sexuality in an unconventional way is really interesting to me. They accept the masculine side of myself as well as the feminine."

—Madonna, 1991

ple in her life. Madonna is the first gay icon who got that way *on purpose.*

Geffen, David: Entertainment mogul and Madonna pal who gushed, "Madonna is the embodiment of the 'modern woman' of legend. Instead of being stultified as an object, Madonna is a trailblazer who has confronted prejudice, smitten the obstacles of convention, and distorted boundaries into challenges with the **power** of her will and inspiration. She is a **beauty** in **control** of her body, her image, and her **art.**" (1991)

Gerardo: Latin-American rapper who—despite his boast that Madonna left an obscene message on his answering machine—had his 15 minutes in 1991 when Madonna summed him up with a caustic, "I'm not into hair extensions." He attended her thirty-sixth **birthday** party in **Miami** with his newly short haircut.

Gibson, Beverly: The high school drama teacher who raves about Madonna's school performances and her "even-then" widely recognized stage magnetism.

gifts: Madonna said in 1990 that the best present she ever received was a handful of "sweaty diamonds and emeralds."

She is known to lavish her close associates with gifts, taking the entire **Blond Ambition dance** troupe on shopping sprees across Europe. While doing *Speed-the-Plow,* she gave floral arrangements to everyone involved in the show, and in 1992 she gave director **Mary Lambert** a teeny-tiny black leather motorcycle jacket with a **crucifix** on the back as a baby-shower gift.

Gilroy, Dan: With his brother Ed (they once performed in an act called "The Bil and Gil Show"), DG formed the core of **The Breakfast Club,** Madonna's first band. A huge Beatles fan, he helped Madonna shape her early **music,** and also helped her keep warm for a year in 1979: Gilroy became her **lover** after meeting her at a party at her ex-lover **Norris Burroughs**'s apartment.

Girlie Show tour, The: Madonna-bashing was at an all-time peak in the last quarter of 1993. Rather than hide from the press, Madonna forged ahead with a limited, nineteen city world tour.

TGS bravely reinvented Madonna as a one-woman song-and-dance, *South Pacific*-in-a-**"Steve McQueen,"** Barnum & Bailey three-cockring circus. As sweet as cotton **candy** and nearly as satisfying, TGS was Madonna's most entertaining concert, ninety minutes of sheer smile and hoot and bump and grind. Not as thematically complex as its predecessor, **Blond Ambition,** Madonna's fourth tour didn't need to be. What it lacked in depth it more than made up for with spectacle and eye-popping visuals.

She must've done something right: It sold out at every single venue.

TGS was a spectacle about spectacle. It incorporated nearly every imaginable element of **voyeurism: stardom,** the circus, public **nudity, boxing,** strip shows, **masks** (which comment on voyeurism by making it harder for you to see the wearer, and easier for the wearer to see *you*), the Golden Era of Hollywood, a gay disco (where everyone has an eye on everyone else), and its own grandiose setting, usually in an auditorium capable of servicing 50,000-plus watchers. It celebrated the pleasure in seeing, and in *looking.*

There were three sections to the show: an opening set of torrid performances that became progressively more amusing, ending with a happy ballad; a seventies disco set that began as a mindless party and ended with a moving representation of **AIDS**; and an all-out Hollywood tribute set. A pair of encores distilled the show's entire sensibility into two minimalist songs.

This concept concert started even before its star appeared onstage, Smokey Robinson's "Tears of a Clown" segueing into a circus aria as barkers offered the audience, "Peanuts, **popcorn,** cotton can-dy!" Never one to mince words, Madonna began her show with a topless dancer performing a gravity-defying shimmy down

a go-go pole. Once she had our attention, Madonna emerged from the floor as an S&M Robin ("Holy Tit Clamps, Batman!"), sleek in black-sequined bra and hotpants and that persona-obscuring mask, standing heavily in enormous platform boots.

"My name is **Dita,**" she began, reestablishing herself as the dominatrix who beat the world into submission in 1992 before the world burned the bed on her. Dita was back on top, crooning **"Erotica"** as aggressively as a **sex** crime. Behind Madonna, in ingenious lightboxes far above the main stage, dancers enacted scenes of stylized violence and sexuality. A mute clown in royal blue made the first of its many appearances at this inopportune moment, like a child inadvertently stumbling upon the Primal Scene. There was no question that our sweet little clown liked to watch, a neat spin on the usual state of the world, since clowns themselves are usually the watch*ees.*

Madonna segued smoothly into **"Fever,"** complete with copious molestation of her two primary male dancers. She presented a *The King and I* **"Vogue"** next, gaily flapping her hands above her head to approximate the fluttering synthesizer groove, wearing a black beaded **Dolce & Gabbana** headdress. The first set was washed away by **"Rain."** When she appropriated a few lines from "Just My Imagination," the Motown girl was truly back home.

A breezy exposition of umbrella-bearing dancers (à la *Singin' in the Rain*) escorted the audience to the next section.

The velocity increased in the second set, with Madonna—in seventies **fashions** and a blonde 'fro—descending on a huge glitterball, inviting crowds to join her through **"Express Yourself"** and **"Deeper and Deeper"** in what resembled a gay disco of the period. As she began a sincere plea for world tolerance in "Why's It So Hard" she pitched unity by engaging in a sizzling mock **orgy.** AIDS smashed the party. Madonna delivered a stirring speech about the disease, begging for awareness. Her performance of "In This Life," which on the album sounds trite, was a showstopper; her dancers disappeared one by one into a cleverly-conceived white light beyond a space in the curtain.

The transition song was the controversial **"Beast Within Mix"** of **"Justify My Love,"** brought to life by male dancers

"*T*he two-hour extravaganza . . . was notable not only as a showcase for the superstar's prodigious talents as a singer and dancer but also for her ability to orchestrate and film an appropriately mammoth production."

—*The Hollywood Reporter*

·

"'*I*n This Life' is particularly spooky and nauseating. Especially the part where she clasps her hands and beseeches us, `Have you ever watched your best friend die? / Have you ever seen a grown man cry?' Even if I had, Maddy, I'd hardly want to share it with 70,000 people. This is the U.K. We don't have group therapy over here, y'know?"

—Everett True, *Melody Maker* (U.K.)

·

"*T*he all-singing, all-dancing Girlie Show even solves the mystery of what Madonna's latest incarnation will be: the Carol Burnett of her generation. Give this woman her own variety hour!"

—Peter Galvin, *The Advocate*

·

"*T*he fascinating thing about Madonna is that she is all-real and all-fake—in other words, pure show biz . . . [The Girlie Show tour is] at once a movie retrospective, a Ziegfeld revue, a living video, and an R-rated takeoff on Cirque du Soleil. . . . Pierrot is your silent host; the calliope music announces that this is a three-ring circus of clowning around. And Madonna, once the Harlow harlot and now a perky harlequin, is the greatest show-off on earth."

—Richard Corliss, *Time*

·

"*W*hy does the rhetoric of fiasco and decline hover over the production like a vulture? Forget the naysayers—the wise thing to do is try to get tickets. Madonna may have failed at other things, but her stage presence—her fluent and daring dancer's imagination, her genius for iconographic playfulness, her libertine expansiveness—is a wonder of our times."

—*The New Yorker*

correctly enacting the violence, confusion, and passion of gay sex.

The third segment of the show was all fun and games. Madonna emerged transformed into **"Marlene Dietrich"** crooning **"Like a Virgin"** in top hat and tails. "Marlene" played a game of visual tag with the impish clown, who hid in a traveling trunk. The next number was the exact performance she gave at the 1993 **MTV Awards**: "Bye Bye Baby" as a sex circus, with Madonna as a barker and an all-girl stage that put the "gal" in galpal.

"I'm Going Bananas," a short, campy Latin-flavored song from *I'm Breathless,* was performed energetically, with Madonna in horizontal stripes and a bandanna, followed by a rendition of **"La Isla Bonita"** (perfect, since the tour traveled to Mexico and much of South America) complete with a James Brown–esque bit where Madonna kept falling and had to be literally dragged from the stage. Her marchlike **"Holiday"** was performed in military **drag,** the cast's severe coats fanning out into the U.S. **flag.** The patriotism was almost surprising considering that "TGS" played only three American cities.

For her first encore, she slinked across the stage in exact replicas of the Cecil Beaton costumes from the Ascot Gavot racing scene in *My Fair Lady,* lip-synching **"Justify My Love."** That smoldering number was tempered by a dressed-down (cutoff

The Girlie Show set:

"Erotica," "Fever," "Vogue," "Just My Imagination"/"Rain," "Express Yourself," "Deeper and Deeper," "Why's It So Hard," "In This Life," "Justify My Love: The Beast Within Mix," "Like a Virgin," "Bye Bye Baby," "I'm Going Bananas," "La Isla Bonita," "Holiday," "Justify My Love," "Everybody is a Star"/"Everybody."

Cities in which The Girlie Show played:

London, England; Paris, France; Tel Aviv, Israel; Istanbul, Turkey; Montreal and Toronto, Canada; New York, Philadelphia, Detroit, and San Juan, Puerto Rico, in the U.S.; Buenos Aires, Argentina; Sao Paulo and Rio De Janeiro, Brazil; Mexico City, Mexico; Sydney, Brisbane, Adelaide, and Melbourne, Australia; and Tokyo, Japan.

Girlie Show tour Mishaps and Scandals:

• Some venues forbade toplessness, so dancer **Carrie Inaba** wore a halter top on those evenings.

• Madonna held up traffic by **jogging** in the street while in Toronto, then later exchanged obscenities with a stockbroker in a Four Seasons **gym.** She'd turned off his **business TV** show so she could better hear her boombox.

• Orthodox Jews staged protests to cancel Madonna's first-ever show in Israel.

• Caught by reporters at the birthplace of Christ in Jerusalem, Madonna called them "sons of whores" ("*bnei-zonot*") and hurled other vicious slurs in Hebrew and Arabic, then dodged a meeting with Mayor Teddy Koleck.

• Puerto Rican **flag** flap! The week Puerto Rico voted whether to seek independence, she rubbed its flag between her legs onstage.

• Pious Mexican students burned Madonna in poster-gy, pissed off that she **fucking** represented vulgarity.

• Madonna received a pretty stick as a welcoming gift, carrying it around Australia before realizing it was a bizarre "men only" Aborigine symbol. Whoops.

• Flick Pest Control Company issued a warning that Sydney, Australia, shows could be besieged by love-starved termites—it was mating season! The pests got ringside seats—you can see one crawling up her chest on the home **video.**

jeans and white tank tops) **"Everybody,"** a sweet, nostalgic way to end—with her very first song.

Madonna has never been more real onstage. She joked with the audience (different jokes at different performances!), smiled warmly, cried real tears throughout her AIDS tribute, and danced like a seasoned hoofer.

TGS ignored hits like **"Like a Prayer"** and **"Into the Groove,"** but that's no criticism—this ain't no oldies show. The concert elevated Madonna's music to emotional anthems. If she could cook *this* up in a **slump,** there was no question that she was still going strong.

The critical reaction to the show was schizophrenic. Several London **tabloids** trashed it despite mind-bogglingly positive fan reaction, and their too-clever negative reviews preceded the show as it traveled across the world. In every other venue, the reviews ranged from "I didn't know she was so good" to "I'll be sure to wipe the slobber off my face when I'm done raving."

TGS required 1,500 costumes for the cast (including $500-per-yard patchwork material for the "Deeper and Deeper" frock) and a 24-hour stage set-up time. The cast rehearsed from 11 A.M. to 11 P.M. six days a week for several weeks before their debut in front of 72,000 fans. Credit **Christopher Ciccone** for his direction and production design, and **Jeffrey Hornaday** for staging the entire thing. Other Madonna regulars involved include singers/dancers **Niki Haris** and **Donna DeLory** and Blond Ambition dancer **Carlton Wilborn**.

HBO televised the concert live from Sydney, Australia, which **Maverick** packaged for home video as *The Girlie Show: Live Down Under.* Madonna made the entire experience on the road into her second book, *Madonna: The Girlie Show,* published by Callaway Editions in 1994.

girlykind: First introduced in the **Girlie Show tour** program, a word Madonna invented to encompass women, girls, and girl-minded boys who strut, preen, pose, mug, and dazzle all boykind.

glamor: "You needn't be conventionally beautiful to be glamorous. It has to do with carriage, grace, dignity, and the way you present yourself. You have to value it to have it."—Madonna, 1988.

Glamour: Glossy women's magazine that in 1990 named Madonna one of its ten "Women of the Year." Madonna's company was **Jane Pauley;** Chris Evert; gun control advocate Sarah Brady; founder of the Children's Defense Fund Marian Wright Edelman; PWA and the late **AIDS** lobbyist Elizabeth Glaser, founder of Teach for America, Wendy Kopp; Chinese expatriate and Tiananmen Square revolt leader Chai Ling; Democratic Maryland senator Barbara Mikulski; and Democratic Colorado representative Pat Schroeder.

Madonna skipped the associated party because she was annoyed that the magazine's art department had seen fit to **air-brush** her cover photo.

God: In 1992 the Agnostic Girl said simply, "Everyone has their own God."

gold tooth: Madonna wore a $10,000 gold tooth—inscribed with a *D* for her persona "**Dita**"—steadily from September 1992 through January 1993.

The tooth (she actually had two, but didn't care for the *M* version) had to be fitted by a dentist each time she wore it, and removed by one each time she tired of it. The jack-o-lantern impression it lent her smile was highly effective in the **"Erotica" video,** but it got in the way of European interviews she gave to promote ***Body of Evidence,*** causing a slight lisp.

golf: She tried her hand at this, the dullest of all sports, in 1994, after receiving golf clubs as a Christmas present. Michael Jordan has nothing to worry about.

"Goodbye to Innocence": Uptempo tune originally recorded for *Erotica* whose beat was initially used for the recording of **"Fever."** Madonna and co-producer **Shep Pettibone** were so taken with the latter that they shelved "GTI" until July 19, 1994, when it was released on **Sire**'s controversial pro-choice compilation, *Just Say Roe.*

Goose and Tom-Tom: David Rabe **play** staged as a work-in-progress in the Mitzi Newhouse Theater at Lincoln Center the last

"*A*n inarticulate and incomprehensible meditation on human grubbiness."
—*The Wall Street Journal*

·

"*T*he best thing about the play was the costumes. . . . Madonna changes outfits all the time, from one beautiful one to another one. And Sean Penn wore a gun holster and fuschia socks and shoes. The play was like a Charles Ludlam, abstract. Madonna was good when she wasn't trying to be Judy Holliday or Marilyn. She chewed gum through the whole two hours and I did, too. She was blowing bubbles and everything."

—Andy Warhol on *Goose and Tom-Tom,*
from *The Andy Warhol Diaries*

week of August 1986, in which **Sean Penn** played "Goose," a jewel thief, to wifey Madonna's gum-snapping moll, "Lorraine." Harvey Keitel, who would costar with Madonna in ***Dangerous Game*** seven years later, played the crooked "Tom-Tom."

The content of the show paled in comparison to the real-life drama of Penn's violent streak, which struck on opening night when he punched **paparazzo** Vinnie Zuffante and spat on Anthony Savignano, an attack for which he earned probation.

The show was closed to the general public, which didn't stop an A-list of celebs from getting a gander at Madonna's stage debut. **Cher, Andy Warhol,** Melanie Griffith, Chris Penn, Robert DeNiro, Martin Scorcese, Tom Cruise, Griffin Dunne, **Keith Haring,** Tatum O'Neal and John McEnroe, Liza Minnelli and Mark Gero, and future lover **Warren Beatty** all saw it, as did best friend **Martin Burgoyne**. In 1994, Penn prepared to direct the film version of *G&T-T.*

Gore, Tipper: Prudish wife of Democratic U.S. Vice President Al Gore.

In the eighties she ran the Parents Music Resource Center (PMRC), a conservative group that lobbied hard for mandatory rating labels on music after serial killer Richard "The Night Stalker" Ramirez was found to have been obsessed with rock group AC/DC. The PMRC also advocated banning "offensive" album covers and having **lyrics** printed on every album sleeve, and pressured record companies to drop raunchy acts. Madonna's **"Dress You Up"** appeared on their "Filthy 15" list of especially egregious affronts to decency.

The fact that the song is universally inoffensive points up that it's Madonna herself—not her music—that riles her fundamentalist detractors. (In 1991, 64 percent of respondents in an *Entertainment Weekly* poll said they would not allow their children to see a Madonna concert.)

Though Madonna is actually in favor of record labeling—calling something naughty is the best way to make it appealing, no?—she has no use for Miss Tipper Gore. When hypocritical Gore gushily greeted Madonna at the Washington, D.C., premiere of **Dick Tracy,** she received total silence in return. Madonna later told **Liz Rosenberg,** "I think I'm going to throw. I think I'm going to hurl some chunks." To Madonna, the only good Gore is a Lesley Gore.

Gotham Bar and Grill: New York City eatery that was the site of Madonna's 28th **birthday** party and the **Who's That Girl tour** post-concert bash in 1987.

graffiti: Graffiti on workers' Port-a-Johns pointed the way to **Castillo del Lago** when Madonna first bought it and it was under renovation.

Graham, Martha: Maverick choreographer/dancer whose sensual, innovative style and whipcord personality dominated **dance** in the 20th century.

Highjinks with Martha Graham and Calvin Klein.

Madonna attended classes at the Graham School when she was an eighteen-year-old naïf, plotting how fearlessly she would react to her first meeting with the great MG. As Madonna wrote in an inspirational piece for **Harper's Bazaar** in May 1994, when she bumped into MG while exiting a class to head for the bathroom, she felt it was her "first true encounter with a goddess. A warrior. A survivor. Someone not to be **fuck**ed with."

Madonna got the chance to meet her idol on more equal footing at MG's 180th ballet, "Maple Leaf Rag," which featured music by Scott Joplin, at **New York**'s City Center in late 1990. Madonna gave MG red roses after the performance, and the two got along famously, holding hands as cameras clicked. Calvin Klein proposed a toast to "the first lady of twentieth-century dance," and Madonna joked, "You're not going to say anything about my **singing**?" Later she said, "It would be the **dream** of a lifetime to portray Martha Graham in a film. She is one of my true heroes,"even as she was developing such a project. It never materialized.

MG died a few short months after their second meeting.

grandparents: Madonna's paternal grandparents were Gaetano (1901–68) and Michelina **Ciccone** (1903–68), who emigrated to Aliquippa, Pennsylvania, a suburb of Pittsburgh, from **Pacentro,** Italy. They had six children, the youngest of whom was **Silvio "Tony" Ciccone,** Madonna's oh father.

Grant, Hugh: Dashing British actor from such films as *Four Weddings and a Funeral*, with whom Madonna was reported to have been infatuated in 1994, sending him romantic **faxes** at all hours. "I've never said anything as pompous as 'no comment' before, but—no comment," he replied to **Michael Musto**'s query on the subject. He did feign jealousy at hints that Madonna had moved on to Ethan Hawke, who has about as much in common with Grant as Fluffernutter does with paté.

GROI: A favorite expression of Madonna's from 1985, meaning "get rid of it."

Grubman, Allen: Madonna's entertainment lawyer—of Grubman, Indursky & Schindler—who also represents Bruce Springsteen, **Michael Jackson**, and ex-Madonna lover **Jellybean**. So loyal is she to AG that she attended his wedding reception (in a leopard-print wrap) at the **New York** Public Library after his marriage to Deborah Haimoff.

AG was sued by ex-client Billy Joel in 1992 for fraud and breach of contract. The suit was settled in 1993.

Guccione, Bob Jr.: Son of the **Penthouse** founder and the publisher of *Spin*, Guccione wrote a scathing editorial in 1992 arguing that "Madonna has overstayed her welcome. Not just in rock culture, or here in America, or even the Western Hemisphere. The planet. . . . She is not an important artist."

Madonna has appeared on three *Spin* covers, including its premiere issue, and was asked by the magazine to write an article to coincide with the publication of **Sex,** but declined. Perhaps BG didn't like the way she said no, or perhaps his diatribe was more principled. Either way, it was a serious attack that heralded more to come.

Guinness Book of World Records, The: In the 1988 edition, Madonna earned the distinction of being the world's most successful female singer of all time.

SEE ALSO: *TRUE BLUE* ALBUM

Gustafson (Ciccone), Joan: Stern, blonde housekeeper for the Ciccones who became Madonna's stepmother after her natural **mother** died. Growing up, Madonna never liked JG, rebelling against her strict rules, the uniformlike outfits she sewed for the **Ciccone** kids, and what Madonna could only perceive as her attempt to take the place of the first Mrs. Ciccone.

Madonna revealed that JG once bloodied her nose, but she was happy for it since it enabled her to skip mass. Wherever JG goes blood follows: Madonna said that her stepmother wouldn't allow her to use tampons when she began **menstruation,** warning that Madonna shouldn't wear such things until she was married.

JG was seen in ***Truth or Dare*** and has given brief on-camera interviews about life as a famous step-relation, always seeming eerily calm to the point of distraction. It's easy to envision JG and Madonna battling like spiders in a terrarium.

gym: The **fitness** freak once said, "If I had nothing to do, I would stay in the gym forever."

hair: Madonna has had a long and tortured relationship with hair. She is a natural dark brunette, but sported longish, streaky, sandy-colored tresses in her first major **videos** and in **Desperately Seeking Susan**. When she chopped it all off and went platinum for her **"Papa Don't Preach" video**, it marked the first of a series of color and length switches, progressing from long, immaculately-kept blonde to shaggy brunette to Shirley Temple curls to auburn to slicked-back black.

"*A* ny lady who chooses to become
a blonde is truly blonde."

—Norman Mailer

·

"*It* looks good onstage."

—Madonna on touring blonde, 1987

·

"*It* wouldn't surprise me if Madonna were a
natural blonde who dyes her roots black."

—Eric Schmuckler, *The Village Voice*, 1984

·

"*With* but a change of hair color . . .
she transmutes from blonde, aerobicized pop
star into some pre-Raphaelite personification
of spiritual beauty."

—Roy Wilkinson, *New Music Express*, 1989

Hair may seem a superficial aspect of a person, but to Madonna, it is a signifier. She feels more down-to-earth and centered as a brunette, more fabulous and playful as a blonde. No word on how she feels as a redhead—maybe confused?

A classic example of the continuing changes to her 'do and of the challenge she presents to a lazy imagination came in anticipation of **The Girlie Show.** Asked what color her hair would be, her response was, "What hair?"

Respondents to a 1994 Neutrogena survey totally missed the point when they awarded Madonna with the Medusa Award for her constant bad-hair days. After all, Madonna doesn't have bad hair days, she sometimes has bad hair*dos* that only last a *day*.

The hair on her head isn't the only hair that gets Madonna in the news. When her nudes appeared in **Playboy** and **Penthouse**, most interesting was the underarm hair on that spindly young baby goddess, the ultimate shock to Middle America. And in 1992, much ado was made by the foreign press about her bleached facial hair, pictured under such snappy headlines as "Hair's That Girl?" and "What's All the Fuzz About? (Being a Superstar Can Get You Down)."

Hall, Arsenio: It's a canceled thing. Madonna graced "Arsenio!" three times, first appearing in a no-holds-barred **Blond Ambition** interview that is legendary **television**. Madonna appeared in AH's stead, a funny gag that was somehow passed off as unplanned. As soon as AH began questioning her about **Warren Beatty** and her supposed passion for spanking, Madonna brought up **rumors** that AH had been Eddie Murphy's **lover**, and also referred to an American Music **Awards** incident between AH and singlet **Paula Abdul**. AH threw the **Sandra Bernhard** rumors back in her face, not a very effective tactic considering Madonna herself had started them.

She cut to the quick by asking about Abdul's bed: "Is it a king-size, or is it a *queen*-size?" She even had the gall to insult his "tired" **hair**style. (Sorry, Arsenio, but that 'do was yawning for years before Madonna mentioned it.) AH later griped to *Ebony* magazine that a bleached-blonde white girl has no business dictating African-American hairstyles, a typically cheap effort to take the event into the realm of race. If Louis Farrakhan told him it was tired, would he change it? Despite the controversy, her appearance was the highest-rated episode ever, attracting almost 6.5 million TV households.

Madonna next showed up on "Arsenio!" in the company of **Rosie O'Donnell** to promote **A League of Their Own**. The exchange was raunchy (connect the bleeps), but was cut short when AH craftily brought out Madonna's father, **Tony Ciccone**. "Now I have to be good!" she moaned. The show's highlight came when Hall asked Mr. Ciccone what Madonna had been like as a child. "A very nice young lady," he replied with a straight face.

Hall's 1,000th-episode special at the Hollywood Bowl attracted Madonna again less than a year later, and this time the appearance was bittersweet. She opened with a traditional version of **"Fever,"** her auburn hair curled under à la Bette Davis, clad in a sleek gown and stiltlike platforms. She kept her footing but stumbled vocally, singing out of place. "I don't usually mess up. But everyone makes mistakes, baby." She muddled through, dramatically snubbed out a cigarette, and got seriously leggy before slinking offstage. She showed up later in an inspired duet with Red Hot Chili Pepper Anthony Kiedis—in **drag**. Both wore horned hats, duetting on "The Lady is a Tramp."

AH is a fan of Madonna's **AIDS** work (his 1,000th-episode show raised $250,000 for The Magic Johnson Foundation), but is very turned off by her **sex activism**.

An artist's rendering of Madonna as she appeared on Arsenio Hall's 1000th episode celebration, 1993.

Hank: The hapless half-wolf, half-Akik dog that Madonna bought for herself and **Sean Penn** in December 1986, only to leave him behind when the marriage went sour.

"Hanky Panky": The second and last single from *I'm Breathless* was this rip-roaring recommendation of light spanking.

The song is simultaneously a comment on **"Breathless Mahoney"**'s status as a woman who thrives on abuse, and a saucy challenge to radio stations, some of which declined to play it. The lack of airplay kept "HP" from rising above number 10, but the single went gold anyway.

Haring, Keith: Young, influential **graffiti** artist who helped revolutionize **art** in the eighties with his quirky, radiant infants and dogs.

KH went from being arrested for defacing **New York City** subways—the halls of which were at one time covered with Haring originals—to commanding $20,000 per canvas, all before the age of twenty-five. Madonna hung around with the street art crowd, and became fast friends with KH.

He designed the cover for the *A Very Special Christmas* album, to which Madonna donated her lippy rendition of "Santa Baby," and also showed up as a special guest at **Don't Bungle the Jungle**.

He contracted **AIDS** and became an early example of a celebrity using his seropositivity to spread the word about safer **sex**, humanizing the face of AIDS by connecting his own harmless mug to it. He lectured to kids on AIDS right up until a few months before he died in 1990.

Madonna owns an elaborate Haring original collage of herself that hangs in **Castillo del Lago**.

"*E*ven with his massive success, Keith still came out and said, 'I have AIDS, I'm gay.' He didn't worry if it was going to jeopardize his career, he just went with it. He gave all people courage to be strong and to stare death in the face."

—Madonna, 1990

Haris, Niki: Enthusiastic backup singer/dancer for Madonna on both the **Blond Ambition** and **Girlie Show tours**. As well as lending vocals to the *Like a Prayer* **album** and songs like "**Bye Bye Baby**," **"Deeper and Deeper,"** and "Why's It So Hard," NH sang Snap's **dance** hit "Exterminate."

NH made a terrific splash in *Truth or Dare*, coming across with potent screen presence and earthy charm. Shortly thereafter, she captured the lead role in a bio-pic of blues legend Billie Holiday, costarring **Bruce Willis**.

Harper's Bazaar: Venerable **fashion** magazine that has featured Madonna on its cover three times.

In 1988, her layout was to show off her demure brunette **look** while performing in ***Speed-the-Plow***. Inside she donned an unconventional straw hat with a big, juicy apple perched dead center like William Tell's son, and, for the first time, a **Jean-Paul Gaultier**–designed bodysuit that perfectly captured her playfulness.

Her 1990 cover spread (shot by **Jean-Baptiste Mondino**) featured her as a metallic siren, cruising the country in **Blond Ambition.**

Peter Lindbergh provided her May 1994 cover and layout, a series of translations of the spirit of **dance** owing much to Man Ray, which illustrated a short piece by Madonna describing her first encounter with **Martha Graham**.

An earlier appearance on *HB*'s hallowed pages was in 1984, in a spread by **Francesco Scavullo** that featured shots of Madonna in black lace and a form-fitting elasticized skirt by Commes des Garçons, her own boots and backwards-turned hat, a wild purple scarf with bronze bird clip, a snake bracelet, and spooky accessories galore. The shoot was done to coincide with the release of ***Like a Virgin***, and the text, which tried gamely to pin down the new "hip-hop" subculture, inadvertently grouped Madonna with Afrika Bambaataa as a "rapper." Seen today Scavullo's work makes one gasp at a lost vision of Madonna, the pagan goddess of lust and all things creepy-crawly.

Madonna would later work with *HB*'s *enfant terrible* **art** designer **Fabien Baron**.

Harry, Deborah ("Debbie"): Sultry, towheaded lead singer of the punk/rock/new wave/disco group Blondie and, later, a solo act. DH was a pioneer in incorporating **sex**ual allure with brains to make beautiful **music**. She is often cited as a "precursor" of Madonna, as if women evolve from one another.

There is no doubt that Madonna was influenced by DH, whose music she has professed to admire, and some of DH's songs with Blondie seem to have inspired some Madonna tunes: "Thief of Hearts" is a bubblegum version of the earlier, more lethal "Rip Her to Shreds," and **"Supernatural"** is an obvious exploration of ghostly intercourse à la "(I'm Always Touched by Your) Presence Dear."

DH always has praise for Madonna—and she is asked her opinion on that subject with every interview she grants—calling her very "commercial" and good at what she does. DH has shown up to several Madonna "events," including the **New York** pre-

miere of ***Truth or Dare*** and Madonna's 35th **birthday** party at **Castillo del Lago**.

"*S*he has mentioned that I was important to her, and that's very satisfying. However, a check would be better!"

—Deborah Harry, 1993

hatred: As successful as she is, Madonna turns a lot of people off. Way off. An entire book was written called *The I Hate Madonna Handbook*, but most of her detractors don't need a manual—for them, it's "loathe at first sight."

"*M*adonna is the kind of woman who comes into your room at 3 A.M. and sucks your life out."

—Milo Miles, *Boston Phoenix*

·

"*M*adonna is an awful, ugly, dull person who by being completely shameless, blatant, and cheap has become successful. . . . If she got a gun and blew her own head off I doubt if anyone would notice."

—Pink Floyd bassist Roger Waters, 1992

·

"*I*f someone becomes hugely successful the public becomes disgusted with them and begins to wish the star would slip on a banana peel."

—Madonna, 1988

For people who hate Madonna, it's frequently her omnipresence they object to, or what they see as the exaggerated importance ascribed to a bleached-blonde singer. Madonna also provokes hatred for her glib enjoyment of her celebrity and wealth, and for her unpopular affection for **nudity** and **sex**ual themes in her **work**.

But at the root of most Madonna hatred is contempt for a pop star who dares to contend that her output is "art," and who refuses to smile, play nice, and behave humbly.

HBO: As past icons have graced **television** with elaborate, self-involved, compulsively watchable "specials," so has Madonna dabbled with the medium. Her efforts have been more elite, restricted to professionally-filmed versions of her masterpiece concerts aired on the cable network HBO. **Blond Ambition,** which was aired uncensored from Nice, France, set the record for the highest-rated non-sports event in HBO history, snagging 19.8 million watchers, or 21.4 percent of all subscribers.

The next time any event would come close was **Michael Jackson**'s Dangerous concert, broadcast the following year. Madonna's concert had already swept through America and had been dissected in the media; Jackson's concert was just kicking off, however, and it had been announced it would never play America. Even with those qualifiers, all he could muster was a tie.

The Girlie Show was also broadcast on HBO, from a performance in Sydney, Australia, before 90,000 fans (holding tickets sold at a rate of 1,000 per minute at $70–200 each). *The Girlie Show: Live Down Under* was another tremendous success, raking in nearly as many viewers as Blond Ambition and $3 million for Madonna, and also providing the basis for a Top Ten home **video**.

headset: When Madonna strapped on a microphone headset to free up her hands for her **Blond Ambition** performances, she single-handedly established it as the standard in the industry. Since 1990, acts like **Janet** and **Michael Jackson, Paula Abdul**, and Whitney Houston (in her Madonna-inspired role in *The Bodyguard*) have used headsets.

The **look** recalls Lily Tomlin's character "Ernestine," but it gets the job done.

healthy: Madonna popularized midriff tank tops with the phrase HEALTHY across the chest in 1985. She appeared in hers on the cover of *Penthouse* and performed in it on **Japan**ese TV, where audiences also saw the slogan on the *back* of the shirt—SWIMMER.

height: Like a midget.

Madonna, such an enormous personality, is actually a diminutive figure, all of 5'4½". That makes her over three inches taller than Prince, about four inches shy of Annie Lennox, and almost nine inches shorter than Boy George. Aside from her "thin lips," small stature is the one thing about her physicality that she has consistently said she'd like to change.

Helena's: Los Angeles eatery owned by Helena Kallianiotes, Jack Nicholson, and a group of other investors. It's one of Madonna's faves, and was her special favorite when married to **Sean Penn**. She hosted a **Who's That Girl tour** wrap party there, even though it was the site of Penn's drunken attack on David Wolinski.

Hepburn, Katharine: Refined *grande dame* of the American cinema, whose film *Bringing Up Baby* was a direct inspiration for *Who's That Girl* and who is cited in **"Vogue."**

In 1993, she admitted to never having even *seen* Madonna (or Kevin Costner or Julia Roberts, for that matter). "The type of thing she does is not of a great deal of interest to me, but I should have seen her. I'm lazy."

Hernandez, Patrick: Cheesy singer behind the huge disco hit "Born to be Alive."

Madonna was recruited by his promoters Jean-Claude Pellerin and Jean Van Lieu to appear as part of his multimedia Vaudeville-flavored "Patrick Hernandez Revue" in Paris in the early eighties. She proved so talented the producers tried to mold her into the next Piaf, even writing a song called "She's a Real Disco Queen" for her. She hated the song, and took off for the U.S. when their promises grew stale.

heroes: Madonna's heroes, circa 1990, were **Spike Lee, Public Enemy**, Mikhail Gorbachev, Mother Teresa, Czech leader Václav Havel, and **Martha Graham**.

Hitler, Adolf: One of history's most reprehensible monsters, Nazi leader AH and his contemporary equal, Persian Gulf War-rior Saddam Hussein, were mentioned in the same breath as Madonna by Boston University president John R. Silber in 1991, in a speech that compared her message with theirs.

Huh? Such a callous comparison is an extreme example of the overblown critical reception Madonna receives. Her next **project** might be X-rated or controversial or even *lame*, but it probably won't be a death camp.

hoax: The greatest Madonna hoax so far was also the most diabolical.

A Massachusetts con artist named Marie Lamour successfully impersonated Madonna for almost six months, convincing a pair of dumbbell bodyguard-**wanna-bes** to protect her on spec and an eager British filmmaker to invest time and money for a proposed sequel to **Truth or Dare**. Lamour, whose children were conditioned to call her by Madonna's **nickname**, "Mo," had been passing herself off as Madonna for five years. She even had prescriptions in Madonna's name.

In 1993 she went whole hog, telling Northampton neighbors she was Madonna and was staying there to take care of her sister's kids (all her own) and to hide out while pregnant. Of course, with

rumors swirling that the real Madonna was expecting, the lie wasn't so farfetched. Whenever Madonna showed up on TV thousands of miles away, Lamour explained it by saying that that other woman was her double, meant to fool the press. That people believed it underscores just one of the many strange myths the public holds regarding celebrities.

Lamour's most evil shenanigan was sending pleas to hundreds of corporations, suggesting a 24-hour, weeks-long "Care-a-Thon" to help raise money for a slew of charities, many of which were also duped by Lamour into believing they'd soon be receiving badly-needed dollars. She wrote a bogus promissory note for a million bucks to San Francisco's Burts Children's Home, signing both her assumed name and that of **Maverick** hotshot **Guy Oseary**.

But the bad girl lost in the end, exposed on "Hard Copy."

"Holiday" song: The song only rose to number 16 (her first Top 20 hit) on its release in 1983, but it has aged remarkably well and still pops up on contemporary pop stations. Helping to keep the song fresh, Madonna has performed this crowd-pleaser on all of her tours, rearranging it each time.

"H" is a prime example of Madonna's reliance on infectious optimism in her early career.

There was a small-scale **video** made for the song, featuring Madonna in Boy George baby dreadlocks against a hot pink backdrop, but the video was scrapped and has never been released commercially.

Holy Water: Long-**rumor**ed name of Madonna's foray into the world of celebrity perfumes, supposedly being cooked up by Prestige Fragrance at Unilever. It's a better name than "Shocking" (or "Uninhibited," for that matter), but according to an anonymous fragrance exec (in ***Harper's Bazaar***, 1994), "It has a slightly better chance of succeeding than a **Michael Jackson** scent."

Still, though cynics may think that Madonna **fans** don't wear scents, it's probably more accurate that we're the ones wearing *all* the scents. **Liz Rosenberg** said, "Madonna's been offered everything from entire continents to the heads of her least favorite people on a platter to get her name on a perfume or some other product. It hasn't happened, and I seriously doubt a deal is in the works."

As for Madonna's own perfume preferences, she was so into Chanel No. 5 that she scented limited copies of "**Material Girl**" with it, and she adored patchouli oil enough to scent *Like a Prayer* with *that*, but if you sniff behind her ears you're more likely to catch a whiff of Tuberose by Jean Le Port.

hommage: Madonna has been the subject of numerous musical *hommages* the likes of which are usually reserved for the sick and the dead.

The first *hommage* came from the loftiest source, "Weird Al" Yankovic, who in 1985 (with Madonna's blessing) turned **"Like a Virgin"** into "Like a Surgeon," complete with a Madonna look-

alike for the accompanying **video**. The following year, Danny Aiello made a video·of a song called "Papa Only Wants What's Best for You," in response to the **"Papa Don't Preach" video**, in which he had played Madonna's troubled father. **Otto von Wernherr** sang the similarly cautionary "Madonna Don't Preach."

Sparks recorded a hilarious fantasy of being picked up by Madonna in her limo (**Christopher Andersen**, take note!) titled simply "Madonna," and Billy Crystal's semihit "You Look Mah-velous" praised Madonna's mah-velous **belly button**.

Sonic Youth went so far as to rechristen themselves **Ciccone** Youth for an EP of Madonna covers (*The Whitey Album*, 1986).

"Justify My Love" was such a radical departure from mainstream pop music it immediately generated at least three answer songs, from rapper D-Melo ("Justify, Satisfy"), Young Black Teenagers ("To My Donna"), and Al B. Sure ("I'll Justify Your Love"). Canadian crooner Corey Hart offered a mystical interpretation of Madonna's **overexposure** with "She's Everywhere" on his *Attitude and Virtue* album.

With so much activity already, it seems safe to say that Madonna-inspired songs will only increase as her legend does. It makes you wonder: *Hommage* is too much?

SEE ALSO: **PARODY**

homes: Madonna currently owns three of them, one in **Miami**, Florida, one in the Hollywood Hills of California, and the other a swank **New York City** apartment.

Her Mediterranean Revival—style six-bedroom Florida mansion is done in gray, dark green, and white, and features a carved-wood ceiling in the living room and keystone details. The home, built in 1928 on "Millionaire's Row," is surrounded by fifty-seven mature palm trees, and is within spitting distance of **Jose Canseco**'s house. But that's a whole different entry.

Madonna's New York apartment at 1 West 64th Street (Harperley Hall) showcases her **art** collection and **Christopher Ciccone**—dictated taste, featuring a yellowish-beige-and-gold master bedroom and hexagonal dressing room. The apartment is

Madonna's secluded childhood home in
Rochester Hills, Michigan.

actually three units: the first she purchased with **Sean Penn**, the second two she purchased on her own. Other star residents of 1 West 64th are **Don Johnson** and Melanie Griffith, Carol Kane, and Ed Asner.

Her most notorious abode is the 10,000-square-foot **Castillo del Lago** in the Hollywood Hills, which was built in 1926 by gangster Bugsy Siegel (whom **Warren Beatty** played in the 1991 film, *Bugsy*). When the first coats of yellow and bloodred went up on the $5-million, four-story manse in May 1993, neighbors groused. Designer/brother Christopher Ciccone replied, "If it wasn't Madonna, nobody would really care. A number of houses in the area are, shall we say, a bit ramshackle."

In the song **"Like a Prayer,"** the word "home" is invoked for its reassuring familiarity. It's a shame that Madonna chose **Maverick** over her company's original working title, Home.

"*M*adonna at home would have pleased Charles Addams."

—James Kaplan, *Entertainment Weekly*, 1991

A wistful Madonna poses on the roof of her apartment in this rare portrait from 1983.

"You have to expect a certain amount of invasion . . . but then you have to draw the line.
I draw the line when I get to my house. Wherever I live, that should be sacred."

—Madonna, 1987

Where Madonna's Heart Has Roosted Over the Years:

childhood
· First home with her parents at 443 Thors Street in Pontiac, Michigan.
· Second home when brood moved to 2036 Oklahoma Street, in **Rochester Hills**, Michigan, a two-story chocolate-colored colonial with forest green shutters, a blue door, and a ranch-style fence surrounding the grounds.

college
· One semester at the University of Michigan–Ann Arbor, spent in student housing at 536 S. University, #10A.

1979
· Stayed with total stranger she met in Times Square for first several days in New York City.
· Spent formative New York years crashing with friends and living with boyfriends (**Dan Gilroy,** et al).

1978—80
· First apartment on the Lower East Side at 232 East 4th Street between Avenues A and B.
· Lived in 13th Street apartment that once housed Yippie leader Abbie Hoffman.
· Squatted in illegal garment-district loft . . . almost died in fire sparked by space heater.

1981
· Lived in apartment known as "the Star Hotel" on West 30th Street between 8th and 9th Avenues, across from Madison Square Garden, which she always **dream**ed of playing . . . and did in 1985. Apartment subsidized ($65 per week) by Gotham, her first management.
· Shacked up with **Steve Bray** in **the Music Building** near Times Square.

1982—84
· Cozy loft in SoHo. Thank you, Sire!

1985
· Attempted to buy $1.2-million apartment from producer Bill Gerber, but was rejected by the **San Remo** co-op board.

1985
· Bought first unit of current New York apartment.

1989
· Bought $2.9-million 10-room Hollywood Hills mansion; later sold in favor of Castillo del Lago.

1992
· Bought Castillo del Lago. Special thanks to all the little people!

1993
· Bought Miami mansion for $4.9 million ($2.75 million more than the owners had paid five years earlier).

homosexuality: Madonna's first reference to same-**sex**uality was the **"Open Your Heart" video**. The setting is a strip club, and in one of the booths watching Madonna are two beautiful sailors, their cheeks pressed together in bliss. Another booth features a lone woman in **drag**, who had also been enjoying the girlie show. The video was extremely controversial, though its homosexual bits were less frequently cited than her character's strange relationship with a young boy.

There is an almost beatific lesbian power in the gaze between Madonna and the African-American preacher/singer in her **"Like a Prayer" video**, which was one more reason to pay close attention to the **Sandra Bernhard**—fueled rumors of Madonna's **bisexuality** that were in full force at the time the video was released.

Her next use of homosexuality was far more explicit, depicting highly charged romantic embraces among men and among women—including her own passionate lesbian **kiss**—in the **"Justify My Love" video**. With *Sex* and its companion video, **"Erotica,"** homosexuality was no longer mere *chic* to Madonna. It became a full-fledged, fully-integrated part of her work in the form of both political and prurient images (involving Madonna directly) and in Madonna's erotic short stories, which were saturated with homosexual desire.

SEE ALSO: GAY MEN, LIPSTICK LESBIANISM

honeymoon: Mr. and Mrs. **Sean Penn** had a fabulous honeymoon at the Highlands Inn in Carmel, California. They stayed (four days and nights) in Honeymoon Suite 429. When they emerged for drinks at Clint Eastwood's Hog's Breath Inn, the **paparazzi** saw to it that their **privacy**—and the honeymoon—was over.

hopping ghost: Chinese in origin, this little guy is the very same sort of puppet that stood up to **"Dita"** in the **"Erotica" video** and was rewarded with a "glove job."

As harmless as these dolls should be, they do emanate pure evil, don't they? The dolls represent dissatisfied revenants of Chinese legend that return from the dead in lethally odoriferous corpse bodies, hopping in search of more psychically comfy graves. If they encounter you (they detect people by the smell of our breath) they will hop toward you

until they have punctured your neck, leaving you to die in breathless agony. "Erotic, erotic . . . " (thud, *whoosh!*)

Hornaday, Jeffrey: Choreographer of *Flashdance* and ex–live-in love of Lesley Anne Warren.

Blond, blue-eyed JH choreographed the **Who's That Girl tour, Blond Ambition,** and also staged the entire production of **The Girlie Show.**

He was romantically linked to Madonna in early 1989, immediately after she filed for **divorce** from **Sean Penn.**

horoscope: According to astrologer Lina Accurso, Madonna is a "Sun-sign Leo who has a Virgo ascendant Moon." Her Virgo streak is responsible for her nose-to-the-grindstone m.o., her neatness, her **love** affair with **control**, and her self-absorption. Her Moon represents maternity, which bears out her much-discussed mom ambition.

That she was born a Leo made her very likely to become a star, and explains her need for attention and for "showing," whether it be her immaculate apartment, her private life, or her breasts. It also signifies leadership, which any **wanna-be** can tell you Madonna has in spades.

hot line: A Madonna news hot line was established by **Sire Records** in 1990: 1-900-98-**VOGUE** (no longer in service). It cost $2 for the first minute (which was taken up by Madonna's prerecorded, breathy introduction) and $1 for each additional minute, during which callers could hear about *I'm Breathless, Dick Tracy*, and **Blond Ambition.**

Howard, Felix: The little British boy who, in the **"Open Your Heart" video**, emulates the glamorous stripper played by Madonna. His **mother** is a former **fashion** model, which helped him make the cover of *The Face* magazine, and meet Madonna backstage at a fashion show in 1986. "She was really, really nice," he said at the time, but he cried his eyes out when his failure to get a work license mandated his replacement on the **Who's That Girl tour**.

He consoled himself for a time by hosting London's "The Tube" **music** show.

Hutton, Timothy: Pal of ex–Mr. Madonna, **Sean Penn. Andy Warhol** recalled receiving a call from TH who, in begging off a social engagement, said he and Madonna weren't going to be able to make it. According to Warhol, TH hung up when Andy asked, "What are you doing with Madonna?"

Ice-T: Controversial rapper/philosopher whose incendiary song "Cop Killer" gave **Warner Bros.** Records major grief just before **Sex** came along to give Warner Books a little more.

"I like Madonna," he says. "She's my idol. She performed in my **club** when she first started. She did ` Physical Attraction,' pulled my shirt off, and kissed me on the chest. Blew my mind. I **love** her, man. If she wants to do a 100-page book of herself butt-naked, licking feet, then do it, baby. That's what the **fuck** you're supposed to do."

"I'll Remember" song: A return to form for Madonna in 1994, this number 2 smash theme from the **Alek Keshishian** film *With Honors* restored Madonna to good graces with the record-buying public after the much-ballyhooed backlash against **Erotica**.

It sounds a lot like "The Look of Love" and is full of the same **lyric**al nostalgia that drives **"This Used to be My Playground,"** but it's a mid-tempo ballad with a vulnerability that so many **fans** find so appealing in the woman of steel. The song was cowritten with **Pat Leonard** and Richard Page.

"I'll Remember" video: The laziest gal in town! Directed by **Alek Keshishian**, this video is a virtual remake of the video that directly preceded it, **"Rain."** We see the techies, behind the scenes at the recording studio, and Madonna looking drop-dead in short black **hair**, emoting as she croons wistfully . . . But where are the **Japan**ese? Another major difference between the **videos** is that in "IR", the hair is really Madonna's—in "Rain," she wears a wig. The most clever bit is that Madonna (thanks to computer finagling) watches herself **singing**. The **voyeur** Madonna is dressed in a man's suitcoat and shirt, the **exhibitionist** Madonna in a clingy black gown; both stand before images of *With Honors*, the film for which the song is the love theme.

Madonna's going for the Louise Brooks **look** with her severe bangs and arch make up, but when she stares into the camera at video's end, it's hard not to think, *"Chita Rivera."*

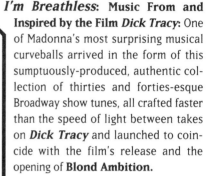

I'm Breathless: Music From and Inspired by the Film *Dick Tracy*: One of Madonna's most surprising musical curveballs arrived in the form of this sumptuously-produced, authentic collection of thirties and forties-esque Broadway show tunes, all crafted faster than the speed of light between takes on **Dick Tracy** and launched to coincide with the film's release and the opening of **Blond Ambition.**

The 1990 album, which is Madonna's least successful full-length album of all-new material, was nonetheless a well-reviewed number 2 smash, eventually selling close to 3 million copies in the U.S., 5 million worldwide. It spawned only two singles, the number 1 **"Vogue"** and the number 10 **"Hanky Panky,"** neither of them among the three tunes written expressly for *Dick Tracy* by legendary composer Stephen Sondheim.

On *IB*, Madonna stretches her vocals to encompass torch songs ("He's a Man," "Sooner or Later"), chirpy Boop tunes ("Cry Baby"), comic flamenco ("I'm Going Bananas"), romantic ballads ("Something to Remember"), dance-hall ditties ("Now I'm Following You, Part I"), and even modern disco ("Now I'm Following You, Part II," "Vogue"). For a woman whose critics often say she can't sing, she pulls off these diverse vocal demands with enthusiasm, style, and aplomb.

IB is a concept album. A soundtrack of sorts (though only three of its songs are actually "from" *Dick Tracy*), it manages to musically explore Madonna's screen persona from the film ("**Breathless Mahoney**") while exploring the definitions of Madonna herself by presenting decidedly un-Madonna offerings. It answers the question, "What if Madonna were legitimate?" with a resounding "Whaddya mean *'if'*?"

Most interesting is the album's flawless immersion in the **music**al sound of the Golden Age of Broadway (and Hollywood, for that matter), followed by its transition to a canny deconstruction of the style of that era in a nineties retooling of a thirties-sounding song ("Now I'm Following You, Part II"), and its grand finale: a commentary on all that has preceded it—both on *IB* and in Madonna's entire career—with "Vogue."

*"M*adonna's latest may not be for Top 40 **fans**, but the music is sophisticated pop, as compelling as the scenes unfolding in a Broadway hit. Good show!"

—Anne Ayers, *USA Today*

•

*"M*adonna now knows how to project Sondheim's characteristic verbal wit. She even invents a new Broadway vocal persona, built around a chest voice not yet perfectly under control but still much richer and duskier than her low range sounded before. *I'm Breathless* is an album ten times more accomplished than any record she has made before."

—Greg Sandow, *Entertainment Weekly*

The album is not as salacious as some of Madonna's work, "Hanky Panky" aside, but it does sample the movie's raunchiest line—"You don't know if you wanna hit me or **kiss** me. I get a lot of that"—and gets away with, "Dick—that's an interesting name. . . . My bottom hurts just thinking about it." Madonna would later admit that because the film was for Disney, she had to delete all references (well, *most*) to sodomy, intercourse, or **masturbation**; where these themes originally fit is a mystery. Frankly, a thirties show tune on jerking off is sorely missed.

Madonna's songwriting is confident and assured. Try picking out the Stephen Sondheim numbers cold—it's difficult. For the record, Sondheim penned the Oscar-winning "Sooner or Later," "More" (a whimsical, upmarket version of **"Material Girl"**), and the album's only turkey, "What Can You Lose?"—a simpering **love**-and-regrets ballad that finds Mandy Patinkin scaling Everest with his mellifluous soprano (*read:* oversinging) and Madonna trying to play catch up (*read:* undersinging). There is a bootlegged early version of this song featuring only Madonna's voice that is catastrophic.

Listen for then **lover Warren Beatty**'s baritone on both parts of "Now I'm Following You," the second part of which features him rapping, "Ten million . . . Twenty million . . . Thirty million . . . " and so on, mocking overblown estimates of *Dick Tracy*'s final budget.

The downer of *IB* is the cover **art**, an uninspired, unflattering mugshot of **Ciccone**/"Mahoney" in chintzy black fur with Beatty/"Tracy" peering over her shoulder: "*I'm Lifeless.*"

Other than one faulty song and a faulty package, *IB* is a compulsively listenable accomplishment, one that makes you long for Madonna in an all-**singing**, all-dancing Broadway extravaganza.

Immaculate Collection, The: The title is classic Madonna, a silly pun that also manages to refer to her position as a pop "goddess." *IC* is Madonna's first greatest-hits collection. Released in late 1990, it lingered on *Billboard*'s album charts for over two years, selling approximately 11 million units worldwide.

The album, whose cover features not Madonna's famous face but a tacky turquoise-and-gold design and logo, was set to bear a **Herb Ritts** photo until Madonna yanked it. The photo, of Madonna in pointy black bangs and a bowler, made her look "like Mike Tyson." Still, **Warner Bros.** preferred it to the racy crotch-grabbing shot Madonna favored, so in the end a compromise was struck, resulting in the plain cover.

No matter. The double album's seventeen songs are such perfect pop the cover is the last thing on your mind. Though many of her hits were sacrificed—**"Dress You Up," "Who's That Girl," "Causing a Commotion,"** and **"Keep It Together"** come to mind—nothing seems out of place on this priceless disc. Its two original tunes are among Madonna's best. In fact, it's disappointing that the radically bass-driven, overheated **"Justify My Love"** and **lyric**ally and vocally challenging **"Rescue Me"** originated on a best-of, but the former's controversial **video** gave this collection a major boost. It was the first record (and one of the last) equipped with **QSound**. Tongue firmly in cheek, Madonna dedicated the album to **the Pope**.

*"S*o there it is: good sex, bad sex, dominance, submission, money, religion, race, image, reality, sleaze, and innocence. Pop culture comes no better and we should be grateful."

—Russell Brown, *Select* (U.K.)

•

*"T*he most exciting and culturally resonant singles collection of the last decade."

—Jim Farber, *New York Daily News*

impersonators: Like Elvis before her, Madonna has inspired legions of professional look-alikes. Unlike Elvis, Madonna has supplied her charges with a cornucopia of **looks** from which to choose, so that there will always be room for another paid **wanna-be.** Don't look for them to inaugurate unveilings of national landmarks just yet, but some of these guys and gals are so good they give the real thing a run for her money.

The best male Madonna impersonators are the best, period. **Gay men,** whose impersonations of other famous divas like Garland, **Monroe,** and Minnelli are famously hilarious, have a leg up in imitating the already androgynous, brittle Blonde One. The best? On a limb, try Viva, an L.A.-based divo.

The best-known female Madonna impersonator (and Madonna herself has been called a female impersonator more than once) is Chris America, who probably fooled you on the cover of *Esquire* magazine's 1991 Christmas issue. Denise Vlasis appears as Madonna at promotional events and played "Shoshonna" in **Sandra Bernhard**'s *Without You I'm Nothing,* and famous British impersonator Sara Lee has thrown Londoners for a loop for years.

Impersonators are not always paid. A Chicago woman named Melissa Totten wreaked havoc when Madonna was in town filming *A League of Their Own.* At least half of local newspapers' Madonna sightings were actually of playful Totten.

SEE ALSO: DRAG, QUEERDONNA

A girl's gotta make a living: impersonators Viva, Chris America, Denise Vlasis, and Annette Pizzo take their show on the road.

In the Realm of the Senses: The true story of an obsessive **sex**ual relationship, this Japanese film ends with its female protagonist castrating her **lover.**

Madonna loves this **art** flick. She referred to it in *Sex* as an intensely erotic movie and also gave a copy of it to **Michael Jackson** to inspire ideas for their aborted collaboration on his song "In the Closet." He told her he liked the movie, but she said his attitude toward it and all her books of nude photographs was that it was "just **pornography.**"

Inaba, Carrie Ann: Sexy, shaven-headed Asian androgyne who slithered topless down a go-go pole at the beginning of **The Girlie Show,** and performed as a backup dancer throughout the tour. Inaba is an ex–*In Living Color* flygirl.

infomercial: In an act of **Cher**-madness, Madonna was tapped by Diane von Furstenberg in 1994 to do an infomercial for a line of lingerie on Barry Diller's Q2 network.

*"N*obody had the balls to tell Mike Ovitz to give up on packaging Madonna for the big screen and start thinking Las Vegas and infomercials."

—*Movieline* magazine's choice for the "number 1 Dumbest Thing Hollywood's Done Recently," 1993

Inglis, Ledbetter & Gower: Los Angeles legal firm located at 611 West Sixth Street that represented Madonna in her **divorce** from **Sean Penn.** Her personal attorney was Michael K. Inglis, Esq.

insomnia: The inability to sleep—a problem that plagues Madonna. She sometimes tries to remember scenes from her childhood in rigorous detail in order to exhaust her mind and bring on slumber, but often loses that battle and is up all night.

"Into the Groove" song: One of Madonna's signature hits, her indelible contribution to the **Desperately Seeking Susan** soundtrack. Through exposure on **MTV** with a movie-montage **video** clip, the song became a major smash without ever being released as a single.

It was eventually released as the B-side of the extended single **"Angel,"** which Warner was pushing in favor of "ITG." The end result was that "Angel" went Top Five, while "ITG" ranked higher in airplay that summer of 1985 than any other unreleased single before or since.

"ITG" is the quintessential Madonna song. It has an irresistible **dance** groove, and Madonna speaks directly to her audience, telling us to use dance for inspiration and exalting music as a near-religious experience, all the while winking at us over the title's vaginal allusion. As if this weren't enough to skewer any adolescent's heart, Madonna possessively tells us she is sure that we are *hers.* Yes, ma'am!

Curiously, Madonna told an interviewer in late 1984 that she had written a song called "Into the Groove" for a **Sire** singer named Cheyne. Cheyne was reportedly devastated when "ITG" was pulled out from under her (albeit by its rightful owner). The song's original title was "Get Into the Groove," and Madonna frequently refers to it as such. It was remade in 1986 as "Into the Groovy" by Ciccone Youth (Sonic Youth).

"'*I*nto the Groove' is as succinct and incontrovertible a paean to the new pop dance as can be. . . . [T]he most profound comment on pop in general."

—Andrew Harrison, *Select* (U.K.)

intolerance: "I want to use my celebrity as a platform so that a lot of the people who are persecuted for their lifestyles will not be so in the future. I don't say it's gonna happen right away, but in five years, or maybe ten, what I'm doing now will have an effect, in a positive way." —Madonna, 1991

IQ: Madonna's is reportedly around 140, which puts her in the "extremely gifted" range.

Island: Madonna's first magazine cover was for this Long Island–based **club** 'zine, whose publisher—Steve Newman—she supposedly dated. Right from the start Madonna knew the **power** of making classical images speak for you: She dramatically holds her face like the famed Greta Garbo pose on this nearly impossible-to-find collector's item.

Italian: That's what she is, and she's proud of it. If you don't believe it, believe that on her **Who's That Girl tour** in Turin, Italy, she shouted, "Io sono fiera di essere Italiana!" And when **the Pope** ix-nayed her **Blond Ambition tour**, part of her speech was devoted to her pride in being a passionate Italian woman. Another source of pride can be found in the slogan on her T-shirt in the **"Papa Don't Preach" video**: "ITALIANS DO IT BETTER."

*Italian girl makes good on national Italian **magazine**.*

Jackson, Janet: Madonna-**wanna-be** pop diva and sister to **Michael**, **LaToya**, and countless other singing Jacksons. JJ has consistently paid *hommage* to Madonna in both her **look** (JJ worked her body into a Madonna-like mold and did a **video** on the beach with **Herb Ritts** à la "**Cherish**" wearing a blond wig), and her **music** (songs like "That's the Way Love Goes" and "Throb" would have been impossible without precursors like "**Erotica**" and "**Vogue**," respectively). Still, JJ does not care for Madonna one little bit. Asked if it were true that she "can't stand" Madonna, JJ went the Thumper route with *Vibe* magazine in its September 1994 issue, saying "If you can't say anything nice don't say anything at all." Her dislike was apparent when she denied hating Madonna, but noted that "If I did hate her, I'd have good reason to."

Jackson, LaToya: Surgical wondergirl, sister to **Michael**, and exotic performer whom Madonna deeply offended in 1991 with speculation that her boobs were a job, not a given.

Madonna first made the call in a *Rolling Stone* interview, wherein she eagerly tore into a preview copy of LTJ's first *Playboy* spread. "She's had a boob job for sure," Madonna said, cattily remarking that the layout might actually land LTJ some work. She repeated the comment on national **television** to **Arsenio Hall**, noting that she knew LTJ's breasts were fake because "somebody told me."

LTJ hurled the same accusation right back at the as-yet surgically untouched (**collagen** doesn't count) Madonna.

Jackson, Michael: Pop's crown prince of entertainment, the one performer Madonna always aspired to match. Little did she know she would surpass MJ's achievements, if not in sheer record sales, in artistic integrity, diversity of material, and output. Madonna initially sought out her longtime manager **Freddy DeMann** only because she was under the impression that he still represented MJ, and her blend of **music**, **dance**, and razzamatazz owes much to MJ's own style.

But the similarities end there. Where MJ keeps making the same records and **videos** over and over, dancing the exact same dance steps (albeit with incredible skill), Madonna retains only her basic modern dance archness, her sound, and a few recurring themes (**love, sex, death,** and pain), bringing new ideas and styles into each new **project**. Even their popularity is different. Until his "special friend" ratted him out for dollars, MJ was popular for being Mr. Clean & Wholesome Child-Champion, whereas Madonna is popular for being reckless and independent.

The music track for Madonna's chestnut **"La Isla Bonita,"** composed by **Patrick Leonard**, was originally meant for MJ, but he rejected the song. Besides that tangential connection, M&M nearly worked together in 1991, when MJ asked her to collaborate on his song "In the Closet." She was shocked at his bold choice of titles but unimpressed by his lackluster ideas, and bailed. Her public comments that his image was badly in need of overhaul may also have cooled their working relationship before it had a chance to warm up. "In the Closet" wound up as one of the best tracks from MJ's *Dangerous* album, featuring a guest vocal by a Madonna sound-alike "Mystery Girl" (it's *not* her).

The two did eventually collaborate—they escorted one another to the 1991 **Oscars**, both in white, both looking otherworldly and plastic and **glamor**ous, like **Japan**ese cartoons run amok. They attended the late Swifty Lazar's after-party, where Madonna sat in the lap of ex-beau **Warren Beatty** and MJ held

Madonna Jackson? The magic of computer imaging confronts us with the best of both worlds, merging Madonna and Michael.

"*I* think Michael Jackson is a very talented man. But he operates in a world that I don't want any part of. I don't want to cut myself off. I don't want to alienate myself from humanity. . . . We're like oil and water. We just don't mix. I think he's killing himself."

—Madonna, 1992

court with **role model Diana Ross**. Madonna cheerfully admitted their appearance was planned when, while dining at the Ivy restaurant in Los Angeles a week before the telecast, they realized that neither of them had a date.

Madonna zinged MJ's stilted "and they said this wouldn't last" appearance with new wifey Lisa Marie Presley on the 1994 **MTV Video Music Awards**. Showing up with **David Letterman**, Madonna repeated MJ's earlier boast, bringing down the house.

Jagger, Mick: When Madonna was a newcomer, Jagger said her work was characterized by "a central dumbness." The two first met in 1984 via mutual acquaintance **Maripol**, and were later reintroduced after he'd made the slur against her. "I don't think he really felt that way when he said it," she told **Jane Pauley** in 1987, "I think he was feeling my threat."

In 1992, Jagger handed out as many as twenty *cases* of *Sex* to his pals.

Japan: Is she big in Japan? Without a doubt. Madonna can't walk the streets in Japan without having Japanese **fans** throw themselves at her. As enigmatic as she seems in the Western world, Madonna's anti-patriarchal ways and her larger-than-life blondeness make her a sensation in the Orient. She opened both her **Who's That Girl** and **Blond Ambition tours** there, and made Japan the last stop of her **Girlie Show.**

Jellybean (Benitez, John): Former DJ at Manhattan's Funhouse, Studio 54, Xenon, and Paradise Garage **clubs**, and the top remixer of the mid-eighties. Madonna was in **love** with J, and both were in love with themselves, from their Funhouse meeting in spring 1983 until she broke it off in 1985. The two were virtually engaged, though both played the field (and the locker room, the parking lot, the bandstand . . .).

The cute, slight, Latin J made his producing debut on Madonna's **"Holiday"** single, which he also wrote. The song went on to become her first Top 40 hit.

An important force in Madonna's early career and a heavy-duty old flame, J's story with Madonna may have a few

"*S*he worked here for two months and was, well, an *okay* hatcheck girl. I asked her to leave because, well, her costumes were outrageous. But I'm still responsible for promoting her career by firing her."

—Gregory Camillucci, former
Russian Tea Room manager, 1990

"*I* keep telling **Michael Jackson**, 'I'd **love** to turn José and Luis on you for a week. They'll pull you out of the shoebox you're in.'"

—Madonna, 1991

·

"*I*t's a highly dysfunctional but terribly rewarding relationship. They're a gold mine that needs to be explored. I think they should have their own talk show."

—Madonna, 1992

·

"*I*'ve never seen anyone give more shit to Madonna and get away with it than José and Luis."

—**Liz Rosenberg**, 1992

more chapters left in it somewhere down the road.

jobs: In high school, Madonna worked as a lifeguard. In **New York**, she worked at such high-class joints as Burger King, McDonald's, Dunkin' Donuts (from which she was canned for playing with the jelly-squirting machine), Arby's, and a Greek chain called Amy's, plus moonlighting as an artist's model. She also checked coats at the Russian Tea Room, one of New York's swankest *spots*, for $4.50 an hour. In the end, she herself was checked by manager Gregory Camillucci for her nutty wardrobe.

jogging: Madonna jogs incessantly, as often as six days a week, ten miles at a time. She does not forego jogging while traveling or on tour, which makes for some guaranteed Madonna sightings at every port of call, not to mention a bounty of unflattering **paparazzi** photos. When *People* magazine's annual hastily-appointed **fashion** committee decides who's best and who's worst dressed, they invariably give Madonna a thumbs-down based on these jogging photos.

In 1990, the British **tabloids** savaged Madonna for daring to jog in Hyde Park, thereby causing run-ins with photographers and **fans**. The Brits remembered this incident—which included her **bodyguards** roughing some folks up—when reviewing her ensuing **projects**.

Johnson, Don: Mr. Melanie Griffith asked Madonna to duet with him on an Otis Redding song in 1986. He asked her at **Helena's**, one of her favorite eateries. We only hope she didn't have her mouth full when she laughed in his face.

Johnson, Lyndon B.: A.k.a. "Elbee," one of Madonna's Wham!-like backing dancers on her **Virgin tour**.

José & Luis: José Guiterez and Luis Camacho. Flaming backup dancers on **Blond Ambition,** the guys wearing **cone bras** during her **"Like a Virgin" masturbation** sequence. They were discovered by Madonna while voguing at the Sound Factory, and later performed for her before-hours at Tracks.

There is no question that their dancing skills—particularly their incredible voguing—lent a real street credibility to the **"Vogue" video** and to Blond Ambition, and they were a hoot in *Truth or Dare*.

These two gregarious souls teamed up to form a musical duo, snagging Madonna to donate a generous backing chorus to their debut single, "Queen's English"—a clever reworking of "Vogue" as a semantic, rather than somatic, experience. Their first three songs were released on a multi-artist **Sire** compilation, *New Faces*, rather than on a full-scale **Maverick** album, as had been presumed when "Queen's English" was premiered at a **Dolce & Gabbana fashion** show in 1992.

Over a year later, after growing amicably impatient with Maverick's slow start-up, J&L struck out on their own with Sire, no hard feelings. Lost in the shuffle was Madonna's scheduled directorial debut at the helm of a never-to-be video of a song of theirs called "Groovin'."

journal: Madonna writes in one daily, recording things that happen to her and things she's read that impress her. She sometimes draws songwriting inspiration from flipping back through the pages.

Juanita: The name of Madonna's troupe's enormous props plane on the **Girlie Show tour.**

"Justify My Love" song: The song that curled Top 40 radio's toes in December 1990, and which foreshadowed Madonna's long-term commitment to explicitly politi-**sex**ual **art** in the wake of an already suggestive career. The song was cowritten by Lenny Kravitz and Andre Betts (with additional **lyrics** by Madonna). **Prince** protégée Ingrid Chavez later sued for a writing credit, saying Kravitz had lifted the song from her wholesale. Kravitz admitted that Ingrid wrote some of the lyrics and would receive 25 percent of the royalties, but that "for personal reasons," they'd previously agreed that he'd get sole credit. Kravitz also caught flak

when it was pointed out that the song's humming [...] lifted from **Public Enemy**. He explained that the bas[...] a tape left lying around at the recording studio and th[...] intentionally appropriated Public Enemy.

Hoopla aside, Madonna's "JML" was an unqualifie[...] sounded like nothing else on the airwaves at the time, [...] a rare *truly erotic* vocal from a woman fonder of [...] Madonna's direct sexual come-on, delivered in a dis[...] whisper, is riveting; her delivery even overcomes a silly ly[...] riding trains . . . *"cross-country."* Irish *Hot Press* magazin[...] it the number 3 sexiest song of all time, and rightly so—lis[...] with the lights off, but don't wear brand-new underwear.

"JML" was a ballistic number 1 song, selling over a m[...] copies and becoming one of Madonna's biggest hits, boosting [...] of her greatest-hits collection (*The Immaculate Collection*[...] which it originated. Would you believe it was originally inte[...] for . . . *Paula Abdul*? "Justify My Jelly Donut"?

"Justify My Love" video: "Poor is the music channel/Whose pleasures depend/On the permission/Of another . . ."

If the song was a naughty smash, the video was a full-scale national incident, so raunchy it was banned by **MTV**, even after the channel had promoted it as the capper of an all-Madonna weekend.

The channel objected not to one specific part of the video, but rather its entire aura, taking a stand despite the **nudity** they had allowed in her **"Vogue" video**, the S&M they had allowed in her **"Express Yourself" video**, and the steady stream of blatant sexism (Warrant's "Cherry Pie") and violence (rap, anyone?—or how about a little heavy metal?) the channel regularly allows. By telling the public "JML" was too **sex**y to be aired, MTV single-handedly made the clip the hottest thing since Duran Duran's X-rated version of "Girls on Film." "Wayne" and "Garth" watched segments of the video on **"Saturday Night Live,"** and Madonna showed up to chat with Forrest Sawyer on **"Nightline"** about the badness she'd borne.

The video is worthy of censure. It's a self-contained sexual netherworld, shot by **Jean-Baptiste Mondino ("Open Your Heart")** over the course of three days spent locked on the sixth floor of the Royal Monceau Hotel in Paris. In it, Madonna—looking like a hyper-Marilyn with white-blonde **hair, glamor** makeup, and newly **collagen**-swollen lips—is a lone woman, a sexual adventurer who mysteriously falls prey to the overheated atmosphere of a clinical hotel that houses the gamut of sexuality.

Topless butch lesbians threaten from here, sexy transvestites cuddle together there, real-life beau **Tony Ward** watches in awe as Madonna is straddled by and deep-**kisses** an androgynous woman. After the lurid affairs fade, Madonna streaks, laughing, from the hotel, invigorated by her experience. Never before or since have Madonna's **music**al and visual statements been so perfectly matched.

The video is wholly sexual, a bit too sophisticated for the

average MTV lunkhead. Still, what's deplorable is not that MTV rejected it, but *why*.

It wasn't the video's sexual nature, but rather the nature of its sex. Pansexuality—**bisexuality**—was a longstanding taboo at MTV (which didn't even play black artists for its first three years, let alone openly bisexual ones, whether real or feigned), and there is no question that the reason the clip was sacked was Madonna's leisurely, undeniably *hot* kiss with model **Amanda de Cazelet**.

Note Roseanne's similar battle with ABC-TV four years later when an episode of her show called for a brief smooch with Mariel Hemingway. MTV isn't anti-sex, it's anti-lesbo. Or at least it *was*. In the wake of the "JML" flap, artists like John Mellencamp, Sheila E., **Sinéad O'Connor, k.d. lang,** and others, have successfully depicted same-sex issues and romance on MTV.

The five-minute video single sold almost 800,000 copies at $9.98 a pop.

"*W*hy is it that people are willing to go to a movie to watch someone get blown to bits, but nobody wants to see two girls kissing or two men snuggling?"

—Madonna

·

"*B*y suppressing erotic dissent, MTV does its best to see that this powerful medium will not communicate the 'wrong' idea about sex. That may pacify the puritans, but it also makes it easier to deny women and gays their full humanity—easier for the metal masses to justify their hate. . . . 'Justify My Love' makes it harder to hurt people. . . . "

—Richard Goldstein, *The Village Voice*

·

"*I* don't think Madonna had any intention of getting this video on MTV."

—MTV mucky-muck Marshall Cohen

KAFM: Dallas radio station that banned Madonna's songs from its airwaves for a weekend in 1985 after research showed that its listeners were burned out on her **music**. Though the station's owners are affiliated with the Mormon Church, the decision was purported to be purely a matter of listener taste, not corporate morality. The event is an early example of the backlash to her **overexposure**.

Kahlo, Frida: Considered by many to be the greatest Mexican painter of all time, just ahead of her husband, Diego Rivera.

Almost all of FK's work is self-portraiture, which portrays her as an enigmatic presence. And check out that single eyebrow! It puts Madonna's former fuzziness to shame. Madonna loves FK's self-reflexive work and owns several of her best pieces, including *My Birth*.

In 1990, Madonna was developing a film project on the artist's life, which was to have starred Madonna herself, with a script by Jeremy Pikser, who wrote that enduring classic *The Lemon Sisters*. But FK was too *too* trendy at the time (and still is), and several other entities (Robert DeNiro's TriBeca Productions; producer Nancy Hardin, New Line Cinema) were developing identical **projects**, one of which would have gone in front of the cameras were it not for Mexican-American outcry against the casting of Italian-American Laura San Giacomo as Kahlo.

Can you imagine how they'd have felt if Madonna had played her?

Kamen, Nick: Remember the Levi's 501 jeans TV **commercial** where a really cute guy strolls into a laundry, strips to his underwear, and sits patiently while his clothes are in the machine? That was NK, a dark-featured, baby-faced model/singer whom Madonna took under her wing in 1986. Much to her (then) husband's dismay, she wrote, produced, and provided prominent backing vocals to NK's first single, "Each Time You Break My Heart," which failed to launch him in the U.S. but made him an overnight sensation in Britain, where it became the first number 1 single ever produced by a woman. She also did backing vocals on his song "Tell Me," another single release.

Did they ever have an affair? Even her biographers stop short of saying yes, probably for a very good reason. He's a dreamboat, regardless, and has a strong, blue-eyed soul voice. Don't tell him you read it here, but his real name is *Ivor*. Nick, for short.

Kamins, Mark: A **lover** from the early eighties, MK is also the former **Danceteria** DJ and struggling producer on whom

Madonna sprang her **demo** tape in 1981. He remixed the **Steve Bray** production, brought the tape to the attention of **Sire Records** honchos (via contact **Michael Rosenblatt**, who'd "discovered" acts like the B-52s), and eventually landed Madonna a recording contract.

Though he produced her first 12", **"Everybody,"** and the aborted single **"Ain't No Big Deal,"** he was passed over in favor of Reggie Lucas to produce her first album. His legwork in "discovering" Madonna has resulted in a billion dollars in worldwide record sales alone. He's still a revered DJ who makes the **NYC** rounds and travels to high-paying gigs abroad, spreading the gospel of the "Downtown sound" to the unenlightened.

Keaton, Diane: Famous lead of *Annie Hall* and ex of **Woody Allen**'s who was the first actress meant to play "Susan" in *Desperately Seeking Susan* when the character was conceived as a (dried) flower child. She was also the only **San Remo** resident to come to Madonna's defense in her effort to secure an apartment in that co-op.

"Keep It Together" song: Madonna's fifth and final single from *Like a Prayer* was remixed to echo the sound of then-influential R&B group De La Soul. The remix made Madonna's ode to the strength of family into a serviceable mid-tempo **dance** number, and helped escort it to number 7 on the pop charts. It served as the finale to **Blond Ambition.**

Kelly, Gene: Legendary broad-shouldered hoofer who came out of retirement to offer advice to Madonna and **Christopher Ciccone** on their **Girlie Show**. GK told Madonna she reminded him of **Marlene Dietrich**, possibly the exact right thing to say to win her undying adoration. Unfortunately, the octogenarian wrenched his leg while demonstrating a step and endured some painful moments for the rest of their meeting.

His ideas were not incorporated into the final show.

Kennedy, John F., Jr.: The Adonis-like son of the slain U.S. President probably made it with Madonna during her first, brief separation from **Sean Penn** in 1987. They met at a mutual fitness salon (Plus One and/or Body Beautiful, depending on who's fibbing), jogged together in Central Park and on the beach near Hyannis Port (Kennedyville), chatted backstage after her **Who's That Girl** show, and are said to have had a brief, mutually unthrilling fling. JFK Jr., supposedly introduced Madonna to his mom, the late, sainted Jackie O, and Madonna is said to have signed the guest register "Mrs. Sean Penn." If a meeting occurred, Jackie had to be shitting bricks. Madonna's parallels to **Marilyn Monroe** were already a daily topic of discussion in the press, and Jackie's husband had a lengthy affair with Marilyn. No need to worry; JFK, Jr.'s biographer later said Madonna found him sexy, but a dud in bed. At any rate, their affair lasted all of a couple of weeks, then she was back for another hell-year with Penn, after which she remained on friendly terms with JFK, Jr. Sean Penn once confronted him at a party and demanded an apology for having slept with his wife; for which Madonna embarrassedly sent a funeral wreath with the message "In Deepest Sympathy."

Keshishian, Alek: Long-haired, Armenian-American café-baby and young **director**. For his Harvard senior project, he produced a rock-opera adaptation of *Wuthering Heights* called *Trouble at the Linton Home*, featuring the **music** of Kate Bush to represent "Cathy," then the music of Madonna to represent

*Madonna with one of her biggest **fans** (note the rubber bracelets), Alek Keshishian, 1991.*

"Cathy" after she marries "Linton." He moved to L.A. where he found work directing music **videos** for the likes of Bobby Brown, Edie Brickell and New Bohemians, and Elton John. He met CAA agent Jane Berliner in 1989 through a former classmate, and when she got a load of a video of his Harvard play, she introduced him and his work to Madonna herself.

Madonna and the aspiring director hit it off and she seemed eager to work with him, but that didn't happen until she called him in March 1990—with only a few *days'* notice—to shoot backstage footage of her **Blond Ambition tour**, an assignment he aggressively turned into the much more ambitious feature-film documentary ***Truth or Dare***. He and his crew wore all-black as they filmed the goings-on behind the scenes of Madonna's grandest concert, producing a priceless piece of work for only $4 million.

The two became good buddies and have since frequently socialized, including scouting strip clubs for ***Sex*** inspiration. (They'd finalized plans for *Truth or Dare* at the L.A. go-go bar The Body Shop.) They even exchanged friendship rings—he gave her one with a cobra emblem, she gave him an antique with a huge precious stone.

Madonna contributed the song **"I'll Remember"** to the **Maverick** soundtrack of AK's sophomore feature-film effort, *With Honors*.

"*J* would constantly disobey her, to show she wasn't directing me. I was completely prepared to be fired. That's when you do your best **work**, when you're not scared of being fired. I wasn't so blinded by the idea of working with Madonna that I would do anything she asked."

—Alek Keshishian, 1991

·

"*Y*ou know more about my life than anybody. You've seen more of me than even Sean."

—Madonna to Alek Keshishian, 1990

·

"*J* wanted the audience of *Truth or Dare* to feel the same emotional roller coaster I felt in getting to know her."

—Alek Keshishian, 1991

key to the city: Bäy City, Michigan, near where she grew up, was set to bestow the key to their "stinky" little city upon Madonna in 1985, but when ***Playboy*** and ***Penthouse*** sneakily displayed old nudes of her from her art-modeling days, the city reneged.

"He had terrible teeth, but I wanted him. . . . It was incredible."

—Madonna
on her first kiss

kisses: Her first was at age eleven, from a boy named Tommy. Much later, the brushing of lips would make several important appearances in Madonna's *oeuvre*. She kisses a man or a woman in many of her **videos**, with the top three most striking ones in **"Open Your Heart,"** where she plants a sweetly innocent one on a pubescent voyeur; in **"Like a Prayer,"** where she is chastely kissed by a black saint; and in **"Justify My Love,"** where she swaps saliva with another woman.

Kitt, Eartha: Mascara'ed, leather-skinned diva. Though she's as famous for making Lady Bird Johnson cry with white guilt after a fiery speech as she is for her wonderfully growly crooning, she has ironic views on the subject of human rights. ("Majority rules.") She also *loathes* Madonna, who covered her old hit "Santa Baby" on the first *A Very Special Christmas* compilation.

She does not write her own material.

EK voted for H. Ross Perot in 1992.

K-Mart: Unglamorous chain store at which Madonna's **step-mom** shopped for the fabric she used to make matching dresses for the **Ciccone** girls.

Knapp's Dairy Bar: Rochester Hills, Michigan, hangout famed for its seasoned french fries and for the fact that Madonna went there all the time on dates with high-school sweetheart **Russell Long**.

knock-knock jokes: Madonna once delighted mentor **Christopher Flynn** by telling a series of knock-knock jokes all through a ninety-minute car ride. "And they were *good*," he remembered fondly.

Konk: Madonna and pal **Martin Burgoyne** appeared as extras, dancing wildly in a 1980 **video** by this early eighties group. The video was shot at a **club** called David's Loft. Konk member Richard Edson later turned up in ***Desperately Seeking Susan***, trading lines with Madonna/"Susan" over a newspaper.

Kravitz, Lenny: SEE: "Justify My Love" song

"It's terrrrribly frustrating when—I call them the crotch-holders— make much more money than those of us making quality artwork."

—Eartha Kitt, 1993

*An unconvincing pair of smiles as Kitt meets **Ciccone** at **Martha Graham**'s final show, 1991.*

"La Isla Bonita" song: Madonna called her fifth and final single off *True Blue* her tribute to "the **beauty** and mystery of Latin American people." In it, she sings (sometimes in Spanish) about a lover she encountered on an island vacation, a romantic sentiment that propelled the song to number 4 in the United States.

"La Isla Bonita" video: Director **Mary Lambert** elicited another fine video performance from Madonna in this precursor to **"Like a Prayer."**

In the video, Madonna is alternately a boyishly-dressed Catholic woman and a colorful flamenco dancer, magically changed by her memories of a summer lover and her working of the rosary. As in her later **"Who's That Girl"** video, Madonna ends by dancing down the street, this time emerging from a band of Latin musicians.

Lambert, Mary: Visionary **music-video** director behind some of the strongest components of the Madonna canon, including **"Borderline," "Like a Virgin," "Material Girl,"** and **"Like a Prayer."**

Before Madonna, ML had whipped up videos for Sheila E.'s "Glamorous Life," and the Go-Gos' "Turn to You."

After, she directed the uncommonly sensual feature film *Siesta*, which Madonna decided against starring in because of all the . . . *nudity.* That was 1987.

lang, k.d.: Androgynous, openly lesbian country/pop singer/songwriter with whom Madonna has shared a casual **friendship**, and possibly a **lover**. lang and **Ciccone** have complimented each other's artistry in the press and both are very good friends of one **Ingrid Casares**, the ex-lover **Sandra Bernhard** accused Madonna of stealing. If Madonna *did* steal her (and Casares does not seem the type that one can "steal"), then lang stole her from Madonna: lang and Casares were lovers in 1993.

Liaisons aside, Madonna threw a bash for lang after her performance at Radio City Music Hall in December 1992 at Remi's (West 53rd Street). Though Madonna showed up with her **gold tooth**, she left before lang even arrived. lang's explanation? "We're having a lover's quarrel."

Their paths also crossed at the 1991 AmFAR benefit, where Madonna was given the Award of Courage and at which lang performed.

"*E*lvis is alive—and she's beautiful!"

—Madonna on lang, 1989

·

"*k.d.* lang is the female version of Sean [Penn]. I could fall in love with her."

—Madonna on first meeting Sire labelmate lang, 1991

Lang, Pearl: Former lead of the **Martha Graham** dancers. For Madonna's tryout at the American **Dance** Festival six-week course at **Duke University**, Madonna strolled up to PL and—feigning ignorance—demanded to perform only for Miss Pearl Lang, the instructor with whom she wished to work.

Now one of the screen's least-admired actresses, Madonna must've been having a good day—she fooled Lang and scored points. Madonna's talent secured her a position with PL's troupe. PL has high accolades for Madonna, whom she remembers as an impetuous yet charming person, but whose dancing definitely had that special something. "She was an exceptional dancer," PL recalls of Madonna's two years under her tutelage.

While performing with the troupe, Madonna had roles in the Holocaust melodrama *I Never Saw Another Butterfly*, in which PL remembers her inspired performance as a starving ghetto child, and in *La Rosa en Flores.*

laserdisc: Pioneer Artists, which sponsored **Blond Ambition** after **Pepsi** dropped Madonna, released a film of the concert exclusively on laserdisc to test the economic feasibility of the then relatively-new format.

"Madonna is the ideal artist to reach the new demographics that we are hoping to attract with the new, low-priced combination CD-and-laser players . . . the young, hip, 18–35 audience," Pioneer said.

She reached the audience, and the popularity of laserdiscs has continued to expand.

Lauper, Cyndi: Quirky, helium-voiced pop/rock belter most famous for her signature song, "Girls Just Want to Have Fun," flamboyant **hair**, mismatched thrift-store glad rags, and an offbeat sense of humor. For her sensational four-and-a-half-octave voice and earnest **lyrics**, CL was widely believed to be the female singer to watch for the rest of the eighties. She was constantly pitted against Madonna by the press, though the two have never attacked each other personally.

"When people say to me, 'Aren't you Cyndi Lauper?' I say, 'No, I'm Madonna, and watch out 'cuz **Sean Penn** is gonna come at ya any second and beat the shit outta ya.'"

—Cyndi Lauper, 1987

Critics ate a lot of crow as Madonna got bigger and bigger and Lauper, unfortunately for us all, did a fast fade. In 1985, *Newsweek* even went so far as to deduce that CL was the truer maverick of the two. Madonna now *owns* **Maverick**.

The two started out in similarly wild outfits and Madonna's hit **"Open Your Heart"** began life as "Follow Your Heart," rejected by CL and retooled for and by Madonna. Madonna and CL often competed on the charts, at one point having similarly-titled albums (***True Blue*** and *True Colors*, respectively) and singles ("Open Your Heart" and "Change of Heart," respectively), but their careers diverged.

When CL went platinum-haired and attempted to be **glamor**ous, it felt like a forced attempt to co-opt Madonna's appeal. But during Madonna's **Who's That Girl tour**, when she appeared in Lauper-esque gear, affected CL's Brooklyn accent, and did a satirical medley of some of her own biggest hits, she assimilated CL in one fell swoop.

CL still makes **music**, but her most appealing qualities (bustier **feminism,** bawdy humor, frankness) live on not in her own work, but in Madonna's.

Laura Belle: A favorite **New York** restaurant of Madonna's, located at 120 West 43rd Street at Sixth Avenue, and the site of the pre-premiere reception for ***Truth or Dare***.

lawsuits: They increase exponentially with wealth. Madonna has weathered her fair share, including innumerable nuisance suits and some fairly major battles. Still, for a woman of her success and visibility, she has avoided the plethora of legal troubles that has plagued some of her peers, largely by sticking with the same creative/managerial team after an early jump.

Madonna was sued by her former management, **Camille Barbone**/Gotham, for backing out of her contract. The suit dragged on for years, effectively keeping the contents of an early **demo** out of earshot until ten years into her career.

Next, Madonna sued **Stephen Jon Lewicki**, director of *A Certain Sacrifice*. She was pissed off that he was capitalizing on her success by selling her early film debut on video, but since she had signed an agreement granting the use of her face and image, she could only resort to suing Lewicki for using her *name* to promote the movie. She lost, and Lewicki won even more notoriety for his film.

Though Madonna was not officially involved, in 1986 songwriter Brian Elliot and his Elliot/Jacobsen Music Publishing Co. attempted to get an injunction against Mia Mind Music on the video and proposed single for the **"Papa Don't Preach"** spoof "Madonna Don't Preach," citing copyright infringement, but backed down when Mia Mind threatened to subpoena Madonna herself.

While married to **Sean Penn**, Madonna was named as a correspondent who "instigated and approved of" an **assault** by Penn against **paparazzo** Lawrence Cottrell, who had staked out their hotel in Nashville, Tennessee, where she and Penn were spending time during the filming of his movie *At Close Range*. This and other Penn-induced lawsuits were washed right out of Madonna's **hair** when she sued Penn for **divorce** in 1989.

The most bizarre Madonna-related lawsuit was filed against ABC-TV by Max Baer, Jr., famous as "Jethro" from TV's "The Beverly Hillbillies." Baer claimed ABC had illegally threatened legal action against the songwriters behind **"Like a Virgin"** (Billy Steinberg and Tom Kelly) if the writers licensed the song's movie rights to Baer. Both ABC and "Jethro" wanted to make a TV movie out of the song. ABC-TV's meddling cost them a reported $2-million decision. The next thing you know, old "Jethro"'s a millionaire.

In December 1990, Madonna lost a lawsuit brought against her by her L.A. neighbor Donald Robinson. Though the judge scoffed at Robinson's claim of $1 million in damages resulting from Madonna's too-high **"privacy"** hedge, the judge (ironically named Judge Sally Disco) did require Madonna to trim her bush and pay Robinson's attorney fees.

That suit was followed immediately by Ingrid Chavez's suit claiming that *she* had written **"Justify My Love,"** not Lenny Kravitz. This suit was the most embarrassing because it unfairly cast aspersions on Madonna's songwriting abilities (though she had only contributed "additional **lyrics**" to the song). Chavez won the right to a songwriting credit.

Madonna's most personally infuriating and disillusioning

lawsuit was waged by **Oliver Crumes**, Kevin Stea, and Gabriel Trupin, three of her **Blond Ambition** backup dancers. You remember—the guys she cuddled with in **Truth or Dare**, and with whom she exchanged vows of undying **friendship** and **love**? Less than a year after the film was released, containing backstage footage of all three, they sued Madonna for invasion of privacy, fraud and deceit, misrepresentation, and intentional infliction of emotional distress.

The trio claimed Madonna had lied to them, telling them the footage was only for her private use and for use in a documentary. "When we heard 'documentary' we thought of Public Broadcasting—like whales," carped Crumes. Trupin was annoyed to be seen French-kissing **Slam** (who wouldn't be?), which effectively outed him to his **grandparents**. The dancers also felt they should be reimbursed for their film performances, despite the fact that they'd already signed forms permitting use of their images in a film. Not to mention that they were well paid to participate in the most memorable tour of the nineties,—possibly of all time—gaining incredible exposure. The suit was settled privately in 1994.

In 1992, paparazzo J. Kenneth Katz sued Madonna when her bodyguard allegedly roughed him up as he angled for shots of her leaving a SoHo pizzeria. Though nobody really cares whether paparazzi live or die, this too was settled out of court.

No doubt about it: Where money goes, lawsuits follow. Look for many, many more in her lifetime, and long after her **death**.

Have a nice day.

lawyer: The firm Madonna uses is Grubman, Indursky, Schindler, & Goldstein, and her personal lawyer is Paul Schindler. GIS&G uses instinctive billing, negotiating their fee *after* a service has been performed, with a $1 million ceiling.

Leach, Robin: Little man with a hyper-Aussie accent, host of TV's "Lifestyles of the Rich and Famous" and similar programs.

In March 1993, he hosted "Madonna Exposed," a TV special that started out as a Madonna-approved tribute, but which degenerated into a "live from the Palladium" attempt to smear her after she decided against cooperating. Cohosted by dunce-like mannequin Eleanor Mondale (who seemed caught in a continuous state of "Huh?"), the show was narrated with *tabloid* clichés and gratuitous vaginal innuendos regarding Madonna's **rumor**ed **bisexuality** (lots of talk about "snatching" girlfriends away, not "beating around the bush," and the tongue-twirler "cunning stunt").

The show was a **fan**'s delight, featuring the first-ever playing of her Gotham **demo**, interviews with all of her Early Years intimates and with **Blond Ambition** dancer-turned-disher **Slam**, and lots of rare footage.

RL attempted to milk **hatred** out of his guests, but even though these were the people so often pointed to as examples of Madonna's ruthlessness—**Camille Barbone** and **Mark Kamins** among them—no one had anything really nasty to say.

After all his work, RL had the profound embarrassment of having to announce that the show's call-in poll (to 1-900-89-MADONNA at $1.95 a crack) to the question, "Has Madonna gone too far?" ended with 79 percent of viewers saying that she had not.

League of Their Own, A: Fun, funny baseball romp directed by Penny Marshall and starring Geena Davis, Tom Hanks, and Madonna.

The film was the biggest hit of the summer of '92, knocking *Batman Returns* out of the top slot and grossing $104,004,245 million. Gallons of ink were spilled over its subject matter: the women's baseball league invented by Wrigley chewing gum king Philip K. Wrigley in 1943, and the **feminist** spirit it engendered. Madonna played a tailor-made supporting role as "All the Way Mae Mordabito" (a.k.a. "Joanne Smith"), the "loose" member of a 1940s all-girl hardball team.

The story, as such, revolves around sisters (played by Davis and Lori Petty), the younger of whom is constantly competing with her more talented sibling for recognition as a ballplayer.

The real charm of the film lies in its inspired game scenes and the exhilarating female camaraderie among cast members. Madonna, who got to be cute and sexy and flirty, even got to do something she should really do more often on-screen: **dance**. She jitterbugged enthusiastically with Eddie Mecca (best known as "Carmine Ragusa" from TV's "Laverne and Shirley").

Madonna doesn't like baseball. She once groused to **Miramax**'s Harvey Weinstein that it "has no relevance to the state of the world." So, to prepare for her role, she sought the expertise of *relevant* major-leaguers like **Jose Canseco**. She also spoke to the woman on whom her character was based, endured batting

"What other film could offer comedy, feminism, the national pastime, period nostalgia,
and Madonna squeezing a Louisville Slugger?"

—Mike Clark, *USA Today*

•

"In the early going, her throwing technique was a choreographed step-step-step-kick-*fling* kind of thing.
She throws like a girl, but she can run like the wind."

—Tom Hanks on Madonna's baseball skills

•

"When casting the part of 'All-the-Way' Mae, I thought, 'Maybe Madonna would be interested,'
so she went to St. John's in New York and tried out for three hours. She was a real good sport.
She worked so hard. She would run every morning, then she'd work out playing ball, then at
night she'd jitterbug. . . . There was no star-tripping, none of that."

—Penny Marshall on Madonna

•

"I mainly talked to the one woman that my character was based on, and her name was
Faye Dancer and she was a wild woman. She's still a wild woman. The way she describes their
games and their touring the country and stuff was just that every city was a party and she
had six boyfriends in every town, and every night they snuck out."

—Madonna

•

"Madonna is the hardest-working human being I have ever seen in my life."

—Lowell Ganz, co-screenwriter

•

"Grotesque. Unflattering. A burlap sack."

—Madonna on her Rockford Peaches uniform

•

"Madonna seems nothing like a virgin on the field, playing with devil-may-care gusto
(watch for her face-first, dirt-in-her-skirt slide into third)."

—Michael J. Bandler, *USA Today Baseball Weekly*

practice at St. John's University with Joe Russo, lost six months to baseball training, suffered a bruised left hand (that's what the mitt's for, dear), and spent three weeks learning to jitterbug with Chicago dancer/choreographer Tony Savino.

She came out smelling like a rose. She even chalked up another number 1 hit with the song **"This Used to be My Playground,"** included in the film but not on the soundtrack.

Madonna and costar **Rosie O'Donnell** bonded like a grilled cheese sandwich, and remain fast friends. Madonna and **Evansville**, Indiana, on the other hand, discovered a mutual dislike for one another.

The filming was relatively uneventful, though a pregnant cow, a key player in the milking scenes, did cause a minor delay, and Madonna was doggedly pursued by the press for the duration of the location shooting in Chicago and other parts of the **Midwest**.

ALOTO was also responsible for Marshall's and Hanks's

debuts on the QVC cable shopping network, where they hawked movie merchandise (over $800,000 worth sold before opening day).

Madonna got warm reviews for her small turn in the film, though her signing had caused **Debra Winger** to bail out because she disapproved of "stunt casting."

Lee, Peggy: Smoldering golden oldie, the white-wigged chanteuse whose big hit, **"Fever,"** Madonna covered on *Erotica* after she saw PL belt it onstage. Madonna caught PL's torchy show in Manhattan in 1992 at Hilton's Club 53 (Sixth Avenue), gave her a bouquet of roses, and brought her along to a party she threw for **k.d. lang**. "I've heard the cut," PL said of Madonna's take on "Fever." "It's wonderful. Hers is disco, mine is not."

Lee, Spike: Provocative, self-absorbed, African-American *auteur* director of such films as *Do the Right Thing, Malcolm X,* and *Crooklyn*. A radical thinker and yet not above commercialism (he's directed **commercials** for Nike), SL shares a lot of common ground with Madonna.

She attended the premiere of his *Jungle Fever* while in **Cannes** promoting *Truth or Dare*, and SL has always given Madonna's spirit of rebellion high marks.

LeFargo, Jason: Then nineteen-year-old production assistant whom Madonna met while filming her **Pepsi** commercial in 1989. They reportedly had a fling. That's better than having your **hair** catch fire.

Leonard, Patrick: Longtime Madonna collaborator who composed the **music** to some of her most emotionally resonant work, including **"Live to Tell," "Who's That Girl,"** "Till Death Do Us Part," "Promise to Try," and **"Oh Father"**; for megahits **"Like a Prayer"** and **"Cherish"**; for some of her more popular non-singles like "Where's the Party," "White Heat," and **"Dear Jessie"**; and for moody ballads like **"La Isla Bonita,"** "The Look of Love," and "Spanish Eyes."

He played keyboards on the **Virgin Tour**, was also musical director of the **Who's That Girl tour**, did much work on *I'm Breathless*, and has always shared production credit with Madonna for the songs they've done together.

Leonard generally brings out Madonna's earthiness and thoughtful-

"Marketing is something I'm very proud of. The only artist that does it better than me is Madonna. She's the champ."

—Spike Lee, 1992

"If you listen to what she says, it instantly becomes a 'Madonna' record, no matter what producer she's working with. She likes bells, and that's a good call, because that kind of high-end information's very important to the ear. And she's adamant about bass parts—that's her key to the song. So put those two elements together with the voice in the middle, and you've got the spectrum covered."

—Patrick Leonard

ness, both absent from the otherwise thrilling, Leonard-less *Erotica*. In 1994, their collaboration **"I'll Remember,"** from the *With Honors* movie soundtrack, was released as a single.

Letterman, David: Smart-assed talk-show host on whose show, "Late Night with DL," Madonna first appeared in 1988 with galpal **Sandra Bernhard**. Their appearance is legendary for its spontaneity, and for their open insinuations that they were lesbian **lovers**. Besides Bernhard saying she'd slept with both **Sean Penn** *and* Madonna and preferred the latter, Madonna joked that they frequented the lesbian bar **The Cubby Hole**. Since the two were dressed identically and Bernhard was known for her **bisexuality**, the scenario could not have been more **shock**ing for its involvement of the world's biggest star, nor more titillating for her **fans**.

*Madonna looked like a socialite but talked like a sailor for her 1994 **assault** on David Letterman.*

DL was visibly in awe of Madonna during the show, though he later soured on her, possibly because he remained good friends with the bitter Bernhard and possibly because Madonna favored **Arsenio Hall** when doing the late-night thing. For Madonna's part, she said in 1991 that she hadn't returned to DL's show only because she'd never been invited back.

She got her big break on April Fool's eve (take note), 1994, when she made a notorious appearance on DL's revamped "Late Show with DL," ostensibly to "defend her honor" against DL's frequent jokes at her expense. After a few more potshots, DL warmly welcomed Madonna, attempting to **kiss** her when she slithered in, only to find physical resistance and a pair of her panties shoved into his mitt.

The rest of the show was excruciating, highly disturbing, and great TV. Madonna—uncharacteristically giddy and witlessly vicious—inquired about DL's "rug," asked if he "smoked **endo**," called him a sick **fuck**, and generally refused to play along. Calling for unscripted, break-all-the-rules questioning, Madonna was rewarded with, "What's the next **look** gonna be?" after she'd already accused DL of growing too soft on his guests in his old, **rich** age.

But though the ensuing media frenzy absurdly concentrated on the fact that Madonna used the word "fuck" thirteen times, more shocking were her leaden wisecracks and her deranged behavior. DL, though gamely trying to seduce her into a normal interview throughout, ended up completely flustered, the studio audience completely annoyed . . . and Madonna? Well, at least for an evening, she was completely insane.

The best that can be said of the whole thing was that Madonna had a regal, serpentine look in a deep green velvet gown and center-parted black **hair**. She showed off her new pierced nose, **smoked** a stogie with gusto, and rolled with laughter at every nasty comeback DL unfurled.

Hers were the highest guest-generated ratings since DL's 1993 move to CBS, and her gift to him inspired a tradition of sorts: The very next evening, Charles Grodin gave him his boxers, and Elvis Costello gave him a sock. Madonna later **fax**ed DL a "Happy fucking birthday." This terrible twosome kissed and made up, appearing arm in arm at the 1994 **MTV Video Music Awards**, which washed away the aftertaste of their March run-in.

"*Y*ou can't get through a show without talking about me . . . or *thinking* about me."

—Madonna to David Letterman

·

"*S*he can't be stopped!
There's something wrong with her!"

—David Letterman, to his audience, about guest Madonna

·

"*M*adonna was extremely nervous and so cold she could barely talk. . . . I think it was nice that she wasn't in control for a change, not that Dave was in control, either. . . . Madonna isn't a seasoned TV performer, but she had fun, Dave had fun, and Madonna has no regrets."

—Liz Rosenberg

·

"*A*ll that was completely set up. Not every word, but he knew I was going to come on and say the word 'fuck' a lot. I was doing it as a protest against **censorship**."

—Madonna

Lewicki, Stephen Jon: Enterprising director of the no-budget *A Certain Sacrifice*, Madonna's first film. When Madonna's career took off, he capitalized by selling **videos** of the raunchy **art** film and successfully fended off a half-hearted **lawsuit** by Madonna.

SJL has the same exact **birthday**—month and year—as Madonna.

LifeCycle™: Stationary Exercycle that Madonna describes as one of her most prized possessions, and which was present at a momentous Madonna moment: **David Mamet** was riding his while considering whether to offer her the part of "Karen" in his play *Speed-the-Plow*.

***Like a Prayer* album:** Madonna's fourth full-length studio album (1989) is her most critically acclaimed to date. Intensely personal **lyrics** and mature vocals and instrumentation characterize the **work**, which has sold over 3 million copies (10 million worldwide). Music critics and closet Madonna **fans** had been waiting for a good reason to *really* rave about her, and in *LAP* they found an admirable excuse.

The album is packaged to underscore the maturing of Madonna. For the first time, Madonna's face does not appear on the jacket. Instead, the cover is a tight close-up of her abdomen, her thumbs hooked into a pair of comfortable jeans, fingers adorned with hippielike rings and beads. On the back of the jacket, Madonna leans toward the camera in a praying pose, her dark brown **hair** running to her shoulders. The imagery is a powerful statement from a woman for whom **looks** are nearly everything. By appearing as a brunette, Madonna was officially back to her roots.

To add a bit of intimacy to the package, the album's inner sleeve was scented with patchouli oil, so that the consumer could smell Madonna's own scent when listening to her **music**. The final serious component to *LAP* was an **AIDS** factsheet in every copy, the first time a pop artist had ever included AIDS information with a product.

Packaging alone does not guarantee respect or praise. But the music—not so much the radical departure some reviewers took it to be as a sobering and perfecting of Madonna's established brand of pop— is impressively sincere, and started Madonna on a long ride as a darling of the critics that would last until the release of *Sex* three and a half years later.

The album's eleven songs were all co-produced by Madonna, with **Patrick Leonard** and **Stephen Bray** sharing production credits with her on seven and two songs, respectively, and **Prince** coproducing both his duet with Madonna and "Act of Contrition" (the production credits of which read, "The Powers That Be").

LAP is full of **Catholic** iconography. The album is also a critical look at the state of the family unit in contemporary America. Unifying the themes of religion and family is the fact that *LAP* is dedicated to "my **mother** who taught me how to pray."

The album's singles, **"Like a Prayer"** (number 1), **"Express Yourself"** (number 2), **"Cherish"** (number 2), **"Oh Father"** (number 20), and **"Keep It Together"** (number 7) dominated the airwaves for the better part of a year, segueing with no break into Madonna's next album.

"Like a Prayer" shows off Madonna's warmer, richer vocals and a soulful refrain provided by the Andrae Crouch Choir. "Express Yourself" was the **dance** song of the year, opening with the indelible cry, "Do you believe in love?" "Love Song" is Madonna's duet with **Prince**, followed by "Till Death Do Us Part," a vitriolic portrait of an abusive marriage that is obviously cribbed from her own marital nightmare. "Promise To Try" finishes out side one, a little girl's tearful remembrance of a mother who died young, another direct reflection of Madonna's real life.

Side two kicks off with "Cherish," a genuinely sweet ditty that flows on to "Dear Jessie," a hallucinogenic extravaganza complete with pink elephants and lemonade. "Oh Father" is a tortured ballad about an emotionally abusive father and the daughter who grows to understand—if never quite forgive—his behavior. "Keep It Together" is a mid-tempo plea for family unity, then comes "Spanish Eyes," a Latin ballad about the tragedy of a gang member's short life.

The final "song" on the album is a twisted and jarring chant called "Act of Contrition" whose music is looped from a backtracking of "Like a Prayer" and whose lyrics are a sort of ironic prayer that ends with Madonna finding that her reservations for a spot in Heaven have been *misplaced.*

Madonna wrote the material for the album while appearing on Broadway in ***Speed-the-Plow***, in a role she has described as incredibly draining and spiritually depressing.

LAP was arguably Madonna's big ploy for respect and career longevity. Madonna has always said that she doesn't plan as

"As close to art as pop music gets. *Like a Prayer* is proof . . . that Madonna should be taken seriously as an artist. . . . If you have trouble accepting that, maybe it's time for a little image adjustment of your own."

—J.D. Considine, *Rolling Stone*

·

"Most of the songs . . . are drawn from my life, factually speaking, but it's fictionalized too. Also, the overall emotional context of the album is drawn from what I was going through when I was growing up —and I'm still growing up."

—Madonna

mance on a par with previous highlights **"Live to Tell"** and **"Papa Don't Preach."**

The song's religious imagery was boldly realized by its controversial **video**, but "LAP" is a prime example of how Madonna's **music** endures even after the controversy surrounding it evaporates.

obsessively as most people think she does, that she simply creates and then makes her output work for her, so it's altogether possible that *LAP* is as straight from the heart as it seems. Regardless, it established Madonna as a legit artist in the **eyes** of many.

"Like a Prayer" song: This lead single from *Like a Prayer* was a number-1 hit in 1989 and led the way for a critical reappraisal of the consummate singles artist of the eighties. The song is stylistically different from anything Madonna had sung before, or has sung since.

While **dance**able, "LAP" is a song more concerned with melody and dissonant structure, and with its feverishly romantic storyline. The song opens with Madonna's extremely vulnerable, little-girl vocals set against the strains of a church choir. She sings of a **love** so compelling it's practically a religious experience, and she delivers a perfor-

"Only those who come to the music and lyrics with a grim determination to find prurience and blasphemy can miss—and then with considerable effort—the God hunger that animates them."

—Andrew M. Greeley, *America*

"Like a Prayer" video: One of Madonna's most scandalous **videos**, "LAP" turned **MTV** and the world on its ear with arresting images of Madonna kissing a black saint (St. Martin de Porres), experiencing spontaneous stigmata, and dancing in a slip in front of a field of burning crosses.

But laundry-listing the video's most **shock**ing bits merely

"*T*he music video is utterly harmless, a PG-13 at worst, and by the standards of rock video, charming and chaste. . . . This is blasphemy? Only for the prurient and the sick who come to the video determined to read their own twisted sexual hang-ups into it."

—Andrew M. Greeley, *America*

helps feed the confused readings the video received at the time of its release. Called sacrilegious and profane by religious leaders and by right-winger Reverend Donald Wildmon of the **American Family Association** (Tupelo, Mississippi), the video actually embraces **Catholicism** with the lusty verve of a medieval passion **play**, and makes an overt plea for racial tolerance.

Madonna's character witnesses an assault and sees that the wrong man—a black man instead of the white perpetrator—is arrested for the crime. With spiritual guidance that is naïvely portrayed as a romantic bond between Madonna and the saint/Jesus figure and which is reinforced by the video's setting in a church, she is able to convince police to release the black man. The burning crosses, which offended some black groups, illustrate the racism the video was attacking; they are not mere adornments. Dancer **Niki Haris** refused to appear in the video because, "As a black woman, burning crosses mean something to me," missing the point.

Madonna's original storyline had her character and the accused being shot in the back by the KKK, but veteran Madonna **director Mary Lambert** softened the content and stepped up some of the religious iconography.

The video was so controversial it sparked **Pepsi** to drop Madonna as a spokesperson and to disengage itself from sponsoring **Blond Ambition.** It was protested and banned briefly in Italy, drawing outraged criticism from the Vatican. It also proved Madonna was serious in her efforts to make important, thought-provoking, artful videos as opposed to glossy filler.

Incidentally, "LAP" is the only video in which Madonna appears with her completely natural brunette **hair** color.

Like a Virgin **album:** Madonna's second LP, the one that aggressively defined her image as a high-gloss bad girl, disco diva, pop cultural *bricoleuse*, and lots of other cool junk.

Already completed months before her debut, **Madonna**, had run out of steam, *LAV* was released in late 1984 hot on the heels of her initial impression and immediately shot to the number 1 slot, alongside its number 1 kickoff single of the same name. It is one of the biggest-selling albums by a woman (over 7 million copies in the U.S.; 15 million worldwide), and one of the top sellers of the eighties.

The first striking thing about the album is the jacket. Stylist

and designer **Maripol** has called it a "bride of Satan" **look**, and it effectively communicates the conflicted views of what a **wedding** dress *should* represent (**virginity**), and what—in this unlikely context—it *does* represent (**sex**ual knowingness). She glares out directly at us, her breasts jutting from within a skintight bustier wedding gown, "BOY TOY" buckle prominently cinched at her waist. **Steven Meisel**'s sepia-toned photography serves to make the shot all the more provocative. It's a sexual dare, not a tease, and the dare was taken up by over 3.5 million U.S. fans in its first 14 weeks of release, selling at a rate of 80,000 copies a day at its peak.

Madonna had Chic alum **Nile Rodgers** produce the album, and it's he who is responsible for the slick, heavily layered sound of its driving hits and classic non-hits. Aside from the coy, infectious title track, there was the number 2 smash **"Material Girl"**— a shrill send-up of materialism, taken literally by many **fans** and haters (SEE: **hatred**) alike—as well as the Top Five confections **"Angel"** and **"Dress You Up."**

"Over and Over" set the pace for Madonna's perceived ambition and drive, the angst-ridden remake, "Love Don't Live Here Anymore," proved that Madonna could wipe up the floor with a "She's Out of My Life"—esque ballad, and "Stay" gets this writer's vote as Madonna's best album track. Even the album's filler is top-notch: Madonna makes fluff like "Pretender" and "Shoo-Bee-Doo" come off as something new and exciting through sheer force of will and her tremendous capacity to sing it like she means it.

LAV is not Madonna's strongest album overall, but its nine tracks feature Madonna at her least self-conscious and most cleverly effervescent. In late 1983, while *LAV* was in the final stages of production, Madonna told a rock journalist that the LP would

"*O*n *Like a Virgin*, Madonna's new record, brilliantly produced and arranged by Nile Rodgers, she and Rodgers realize that she's turned out to be a spunky, beat-conscious sex kitten instead of a disco pet. . . . She wants to make captivating girl talk with its own dance-music edge. . . . Another part of her success lies in her peculiar charm—despite her punkiness she doesn't really sound like a bad girl at all. . . . It should keep Madonna dancing all over the airwaves for a long time."

—James Hunter, *Record*

have a more "open feeling . . . like Hall and Oates"—except horny.

LAV was not her first album, but since it was the first album over which she had considerable control, it can be considered her first complete musical "statement." For this, and in honor of the title track, Madonna dedicated the album to "the virgins of the world."

"Like a Virgin" song: Until **"Vogue"** came along, "LAV" was the biggest hit of Madonna's career, a multi-platinum single that stayed at the number 1 position for six straight weeks from December 1984, making it the second most popular song of 1985 (after Wham!'s "Careless Whisper").

"LAV"'s relentless hook is similar to **Michael Jackson**'s "Billie Jean," and though Jackson's song is about a man denying parental responsibility and Madonna's is about a reality-altering **love**, hers was the more scandalous.

Why? In these days of **condom** ads more explicit than those old embarrassing tampon ads ever dared to be, it's hard to remember just how **shock**ing it was to hear the word "virgin" on the radio, much less on the boomboxes of Madonna's then mostly teenaged fans. (Mary Tyler Moore had been the first to utter the word on **television** less than ten years previously.) "LAV" is not only allusive, it equates **virginity** with the pureness of true (but **sex**ual, don't forget *sexual*) love.

Madonna premiered "LAV" on the first **MTV Video Music Awards** telecast, bringing down the house with an audacious roll on the stage and salacious fondling of her nether regions—way before this was precisely what was expected of her.

Though the original "LAV" is hopelessly 1984, Madonna has kept the song strangely *au courant* by reinventing it with every tour, including an extremely effective Middle Eastern version (accompanied by simulated **masturbation**) on **Blond Ambition** and a hilarious **Marlene Dietrich** send-up in **The Girlie Show**. "LAV" may be Madonna's "Falling in Love Again," the first few lines of which she incorporated into the latter live performance.

"Like a Virgin" video: Evocative of the ferocious **sex**uality (at least in the eyes of a **Midwest** girl) of Venice, Italy, the allure of **masks**, the masculine libido symbolized by the King of the Jungle, and the implicit eroticism of the act of marriage, "LAV" was Madonna's first **video** sensation.

In it, Madonna stalks skulkily in a revealing **wedding** gown, dramatically unveiling covered furniture, and dances ecstatically on a gondola. She looks gorgeous in a ten-pounds-of-makeup sort

of way, and the video itself is a feast of symbolism with no particular message. It's still far more intriguing than the **commercials**, which is more than you can say about most of **MTV**.

Mary Lambert directed the clip, so thank her for the brilliance of a lion's pink tongue panting in sync with the song's catchy hook.

As for **analyses**, Madonna explained the presence of a lion as being "the symbol of Venice. There are statues of lions all over Venice," exposing the charming literal-mindedness that tempts academics and dreamers to fill in the more speculative blanks for her.

The video was cannily roasted by Dire Straits in their "Money for Nothing" video, which features clips of a Madonna-ish woman in an "LAV"-ish video when they sing of a famous slut shoving her privates into the camera.

There was a second "LAV" video, a straight performance segment culled from **Blond Ambition** released to promote ***Truth or Dare***.

lipstick lesbianism: A term meant to encompass all women who are lesbians, but don't "look" it i.e., wear makeup, look sexy, have hot bodies—as if lesbians don't come in every conceivable package. Along with the **bisexuality** in Madonna's work, there is every indication that as a cultural icon she encourages a large number of straight women to 'fess up to their lesbian urges (even if they are just that: *urges*).

In 1994, *Esquire* conducted an infamous poll of women aged 18–25, which with two of its questions, proved Madonna's lesbociousness. Of the women interviewed 14.4 percent were either lesbians or had had at least one lesbian encounter, and yet, when asked which famous woman they'd rather sleep with, 34 percent of *all* the respondents chose Madonna, almost twice the number who chose publicity-shy Jodie Foster, over four times as many who chose demure Jessica Lange, over eight times as many who chose **k.d. lang**, and let's not even talk about poor Martina Navratilova, with only 2.7 percent. Lesson learned? A third of all young women are closet lipstick lesbians . . . or at least, if given the shot at momentarily lezzing out, they'd much rather deal with Madonna's mug than Martina's.

Live Aid: Enormous, bi-continental rock concert to benefit Ethiopia, organized by Bob Geldof and staged simultaneously in Philadelphia's JFK Stadium and London's **Wembley Stadium** in August 1985.

Madonna shared a dressing area with Ashford and Simpson

> "*W*e were looking for her clothes, but we hear she doesn't wear too much."
>
> —Beach Boy Mike Love on dressing roomie Madonna

(with whom she was once going to collaborate on a never-realized movie musical), Eric Clapton, and the Beach Boys. She appeared as a brunette for the first time since becoming famous as a blonde, wearing a pastel paisley suitcoat with tails and toreador pants. Her appearance coincided with the unwelcome publication of early nudes in **Playboy** and **Penthouse**. Though it was ninety degrees in the shade, Madonna refused to remove her jacket. "I ain't takin' *shit* off today," she said defiantly to a live audience of billions, clearly emotional. "You'd hold it against me years from now."

She sang **"Holiday"** and previewed a track from her forthcoming **True Blue** album—"Love Makes the World Go Round"—using the Thompson Twins as backup and returning the favor for their set.

SEE ALSO: ACTIVISM

"Live to Tell" song: Regarded as one of Madonna's finest singles, this searching, sweeping romantic ballad is charged with what was at the time (1986) an uncharacteristic sense of fatalism and psychological depth.

Madonna originally intended for a man to sing "LTT," a song about the haunting secrets learned in a tumultuous **love** affair. But it became the first single from Madonna's biggest-selling record, **True Blue**, and was also on the soundtrack of **At Close Range**, starring **Sean Penn**. Despite doubts among some **Sire** execs at the wisdom of launching a new Madonna album with a ballad, the radically vulnerable single went straight to number 1.

On the **Who's That Girl tour**, Madonna dedicated her live rendition of the song to her friend **Martin Burgoyne**. Live, she turned the song into an aching **AIDS** metaphor, her hyperextended pauses creating enough dramatic tension to incite a frenzied crowd response. On **Blond Ambition**, the song was blended with **"Oh Father"** to tease out its redemptive qualities.

"Live to Tell" video: To go along with the vocal and **lyric**al quiet of the song, the **video** for Madonna's second big-hit ballad (after 1985's **"Crazy for You"**) was shot by director **James Foley** as a minimalist portrait of the "new" Madonna, who croons the haunting song while emoting the enigma of Garbo's "Queen Christina."

Shot against a black backdrop, the video is filmed by a sweeping camera that catches its star sitting serenely in a simple frock, looking ultra-feminine with long **hair** and pastel makeup, all dressed down and everyplace to go.

The image switch, the simple video, and the moving song ushered Madonna on to even greater success.

Loder, Kurt: Respected rock critic and stone-faced **MTV** correspondent who has been one of Madonna's most consistent boosters. Loder gushed over her **Blond Ambition tour**, even though Madonna flipped him the bird on MTV's live coverage.

His MTV interviews with Madonna ("Breakfast With Madonna," 1990; "Dinner with Madonna," 1991) are notable for his serious questions and Madonna's comfortable, articulate replies. His interview with her for *TV Guide* lost Madonna all of her **Evansville**, Indiana, **fans**.

lollipop: **Candy** fiend that she is, Madonna can often be seen slurping on one of these while avidly watching **basketball** games. She also sucked one all through her brief appearance at **Miami**'s White Party at the Biltmore Hotel in Coral Gables in December 1992.

London, Rachel: Designer of the outrageously 3-D, attention-grabbing floral gown Madonna wore on the **Tony Awards** telecast.

When she heard Madonna would be appearing on the Tonys the following evening, RL brazened her way past security at the Royale Theatre where Madonna was appearing in **Speed-the-Plow**, and confronted Madonna in her dressing room with the frock in question. "This is the dress you should wear tomorrow," she said confidently, and so Madonna did, along with an $835 (*cheap* compared to **Gaultier**!) floral bolero jacket.

Long, Russell: Madonna's first-ever **lover**, when she was fifteen and he was sixteen. The two were a notoriously tight couple in high school—so much so, that classmates assumed they were "doing it" long before they actually were.

Involved from December 1973 until June 1974, they started by making out in his light blue 1966 Cadillac. This progressed until Madonna invited Long to deflower her. Little did she know he would sell all the intimate details to the British **tabloids** sixteen years later, going so far as to recount that she called him "baby" throughout and sighed, "Oh, honey," when he climaxed.

He ended up a United Parcel Service delivery man. One only hopes that for his ungallant **kiss**-and-tell behavior he at *least* lived up to his name.

looks: As proof of Madonna's influence on **fashion**, note that she has taken the "look" to new levels: the image-makeover as an **art** form. While **fans** have always commented on the various **glamor**ous, unglamorous, inspired, and insipid looks tried out by their favorite stars, Madonna is the first star to engage in that discussion herself *of* herself.

It all started innocently enough. Madonnamania began with the **Boy Toy** look: tons of rubber bracelets, mesh hair ties, and navel-surfing belts. This early look survived with only minor adjustments until she started filming **Shanghai Surprise** and her demure, classical "Lana Turner" look took over, complete with bleached, neatly-coiffed locks.

But the first major to-do made over a new Madonna look was in response to her appearance in *Rolling Stone* magazine, which in 1986 bore the cover story "The New Madonna," with a gamine Madonna smiling from the front cover. Thousands of gallons of ink were spilled over Madonna's new taut build, short platinum **hair**, and glamor makeup, all shown off to maximum effect in her **"Papa Don't Preach" video**. The change was enormously **shock**ing to the public, who'd come to expect grungy, lipsticky *tack* from Madonna.

With so much interest devoted to her sudden appearance-shift, it became obvious that the world had a major-league interest in Madonna. The uproar over that first "new Madonna" has undoubtedly ushered the way for the countless new Madonnas that have emerged on a regular basis since then. She began experimenting with new looks with each new **project**, eventually changing almost week to week. In her biggest image coup, she appeared at her Los Angeles **Truth or Dare** premiere with ghoulish makeup and straight black hair one night, and at the **New York** premiere two days later with a classic Hollywood look (except for her jazzy, beaded minisuit).

That Madonna has incorporated the "look" into her artistry is telling. She's a very literal-minded creator despite the speculative elements of some of her **videos**, so to Madonna, images are extremely important. Though she has been criticized as "superficial," it's plain that appearances—superficial constructions—dictate how we see things. This is a concept not lost on the art of voguing, nor on **drag** queens, nor on Madonna's non-straight fans.

As for the **power** of looking a certain way, the critical reception of **Like a Prayer** unquestionably benefited from its creator's natural brown hair, an aspect of her appearance that was noted in almost all reviews that argued the album's sincerity.

More obviously, Madonna proved that simply by looking like a star, you are one. By looking exceptional (not necessarily classically beautiful), Madonna captivated her myriad of self-proclaimed "discoverers" and engaged the imaginations of her fans. By co-opting the looks of other great stars, she immediately insinuated herself into their company, though she couldn't have kept that company if she *merely* looked the part.

"I sat next to Madonna at a Laura Nyro concert and she was further from her stage persona than anyone I've ever seen. She looked so different it was unbelievable."

—Elayne Boosler, comedienne, 1991

·

"It would be my guess that Madonna is not a very happy woman. From my own experience, having gone through persona changes like that, that kind of clawing need to be the center of attention is not a pleasant place to be."

—David Bowie, 1992

·

"What she does is, she took a leaf from Detroit—the auto industry—which the auto industry forgot, and that is the annual model change."

—Malcolm Forbes, Jr., 1993

Her image-changing points to an even more elemental aspect of her **stardom**, and of stardom in general: The only way to tell a real star is by how many people are looking at her. Madonna has a unique tendency in photos and videos to stare directly at the camera, whether she's a blonde, brunette, or redhead, whether buried in **crucifixes**, dancing in lace, or stark raving naked. This is what makes her one of our most compelling stars: When we look at Madonna, Madonna looks *back*.

Loren, Sophia: Madonna solicited a vintage gown worn by this **Italian** institution of international cinema for her 1986 *Vanity Fair* spread.

Los Angeles riots: Violent outbursts and opportunistic looting that shook L.A. in May 1992. Despite the ensuing curfew, Madonna was one of many star patrons to be served after-hours at Santa Monica's Ivy At the Shore restaurant.

Perhaps she was eating to displace her worries over her missing bustier, the one she wore in her **"Open Your Heart" video**. The garment was looted from Frederick's of Hollywood's Lingerie Museum, which offered a $1,000 reward for its return. Like the family cat accidentally abandoned at the Grand Canyon, the bustier made its way back to Frederick's, and Mayor Tom Bradley declared December 1, 1992, "Frederick's of Hollywood Day."

Louise: Madonna's middle name.

love: You don't really expect to find an adequate definition of love in here, do you? Let's assume we all know what it is. In terms of Madonna's life, she has been extraordinarily gifted with love.

In 1991, she asserted that she'd never slept with anyone for whom she didn't have feelings of love.

She loved **Sean Penn** so much she married him, and called him the love of her life even after they'd been divorced two years.

In early 1993, she cryptically confessed that she was in love, that it had been love at first sight, and that she felt the love would last forever. Only problem is, she wouldn't say who it was. Gossips

"Love is like breathing. You just have to do it."

—Madonna, 1989

suggested longtime L.A. pal **John Enos**, or even **rumor**ed **lover Ingrid Casares**.

But whoever it was, or whoever it will be, Madonna is a romantic. So many of her songs *are* about love that in both "Love Song" and "Bye Bye Baby" she has to remind listeners that they are *not*.

Love, Courtney: This grungy lead singer of the L.A.-based rock group Hole and widow of Nirvana's Kurt Cobain was on Madonna's wish list of acts for her **Maverick** label.

"*S*he's a bad enemy to have. I don't want her to know anything about me, because she'll steal what she can. What I have is mine and she can't fuckin' have it. She's not going to be able to write lyrics like me, and even if she does get up onstage with a guitar, it's not going to last. I don't care how vain and arrogant this sounds, but just watch: In her next video, Madonna's going to have roots. She's going to have smeared eyeliner. And that's me."

—Courtney Love, 1992

·

"*W*ho is Courtney Love?"

—Madonna, 1992

love letter: In 1992, "Hard Copy" offered free color copies of a sexy **love** letter Madonna inscribed in a high-school classmate's yearbook. She wrote the letter in purple ink because "purple is a sign of lustfulness," implored the object of her affections to think of her often, bemoaned the fact that despite their obvious mutual interest they never had the chance to get together, and urged, "Please don't get the wrong idea of me. I'm really a sincere person."

An early example of her coquettish ways, the love letter is probably exactly what it took to make "Mike, (alias Chomp)" cream in his pants. And it probably earned him a month's wages when he licensed it to "Hard Copy." Ah, yes, I remember it well . . .

lovers: "I read about people I'm dating I've never met." — Madonna, 1990

The ones we can definitely pin on her?
· high school: **Russell Long**

· college: **Steve Bray**
· adulthood: **Jimmy Albright, Jean-Michel Basquiat, Warren Beatty, Jellybean Benitez, Norris Burroughs, Ken Compton, John Enos, Dan Gilroy, Vanilla Ice, Mark Kamins, Sean Penn, Dennis Rodman, Tony Ward**
The ones we can fairly assume?
· **Billy Baldwin, Charles Barkley, Jose Canseco, Jeffrey Hornaday, John F. Kennedy, Jr., Bobby Martinez, Sasha Mitchell**
The ones that are at least possible?
· **Ingrid Casares**, Simon F., Esai Morales
As for the rest, you know who you are.

"Lucky Star" song: Madonna's first Top Five smash (number 4) is this perky **love** song, a 1983 knockoff of the old nursery rhyme, "Star light, star bright."

"Lucky Star" video: The 1983 video that immortalized Madonna's **belly button** and whose all-white backdrop served the purpose of setting off Madonna's dancing skills. Her **Boy Toy** appearance is captivating, right down to the swinging, star-shaped earring and suggestive wink.

LuPone, Patti: Broadway belter who originated the role of "Evita," a role Madonna would later vie for on the screen.

While performing in *Anything Goes* in the Vivien Beaumont Theater at Lincoln Center, a hop-skip-jump away from Madonna's originally-scheduled Mitzi Newhouse debut in ***Speed-the-Plow***, PLP posted a satirical note to the management, grumping that there wasn't enough room at the Center for *two* Sicilian divas.

She wasn't joking later, though, when she publicly trashed the possibility of a Madonna-driven *Evita* film.

The movie world got even in 1994 when PLP was humiliatingly bumped from Andrew Lloyd Webber's musical version of *Sunset Boulevard* by film star Glenn Close, and from *Evita* by Michelle Pfeiffer.

Lypsinka (Epperson, John): Popular **drag** artist whose shows are a series of cleverly-arranged lip-synchs to various **camp** tunes, **commercials**, and sampled sounds.

Madonna was an investor in L's first one-drag-queen show in L.A.—"*I Could Go On Lip-Synching!*"—and is as responsible as anyone for bringing L to national prominence.

lyrics: Unlike most of her peers, Madonna has always written most of her own material. Though her songs always have collaborator credits, she usually does the lyrics, leaving the **music** to her collaborators (with her direction).

Since *True Blue*, only a few of the tunes on Madonna's albums were written by someone besides herself, and she often goes out of her way to write "additional lyrics" to Madonna-ize those that are (**"Papa Don't Preach," "Justify My Love"**).

Madonna: The 1983 debut album that got the ball rolling—dedicated to her **father** and recorded in a hurry. Madonna already had two 12" **dance** singles before *M* was assembled, so the enduring dance-club hits **"Everybody," "Burning Up,"** and "Physical Attraction" merely had to be boiled down to album-sized lengths. **"Holiday"** was given to Madonna by producer/soon-to-be-boyfriend **Jellybean; "Borderline"** was the second song written by Reggie Lucas for Madonna (after "Physical Attraction"); and Madonna wrote the remaining tracks—**"Lucky Star,"** "I Know It," and "Think of Me." **"Ain't No Big Deal"** was to have appeared on the album, but was replaced at the eleventh hour by "Holiday." Good choice.

M was one of the most auspicious musical debuts of the eighties, though it underwhelmed critics at the time. It's a seamlessly sweet, lyrically coy, infectiously kinetic dance album with a difference. Instead of only good grooves, the album has charming girl-group heart, the kind of overemotional angst that young people eat like **popcorn.**

M took its time to bloom into a major hit, starting out in the nether regions of the Top 200. It was months before it crawled into the Top 40 and didn't hit the Top Ten for over a year, but it went on to sell four million copies (eight million worldwide). Not half-bad for a first-timer some male critics were openly branding a slut. (As if chastity affects musical credibility!).

Besides the record's prefab **club** hits, it spawned Madonna's first Top 40 hit "Holiday," (number 16); her first Top Ten hit, "Borderline," (number 10); and her first Top Five hit "Lucky Star" (number 4), which was the album's original title. The hits just got bigger with each single release, and remained unbroken

"The musicians were all guys who are making a thousand dollars a day in the studio so we couldn't rehearse much. Halfway through we all started doubting each other."

—Madonna, 1983

·

"Without overstepping the modest ambitions of minimal funk, Madonna issues an irresistible invitation to the dance."

—Don Shewey, *Rolling Stone,* 1983

with the immediately subsequent release of her follow-up album.

If critics were unkind at first, they've now mostly forgotten their initial impressions, or changed their minds. *M* is now regarded as a must-have for any pop collection.

The packaging of the album prefigures a lot of later Madonna motifs. She has short-cropped, platinum **hair** on the front and back covers (1986's "new Madonna" was really just a throwback to the original), and stretches a dog chain roughly around her throat (baby **"Dita"**). Most importantly, Madonna's navel is prominent on the inner sleeve, and that **belly button**—especially in her **"Lucky Star"** video—was the umbilical to a career built on the public's fascination with her body.

The album was produced by Reggie Lucas, renowned for his work with female singers, at the expense of both **Steve Bray,** who'd been a musical and romantic partner of Madonna's, and **Mark Kamins** (ditto). But the most sensational credit on the album belongs to Madonna herself, who cowrote five of the eight songs and still found time to play the "cowbelle" (*sic*). *M* is known as *The First Album* in the U.K.

Madonna Diet: Collaborator **Steve Bray** coined this term to describe everyone's eating habits while working on *True Blue*—namely, *none*. He reported that Madonna demanded total immersion in the album which included working foodless until 9 P.M. every day.

Madonna money: In Madonna we trust? That's what Madonna money asks of us. Loads of the phony stuff—bearing Madonna's image—were printed up for her **Virgin tour** and dumped on audiences at the end of **"Material Girl."**

Her official **fan club** also presses

Madonna money for use in buying merchandise from their catalogue.

Don't knock it—it sure outclasses that funky cyclops pyramid thing.

Madonna queen: An over-the-top Madonna **fan**, especially *apropos* for **gay men**, but it has become generic. If you find yourself calling hotels while Madonna's on tour to see if **Liz Rosenberg** is registered, buying every format of every Madonna song available, and/or have recently started a letter-writing campaign to get Madonna a star on the Hollywood Walk of **Fame**, you are one!

Madonnathon: You've heard of Star Trek conventions? Well, they're positively earthbound compared to the antics at these Madonna appreciation celebrations, staged since 1992 in Southfield, Michigan, the weekend of Madonna's **birthday**. About 1,500 **fans** converge to buy Ma-merchandise so fabulous it might have been offered up to a certain newborn in a manger, to discuss their mutual heartache over the latest Madonna strike-out or to toast her latest home run, to watch **impersonators** of both sexes strutting their stuff, and simply to get in touch with other fans.

The event is well worth the trip for any diehard fan. Aside from great bargains, the event sponsors a **"This Used to be My Playground"** bus tour of Madonna's childhood home, her schools, the site of her first **kiss**, and the Dunkin' Donuts where she . . . well, ate donuts.

MTV calls its weekend-long Madonna-only events Madonnathons.

magazines: When she's not appearing on the cover of one, she's buying them by the armful. Madonna loves to keep up on contemporary culture (a job requirement, since she dictates so much of it), and there's no better way than leafing through her favorites, which in 1990 included *Vanity Fair*, *Vogue*, *Details*, *Tatler*, and *Spy*.

SEE ALSO: CENTERSPREAD

Mailer, Norman: Grizzled *auteur* of *The Naked and the Dead* and the most famous **Marilyn Monroe** "biography" of all time. NM proclaimed Madonna to be our "greatest living female artist" in an August 1994 cover story for *Esquire* magazine's "Women We Love" issue. NM's portrait with Madonna for the issue featured him in black tie and she in a deep green (**black-and-white** film) evening gown and matching dog collar. NM hilariously wrote of photographer **Wayne**

"*I* think it's fairly evident she had a lot going for her in the audition. Does this mean I'm a big, fat whore? Maybe."

—David Mamet
on his practical-minded casting of Madonna in
Speed-the-Plow, 1988

*Mantegna signing **autographs** outside the Royale after a performance of **Speed-the-Plow**.*

Maser's attempts to get a "stunt photo" of the famous pair, with Madonna on NM's lap, her breast exposed. But NM recoiled at the unceremoniously unsheathed breast, not out of modesty, but out of a wounded ego at its flaccid nipple! The lengthy essay/interview served to defend Madonna against the talons of the press in the backlash after her **David Letterman** appearance, but it was also a rare in-depth interview with Madonna that allowed her to get real about **condoms**, discuss her amazing resilience after a dozen years of intermittently bad press, and admit that *Sex* was at least partially made-up of concessions to practicality. The article was a watershed piece that paved the way for Madonna's seventh full-length studio album.

Malibu: Madonna and **Sean Penn** lived in a $4-million Malibu beach house in Carbon Canyon at 22271 Carbon Mesa Drive as young marrieds. It was the site of their most loving moments, as well as the abusive times that led to their **divorce**. Madonna signed it over to Sean when they split, and he lived there with girlfriend Robin Wright and their children until it was burned to the ground in the brushfires of November 1993. Madonna was said to have offered Sean financial help in rebuilding.

While living there, Madonna often indulged in the Malibu eccentricity of wearing around her neck a tiny vial of soapy water with a little wand for blowing bubbles.

Mamet, David: Intense playwright and film director best known for his plays *Glengarry Glen Ross* and *Sexual Perversity in Chicago*, and his film *House of Games*.

In 1988, he cast Madonna in the role of "Karen" in his ***Speed-the-Plow***, ensuring the **play**'s financial success for her entire run.

Madonna later described him as a misogynist (along with Oliver Stone), and her meek, willingly exploited character certainly didn't do much for women's lib.

Manilow, Barry: The man who played the piano for **Bette Midler** during her gay bathhouse performances in the early seventies played for Madonna the night the American Foundation for **AIDS** Research (AmFAR) honored her with its Award of Courage in 1991, just a few months after he attended the Los Angeles premiere of ***Truth or Dare***.

Mantegna, Joe: Tony Award—winning "Ordinary Joe," **Italian**-American actor, and **David Mamet** player who was "Bobby

Gould" (rumored to be based on Paramount bigwig Ned Tanen) to Madonna's "Karen" in **Speed-the-Plow**. He later played the snarky homicide detective in **Body of Evidence**.

Maripol: American-based French designer/stylist responsible for Madonna's early ensembles *avec* rubber bracelets, neon, heavy **crucifixes**, and mesh **hair** ties. She operated a boutique at 59-65 Bleecker Street in Greenwich Village called Maripolitan, from which she sold all the components of the Madonna look circa 1985, including jackets like those she provided for **Desperately Seeking Susan**.

M styled Madonna for the covers for her first two albums and also for her appearance at the first annual **MTV Music Video Awards**. It was M who first introduced Madonna to Downtown regulars **Andy Warhol, Mick Jagger**, and **Deborah Harry**.

When Madonna streamlined her image, Maripolitan folded, in late 1986, but there was never acrimony between the two women. The gracious Maripol remains great friends with Madonna to this day. In a rare TV interview in 1993 after the airing of **Robin Leach**'s "Madonna Exposed," M defended Madonna against bad press, flashing personal photos of Madonna with M's children.

Marky Mark: Impossibly-built Boston rapper, famous for his shirtlessness and the playful wink of his peekaboo **underwear**. He hit it big with his Funky Bunch and their "Good Vibration" in 1991, and even bigger as a Calvin Klein underwear model along with waif Kate Moss from 1992 to the end of 1993.

MM sparred with Madonna at **Alek Keshishian**'s **birthday** party thrown by Gerry and Angela Janklow Harrington in 1993. The

story, depending on whom you believe, is either that (1) MM, fresh from making public amends for black- and Asian-bashing he indulged in as a teen, called **Guy Oseary** a "homo," decked him, exchanged obscenities with Madonna, and was ejected from the party; or (2) Madonna, smarting from MM's snotty slams against her in the British press, flirted with him, got pissed off at his polite refusal, and deliberately provoked a brawl that got Mark ejected from the party and earned him grief from his gay following.

That MM defended righteous **dance**hall rapper Shabba Ranks for his belief that gays should be crucified does not help his cause, but MM has since denied being homophobic, whether sincere or just wise. Madonna is mum. You decide. The lady . . . or the rapper?

"*J* turn the **TV** on and there's a boy in his underwear—for twenty minutes. I thought *I* was bad. He's *very* cute. He's adorable. What else can he do?"

—Madonna, 1991

·

"*J* always thought she was at least 'cute.' When I met her she looked like fucking *Beetlejuice.*"

—Marky Mark on Madonna, [attrib.] 1992

·

"*J* was like, 'What's up, Madonna?' She was like, 'Don't **fuck**ing say hi to me. You know what the fuck you fucking did. You dissed me. You're a fucking asshole, a fucking fake. . . . I'm going to get somebody to kick your ass.' . . . I mean, honestly, I had a lot of respect for her. I think she's very talented. She's very smart. She does a lot of good. As much as she promotes wild **sex**, she does a lot for **AIDS** research. . . . "

—Marky Mark, *The Advocate*, 1994

·

"*T*hank **God** that happened. It was such a bad party!"

—Angela Janklow Harrington, 1993

Martin, Marilyn: The blonde singer who duetted with Phil Collins on "Separate Lives" provided backing vocals for the *Like a Prayer* album. In return, Madonna wrote and produced the song "Possessive Love" for her, which became MM's first solo single.

SEE ALSO: DISCOGRAPHY

Martinez, Bobby: Extra-young **graffiti** artist who told biographer **Christopher Andersen** of Madonna's voracious **sex**ual appetite, including a **bisexual orgy** in Madonna's Jacuzzi in which he participated. . . . Except, of course, Madonna doesn't *have* a Jacuzzi.

Ask any number of kids in Alphabet City and they'll tell you Madonna used to cruise through with her limo and pick them up for sexplay. BM is an example of why that's neither surprising nor particularly credible.

masculinity: Like all great stars, Madonna's androgynous. Her masculinity is overt: She has bulging biceps, a strong face, a macho swagger, even an unsisterly fondness for women. As a child, she enjoyed peeing while standing up (please don't try this at home, ladies); as an adult, her accessing of masculinity includes wearing male clothing like top hats and suits, using male props like cigars, and impersonating men often, as in **Blond Ambition** when she grabbed her crotch and "**assault**ed" her female dancers.

Madonna does not simply embrace masculinity, she wears it like a costume, provoking an evaluation of the nature of "maleness."

A sterling example is the "**Bye Bye Baby**" number from her **Girlie Show.** Madonna, **Donna Delory**, and **Niki Haris** were dressed as men in tuxedos, groping and ogling a group of women in scanty teddies. Because the audience was aware that these "men" were imposters, every stage movement that could be defined as masculine was immediately identifiable; seeing women behave as men do throws that behavior into sharp relief.

As for assuming physiological masculinity, Madonna said in 1991 that despite initial curiosity over the feeling of having a penis: "It would be like a third leg. It would seem like a contraption that would get in the way."

Maser, Wayne: The photographer who has taken some of Madonna's most daring and abrasive portraits, though he has been in the shadows of **Herb Ritts** and **Steven Meisel**. WM gave us Madonna chomping a stogie, posing as Christ with a crown of thorns, and the stunning *Esquire* '94 cover of Madonna in leather bikini and dog collar.

SEE ALSO: MAILER, NORMAN

masks: Madonna's fetish for posing and for assuming new identities is a sort of mask, and she has employed actual masks at two key points in her career.

First, a lion's-head mask helps to hammer home the theme of **sex**ual voracity in the **"Like a Virgin" video**. Eight years later, a black eye-mask was all she needed to thoroughly obscure her super-familiar face in her **"Erotica" video**.

The **Girlie Show** program was full of masks to echo that of the mirthsome Pierrot who appeared throughout the show, a metaphor for the stage personae adapted by all entertainers.

"*F*eminism says, 'No more masks.' Madonna says we are nothing but masks."

—Camille Paglia, 1990

The Tragic Saga of John Edgar Wideman, by Chip Brown

Esquire

Man At His Best
August 1989 Price $2.50

WOMEN WE LOVE And Women We Don't

Who Knows?
Roseanne
She's awfully tough to get a handle on!

Who Else!
Madonna
One of the century's great inventions!

Who Cares?
hopesomething
Really, we'd like to stay and chat, but we're only in town for a month!

masturbation: Madonna abused herself so unabashedly during her **Blond Ambition** performance of **"Like a Virgin"** that Toronto authorities threatened to arrest her for indecency. They backed down, and Madonna jerked all the way to the bank.

At the 11th Annual **MTV Video Music Awards**, Aerosmith's Steve Tyler accepted an award from Madonna with a jerk-off joke. Holding up his index and middle fingers, he queried, "Why does Madonna masturbate with these two fingers?" The answer: "Because they're *mine*." Madonna giggled and retorted that that wouldn't be masturbating it'd be "sexual abuse." They were just joshing and the audience ate it up.

SEE ALSO: DEMANN, FREDDY

"Material Girl" song: The number 2 smash from *Like a Virgin* launched a **nickname** that has followed Madonna to virtually every article written about her. The fact that she only gets **rich**er doesn't help shake the "material girl" image, which itself resonated sharply with the yuppie mentality so prevalent in the eighties.

The public reception of this song—though extra positive—may be the earliest example of people not "getting" Madonna, as she has often complained. "MG" is widely misinterpreted as an unabashed ode to wealth along the lines of "I Wanna Be Rich." Quite the contrary, the song is a fairly broad send-up of the type of gold digger that **Marilyn Monroe** played so often and so well, an affectionate *hommage* to a hopelessly outdated type of girl. That material girls (and boys) thrive to this day doesn't make them any less *passé*, or any less pathetic.

"Apparently, Madonna doesn't limit her financial affairs to old money."

—James Hunter, *Record*

True materialism is the absolute antithesis of Madonna. Madonna is about take-no-prisoners self-reliance, and material girls are about lazy dependence. The first clue that "MG" is not dead serious is Madonna's vocal, a forced chirp made even more hilarious by several excited hiccups. The second clue is the sheerly cotton-**candy** music.

The song has become a staple of Madonna's tours, performed straight on **The Virgin Tour,** as a **Cyndi Lauper parody** on **Who's That Girl,** and as part of a medley on **Blond Ambition.**

"Material Girl" video: The first **video** that proved Madonna was a star. In "MG," Madonna's turn as **Marilyn Monroe**—in a restaging of the famous "Diamonds are a Girl's Best Friend" sequence from *Gentlemen Prefer Blondes*—is completely credible. In fact, Madonna's cool enough not only to play MM, but to *correct* her.

In the video—which was directed by **Mary Lambert** after Jean-Paul Goude fell through—an enigmatic artist character, played by Keith Carradine, obsesses over how to win the Madonna character's heart.

While watching footage of her performing, he checks a studio underling who makes the mistake of saying she "could" be a star. "She *is* a star" he drones, and soon we see that she is such a star she is unimpressed by the 14-karat gifts bestowed upon her by other suitors. She tells a friend on the phone about one bauble, "He thinks he can impress me. . . . It's nice though. . . . You want it?"

Carradine eventually wins her over by taking her for a ride in a jalopy he buys off an old man, and by handing her a humble bouquet. In the end, we see them **kiss**ing beyond the truck's rain-streaked windshield.

This storyline is intercut with splashy performance sequences of Madonna reinventing the Marilyn scene. The scene is so carefully evoked that the hot-pink gown Madonna wears was copied exactly from designer Bill Travilla's original, which annoyed him to no end. But Madonna's character is very different from Marilyn's. Madonna directs the fawning millionaires around her, taking charge in a way that the merely gold-digging Marilyn character never could have—she doesn't dig gold, she picks pockets!

Though most pop summaries of the video take for granted that it is a direct imitation of the Monroe scene, "MG" is about a lot more than greed. It's about independence and true **love**, two of the most consistently recurring themes in Madonna's **work.** The video is also about super**stardom**, which Madonna assumed as soon as "MG" hit **MTV.** "MG" earned Madonna her first *TV Guide* cover, illustrating an article on how to tell good videos (like "MG") from bad.

Maverick Entertainment: Madonna's multimedia company, born in April 1992 with her $60-million deal with Time-Warner Inc. Maverick is a record label home to such star acts as UNV (the first act signed), Proper Grounds, Candlebox, **Me'Shell NdegéOcello,** and Madonna herself; the film production company behind *Dangerous Game* and cosponsor of the American distribution of *Farewell, My Concubine*; as well as the publishing

Madonna steps out with Maverick honcho Guy Oseary.

imprint under which *Sex* was released. The company also develops **video** and TV **projects**.

Make no mistake: Madonna *runs* Maverick. Manager **Freddy DeMann** comanages, with Anna DeRoy as its director of creative affairs, and Guy Oseary as its director of Artists and Repertoire (A&R). **Sire**'s **Seymour Stein** serves as a scout, and Madonna snagged **MTV** exec Abbey Konowitch as a vice president.

Maverick is bicoastal, based in Los Angeles at 8000 Beverly Boulevard—what used to be a senior-citizen home—and in **New York** at 75 Rockefeller Plaza. Don't try sending in unsolicited materials: like most other companies, Maverick will send them back unopened. In the first two weeks of operation, Maverick received—and rejected—over 5,000 unbidden projects.

The interiors of the L.A. office are extremely chic, with delicate Euro-style furniture and wall-to-wall Madonna portraits, including an enormous **"Justify My Love"** subway poster with a long-winded inscription, in Oseary's office. Madonna's own office boasts a trio of TV monitors for easy viewing of what Oseary describes as "young, raw talent."

"*M*averick Entertainment sits squatly and
conspicuously on a corner, looking like a
cross between a late-eighties Comme
des Garçons boutique and the bunker
where Eva Braun killed herself."

—Danny Sommers, *Sky* (U.K.), 1993

.

"*M*averick will be an intellectual think tank.
It started as a desire to have more **control**.
There's a group of writers, photographers,
and editors that I've met along the way
in my career who I want to take with
me wherever I go. I want to incorporate
them into my little factory of ideas.
I also came in contact with a lot
of young talent I feel
entrepreneurial about."

—Madonna, 1992

Mazar, Debi: Scrupulously-browed, Queens-born actress and former makeup artist (as "Debi M.") to Madonna. She did

Madonna's face so well the two became pals—DM even went to Madonna's **wedding**, where she caught some of Steve "Studio 54" Rubell's vomit on her dress.

The **acting** bug bit DM after she did Madonna's face for ***Speed-the-Plow***, though she'd already appeared in the **"Papa Don't Preach"** and non-U.S. **"True Blue"** videos. Since then, she has had memorable roles in *GoodFellas*, *Little Man Tate*, *Jungle Fever*, and on TV's "Civil Wars."

She stopped working for Madonna way back when, but as one of Madonna's best buddies, she often shows up in the company of the Blonde One.

Mazar made a big splash at the ***Sex* launch party** in a leather bustier; Madonna accompanied her to the **New York** premiere of *Malcolm X*; and the women can often be spotted taking in a **basketball** game.

"*W*e're good friends, and not working
together was the best thing we ever did.
Two Leo women, one working for the other?
Forget it!"

—Debi Mazar on ex-boss Madonna, 1993

McArthur, Alex: Lanky, **sex**y, **Italian** guy who played Madonna's underaged beau in the **"Papa Don't Preach" video**. He's the one her **father** warned her all about, and his baby blues make a good case for teen **pregnancy**.

Madonna chose him for the role after seeing him in the lesbian romance *Desert Hearts*. "I was in my garage working on my motorcycle when the phone rang," he remembered. "I answered the call and a voice said, 'Hi, this is Madonna and I would like you to be in my next video.' She's sweet, yet very professional, and I was impressed with the fact that she knows exactly what she wants."

measurements: On a **Japan**ese talk show in 1985, a giggling group of adolescent girls asked Madonna her measurements. Shocked by their forwardness, she stammered that that information was top secret, even as the cameraman zoomed in on her barely-there bustier. She's actually 33(C)-24-34, figures that shift depending on her **fitness** regimen.

mediocrity: "My drive in life is from this horrible fear of being mediocre."—Madonna, 1991.

Madonna, the only thing you have to fear is fear itself—you

couldn't be mediocre if you tried. But just to stave off any middle-of-the-road doldrums, she keeps a framed quote from Sir Arthur Conan Doyle on her desk at **Maverick**: "Mediocrity knows nothing higher than itself, but talent instantly recognizes genius."

Meisel, Steven: Controversial **fashion** photographer who made the leap into fine-**art** photography with Madonna in their *Sex* collaboration. SM became Madonna's photographer of choice after their 1991 *Vanity Fair* shoot, but he was actually instrumental in establishing some of Madonna's early memorable images. He took the photo for her first-ever promotional poster in 1983 and the famous "satanic bride" cover for 1985's *Like a Virgin* LP.

"*B*eing a good artist is not about being **powerful** or **rich** or well respected by your peers. It's about taking chances. Steven has done this since the beginning of his career as a photographer. There is nothing more exciting than collaborating with an artist who is willing to risk everything."

—Madonna, in the Council of **Fashion** Designers of America **Awards** program, 1992

In many ways, SM is the Madonna of photography, an intensely creative but derivative co-opter of images whose work often reflects a preoccupation with brazen **sex**uality and harsh stylization. Of *Sex*, he said, "After this, no one ever needs to do another book on erotica," with a bold confidence that surpassed even Madonna's own.

memories: Madonna's earliest memory is of her beautiful **mother**, and of sleeping soundly between her parents in their bed.

Her second memory, quite the opposite, is of being four years old and knocking down a younger girl who was attempting to give her a **dandelion**.

men, most influential: Asked by Brazil's *Veja* magazine in 1993 to list the most prominent and influential men in the world, Madonna answered, "Michael Jordan, **Spike Lee**, **Bill Clinton**, Bill Gates [of the MicroSoft corporation], and Steven Spielberg."

Menem, Carlos: President of Argentina who refused to meet with Madonna when she blew into Buenos Aires with her **Girlie Show**, after Catholic archbishop Antonio Cardinal Quarracino had branded her sacrilegious and an insult to Argentine women.

Menjo's: Menjo's is the first gay bar Madonna ever pranced in, on the arm of mentor **Christopher Flynn**. It's still standing at 928 McNichols (Six Mile) Road in Ferndale, Michigan.

If you want to see Menjo's full of Madonna **fans**, attend the **Madonnathon**'s opening-night bash, held there.

menstruation: Madonna first bled at age ten.

merchandising: Since Madonna has never made any bones about her capitalism, it makes perfect sense that her image should be expertly merchandised. From the beginning, there has been no limit to the amount of Madonna-related merchandise available to those interested.

*The only thing not-for-sale on The **Who's That Girl** tour was this official merchandise banner. Talk about merchandise . . . look at all those stickers!*

Aside from all her regular film and record releases and all the ensuing promotional and commercial items available with each, there have been literally hundreds of posters, stand-ups, nudie pens, T-shirts, concert programs, bicycle shorts, caps, sweatshirts, postcards, buttons, magazine covers, bandannas, patches, temporary tattoos, towels, **books** . . . you name it, she sells it.

Though many Madonna items you'll run across are unofficial (*read*: illegal bootlegs), the official stuff is handled by **Boy Toy, Inc.**—the marketing branch of "Madonna, Inc." Don't scoff at Madonna merchandise: today's **Girlie Show** peep-box key chain is tomorrow's valuable **artifact**.

In October 1992, readers of **England**'s respected *Record Collector* magazine voted Madonna the sixth most collectible artist of all time, ahead of Elvis Presley.

Meyer, Ron: Top **Creative Artists Agency (CAA)** agent who, in tandem with Jane Berliner, represents Madonna in her film career. RM also handles stars like **Barbra Streisand**, Jessica Lange, and Jane Fonda, but he is perhaps better known for his **rumor**ed philandering. His relationship with Cyndy Garvey (the ex–Mrs. Steve) ended with her filing an abuse complaint with the

**MADONNA
SEAN PENN**

sortie
29
octobre

SHANGHAÏ SURPRISE

Réalisé par
JIM GODDARD

WILLEM DAFOE **El cuerpo del delito** MADONNA

A FILM BY ULI EDEL

NEW AL
TRUE BLU
トゥルー・ブルー 7.2
ON S

マドンナ
MADONNA

PLAYBOY

マドンナ

12

MITSUBISHI

Yes!
Beautiful

VASS

MITSUBISHI
Hi-Fi VIDEO

Una vez en la vida,
llega la oportunidad de hacer algo diferente.

ELLAS DAN EL GOLPE

MADONNA

MADONNA

NAME
AUTHORIZED SIGNATURE

MADONNA

Hi there!
Thanks for joining my fan club.
I thought I'd tell you about what I've
been up to lately. My latest album
True Blue I hope is a hit. I owe you all
been a big hit! This is especially
exciting to me because it was the
first time I coproduced a record.
Hopefully you get the chance to see all
my new videos. Right now I'm in
Hollywood finishing a new movie
called Shanghai Surprise. My co-stars are
Griffin Dunne and the other co-star
isn't of a romantic comedy set
with out giving away the story I got
into and but a lot of trouble. My albums
written some songs for the soundtrack they
should both be out this summer I
do check em out! I hope to be doing
a world tour during the summer of '87
so stay tuned —
And Don't forget - Dreams come True!
love/Madonna

Johnny will be away for the night. I absolutely must see you. I am desperate, and if you don't come I won't answer for the consequences. Don't drive up.
Dita

madonna!

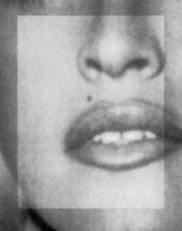

SPIN

MADONNA

U2

¡NUEVO!
RETIN-A

ADVOCATE

MADONNA

The X-Rated Interview

STEVE RENOUF · NAOMI CAMPBELL

Who
EXCLUSIVE PREVIEW

MADONNA'S
X-RATED
TOUR

IN DUBLIN

max

Time Out

The Cloning of
Madonna

PENTHOUSE

MADONNA
NUE !!!

EARTHY

Time Out

MADONNA'S
BACK

Rolling Stone

PLAYBOY

MADONNA

THE FACE

EXCLUSIVE!
MADONNA
ON THE
SET OF
DICK TRACY

10

ROCKSTAR

MADONNA

max

MADONNA!

Los Angeles County Sheriff's Department, and it's said he's had his assistants make and break dates for him with CAA starlets.

Spy magazine also reported that a hireling, having seen Madonna in RM's **office**, said, "I didn't recognize her. She was more . . . more . . ." "More hideous than you thought?" RM finished.

Mia Mind Music: Production/promotion facility that hired Madonna, on the recommendation of The System's David Frank, in 1981, to provide backing vocals to songs by **Otto von Wernherr**. When Madonna hit it big, Mia Mind cashed in, licensing the von Wernherr songs, newly remixed to bring Madonna's vocals to the fore. This "early years" material is anything but vintage Madonna, a collection of jarring, tuneless compositions with titles like "We are the Gods" and "Cosmic Climb" that are nonetheless must-hears for Madonna **fans**.

Founder Steve Bentzel went on to pen the **"Papa Don't Preach"** spoof "Madonna Don't Preach," the **video** of which featured von Wernherr performing as a priest hounded by pregnant teens in front of **New York**'s club Limelight.

Mia Mind also did individual work with Madonna at Evergreen Studios on the Upper West Side of Manhattan, and eventually licensed several Madonna solo performances—"Shine a Light," "Little Boy Lost," "On the Ground," "Time and Time Again," and "The Da-Da-Da-Dance"—written by missing-in-action Daniel Giorlando. All of these Madonna songs lack her personal touch, but stand on their own as credible rock tunes with stronger vocals than she mustered for *Madonna*.

Bentzel has high praises for Madonna: "I think we paid her less than union wages. I always found her nothing less than professional, and I've always felt that she's very talented. I never had a problem with her."

Miami Beach: After doing an extensive photo shoot in Florida's swankiest city, Madonna spent almost $5 million for a sprawling, Spanish-style mansion on fashionable Brickell Avenue in Coconut Grove to add to her collection of part-time residences. The mansion overlooks Biscayne Bay. Since the mid-eighties, Miami has become a mecca for wealthy party-types and a wide-out-in-the-open gay culture, neither of which have suffered from Madonna's proximity.

Midler, Bette: The Madonna of the seventies who became the Minnie Mouse of the eighties with a string of Disney films, and tried to be the **Barbra Streisand** of the nineties with more serious film roles and diva-ish ballads and concerts. BM tweaked Madonna's pride with a funny introduction at **Live Aid** which referred to her recent nude photo flap.

Later, BM was at the premiere of **Speed-the-Plow**, where she was so besieged by **paparazzi** that she sobbed with frustration.

A happier occasion saw BM handing Madonna a lifetime achievement award on behalf of **AIDS** Project Los Angeles in 1991.

Midwest: She was born and raised there (in Michigan), and later filmed *A League of Their Own* there (in **Evansville**, Indiana, and Chicago), but she can never be accused of sentimentality for her roots, or of sucking up to the all-important heartland record-buyers: "I prayed for seventeen years to get out of the Midwest and I don't want to go back."

Miramax: The class-act distributor of such prestigious films as *The Piano* and *The Nasty Girl* also distributed Jennie Livingston's voguing documentary *Paris is Burning* (on Madonna's advice), and *Truth or Dare* in 1991. Since then, Madonna has been ultra-sympatico with Miramax bigwigs Harvey and Bob Weinstein, the former of whom enthused in 1993: "I **love** Madonna! And we're a great team, she and **Alek Keshishian** and I," while employing Madonna's **Maverick** Films as codistributor of *Farewell, My Concubine*.

The success Miramax had with *Truth or Dare* has been repaid with Madonna's appearances at various Miramax functions, including their 1991 launch for *Hear My Song*.

"**M**adonna is honest. She says what she feels, doesn't censor herself, and has an adventurous spirit."

—Harvey Weinstein, on why the excitement for Madonna arriving at **Cannes** in 1991 was greater than for any star since Brigitte Bardot

Miriam, the Weinsteins' mother, has offered to fix Madonna up with a single doctor. "Fine. I've had no luck with actors and models," was Madonna's reply.

Look for Miramax, Maverick, and Madonna to collaborate in the future.

miscarriage: Fine institutions like *The News Extra* reported that Madonna miscarried **Warren Beatty**'s baby in August 1990, and also that she was forced to terminate a **pregnancy** by **Tony Ward** six months later, which would have resulted in a miscarriage otherwise. Madonna has never discussed any **pregnancies** she may or may not have had.

Mitchell, Joni: Madonna frequently lists this singer's *Court and Spark* as an influential and favorite album, but JM told *Rolling Stone* that

"**A**nd now for the woman whose name has been on everyone's lips for the last six months: She pulled herself up by her bra-straps, and has been known to let them *down* o-ccasion-al-ly. . . . She's great, she's hot, she's a *lot* like a virgin . . . she's Madonna!"

—Bette Midler, **Live Aid**, 1985

Madonna "flirts with humiliation and degradation. And perhaps that bravado is in some ways to be applauded; but at what cost to her soul, is my question."

Mitchell, Nancy Ryan: Madonna's high-school guidance counselor. She does *not*, as you might guess, wonder, 'Where did I go wrong?!?' Instead, she remembers Madonna as a gifted student who projected an extremely positive outlook and, closer to graduation, a flamboyant **fashion** sense.

She also remembers the time that **cheerleader** Madonna wore flesh-colored tights and **shock**ed the entire **gym**nasium with a cartwheel.

Mitchell, Sasha: Strapping male model/actor and star of the Paul Morrissey film *Spike of Bensonhurst*, with whom Madonna was purported to have "affaired." Whether she did or not, she styled him for over four hours for his profile in *Interview* magazine in 1987, which amounted to touches like removing his shirt and tearing his jeans artistically.

She described him to a *Vogue* reporter with affectionate condescension as an eager Downtown actor-type.

Mitsubishi: Japanese corporation whose stereophonic equipment Madonna endorsed in 1986 and 1987. As part of her $3-million deal, she made a TV **commercial, dancing** and lip-synching to **"La Isla Bonita,"** and appeared in print ads wearing a leather jacket with silver studs forming the letter *M.*

An oversized poster-book of **Who's That Girl tour** photos was given away with each purchase of a Mitsubishi stereo; Madonna/Mitsubishi phone cards were sold (flimsy, colorful credit cards which are punched with each use of a pay phone); and silk banners bearing unique photos of Madonna were used to attract young buyers.

No Japanese Christian groups threatened to boycott Mitsubishi for associating with Madonna.

Mitzelfeld's department store: Located at 401 Main Street, opposite the Rochester School of Ballet, this Michigan store is where Madonna **shoplift**ed and hung out as a teenager.

Moira: In *Truth or Dare*, Madonna giddily tells of her sexual experimentation with her childhood pal Moira (McPharlin) when the two, as little girls, used to finger-**fuck** each other on Moira's

mom's bed. In the film, Moira lovingly recalls her innocent friendship with Madonna, then appears quite surprised—but always a good sport—when asked about the purported finger-fucking.

Later, a pregnant Moira meets Madonna for the first time in over ten years as Madonna strolls through the lobby of her hotel while on tour. Madonna is a trifle patronizing, barely able to contain laughter as Moira begs her to bless her fetus because she plans to name the child after her. Madonna blows her off and Moira mutters, "That little shit."

Used and abused for our amusement, Moira still comes off as a genuine person, shedding real tears for Madonna's long-dead **mother**, and recalling her own less-than-**glamor**ous life in sharp contrast to Madonna's groovy one. Moira's brother, Pat, later fumed to the *National Enquirer* that Madonna was lying, and that "I don't want people thinking my sister is a sexual pervert."

SEE ALSO: BISEXUALITY, HOMOSEXUALITY

Mondino, Jean-Baptiste: French photographer and **director** who brought to life Madonna's first really subversive **sex**ual vision (the **"Open Your Heart" video**) and her celluloid bacchanal, **"Justify My Love."** He won the Gold Lion **Award** at the **Cannes** Film Festival in 1993 for his TV **commercial** for **Jean-Paul Gaultier**'s fragrance "Parfum."

Monroe, Marilyn: Madonna, Senior. Fluid, voluptuous blonde movie actress whose winning comedic roles, steamy aura, desire to be taken seriously, and tragic demise (**suicide** or murder, depending on what book's on the best-seller charts this month) have made her the world's most indelible star.

Madonna is frequently measured against MM for lack of a better comparison. The similarities, according to Madonna, are that both are blonde, and that's it. But Madonna isn't even always blonde, so there must be other parallels to attract such persistent comparisons.

Madonna, like MM, is the biggest star of her generation. Madonna's name and face—even with the rapid-fire changes—are probably as recognizable the world over as MM's, if not more. Both stars are undeniably **sex**ual, MM as a submissive kitten and Madonna as an aggressor. Like Madonna, MM sought **control** over her life and career and yearned for artistic kudos. MM achieved the latter more easily than the former, and Madonna vice versa. It's even fair to compare their marriages—MM's most famous pairing was with hotheaded slugger Joe DiMaggio, and they **divorce**d after less than two years of infamous rows. Madonna and **Sean Penn** lasted longer, but their **marriage** was every bit as stormy. Both unions were **rumor**ed to involve physical abuse.

Besides the uncontrollable similarities, Madonna has actually cultivated a Marilyn-esque impression for herself many times. From the time she incorporated MM's "Diamonds are a Girl's Best Friend" routine into her **"Material Girl" video**, MM's ghost has haunted her. When she went platinum blonde, some nearsighted writers actually felt Madonna resembled MM, which is preposter-

> *Madonna is the world's greatest Marilyn Monroe **impersonator**.*

ous—Madonna is all cool angles and exacting style, whereas Marilyn was rounded, almost blurred when emoting at full throttle. But costumes like her off-the-shoulder gown in **Who's That Girl** and her appreciation for MM's favorite designer, Pucci, have lent Madonna a distinctly Marilyn air.

Never one to discourage echoes of other pop institutions, Madonna has posed in dozens of classic MM settings. Bruce Weber recreated MM poses for Madonna's 1986 *Life* magazine cover story, and **Steven Meisel** orchestrated a stunning series of Marilyn-esque poses for her appearance on and in **Vanity Fair** in 1991. Some of the shots were close copies of Monroe's last sitting with photographer Bert Stern. An *Italian Vogue* sitting with Meisel yielded poses titled *"Madonna Come Marilyn."*

But Madonna's similarities to MM are, like her clever appropriations of MM's external trappings, superficial. Madonna's strength of will, her resilience, her self-reliance, and her confident vision would have been alien to MM, who is loved for her vulnerability. In fact, one reason Madonna is either intensely loved or hated may be that it's difficult for some people to feel affection or even empathy with such a fierce figure, who seems to dare us to like her, and whom we can imagine surviving handily without our support. Weakness is rewarded and strength frozen out.

The greatest difference between the two biggest Ms of the twentieth century is that MM is an unreal, untouchable, flicker on a screen. From the beginning, MM was all fake. Her **hair** was always peroxided, her makeup was always intense, and her film characters were almost always cute dimwits. Her real personality was at odds with her public persona so drastically that she discussed her ability to "turn on" her "Marilyn Monroe" aura. Madonna's artifice is pretty obviously artifice; we all know that she dresses up, and that when we see a radically altered vision of

her, it's just another fun pose, an inspired contribution to a photograph, or a bad **hair** day.

Madonna, despite her steely reserve, is not all fake. . . . She's one of us. Madonna has been elected a generation's icon—rather than gradually becoming one, as with MM—so she is our link to the realm of **stardom**, our girl on the inside.

One of the reasons Madonna strikes such a chord in people is directly related to her MM poses: When she re-creates famous Marilyn photographs, her audience can't overlook the fact that Madonna adores and is fascinated by MM too. She is outside it all at the same time she is at the center of it.

Despite glaring differences, Madonna and MM will be linked forever. Why not? Their first names do have the same number of letters. Except, of course, MM's first name is made up.

"**J**'d like to be memorable in some sexual comic-tragic way. I'd like to leave the impression that Marilyn Monroe did, to be able to arouse so many different feelings in people."

—Madonna, 1984

·

"**S**he . . . thinks she's Marilyn Monroe; I guess she came back to get her money."

—Sandra Bernhard, 1994

·

"**J**oe DiMaggio's rose was there. He really loved her."

—Madonna on visiting Marilyn Monroe's grave in Westwood, California, with Sean Penn, 1985. In 1991, it was rumored that Madonna was trying to buy the crypt next to Marilyn's

Montand, Yves: Late French actor who was notorious for his indiscreet affair with **Marilyn Monroe** on the set of *Let's Make Love* in the early sixties. When Madonna was on tour in Paris in the early nineties, Montand was quoted as saying wistfully, "I wish I had known her thirty years ago."

Morrissey: Brooding, postmodern, androgynous **sex** symbol and former frontman for the British group the Smiths. In 1986, he observed of his fellow one-named icon, "Madonna is closer to organized prostitution than anything else."

Mosher, Gregory: Lincoln Center artistic **director** who produced and directed many **David Mamet plays**, including *Speed-the-Plow* on Broadway.

"*I*t's scary how much talent she has."

—Gregory Mosher on Madonna, 1988

mother: SEE: FORTIN (CICCONE), MADONNA LOUISE

motorcycle: As a wild young thing during her Paris years, Madonna described her favorite leisure-time activity as riding with Algerian and Vietnamese motorcycle toughs and swerving within inches of pedestrians, screaming epithets.

movie, favorite: In 1985, she listed hers as the classic fifties **Liz Taylor**/Montgomery Clift potboiler *A Place in the Sun*.

MTV: **Music**-television cable channel that started as a 24-hour video station but has become a purveyor of talk shows, "The Real World," game shows, "Beavis and Butthead," and Spring Break coverage, all of which is beamed into over 210 million households in over 70 countries.

Madonna was one of the first artists to build up a canon of provocative and artistic music **videos** (after Duran Duran), and from her earliest hit video for **"Borderline"** she has been a staple of MTV programming.

The network often runs entire weekends full of nothing but Madonna videos, frequently world-premieres her new videos with great fanfare, and, via correspondent **Kurt Loder**, has been granted exclusive interviews with Madonna. Though she told Loder in one interview that she never had time to watch MTV, she complained to him in a *TV Guide* session that while filming *A League of Their Own* in **Evansville**, Indiana, she was deprived of MTV, a complaint the local cable company refuted.

"*I*'m your motherbrothersisterloverdaughter-auntieunclegrandmagrandpalittlebabyJesus."

—Madonna to MTV, 1991

In 1990, MTV had to back out of its much-ballyhooed plans to debut her **"Justify My Love" video** after its censors deemed the clip too hot to handle. Nonetheless, Madonna has performed on four of their annual **awards** telecasts, and for MTV's 10th anniversary special on November 27, 1991, she lensed a hilarious personal message to MTV.

SEE ALSO: **MTV MUSIC VIDEO AWARDS**

MTV Video Music Awards: Madonna performed at the very first telecast in 1984, emerging from a gigantic **wedding** cake in full bridal bustier to perform **"Like a Virgin"** while slithering onstage like a cat in heat. It was momentous TV and helped establish her as one of pop's most ambitious, outrageous, and shameless performers.

She showed up next in 1986 to accept the first Video Vanguard Award for her visionary **videos**. In 1989, Madonna appeared with shaggy blonde **hair**, men's pants, and a studded bustier to belt **"Express Yourself"** while voguing for the first time, along with faithful sidekicks **Niki Haris** and **Donna DeLory**. The performance was one of her best live takes, including M's tucking her mike in her cleavage for safekeeping and her triumphant finale with a fist raised defiantly skyward (Blonde Power?). She even handed George Michael a Video Vanguard Award later in the evening while facetiously **smoking** a cigarette.

Madonna appeared on the awards the very next year to lip-synch **"Vogue"** along with her entire **Blond Ambition** entourage in full eighteenth-century French gear à la Marie Antoinette. She performed her **Girlie Show "Bye Bye Baby"** routine dressed in top hat and tails in 1993. After the latter, during which she felt up a bevy of barely-dressed women, Madonna turned to face the audience and the world with the clipped query, "Get the picture?" *Mmm-hmm*. And it's suitable for framing.

At the 11th annual ceremony in 1994, Madonna stole "surprise" guest **Michael Jackson's** thunder by showing up at the last minute to hand Aerosmith their Best Video award. Looking every

"*A*n alumnus of the **Alvin Ailey** dance group . . . a queen of **music** and motion . . . and every biker's dream guest rider . . . Madonna!"

—Dan Aykroyd, introducing Madonna at MTV's First Annual **Video** Music **Awards**, 1984

"*I* guess you like me, you really, *really* like me!"

—Madonna, accepting MTV Viewer's Choice **Award** for **"Like a Prayer,"** 1989 inch a superstar, she strolled to the podium on the arm of **David Letterman**, eliciting a standing ovation and catcalls.

Murray: The 160-pound wild cougar supplied by Hollywood Animals, Inc., that was Madonna's sidekick in ***Who's That Girl***. Actually, "Murray" was played by at least four different cats, all of which demonstrated an amazing affinity for Madonna.

"*T*hey're only dangerous if you provoke them."
—Madonna on cougars, 1987

music: With all the hubbub over her **looks**, her **acting**, her politics, and her attitude, Madonna's mainstay is often overlooked: her music. It's been said that Madonna, who neither reads nor writes music, never would have been so popular without her **sex** appeal and her controversy, but even a casual reassessment of her hit records proves otherwise. She has a remarkably sincere and likable **singing** voice, writes accessible and engaging **lyrics**, and chooses **dance**able or romanceable arrangements by masters like **Shep Pettibone, Patrick Leonard**, and **Steve Bray**. Music may not be the only important thing to remember about Madonna, but she certainly knows how to make it beautifully.

Madonna has often referred to her own favorite musicians and singers, some of whom she describes as influential.

Circa 1985, she was gaga over Stevie Wonder, the Supremes, Marvin Gaye, the Jackson Five, "The Letter," by the Boxtops, "Sugar Sugar," by the Archies, Gary Puckett's "Young Girl, Get Out of My Heart," Bobby Sherman, "Happy Together" by the Turtles, Nancy Sinatra, Bronski Beat, Johnny Mathis, Harry Belafonte, "Incense and Peppermints" by the Strawberry Alarm Clock. Also, "The

Mighty Quinn" by Manfred Mann, twist records (the first kind she ever bought on her own), Marianne Faithfull, Lulu, **Diana Ross**, Sarah Vaughan, Ella Fitzgerald, early **Frank Sinatra**, Tom Waits, B.B. King, Chaka Khan, **Prince**, **Joni Mitchell**, Don Henley, Chrissie Hynde, and **Deborah Harry**.

Contemporary favorites (circa 1990) were Technotronic, NWA, Neneh Cherry, and Tanita Tikaram. In 1991, she claimed to like the kind of New Agey music you'd "find at the Bodhi Tree," a shop in Los Angeles.

The best music to wake up to, she believed, was "Moments in Love" by the Art of Noise (which played at her **wedding**). The best music to work out to included Bruce Springsteen and Lime, and the best music to make out to was the Gap Band, the Isley Brothers, and Prince.

In the realm of classical music, Madonna especially likes baroque stuff: Vivaldi, Bach, Pachelbel, and Handel.

A strange brew, but then it's hard to envision a stack of **Sinéad O'Connor** tapes next to her boombox.

"*M*y musical career was an accident. I got a record deal in 1982 and just veered off that way. But the more I did it, the less interested I became in being superficial. And as I've delved more into my unconscious, so my music has evolved."
—Madonna, 1991

"*I*n music and dance, Madonna does her deepest thinking. This is her emotional bond with her audience, a marriage of true minds on a global scale. And no matter how she acts, we will never **divorce** her."
—**Camille Paglia**, 1992

"*I* don't care what anyone says, there is something valid and artistic about a Lionel Richie song."
—-Madonna, 1986

Music Building, The: Recording studio/artist space in Manhattan where Madonna hung out in her early days as a singer. The place is twelve stories tall, with five or six rooms on each floor, all chock-full of musicians in various states of creation. Madonna camped out there with **Steve Bray** briefly, and it was there she bumped into bands like Nervus Rex, The Dance, and The System. SEE ALSO: **Mia Mind Music**

Musto, Michael: *Village Voice* wit and Madonna-watcher, who is one of her most avid supporters. He wrote a seminal essay on Madonna and **gay men** for the now-defunct *Outweek* in 1990, posed as a nude hitchhiker in a send-up of *Sex* for a poster benefitting **AIDS** causes, and generally has all the dish on Madonna, thanks to his glamorous **New York City** locale.

Madonna posed for a series of rare **fashion** shots by Fred Seidman that accompanied an article by MM in the *Voice* in 1982.

"*O*ur greatest hero in the entertainment world continues to be an apparent heterosexual—Madonna, who seems to wield even more power to impact change than all our closeted queer icons and do-nothing politicians *combined.* . . . Her `I'm not ashamed' approach to potential controversy has helped rub us in the faces of every household in America. Strike opposers."

—Michael Musto, *NYQ,* 1992

Napolitano, Jill M.: Los Angeles County Notary Public who witnessed Madonna's signing of the Marital Settlement part of her **divorce** papers in January 1989.

Nars, Francois: Makeup artist behind Madonna's browlessness. He worked with her on *Sex* and on her **"Rain" video**. His make-overs will set you back about $250, but *hey—you're worth it.*

Nasty Girl, The: Nervy drama about a woman who returns to her childhood home in Germany and forces the town to come to terms with its Nazi past.

Madonna loved this 1991 German picture ("I saw it because it was two blocks from my house, and I liked the title.") and presented the 56th Annual **New York** Film Critics Circle **Award** to its **director**, Michael Verhoeven, for Best Foreign Film.

To arrive at the ceremony quietly, she used the trash elevator and slipped through the kitchen, showing up at Rockefeller Plaza's Pegasus Room. She sported two inches of dark roots and a fetching black **hair**band, the same outfit she wore when posing for **Italian** *Moda* with then-boyfriend **Tony Ward**, pal **Debi Mazar**, and assorted tragic young things. Rex Reed introduced Madonna as "living proof that living right doesn't always pay off." He also referred to Kathy Bates's character in *Misery* as the "meanest bitch this side of the Rockies," to which Madonna quipped, "But I thought *I* was the meanest bitch this side of the Rockies!"

NC-17: Movie rating meaning "Not quite porn, but pretty close. Age 17 and over."

Body of Evidence was slapped with an NC-17 six months prior to release, and for a short time it looked as though MGM would release it intact. MGM got cold feet and **director Uli Edel** snipped a few racy seconds. "I think there should be ratings for violence," Madonna snapped. "I just think the ratings are arbitrary in what they cut. I saw the NC-17 version and the R version, and it was ludicrous what was cut and what was acceptable." If you just gotta see the whole, raunchy thing, the "ludicrous" version is available on videocassette.

Billy Crystal referred to Madonna as "the NC-17 portion of our

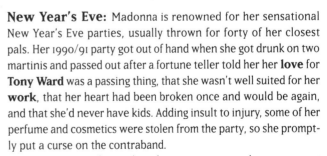

Just brow-sing.

really big show" in his best "Ed Sullivan" on the 1991 **Oscars**.

NdegéOcello, Me'Shell: Her last name means "free like the bird" in Swahili, and her arresting blend of hip-hop, rock, jazz, and rap made her album, *Plantation Lullabies*, one of the most critically acclaimed debuts of 1993. She was one of the first artists signed to **Maverick**.

Her **bisexual lyrics** and intense songs (all of which she sings, writes, and plays instruments for) place her as a Madonna-in-the-making.

nerves: Always a confident performer on tour, Madonna has nonetheless succumbed to nerves on occasion.

She was trembling like a sapling in a hurricane onstage at the **Oscars** in 1991, stumbled over a chorus of **"Fever"** on **Arsenio Hall**'s 1,000th-episode special, and is a nervous wreck on talk shows, where she has been known to sit with arms folded protectively over her abdomen, giggling and grasping for words. Toward the end of her **Girlie Show tour**, she joked with **Japan**ese audiences that she was ready for a nervous breakdown. "Why not? I could do it. Judy Garland did. Elvis did."

SEE ALSO: Letterman, David

New Year's Eve: Madonna is renowned for her sensational New Year's Eve parties, usually thrown for forty of her closest pals. Her 1990/91 party got out of hand when she got drunk on two martinis and passed out after a fortune teller told her her **love** for **Tony Ward** was a passing thing, that she wasn't well suited for her **work**, that her heart had been broken once and would be again, and that she'd never have kids. Adding insult to injury, some of her perfume and cosmetics were stolen from the party, so she promptly put a curse on the contraband.

For New Year's 1991/92, she gave a party at her apartment where she appeared as a topless S&M mistress. Guests included **Sandra Bernhard**, **Ingrid Casares**, Andre Leon Talley, designers Isaac Mizrahi and Gianni Versace, **Naomi Campbell**, **Diana Ross**'s daughter Tracy, **Rosie O'Donnell**, **Christopher Ciccone**, and DJ/remixer Junior Vasquez (Secret).

For both 1992/93 and 1993/94, she hosted at her **Miami** mansion; the former a "foodless fiesta" and the latter an elaborate affair catered by restaurateur Larry Forgione.

New York: The early years.
A breathtakingly brunette Madonna modeled vintage
clothing for **The Village Voice** in 1980 and 1981.

Photographer Fred Seidman was paid "$35 or so" for providing a girl in retro couture, and Madonna used the stunning photos as headshots.

Madonna spent a surreal New Year's Eve 1989/90 at artist Francesco Clemente's party, where she, **Warren Beatty**, and poet Allen Ginsberg discussed the West's exploitation of the Eastern European work force. Ginsberg had previously introduced Madonna to controversial writer and beat icon William S. Burroughs.

New Year's Eve 1988/1989 was less fun: Madonna allegedly spent it being **assault**ed by **Sean Penn**.

SEE ALSO: ALCOHOL

"To my eternal shame, I didn't ask her if she'd spent New Year's Eve trussed up like a turkey."

—Vicki Woods, *Vogue*, 1989

New York City: Madonna referred to it as "the center of the world" in 1987. New York has been her adopted **home**town since July 1978, when she arrived with $35 in her pocket and told the cab driver to take her where all the action was. She wound up nearly penniless in Times Square.

Madonna has an apartment in New York where she spends most of her free time.

"Coming to New York was the bravest thing I'd ever done. My goal was to conquer the city, and I feel I have. I can't believe how frightened I was when I look back on it, but I was."

—Madonna, 1986

nicknames: Besides the many **aliases** used to keep her movements secret, Madonna has had several notable nicknames in her life. Earliest was "Little Nonni," which her family called her as a baby. Upon learning to speak, her nickname became "Mouth." The first nickname she invented for herself was "Mudd" in Junior High.

Madonna called **Sean Penn** "Pal" and he called her "Bud" when they were doing *Goose and Tom-Tom* in October 1986. Penn also went along with her desire to go by literary nicknames like "Daisy" for Daisy Miller and "Kit" for Kit Moresby, tattooing the letters of the former on the toe-ends of one foot. Together, they

were dubbed "the Poison Penns" for their press-*un*friendly attitude, and also "S & M" by friends.

Madonna concocted an entire persona, **"Dita Parlo,"** for her *Sex* book, and even signed her name "Dita" for a while, including on her notorious hate **fax** to Joe Roth.

Madonna's longest-lasting nickname is simply "Mo," which has followed her throughout her life. Against her wishes, the world press refers to her as the **"Boy Toy"** and the **"Material Girl,"** but worse are the British media, who call her "Maddy," "Mads," and even (impossibly) "*Madge.*"

Clue: When you are first introduced to Madonna, don't say, "Nice to meet ya, *Madge.*"

"Nightline": In one of her most infamous **TV** appearances, Madonna went head-to-head with Forrest Sawyer on "Nightline" in December 1990 to discuss the **censorship** issues behind **MTV**'s banning of her **"Justify My Love" video**. She wore a severe, high-buttoned black blouse, her honey-blonde **hair** tastefully upswept, and did her very best to defend her **art**istic integrity as well as to champion the cause of less-restrictive programming of erotic material.

Madonna's sincerity was obvious, but her legendary anti-alacrity with words, her frequent "*you know*"s and "*okay?*"s, and her assertion that crawling under a chair in her **"Express Yourself" video** wasn't demeaning because, "I crawled under my own chair, okay?" made her seem less intelligent than she is.

The money shot of the program was toward the end, when Sawyer pointed out that losing MTV exposure had helped make her video into an even bigger money-maker as a video single. Madonna just smiled and cracked, "Yeah—so lucky me."

"It was very **nerve**-wracking because the interviewer was in another state. I would hear his question in my earphone, but everything was delayed. So when I answered him five minutes later, it sounded like I was retarded."

—Madonna, 1991

Nightporter, The: Stylish S&M-themed film to which **"Justify My Love"** and *Sex* owe their visual sensibility. As early as 1984, way before Madonna went from tease to **sex** activist, she was raving to the British teenybop magazine *Record*, "Oh my God! . . . What an incredible movie! . . . Just like *Salo* . . . absolutely sick! *The Nightporter* touches on a subject people don't like to talk about—that people are drawn to things that cause them pain. They *want* it."

No Entiendes Cabaret: Madonna's first-ever performance of her solo act was at this eclectic, neopunk variety show staged at **Danceteria** by promoter Haoui Montaug in 1981. The translation is: "You Don't Understand" Cabaret—an echo of Madonna's **excuse** that her harshest critics don't "get" what she's doing.

nudity: Uli Edel said it best (if not properly) when describing Madonna's nude **sex** scenes for *Body of Evidence*: "It was no problem for Madonna to pose without dresses."

From all accounts, Madonna has always been very comfortable with her body. As a kid, she and a pal named Carol went to church naked under their raincoats.

She was a skinny artist's model during her early days in **New York**, posing for photographers who later capitalized by selling their photos to **Penthouse** and **Playboy**, and marketing posters and prints of their handiwork. She wasn't paid very much for the nude modeling ($25–30 per session) or for the tons of nudity she provided in her underground film debut *A Certain Sacrifice*, but she had the sense to turn down a $1.2-million offer to pose nude for *High Society* magazine, which later ran secondhand nudes under the headline MADONNA SHOWS YOU HER **PUSSY**!

Though she showed plenty of skin (including some in a 1985 *Rolling Stone* **fashion** layout, where her breasts are visible through a lacy top), she didn't allow herself to be photographed nude again until she flashed a breast for Helmut Newton and *Vanity Fair* at Small's K.O. Bar in Los Angeles in 1990.

Since then, she has appeared in a diaphanous garment in **Dick Tracy**, topless in **Truth or Dare**, fully nude in **Body of**

"When I modeled nude for **art** classes, I felt like I was being really feminine. . . . It was em**power**ing for me to take my clothes off and then to put my clothing back on and go home and carry on with my day and not feel like I lost any dignity or self-esteem. It made me think of my body as a work of art."

—Madonna, 1994

·

"I was really naive and I read *The Village Voice* and it said DANCERS WANTED and I was a dancer at the time . . . and I thought, 'God, a hundred bucks a night! That's good money.' So I'd go to these agencies and these big, fat, disgusting, bald men would be in these offices and they'd say, 'Okay, take your clothes off.'"

—Madonna

·

"If you have such a lovely body, why not make the most of it? I was not the least bit appalled by her pictures in *Penthouse*. She never pretended to be Miss America."

—Helen Gurley Brown, publisher of *Cosmopolitan*, 1985

Evidence and *Dangerous Game*, in various stages of undress for **Herb Ritts** and **Steven Meisel** shoots, and, of course, naked as a jaybird all through *Sex*, for which she rode a bicycle topless and hitchhiked naked on the streets of **Miami**. Just prior to the release of the book, Madonna appeared in public in a breast-baring garment by **Jean-Paul Gaultier**.

Nudity is not always for **sex**ual titillation. The fact that Madonna made *Sex* proves as much; the real issue with that book was the incredible **power** behind the fact that so famous a woman—with so much to lose by posing nude—could strip, not for attention or praise or to turn men on, but because she felt like it. Nudity in the nineties is as much about power and liberation as it is about lust.

At this point, Madonna is synonymous with nudity, and critics have reacted by claiming that her now-familiar nude body is devoid of sexuality or eroticism. If anything, her body has *transcended* the merely prurient. Madonna's so much a part of our daily culture that her nipples are like familiar coworkers, or like old friends we expect to see frequently and welcome warmly when we do.

Nude photos of Madonna, like nudes of **Marilyn Monroe**, do not provoke nearly the amount of outrage as would nude shots of an unknown model. She is an icon, so everything that touches her becomes iconic. In this way, instead of being just another naked lady, Madonna nude also represents an evaluation of nudity as a concept. That doesn't mean you shouldn't get turned on, but it does mean you might consider why.

nuns: "When I was growing up, I wanted to be a nun. I saw nuns as superstars," she told *Rolling Stone* in 1991.

SEE ALSO: CATHOLICISM; CRUCIFIXES; POPE, THE

O'Brien, Glenn: The editor of *Sex* who somehow missed a glaring its/it's error halfway through the book (page 53), but whom Madonna still thanked for "teaching me how to spell." GOB knew Madonna from at least 1983 when she attended a party at his home with **Jean-Michel Basquiat**. As an editor at *Interview*, he chatted her up for a 1990 cover story.

"*I* love Madonna. I'd rather win a date with Goldie Hawn, but I love Madonna. She's saucy and professional. She's gesturally articulate."

—Glenn O'Brien, 1985

Ochs, Michael: A pal of Madonna's under whose name the Penns registered for their **honeymoon** at the Highlands Inn in Carmel-by-the-Sea, California.

O'Connor, Sinéad: Cantankerous Irish muse whose aching vocals and bald head made her famous, and whose politically-charged actions (refusing to allow the U.S. national anthem before her concert, tearing up a photo of **the Pope** on **"Saturday Night Live"**) have made her a much-reviled figure. She's so controversial even Madonna hates her, and has more than implied as much on several occasions. Despite the fact that SOC once picked **"Live to Tell"** as one of the ten best songs of 1986 for a teen magazine, Madonna savaged her in an early version of **Truth or Dare**. Her caustic remarks were edited before the film's final release. Later, she took SOC to task for tearing up the Pope (look who's talking!), saying, "I think there is a better way to present her ideas rather than ripping up an image that means a lot to other people." No word on whether Madonna was fellating a **crucifix** as she said this. Madonna parodied SOC again by tearing up a photo of Joey Buttafuoco on "SNL." One common denominator the divas share is Karl Geary, a former waiter at **New York**'s Siné Café who is a great friend of SOC's and who appeared in both the **"Erotica" video** and in *Sex*.

O'Donnell, Rosie: Madonna's beloved sidekick ever since they co-starred in *A League of Their Own*. ROD, a brassy stand-up-comic-turned-film star (*Sleepless in Seattle*, *The Flintstones*) and "Star Search" runner-up in 1985, met Madonna three weeks after seeing *Truth or Dare* and telling a companion she'd *never* meet her.

"*I* love, adore, and respect her. I feel a little sorry for her for all the **analysis** she goes through. . . . "

—Sinéad O'Connor on Madonna, October 12, 1992, hours before she was booed off the stage at a Bob Dylan tribute concert

·

"*S*he's about as sexy as a venetian blind."

—Madonna on Sinéad O'Connor, 1989

"*H*i, my mom died when I was little, too."

—Rosie O'Donnell to Madonna at their first meeting, 1991

·

"*S*he's asked me to cover a coupla her tunes, but I said, 'Hey, Mo, only *you* can sing like a virgin.'"

—Rosie O'Donnell, 1992

The two frequently socialize, and made a dual appearance on **Arsenio Hall**'s talk show in 1992.

They have lots in common: Both lost their **mothers** as children, both are named for their mothers, both are the eldest girls in their families, and both are adult survivors of **Catholicism**. It's a match made in heaven! Here's hoping she doesn't become the next **Sandra Bernhard**.

To Madonna: Don't piss off a comedienne or you'll end up as *material*, girl.

office: Comedienne Margaret Cho reported to *Detour* **magazine** that after a meeting at **Maverick** in L.A., she was allowed to roam around in Madonna's office. She said it was small, that it reminded her of the **"Express Yourself" video**, and that it had a really "tacky" magnetic paper-clip holder. "I twirled around and picked up the phone. It was weird, because I had been very business-like through the whole meeting, and then when I got in the office, I all but peed on the carpet because I was so excited."

"Oh Father" song: This dirgelike ballad "only" made it up to number 20 on the pop charts, shattering Madonna's record-breaking string of Top Ten singles. Still, the song packs an uncommon emotional wallop, sung from the perspective of a woman trying to forgive her abusive **father** after his **death**.

"Oh Father" video: An elaborate **black-and-white** approximation of Orson Welles's classic film *Citizen Kane*, right down to its use of complicated "deep focus" camera work and a wintery setting. In the video, Madonna plays a woman coming to terms with the abuse she's suffered at the hands of her **father**. The woman is also shown as a young girl who squirms at the sight of her **mother**'s corpse's sewn-together lips, and who eerily dances on her mother's grave.

The video includes a scene where Madonna's character is slapped by her **lover**, suggesting that abused children sometimes fall into abusive relationships as adults. That allusion is not made clear in the song, an example of how Madonna's **videos** are used less to illustrate than to re-imagine her **music**. "OF," intentionally or not, lends credence to reports that **Sean Penn** was violent with Madonna during their marriage.

Ono, Yoko: John Lennon's controversial widow threw a party in 1985 attended by Bob Dylan, **Andy Warhol**, David Bowie, and Madonna, where YO asked that all guests remove their shoes.

Madonna complied reluctantly, but piped up that she'd feel more comfortable shirtless than shoeless.

"Open Your Heart" song: An enormous number 1 hit in 1986, the song's success was doubly incredible since it was the fourth release from **True Blue** and the third to hit the top spot. A straightforward tale of a girl struggling to win the attention and affections of a self-involved guy, it's very "high school" and not one of Madonna's best-written songs. But therein lies a major part of the Madonna magic: She is capable of **singing** about a simple situation and imbuing it with heartfelt emotion.

Madonna's vocals are comparable to those on **"Papa Don't Preach,"** full of pleading and yearning and infectious urgency. The sleeve of the single represented a radical image change—a sultry photo of Madonna wearing a blue-black feathered skull-cap, a still from the unlikely **video** that accompanied it.

"Open Your Heart" video: One of Madonna's best, among her most provocative, and the first glimpse of how far she was willing to go to make cutting-edge artistic **videos**. The song is a cute **love**-angst number, but the video not only pushes the envelope, it addresses, **stamps**, and mails it.

Madonna plays a white-blonde peep-show stripper who is the object of admiration and—murkily—**love** for a young boy, played by **Felix Howard**. The boy falls in love with the apparent **glamor** of the stripper's life, caressing her image on a poster in front of the strip joint and even mimicking how he imagines she dances for the men inside.

Meanwhile, the stripper is performing in a gold-studded bustier, strutting and dancing with a chair for a prop. Most **shocking** is the view we are afforded of the show's audience, ensconced in booths. Among others, we see a grinning cowboy, a pair of beatific sailor twins who watch with hands clasped and heads pressed together, and a lesbian in male **drag**. As her act comes to an end, there is even a shot that clearly suggests a man reassembling his clothes, as if he'd just been **masturbating**.

For all the raunchy elements, the video, directed by French photographer **Jean-Baptiste Mondino**, is too stylized to be prurient, which is precisely the point. When the stripper emerges from the theater, her **hair** is tousled and she looks like a little boy herself. She chastely **kisses** her young admirer, who had dozed while waiting for her to finish, and the two **dance** off together, playing like children.

Though there were indignant whispers that the video pushed **pedophilia** at the time, it's pretty clear that the boy-child is

"*Extraordinarily provocative.* In a brisk, haiku-like four minutes and twenty-two seconds, 'Open Your Heart' presents Madonna as every adolescent boy's wildest, sweetest fantasy. It's a tiny, comic, **sexy** classic."

—Vincent Canby, *The New York Times*, 1987

heroine-worshiping the stripper—coveting her feminine allure, even—a phase common in boys. That the stripper's "real" persona is that of an androgyne rather than a siren only underscores the false allure of the strip show and the artifice of performance as opposed to the genuine feelings of the boy. Just to blur the line between **acting** and real life, the stripper's name is "Madonna."

For her part, Madonna said "OYH," shot in Los Angeles's Echo Park, reminded her of her days on **New York**'s Lower East Side when she would try to overcome the race barrier and make friends with her young Latino neighbors.

The innocence of the video remains untarnished in light of a scene in *Sex* where **"Dita"** professes her penchant for the very young, even describing her seduction of a willing Latino adolescent on the Lower East Side.

opportunism: A hallmark of early criticism of Madonna was the accusation that she had "used" her boyfriends to achieve success, since she had dated the head of her first band (**Dan Gilroy**), her most important early collaborator (**Steve Bray**), the DJ who brought her to **Sire** (**Mark Kamins**), and her best-known remixer (**Jellybean**). However, these relationships all seem to have been genuine, if advantageous, as the men themselves (except Gilroy, who hasn't gone on record) will admit. Madonna was surrounded by people in the industry she sought entry to, dated some of them, and didn't let any advice or knowledge they had go to waste.

"*T*o me the definition of being an opportunist is someone who seizes the moment and gets the most out of what they can, and certainly never having the intent of hurting anyone."

—Madonna, 1987

orange: According to astrologer Daphne Weld Nichols in *Star* magazine, this is Madonna's personal color, corresponding with her personal number, 2. Oranges "like to seek out as much **beauty** as possible in life, but are also materialistic and moody."

Sorry, Madonna, but Mel Gibson is a fellow orange.

orgy: In *A Certain Sacrifice*, Madonna's character "Bruna" owns a pack of **sex** slaves, and in one climactic scene, they pleasure her from all angles as she writhes ecstatically on the floor. Much later, on **The Girlie Show tour**, after a piece depicting the *joie de vivre* of the gay club scene in the seventies, things wound down into an amazingly erotic implied orgy, with male and female

members of Madonna's troupe simulating a slow, sensual, mutual exploration of each other that appeared loose enough to seem unchoreographed.

Oscars: Madonna attended the Oscars in 1991, sitting front and center with her escort, **Michael Jackson**. The pair were dressed all in white, looking like **Japan**ese cartoons, with Madonna in an extremely low-cut Bob Mackie gown and 20 million dollars' worth of borrowed Harry Winston diamonds. She was there to see how her hit, *Dick Tracy,* fared and to perform Stephen Sondheim's nominated song, "Sooner or Later (I Always Get My Man)."

"A girl could get awfully . . . AWFUL . . . in this spotlight." Madonna at the 1991 Oscars.

Madonna's performance was one of the most exciting and well-received in the history of the Oscars. She emerged from a lift in the stage floor, slinkily removed a white glove, and launched into the single best live vocal performance she's ever given, belting the tune in tandem with a twenty-piece orchestra.

Midway through, she stopped the song to purr, "A girl could get awfully *awful* in this spotlight," and later mimicked **Marilyn Monroe** by cooing, "Talk to me General Schwarzkopf, tell me all about it, *oooh!*" At song's end, she vamped offstage, even shaking her rear at the audience. The votes had already been cast, and "Sooner or Later" took Best Original Song.

Madonna was visibly nervous at the start of her performance because a stage hand had told her that her microphone was malfunctioning, one of her earrings fell and caught in her **hair**, her breasts kept popping out at rehearsal so her nipples had been covered with concealer, and she was facing an audience of over a billion people.

But the **nerves** couldn't detract from a winning moment. Jeremy Irons apparently liked Madonna's performance—he **kiss**ed her when he won for Best Actor in *Reversal of Fortune*. That's probably because at the time he was set to play opposite Madonna in *Evita*.

Madonna had had an earlier run-in with the Oscars. She was

asked to present the award for Best Visual Effects in 1987, with clips from **"Material Girl"** used in the background. The response producer Samuel Goldwyn, Jr., got was that "Madonna is not a singer, but she's an actress and will only give a Best Acting award." The quote is probably poorly remembered, but you get the idea: "No thanks."

overexposure: As a woman who has been before the cameras and in our faces almost nonstop for over a dozen years, Madonna should be concerned about overexposure, right? Isn't it career **suicide** to "show too much"? Not in her opinion.

Madonna's critics can't resist offering advice on how best to prolong her career, or how to win favor with the public. Invariably, taking time off to allow her image to cool down is the first suggestion. This advice presumes that Madonna, long considered a shrewd marketer, goes out of her way to court **fans** and popularity. To the contrary, Madonna creates impulsively and is then marketed by **business** entities around her. She also creates *compulsively,* so despite warnings that there is such a thing as too much of a good thing, she continues to work, continues to move about in public, without a care in the world.

Q: "Do you worry about being overexposed?"
A: "Only at the gynecologist's."

—Madonna to *YM*, 1993

·

"*I*'m sick of celebrities. . . . I can't even bear to say their names out loud. Read my lips: The one who shaved her armpits and got married under a helicopter attack. . . . You know who they are—overexposed, almost generic faces who have become as predictable as winter's first set of chapped lips."

—John Waters, *Crackpot: The Obsessions of John Waters*, 1987

In 1991, she made **Truth or Dare**, which should have destroyed any lingering doubts about her lack of a commitment to maintaining any sense of a cobwebby "star mystery." Her harnessing of the **power** of **nudity** also contradicts standard notions of how far is too far.

Though **Sex** enraged many, and though the logical thing to do after **Body of Evidence** flopped would have been to take a **vacation** from the media, Madonna instead launched a tour. Only three months after **The Girlie Show** drew to a close, she was back with the hit song and **video "I'll Remember."**

Though Madonna will undoubtedly sink from the public eye for a period of time at some point, she's proven that she doesn't *have to,* and that she doesn't, for better or for worse, even think in those terms.

overhead: *Entertainment Weekly* in 1993 calculated Madonna's overhead for living expenses at a reasonable $377,012 per year, including: $52,000 for a cook, $182,500 for clothes, $35,880 for a **personal trainer**, $21,185 for jewelry, $832 for Evian, and a mere $41,840 for shoes.

Haven't we all seen this beautiful publicity photo a million times?

Pacentro: Italian village sixty miles northeast of Rome on the Pescara River, where Madonna's paternal **grandparents** (Gaetano and Michelina Ciccone) were born and raised, and where Madonna met with relatives who were complete strangers while on her **Who's That Girl tour** in 1987.

The older relations were not impressed. "That girl sings, dances, and shows her thighs. . . . No Madonna, she! The devil is more like it!" grumped one old geezer, and Madonna's own great-aunt seethed, "The girl is a singer, just a singer. In my times we didn't behave like that." Scratch **"Keep It Together"**: sometimes, it's better not to forget that your family is *fool's* gold.

Paglia, Camille: The Madonna of **Academia**, author of *Sexual Personae* and *Sex, Art, and American Culture*, and professor of humanities at the University of the Arts in Philadelphia.

CP, a radical intellectual whose writings are among the most consistently provocative in her field, believes **feminism** has come to consist of Stepford Wives, that the animal **sex**uality of men is to be admired, and that date **rape** is a joke. She leads the faction of academics who feel Madonna and her phenomenon are worthy of rigorous **analysis**.

Though she viewed Madonna as a polymorphously perverse goddess (and is among the few who realize that Madonna never does anything *only* for publicity), her estimation of Madonna's wit and vision has faded—she intelligently trashed *Sex* in *Us* magazine and has no use for Madonna's occasional brattiness. More infuriating to CP is Madonna's refusal to meet with her, as Madonna believes CP just wants to sleep with her.

Madonna wisely realizes CP has overbilled her from the beginning: CP may be exactly correct in her analysis of the effect of the Madonna zeitgeist, but Madonna knows or at least senses that she, as a *person*, could never live up to Paglia's theories on Madonna the Phenomenon.

"Papa Don't Preach" song: Some of the strongest vocals Madonna ever

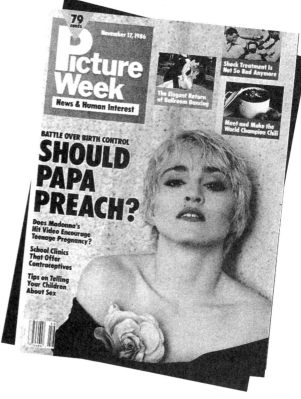

"*M*adonna and I are workaholics, okay. We are **drug**-free, okay. We are strong women who have projected our hallucinatory, pornographic visions to the world, okay. . . . It's like she needs me to open up her life, I'm telling you. She needs help. Because all she ever sees are people in the performing arts. You know, there's no substance."

—Camille Paglia, 1992

.

"*I*'ve heard her say things under the guise of being adoring that make it very clear that she doesn't get me at all. Sometimes I think she's full of shit."

—Madonna on Camille Paglia, 1992

recorded appear on her first politically controversial song, the second single and second number 1 hit from *True Blue* (1986).

The song is sung from the perspective of a pregnant teenager pleading with her **father** not to preach at her, but to listen and offer rational advice. She does assert that she's keeping her "baby," an ambiguous phrase that could refer to the boyfriend her father hates, or to her fetus.

Planned Parenthood and other abortion-rights groups (including the National Organization of Women [NOW]) blasted the song for encouraging **pregnancy**, but "PDP" does no such thing; because Madonna sings it as a teenaged girl, the defiance and the **shock**ing naïveté regarding how well things will work out are expected.

Madonna is not saying she believes things will always work out for pregnant

"*T*o me, the song speaks to a serious subject with a sense of urgency and sensitivity in both the lyrics and Madonna's rendition. It also speaks to the fact that there's got to be more support and more communication in families about this problem, and anything that fosters that I applaud."

—Tipper Gore

·

"*T*he reality is that what Madonna is suggesting to teenagers is a path to permanent poverty."

—Alfred Moran, Planned Parenthood

"'*P*apa Don't Preach' is Madonna's finest three minutes, not merely because it addresses teen pregnancy but because it suggests that a portion of the blame rests on parents' reluctance to discuss, not lecture about, **sex**."

—Joyce Millman, *Boston Phoenix*

·

"*J* give Madonna a hard time because I have a problem with 'Papa Don't Preach.' Not only does she tell young girls to have children, she tells them they can keep their girlish figures afterward."

—Sandra Bernhard, 1987

teens—the teenager of the song is arguing with her father that *her* boyfriend and *her* situation will be different . . . even though we know probably neither will.

"Papa Don't Preach" video: Shot on Staten Island in **New York**, this illustration of one of Madonna's signature songs features her best silent **acting** in a **video**. The then twenty-eight-year-old singer passes herself off convincingly as a sixteen-year-old pregnant teen, emoting to great effect as she bites the bullet and tells her **father** of her surprise **pregnancy** by a boyfriend he had told her not to hang out with.

Madonna's character is a working-class girl, cheesily attired in an ITALIANS DO IT BETTER T-shirt, and wearing a short, cute, pixie haircut. Before she tells her father, there is a striking shot of Madonna walking with determination up a huge outdoor stone staircase, from which the camera springs outward to pan the neighborhood.

Interspersed with the common scene and, intentionally or not, successfully removing Madonna from her character, are breathtaking shots of a white-blonde Madonna in a form-fitting black leotard and bustier, sporting orange-red lipstick. She performs with gusto, dancing archly and showing the strain of the song. "PDP" was the launch of Madonna's first major "new **look**," after slimming down and blonding up.

An annoyed Madonna, caught after the filming of the "Papa Don't Preach" video, 1986.

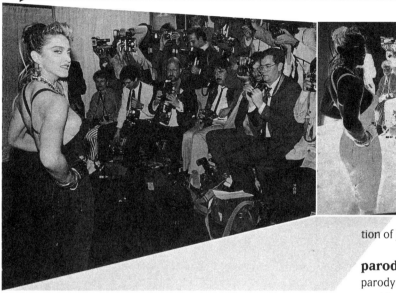

paparazzi: Italian word meaning "vampires." (Just kidding.)

Paparazzi are those wily shutterbugs who chase after celebrities for all those fabulous candid shots we **love**. Some paparazzi are good, honest, hardworking folks who never pester stars unnecessarily, and even get to be on friendly working terms with them. Others are so consumed by their lust for the perfect shot they will stop at nothing.

Paparazzi have been known to follow Madonna, chanting epithets at her to provoke a great visual response, a ploy that is partially responsible for **Sean Penn**'s violent behavior toward them during his **marriage** to Madonna. During the feeding frenzy for photos of Madonna and Penn in **London** in 1987, paparazzo Dave Hogan was injured by Madonna's car. Penn personally manhandled Vinnie Zuffante while spitting on Anthony Savignano.

"*P*hotographers are always scaring me! Every time I go out they're waiting for me. . . . All of a sudden they jump out from behind a tree. I have to deal with that constant fear. It takes me at least an hour to calm down from that **shock** every time it happens."

—Madonna, 1986

.

"*T*hey treat her like wild game."

—Joseph Blasioli, director of *Blast 'Em*

Still, when they behave professionally, you can't blame paparazzi for being persistent—great shots of major celebrities like Madonna can earn them thousands of dollars, both for initial and reprint sales.

Parlo, Dita: Madonna's infamous persona for *Sex* and **"Erotica"** was a gravel-voiced, jaded dominatrix named "Dita Parlo" who was willing to give lessons on **fuck**ing. The name was lifted from a real woman, a German actress (1906–71) who starred in French film classics like Jean Vigo's *L'Atlante* and Jean Renoir's *Grand Illusion*. She might've crossed over to the U.S., but her proposed big break (in the never-made Orson Welles film adaptation of Joseph Conrad's *Heart of Darkness*) never materialized.

parody: You know you're important when someone sees fit to parody you. Madonna must be the most important woman in the world, then, because parodies of her abound.

In response to **Truth or Dare**, **Julie Brown** came up with a hilarious spoof, *Medusa: Dare to be Truthful*, and *Musician* **magazine** proposed a **stamp** featuring Madonna fellating a bottle of Evian.

Sex provided more fertile ground for send-ups. Ann Magnuson parodied it before it was even published, appearing on and in *Paper* magazine nude, straddling a corpse whose toe tag is clearly visible. *Entertainment Weekly* had **Anna Nicole Smith** pose with Larry "Bud" Melman next to a phony page from the book, describing how as a little girl in confession, Madonna hadn't done anything naughty, so she invited the padre to tell her what badness she *could* be committing.

Jackie Mason started (but never finished) a send-up that would have featured him and two of his friends parading shirtless, Matt Groening's "Akbar and Jeff" characters offered a book of "grim and joyless pseudo-sadomasochism," and **"Saturday Night Live"** imagined Charlton Heston reading the audio version of *Sex* with Al (*Screw* magazine) Goldstein describing the pictures.

More viciously, Diesel Jeans and Workwear designed an ad that offered a **sex** book designed to "turn any idiot into a star or make fading stars shine new again." After her 1994 **David Letterman** appearance, a Chicago restaurant called Dixie Q commissioned a life-sized Madonna made out of . . . *ham*.

Most of Madonna's actions are so different from the typical star's that they become the subject of proportionately grandiose dis-

cussion, praise, and criticism. As long as Madonna matters, parodies—which contain elements of all three—will proliferate.

Passion Pack: The Queen of Promotion had nothing to do with this one, a selling tool provided by MGM/UA Home Video to help move copies of the R-rated and unrated (NR) versions of *Body of Evidence* when it hit stores in June 1993.

The pack is a sturdy cardboard box filled with a candle and holder, handcuffs, plastic champagne glass, and a plastic champagne bottle filled with pink bubble bath, whose label depicts Madonna on the verge of the big O.

The movie sucks, but the Passion Pack is a highly-prized collectible.

Paterson, Vincent: The choreographer of Madonna's tours, including the precocious **Blond Ambition,** whose every tiny movement was choreographed. "Safe **art** is dull art, it's entertainment," VP said at the time; "Madonna's an artist."

Pauley, Jane: Chilly NBC News correspondent who in 1987 interviewed Madonna on the "Today" show to promote the **"Who's That Girl" song, video, album, tour,** and **film.**

Liz Rosenberg later confessed she'd goofed, and that the interview came off like the meeting of the "ice maidens." Madonna never seemed more remote, looking untouchably beautiful, dead white and platinum-coiffed. She responded very guardedly to JP's generally skeptical line of questioning. At the end of the three-part interview, JP's summary was the brittle one-liner: "A self-made woman."

Still, the interview is priceless for Madonna's foot-in-the-mouth branding of close-to-**home**town Bay City as "a smelly little town in Northern Michigan." (The interview was telecast to coincide with her arrival in Bay City, where she apologized and reaffirmed her love for the place.)

The tensest moment came when JP implied that Madonna's success may have made her forget some of the "little people." Madonna asked JP if she herself still called and wrote and sent Christmas cards to everyone she'd met along the way to her own success. We never got an answer to that one, but we also never got a Christmas card from Jane that year.

pedophilia: Madonna has **flirt**ed with underaged **sex** in her **work.** Her **kiss,** planted on the lips of young **Felix Howard** in the **"Open Your Heart"** video was done with the knowledge that her sexual image would invite speculation as to the chastity of the smooch, and in *Sex,* Madonna/**"Dita"** goes so far as to opine that

"Sex with the young can be fun." How fun, we're not sure, but certainly *too* young.

A coinciding cover story in **Vanity Fair** featured Madonna as a dewy pubescent in stockings and perched on various kiddie contraptions, a spread that some deluded critics likened to pedophilia, despite the fact that Madonna was thirty-four, and that women (and men) have always had the option of dressing or behaving like the very young to tease and arouse their **lovers.** It's called fantasy, and it has nothing to do with pathological or abusive sexual behavior.

In real life, Madonna has either indulged in younger men or her sexually-charged image has led reporters to misconstrue two of her friendships: A twenty-six-year-old Madonna was linked with **Bobby Martinez,** a decade her junior, and a thirty-five-year-old Madonna was linked with fifteen-year-old **Rodrigo Freire,** *two* decades her junior.

Penn, Sean: She always gets her man, but she doesn't always want him once she's got him.

They met at SP's request on the set of her **"Material Girl" video** on a day when Madonna also first met **Elizabeth Taylor** and chicken entrepreneur Frank Perdue, then spent their first **date** at **New York**'s **Private Eyes club.**

After a whirlwind courtship, Madonna married SP on her **birthday** in 1985, launching one of the unlikeliest and stormiest pairings in Hollywood history. Madonna enjoys the spectacle of performance, Penn the quietude of being the lone wolf. Madonna is a liberal provocateuse, and was an early proponent of gay and **AIDS** rights—Penn is a well-documented homophobe. Madonna is a lover, Penn is a fighter. As the lover herself explains, "Opposites attract."

Together, they were an irresistible mark for **paparazzi,** some of whom SP brawled with: He slugged and expectorated on Anthony Savignano, and he was sentenced to sixty days in jail in 1987 for beating up Jeffrie Klein, a Polaroid-wielding extra on his film *Colors.* The latter incident was complicated by his arrest for charges of reckless driving under the influence in his '83 Chevy Impala. SP served five days, filmed scenes of his **director**-father Leo Penn's film *Judgment in Berlin* in West Germany, then returned to serve twenty-eight more days, getting the rest off for good behavior.

More disturbing to Madonna had been SP's attack on her friend David Wolinski at **Helena**'s in 1986, when Wolinski kissed Madonna hello. SP's outburst cost him a $1,000 fine and probation, which he violated when he brawled with Klein.

By late 1987, the marriage was obviously coming undone. Penn showed up to spend Thanksgiving with Madonna after being absent for days, only to find she was spending it with her sister

"*E*very woman wants to be Lolita for a year."

—Madonna, 1986

"Sean . . .
Sean. "

Melanie in Brooklyn. Madonna filed for **divorce**, but they made up until an alleged **assault** led to her refiling at the tail end of 1988. The marriage had lasted about three and a half years.

Since the Penns' breakup, the **tabloids** can't stop predicting a reunion. Fueling predictions was Madonna's own frank admission of continuing feelings for SP. In *Truth or Dare*, when asked who the **love** of her life has been, she sighs wistfully and whispers, "Sean. . . . *Sean.*"

Before Madonna, SP had been linked to several famous faces, including Susan Sarandon and Bruce Springsteen's sister Pam. After Madonna, he set up house with *Princess Bride* starlet **Robin Wright**, with whom he has two children, and later dated Naomi Campbell. SP deserves "credit" for introducing Madonna to two people with whom she'd form important relationships: **Sandra Bernhard** and **Warren Beatty**.

Among his film projects are *Bad Boys*, *The Falcon and the Snowman*, *Carlito's Way*, and his directorial debut, *The Indian Runner*. Before **Jean-Baptiste Mondino** stepped in, Penn had been slated to direct **"Open Your Heart."**

"*H*e's wild. . . . He'll probably die young. I feel like he's my brother or something."

—Madonna, 1985

•

"*S*ean is my hero and my best friend."

—Madonna, 1985

•

"*I* wish I had **AIDS** so I could shoot you. I wouldn't do it fast, but slow, from the toes up."

—Sean Penn to paparazzo, 1985

•

"*M*ost passionate people are headstrong. We were two fires rubbing up against each other. It's exciting and difficult."

—Madonna, 1989

•

"*E*very once in a while I wake up and go, 'My God! I was married, and he was the **love** of my life.' It is like a **death** to deal with."

—Madonna, 1990

•

"*S*ean really wanted a wife, someone to be more nurturing than I was prepared to be. I was fighting that conventional idea of how a woman behaves, and I realized it wasn't possible for me to have a relationship if the man isn't in touch with his feminine side."

—Madonna, 1991

•

"*I* still love him, but I have to be realistic: He has his own family now. I don't think you could spend many years of your life with someone and then, even if you're not together, just stop having feelings for them. I'll probably love him till I die—I'm afraid I give away my heart easily."

—Madonna, 1991

Penthouse: Men's **magazine**—the dirtier **Playboy**, if you will—that in 1985 unveiled six-year-old nude photos of Madonna by the late photographer Bill Stone. Publisher Bob Guccione's announcement that he would publish the first set of Madonna nudes alerted *Playboy*, which in turn beat *P* to the newsstands with its own selection.

Guccione claimed to have offered Madonna a million dollars to pose in the buff shortly before he went to press with the first nudes.

Madonna later complained that he had snidely sent her volatile husband **Sean Penn** copies of a 1987 *P* follow-up issue featuring more nudes. Penn was in jail at the time.

Pepsi: Though Madonna drinks Diet Coke, she signed a lucrative $5 million deal to star in three Pepsi TV **commercials** in 1989. Pepsi was also to have sponsored her **Blond Ambition tour**. The first commercial—a lush, **black-and-white** fairy tale of an eight-year-old girl making a wish at her **birthday** party that she could trade places with Madonna—featured Madonna with a natty blonde streak through her back-to-brunette **hair**, dancing down the halls of a **Catholic** school, and urging consumers to "Make a Wish." It is a stunning example of TV advertising, the perfect blend of **art** and commerce, and a rare example of Madonna presented as a wholly sweet force of nature.

It was not long-lived. The commercial was set to the strains of **"Like a Prayer,"** Madonna's first single off the eponymous album, and represented the listening audience's first exposure to the song. It was a first: a song launched in a commercial. After weeks of hype and expensive teaser ads featuring clips of the commercial playing in the desolate Australian outback (actually

Madonna frolics on Interview in 1989, sporting the same blonde streak from her Pepsi commercial.

*"*The story is definitely worthy of the attention of the proletariat."

—*The Revolutionary Worker* on Pepsigate

*"*Pepsi made the wrong conclusion. There is certainly no better time—and there may never be a better opportunity—for responsible advertisers to stand up to irresponsible boycotters. For starters, the spot in question is testimony to all that's good in advertising. It's a `Mean Joe Greene' for little girls, a media `must-see' for impossible-to-reach teens. It's soft-sell imagery that hits hard, a hometown message that works around the globe."

—Richard Morgan, *Adweek*

Arizona) to an audience of a single aborigine, the two-minute commercial aired only twice—during TV's then-biggest hit, "The Cosby Show"—before Pepsi canned it.

At least 250 million viewers got a glimpse; but because Madonna's own **music video** for the song featured such unpalatable themes as miscegenation, and harnessed sacred **Catholic** images for its own purposes, conservatives led by the Reverend Donald Wildmon's **American Family Association** successfully pressured Pepsi to drop their association with Madonna under threat of a nationwide boycott of all Pepsi products.

Madonna was released from her contract, the other two proposed commercials were scrapped, and she kept her fee. PepsiCo of Canada, however, continued showing the commercial throughout the summer of 1989.

Perea, Michael: Along with "Elbee," one of Madonna's **Virgin Tour** dancers who got to wear all those fabulous brocade jackets and do calisthenics with Madonna across the globe. He sometimes spells his name "Mykal."

Perry, Luke: "Beverly Hills 90210" star with an enormous forehead.

He was Madonna's **date** for the evening when the American Foundation for **AIDS** Research (AmFAR) gave her its **Award** of Courage in 1991. LP had the honor of handing the statuette to her. Later, when asked about a possible Perry affair, Madonna sniffed that she doesn't go out with people who pose with guns on magazine covers, referring to the *Vanity Fair* featuring LP cuddling up to a gun.

perseverance: "I went through a lot of pain when I was a very young girl and the only way to get through it was to tell myself that this was an education; this was a test for me. If I could get through this, then I would be rewarded in the end; when I'm older, I would get all the things I wanted." —Madonna, 1984

personal trainer: Madonna has worked with several to help keep her body lean and mean. First and most famous was her partnership with dashing Rob Parr for five years from 1985. In 1990, **Liz Rosenberg** said "All people want to know is about that body. How did that body happen? On the seventh day, **God** created Rob Parr."

Since then, Madonna has switched to Ray Kybartis. It's Kybartis who's most responsible for her more recent, over-the-top muscles. For aerobic enhancement, Madonna has also worked sporadically with **New York**–based trainer Pat Manocchia.

Pettibone, Shep: Hot remixer who's jazzed up Madonna tunes from his work on *You Can Dance* to his classic mixes of *"Express Yourself."* SP cowrote most of *Erotica* with Madonna, with whom he also shares production credits.

Madonna has said she likes the work he does on her **music**, but doesn't care for mixes he's done for other divas like **Janet Jackson**, Kim Wilde, and Cathy Dennis.

*Madonna and Shep Pettibone en route to his apartment during the **Erotica** album sessions, summer 1992.*

Philbin, Regis: Jaunty daytime talk-show cohost of "Regis and Kathie Lee" who welcomed Madonna on the show in 1991 to promote *Truth or Dare*. RP—a close pal of **Warren Beatty**'s—interviewed Madonna on top of a building in Los Angeles. She arrived in a black negligee for the segment, which was filmed in **black-and-white**. The gown echoed the theme of anti-**privacy**, the film stock used the device of "black-and-white = the personal" that

were hallmarks of the movie, and RP's **flirt**acious banter with Madonna helped present her as a **glamor**ous siren.

Madonna later dubbed him "really sweet" for his effort, but there was nothing sweet in Kathie Lee Gifford's expression when the segment was introduced.

phone calls: Madonna usually makes all her personal and **business** calls for the day between 9 and 11 A.M.

piano: Though she doesn't play now, Madonna sulked through a year of tortuous piano lessons as a kid until her teacher made her quit because she kept ditching the lessons.

Pioneer: Electronics corporation that sponsored Madonna's **Blond Ambition Tour** after **Pepsi** got religion.

***Playboy*:** The men's **magazine** that featured **Marilyn Monroe** as its first cover girl and which everyone reads "for the articles" beat *Penthouse* to the punch with their issue of Madonna nudes in 1985 . . . by one day. *Playboy*'s nudes were by Martin Schreiber and Lee Friedlander.

*Madonna made the **cover** of nearly every international Playboy as well as the American edition.*

playing the field: "The best thing about single life," she told *Harper's Bazaar* in 1984, "is there's always someone else. And, besides, I wouldn't wish being Mr. Madonna on anybody!" Next!

plays: Before she tackled Broadway as "Karen" in **David Mamet**'s *Speed-the-Plow*, Madonna was a stage star back at Rochester Adams High School. She had lead roles in their high school productions of *Cinderella*, *Godspell*, *The Wizard of Oz*, *My Fair Lady*, and *The Sound of Music*, and also appeared in more challenging fare like *Dark of the Moon* and *The Night Thoreau Spent in Jail*.

SEE ALSO: GOOSE AND TOM-TOM

poetry: Madonna is a poet, as are all songwriters (take away the **music** and indent, and **lyrics** become poems). She also offered some light erotic poetry in *Sex*. Her own favorite poets include Rainer Maria Rilke, James Ayce, and the late Charles Bukowski, whose gruff, cheerfully misogynist work rubbed off on her via **Sean Penn**.

But Madonna's very favorite poet is Anne Sexton, a somber word technician who committed **suicide** when Madonna was a young girl. "I worship her," she told *The Advocate* in 1991, and ended her "X-rated interview" with that **magazine** with a recitation of the Sexton poem "For John, Who Begs Me not to Inquire Further."

popcorn: Madonna's favorite snack, which she claims to eat all day long.

In 1986 she said that the one thing she missed most about America while filming scenes for *Shanghai Surprise* in the Orient was cheese popcorn, and designer **Milena Canonero** said that in order to keep her attention while fitting her with her *Dick Tracy* wardrobe she had to "hold on to her with popcorn and other goodies."

Madonna also admits to using popcorn to liven up meetings with industry executives. "I walk in there with my orange leggings and drop popcorn in my cleavage and then fish it out and eat it."

Pope, the: The most pious being on earth if you're **Catholic**, and not one to keep his opinions of Madonna to himself. After Madonna joked that "if the Pope wants to see me, he can buy tickets like everybody else," he preached against her **Blond Ambition tour**, branding it blasphemous and successfully dissuading thousands of **Italians** from attending her Rome shows in 1990.

"*J*'m convinced he has a sense of humor."

—Madonna of the Pope, 1989

·

"*J* ask you, fair-minded men and women of the Catholic church, come and see my show and judge it for yourself. . . . If you are sure I am a sinner, let whoever is without sin throw the first stone."

—Madonna at a Rome **press conference** in response to the Pope's statement against **Blond Ambition**, 1990

pornography: Literally, prurient material with no redeeming social value save for erotic titillation. Popularly, anything mildly dirty that you might find on European television but is likely to incite obscenity charges in the U.S.

Madonna, for her **sex**ual image, has been called pornographic from the earliest days of her *Like a Virgin* media saturation. "A porn queen on heat," one critic branded her, though at that point the most X-rated of her maneuvers was flashing a lacy bra under a cutoff T-shirt, or keeping her **eyes** half-shut while emoting desire. Typically, instead of retreating from the sexual element of her **work** to disavow such troubling criticism, Madonna turned up the heat. She continued looking (to quote her **"Nightline"** appearance) "like your typical bimbo," posed as a stripper in her **"Open Your Heart" video**, appeared nude (though cleverly concealed) and lapped milk from a bowl in **"Express Yourself,"** and appeared in sexually provocative roles in *Body of Evidence* and *Dangerous Game*.

With *Sex*, Madonna fully incorporated pornography into her work. She—and it's obviously more Madonna than Dita—argues in *Sex* that pornography is a healthy thing that does not degrade women, while at the same time saying she herself doesn't enjoy it because the artificiality of it "makes me laugh." Her critique of pornography represents only embryonic thought on the matter—theorizing that women who are involved in it don't have guns pointed at their heads—but it also makes an important statement about Madonna's outlook.

"*J* have never **masturbated** to pictures of naked people."

—Madonna, 1992

Madonna assesses the relative good of porn from the point of view of a person who can't conceive of being forced to do anything against her will. To illustrate the point, note that she used *Sex* to exploit pornography to em**power** herself, an ironic twist on how some feminists view pornography as an exploitative act against women.

In discussing *Sex*, Madonna told *Newsweek*—and she's clearly defining "pornography" as "obscene," as opposed to "erotic" material—that her definition of pornography is a snuff movie: an underground film where—supposedly—a kidnapped person is actually slaughtered just for the kicks of its viewers. Madonna uses snuff movies to indicate her limitations in *Sex* as well, saying she wouldn't want to see one because she "wouldn't want to watch anyone get really hurt"—cannily polarizing violence and **sex**, and *true* pain with her own *fantasy* of sadomasochism.

In October 1990, erotic "extra" actor Mike Rick tried to auction a 1978 hardcore porn video, allegedly starring Madonna getting it on in the john with two guys and with another woman. He wanted to start the bidding at over $50,000, but the tape's poor quality and the fact that the actress looked more like Chuck Connors scuttled plans for the auction, and for black-marketeering.

Madonna's favorite pornographic material (that presumably doesn't make her laugh) includes the blue writings of George Bataille, Anne Rice (who wrote S&M porn under the pen-name

"A. M. Roquelaure"), Margaret Atwood, Angela Carter, and Marguerite Duras (*The Lover* being Madonna's choice as the sexiest novel ever). She also adores the *Herotica* collections, Mary Gaitskill's *Two Girls, Fat and Thin*, and Vladimir Nabokov's infamous ode to cradle-snatching, *Lolita*.

SEE ALSO: FEMINISM

power: One of the hallmarks of Madonna's impact is her embodiment of power. Especially gripping to young women (and closet cases) in the mid-eighties was the notion that a woman, a physically *small* one at that, dressing and behaving independently, could catch the world's attention, make **music** and **videos** that dictated international popular culture, and be in complete control of all aspects of her **art**, career, and life. The fact that Madonna is a woman who has achieved power is behind readings that interpret her as necessarily "**feminist**."

Madonna's power in the recording industry has always been supreme, with a record-setting string of Top Ten and number 1 hits and albums that never fail to go multi-platinum, but it has increased with her tenure at **Maverick**. Now she not only dictates how popular music will sound, by launching influential hits of her own, she even has the power to sign and develop new acts like ultra-popular Candlebox.

In filmdom, Madonna flexed her power by demanding and receiving star vehicles that were still forthcoming even after her second and third films were major flops, and flexed it again by negotiating a $60-million multimedia deal that granted her CEO status in her own entertainment division. Her interest in any film project still draws attention to that **project**: It was her initial agreement to do *Boxing Helena* that brought that film to the public eye, and Madonna's interest in *Tank Girl* incited campaigns from other top actresses to play the juicy title role.

Madonna's power over the **fashion** world, in *haute couture*, the **clubs**, and on the streets, is undeniable. Her first, famous **Boy Toy look** launched a line of clothing and Madonnamania, with "**wanna-bes**" mimick-

"*W*e're tired of being good all the time. When you deprive women of any notion of threat, it pretty much puts them back in the Victorian Age. All innocent, and without power, except the power of being good."

—Margaret Atwood on Madonna's popularity, likening her to the female outlaw "Zenia" of her book, *The Robber Bride*, 1993

•

"*I* love the fact that she is a woman who is fearless of her own power."

—Mink Stole, 1993

•

"*P*ower is a great aphrodisiac, and I'm a very powerful person."

—Madonna, 1991

*Madonna and Child, as conceived by the **Italian artist** Antonio de Felipe.*

ing her appearance down to the last rubber bracelet and gooey **beauty mark**. When she cropped her **hair** and bleached it nearly white, the look immediately took over the sidewalks. **Jean-Paul Gaultier**'s designs for **Blond Ambition** were based on Madonna's own stick drawings, and he went on to make some of her ideas staples of his line. Even women who pay no attention to how Madonna looks end up being affected by her sense of style as they incorporate elements from the looks of women who do.

Madonna isn't afraid to use her power to promote her **work**, nor is she afraid to use it to promote awareness of issues close to her heart: **self-expression**, **sexual** freedom, and **AIDS** awareness. In her earliest **MTV** interview, Madonna said cheekily of her ambitions, "I want to rule the world." A short time later, she did.

Madonna's highest position on *Entertainment Weekly*'s "101 Most Influential People in Entertainment" list was number 10 in 1992, making her the highest woman on the list. By the very next year, after losing public favor with *Sex* and *Body of Evidence*, she had fallen off the fickle list completely. However, her ability to create influential and successful musical projects has not faltered, nor has her potential to bankroll films.

pregnancy: Though she admits to several **abortions**, Madonna has never been announced a pregnancy, and in fact has had to squelch **rumors** of little Madonnas more than once.

A month after her **wedding** to **Sean Penn**, she denied being pregnant during her opening monologue as host of "**Saturday Night Live**," using publicist **Liz Rosenberg** to issue further denials virtually every month of her marriage. Penn later admitted to *Fame* **magazine**, "I wanted to have a kid, she didn't." To make sure his next squeeze *did* want kids, he knocked her up before popping the question, then never married her at all.

Star magazine reported that Madonna was pregnant by ex–football pro Tony Longo in August 1989, so thoroughly detailing their visit to Dr. Walter F. Jekot's office for a test, they could have been reciting a case history. But, if she *was* pregnant, she made up her mind to *not* keep her baby.

The strongest phony rumors of "Madonna With Child" came in June 1993, when photos of her in an Adidas dress showed a slight belly and the press went wild. Who the **father** was supposed to have been, and how the **condom**-toting icon would have explained a surprise pregnancy are anyone's guesses. There *was* that coed pool party . . .

It's no secret that Madonna would like to become a **mother**, and some cynical media-watchers believe that motherhood would go a long way toward endearing Madonna to the heart of Middle America. They're absolutely right, but if Madonna endures a pregnancy and commits to motherhood, appeasing landlocked straight-and-narrows will be the last thing on her mind.

press conferences: Gone are the days when major stars call press conferences willy-nilly, ostensibly to address the press but actually to generate interest in themselves. Case in point is Madonna who, as the biggest star in the world and supposedly the most publicity-crazed, has called very few in her lengthy career.

Madonna and George Harrison ran a press conference in **London** in 1986 to diffuse media antipathy toward the "Poison Penns" whose exploits while filming **Shanghai Surprise** were threatening the film's production. Madonna appeared in costume as a missionary, nervously but charmingly answering a barrage of queries about the film's subject matter and purring to one reporter, who'd asked if Harrison would consider buying Madonna's recording contract, "You're a little troublemaker, aren't you?"

She held a terse press conference in Rome in 1990 immediately after deplaning, in order to appeal to **Catholics** not to heed the **Pope**'s call for a boycott of her **Blond Ambition tour**. The press and onlookers were so boisterous, she bitterly snapped that she would not speak without total silence, and peppered her prepared statement with commands in **Italian** to "Shut up!"

As early reviews excoriated **Body of Evidence** as Madonna's lowest moment on film, she canceled all her scheduled one-on-one interviews (some of which were with foreign journalists who'd traveled overseas to meet with her) in favor of a press conference.

When one reporter asked her about the flops in her past, she joked, "What, you want me to *name* them?" At the conference, she stood behind her films: "**Desperately Seeking Susan** is a good movie. **Dick Tracy** is a good movie. **Truth or Dare** is a good movie. And *Body of Evidence* is a good movie."

Madonna dislikes press conferences because they're **nerve**-wracking. Still, footage of her rare press conferences reveals that despite her unease, there's no more compelling viewing than the spectacle of a star speaking directly to her subjects.

Prince: Every star of any importance has crossed paths with Prince (or whatever he's calling himself this week), and, more than likely, has worked with him. Many have also slept with him. Though there was once the suggestion that pop's Prince and Queen had a brief fling after a dinner they shared at Yamashiro sushi restaurant in Los Angeles, it looks like Madonna is merely one of the millions who has had the good luck to work with the mysterious genius.

They met backstage at the 1985 American **Music Awards** and got together every once in a while in the hopes that they would collaborate. When plans to cowrite a musical fizzled, Prince visited Madonna after a performance of **Speed-the-Plow** and handed her some rough tapes of songs they'd recorded mostly via phone from opposite coasts.

The result was "Love Song," a funky little number on her **Like a Prayer album** which is a standout—a disturbing and tense song with a pair of vocals that sometimes seems to be coming from the same mouth. The harmonizing is perfect and Madonna's performance is extremely embittered-sounding, complementing Prince's defiant apathy. Madonna played the keyboards herself, which she felt contributed to the song's appealing strangeness. They coproduced "Act of Contrition," which Madonna sang and cowrote, and to which Prince lent some Jimi Hendrix—esque guitarwork.

"*T*ime to go visit the midget."

—Madonna to a *People* magazine reporter just before taking off for a meeting with Prince, 1985

In 1990, a year after the phenomenal success of Prince's "Batdance" single from the *Batman* soundtrack, Madonna turned in a similarly meandering and catchy movie song, "Now I'm Following You, Part II" from **I'm Breathless**. She was directly inspired by Prince's song, sampling dialogue from **Dick Tracy** and using distorted vocals and instrumentation.

Madonna has attended Prince's too-rare concerts, and was photographed at his March 24, 1993, performance at Radio City Music Hall, where she chatted amiably with fellow spectator Whitney Houston-Brown. This in spite of the fact that Madonna admires P's *older* stuff from *Purple Rain*, which she considers "the real shit." Madonna loathes his **videos**, which she brands "silly and cheap and below his ability."

Madonna has invoked Prince's name more than once as an excellent example of a **sex**ist double standard: Prince is a *man* doing virtually the same sexually-explicit performing that Madonna is doing, and yet receives little or no flack for his sexual tastes, provocative clothing, and X-rated stage persona.

Based on her few encounters with Prince, Madonna has described him as "very strange," refusing to elaborate, perhaps recognizing that the observation is self-explanatory. Some may think that's the pot calling the kettle black, but in reality, Prince *is* strange and Madonna just does strange things.

privacy: Unlike the stars of the Golden Age of Hollywood, who hid shamelessly behind stainless-steel images and the **power** of their studios, Madonna's private life is thoroughly vivisected by the press. Unlike many stars of today, who tremble at the appearance of any invasion of their cherished privacy, Madonna moves about with an amazing degree of freedom in public, shopping for **books** and **magazines,** seeing movies, and **club**bing despite the constant threat of being bogged down by clusters of **autograph** hounds and diehard **fans.**

Moreover, Madonna has been remarkably forthcoming about her personal history. She mentioned her **mother**'s untimely **death** in her first interviews in 1982 and 1983, has detailed her **first kiss,** first boyfriend, and personal opinions, has talked about such radically personal habits as picking her nose and, to **David Letterman,** peeing in the shower—the kinds of untidy realities that most nonstars wouldn't admit to their closest friends, much less announce to the planet. Madonna's motto seems to be that no matter how "private" the intricacies of her existence may seem, no amount of disclosure could ever reveal her true self.

She mined that vein to an extreme degree with **Truth or Dare,** about which she asserted that what's most revealing are the parts where she is *not* truthful. "Lies are telling," she claimed cryptically, leaving audiences and critics to paw through scenes of Madonna visiting and talking to her mother's grave, slurping soup while completely *sans* makeup, flashing the camera while her **father** and **stepmother** await her patiently in the next room, fellating a bottle of Vichy water, and being examined by a doctor.

Warren Beatty, Madonna's reluctant costar, acidly comments to the physician that Madonna doesn't see the point of existing off-camera, an oft-quoted observation that failed to see the irony in *Truth or Dare*: The star most devoured by the press was taking control of the situation, flaunting her unattractive

"*T*he biggest trade-off is just a lack of privacy, not being able to walk down the street without being bothered, my loss of anonymity. It's really weird."

—Madonna, 1989

.

"*I* still have my sanity. I'm willing to sacrifice my private life if it will change people's point of view about life and the phobias they have."

—Madonna, 1991

attributes (as well as unguarded, appealing moments) in scenes that would leave most of her peers ripe for blackmail.

Madonna further tested the concept of privacy by publishing a book of written and visual erotica, **Sex,** which marked the first time a star published sexually-explicit photos of herself. Madonna seemed to be saying, "I am public property right down to my short-and-curlies."

And yet—with her **overexposure**, with the true invasions of her privacy, which include covert publication of personal medical documents, sneaky photos of her cavorting in the nude with **John Enos** and **Ingrid Casares,** and publication of the contents of her **garbage** pail, as well as the self-invasions she has mounted in her **work**—Madonna is an enigma. We know nothing of the private Madonna because we only know what's she's been willing to tell us.

To help keep some things private (she hates having the **business** aspect of her career discussed), Madonna has all those around her sign privacy agreements, guaranteeing that the individual will not discuss his/her dealings with Madonna. All of her personal staff have signed them, and it will be interesting to see how they hold up in court if anyone decides to buck his or hers and squawk.

Private Eyes: Video club once situated at 12 West 21st Street that Madonna frequented during her early days in **New York.** It's the site of her first **date** with **Sean Penn.**

prized possessions: Madonna said in 1984 that her most prized possession was a photograph of her **mother** smiling and laughing when she was young.

But, a few years later, when asked what she'd rescue if her house were on fire, she said her Filofax, her **Frida Kahlo** self-portrait, and her **Lifecycle™.**

Maybe that picture of Mom is in a safe-deposit box.

Project X: Underground **magazine**, which for several issues ran full-page pleas to Madonna to support their hip subversion. They even thoughtfully provided a checklist for Madonna to use, ranging from "You're pretty cool, here's $50,000!" to "I'd rather die than give you one red cent for your faggy little magazine, and I might even sue you!"

projects: In the entertainment world, and especially in the world of multimedia artists like Madonna, the simple word "project" transmogrifies into a grandiose concept. A project becomes not only the film, **video,** song, or **book** on which the artist is **work**ing, but the often turbulent road from conception to retail, and involves all the bad press, gossip, hype, hard work, and good luck in between.

For Madonna, a project is rarely a single piece of work. She is famous for, among other things, launching poly-tiered projects whose pieces comment on, relate to, or negate each other: the

Who's That Girl film/soundtrack/tour is one; ***I'm Breathless/ Dick Tracy/*Blond Ambition** is another. But despite her stick-to-it–ness, even Madonna embarks on projects—almost exclusively in the world of film—that sink without a trace. Some of them are classic woulda/coulda/shoulda.

Before she became famous, she was turned down for a role in the "Fame" TV series (in which **Janet Jackson** cut her **acting** teeth) and the Lori Singer role in *Footloose*. In 1985, she was collaborating with Ashford and Simpson to co-screenwrite a big-budget urban musical called *Street Smart*, in which she would have starred and to which she was to contribute songs. It fell by the wayside.

Over the following year and a half, she backed out of *Ruthless People*, was strongly considered for the title roles in a Libby Holman bio-pic that was already a pet project of **Bette Midler**'s, and for *Blaze*, which later became a Paul Newman–starrer. She turned down the female lead in the musical *My One and Only* (to Twiggy's eternal relief) because it paid only $20,000 per week.

By 1987, despite the disastrous ***Shanghai Surprise***, Madonna had set up a production studio, **Siren Films**, and still had the star **power** to command consideration for a variety of films . . . which never made it to the screen.

She was ready to sign on for *Angel Flight*, to costar **sex**y Jean-Hugues Anglade, but it never got off the ground. She was actually signed as the star of the farce *Blind Date*, but when producers signed **Bruce Willis** without giving her her contractual right to approve of the leading man (she wanted hubby **Sean Penn**), she backed out and the role went to Kim Basinger.

Madonna foolishly turned her nose up at *The Fabulous Baker Boys*, a hit for Michelle Pfeiffer, whose script Madonna admired despite the finished product's overabundance of "boring California people." Madonna loved the script to **Mary Lambert**'s *Siesta*, but at the time couldn't "deal with all the **nudity**" required, so Ellen Barkin stepped into a plum leading role in that widely unseen gem (1987).

She was asked to play the Isabella Rossellini bit in David Lynch's *Wild at Heart* but has never been a Lynch **fan**, complaining that the nudity in his *Blue Velvet* was "only done to **shock** the audience" (1989); signed up for *She's Da Lovely* but backed off when by-then ex Sean Penn signed on too (1989); and was turned down by Francis Ford Coppola for the role that went to his daughter Sofia in *The Godfather Part III* (1990).

Things also didn't work out for roles in *Three of Hearts* (which Sherilyn Fenn took) and Gus Van Sant's fiasco, *Even Cowgirls Get the Blues*, (casting began for both in 1991), in which she would have had the opportunity to make time with Uma Thurman. After publicly grousing that Tom Cruise's *Far and Away* bored her ("Sleeping!" was her one-word review to **Arsenio Hall**), Madonna was considered for a starring role opposite him in the 1992 remake of *The Three Musketeers*, but the mismatch became obvious and neither went on to make the film, which became a modest hit for producer Joe Roth.

Kim Basinger got Madonna's sloppy seconds again in 1992 when Madonna stepped out of ***Boxing Helena***, but then Basinger stepped out. Sherilyn Fenn filled in.

Madonna campaigned to be *Tank Girl* in 1994, but was outgunned by Emily Lloyd, who was unceremoniously replaced by ex–**Rockford Peach** Lori Petty.

In the casting-against-type department, Madonna was working on film projects that would have cast her as a mother who sacrifices everything for her children, and as an Auschwitz survivor opposite **Willem Dafoe** (both 1987), and was very interested in a Joel Schumacher screenplay featuring Madonna as a woman who learns her brother is gay when he announces he has **AIDS**. It would've been the first major Hollywood film on the subject. All concerned felt that the role in the latter called for a much older woman, and the studios were too AIDS-shy to forge ahead with the concept (1990).

Maybe out of gratitude, Schumacher wrote a female buddy movie about a wisecracking pair of policewomen called *Leda and Swan*, which came within weeks of going into production with Madonna and Demi Moore, stumbling when Moore got pregnant, and never regaining momentum (1991).

There was also talk of Madonna playing hefty opera diva Maria Callas in a Ken Russell film.

Perhaps because so much of Madonna's work is ***hommage***, she has had several opportunities to remake famous and not-so-famous films from the past, and from abroad. In 1986, it was widely reported that Madonna would play "the Artful Dodger" in a remake of *Oliver!* (adapted from Dickens's *Oliver Twist*), costarring Sting as "Bill Sykes" and Tina Turner as "Fagin."

Madonna was proposed as the lead in a never-made Goldwyn remake of the Barbara Stanwyck stripper-with-a-heart-of-gold classic, *Ball of Fire*; the role of "Tiger Lily" in an update of *Peter Pan* (which years later became *Hook*); and as the female lead in a remake of the Israeli film *Dead End Street* to costar Sean Penn and to be directed by his father Leo.

She nixed plans to remake the Agnes Varda French film *Cleo from 5 to 7*, and *I Married a Dead Man*.

Wiser still was her decision to bow out of a proposed *second* remake of **Marlene Dietrich**'s breakthrough role as *The Blue Angel*, which would have costarred Robert DeNiro in the Emil Jannings role, been directed by Alan Rudolph, and been produced by **Diane Keaton**. Dietrich herself snarled her disapproval, and the subject was considered *dropped*.

It's still possible that Madonna will hook up with **Miramax** to star in a remake of the Swedish blockbuster *House of Angels*, playing a **glamor**ous singer who shows up in a gossip-infested town to claim her grandfather's inheritance.

Since the late eighties, and especially since the birth of **Maverick** (1992), Madonna has looked more and more at the possibilities of film adaptations of **books** and novels. She has considered starring in and/or producing adaptations of Lorrie Moore's novel *Anagrams* (1987); Erica Jong's racy, critically panned *Any*

Woman's Blues (1990); James Baldwin's literary classic *Giovanni's Room* (1991); Kristin McCloy's briefly trendy *Velocity* (1990); Jeane Westin's forties all-girl-band saga *Swing Sisters* (1991); and biographies of her idols **Martha Graham** and **Frida Kahlo** (1991).

Also up for consideration have been Michael Korda's *The Immortals*, which would have starred Madonna as **Marilyn Monroe**, and which even Madonna herself realized "probably isn't a good idea" (1991); transvestite **Warhol** Superstar Holly Woodlawn's hilarious memoirs *A Low Life on High Heels,* as transsexual Candy Darling (1992); and, in a favorable telling of the tale of junk-bond dealer Michael Milken, *Fall From Grace,* which Maverick wanted to **fashion** into a Ted Danson–starrer for TV (1992).

Screenwriter Adam Greenman (*Three of Hearts*) did a still-unfilmed script for her based on Joseph Koenig's *Little Odessa,* about a Russian immigrant who gets swept up with expatriate spies. Greenman cleverly sold it as "a story about a girl who is desperate to make it in America."

Also interesting is Madonna's possible involvement in an adaptation of Robert Plunkett's *Love Junkie,* about a Bronxville *hausfrau* who ditches her hubby after becoming obsessed with the gay underground of 1980s **New York**, falls madly in **love** with a gay **porn** star, and produces his directorial debut. The film was to have been coscripted by Plunkett and coproduced with Amy Robinson and Griffin Dunne, Madonna's straight man in *Who's That Girl*. The role is tailor-made and resonates fortuitously with *Desperately Seeking Susan*, but has floated for ages with no decisions being made (1993). Madonna has said she will probably not act in the film herself if Maverick makes it.

She has also pursued *Bag of Tricks*, David France's nonfiction account of art dealer Andrew Crispo and the "**death**-mask slaying" of Dag Eigil Vesti.

Other Maverick misfires include the much-anticipated "Madonna: The Early Years" ABC-TV miniseries, (pirated away from her by the Fox Network) and her proposed "Peep Show" **HBO** showcase for new talent from around the world. Both reportedly fell through when Madonna had differences of opinion with ABC and HBO (1994).

Television has been risky in general for Madonna. In 1987, she was **rumor**ed to become the next überbitch on "Dynasty," but thankfully deemed such a career move to be a definite step down, and the series ended soon thereafter. More interestingly, Madonna was thinking of providing the voice of prim and proper **Catholic** schoolgirl "Mary Elizabeth" for "The Simpsons," but no acceptable agreement could be forged (1991).

Even TV-to-film concepts are troublesome for Madonna; one that fell through was a brilliant idea in 1992 which had Madonna reinventing Anne Francis's sleek, curvy, Emmy **Award**–winning "Honey West" on the big screen.

Besides unrealized songwriting endeavors, Madonna has also failed to follow through on other writing projects, including a first novel she started in the early eighties (she could only complete "about thirty pages"), and a screenplay of her early years she was to have cowritten in 1985.

proposal (marriage): Sean Penn never officially proposed to Madonna.

While she was jumping on the bed of their room at the "Something Inn" in Tennessee, she caught a look in his eyes. "Reading his mind," she said, "Whatever you're thinking, I'll say yes to." They celebrated their engagement with jawbreakers from the 7-11.

At her third **Girlie Show** at Madison Square Garden, Madonna made dancer Michael Gregory propose to his flame Ungela Brockman, instructing him to sing "You Are the Sunshine of My Life." To celebrate that engagement, Madonna commanded twenty-five push-ups from each of them since no jawbreakers were at hand.

protest: In spring 1989, over two-hundred high-school students walked out of classes in Stamford, Connecticut, to protest the school library's decision to ban the *Rolling Stone* cover story that included revealing photos of Madonna.

Public Enemy: Madonna called them "my number-one favorite rap group" as she defended herself against charges that she'd lifted the bass line from their "Security of the First World" for **"Justify My Love."** It turned out that **Lenny Kravitz** had taken the bass from a discarded tape in the recording studio, and PE never sued.

Madonna challenged any rapper to gripe about sampling, pointing out rightly that rap is largely composed of found material refashioned into something new and fresh.

It was, however, noted in a *Vanity Fair* interview months earlier that one of the cassettes on display in Madonna's living room was the same PE album from which the bass line was supposedly lifted.

public service announcement: Besides her involvement in **Rock the Vote**, Madonna did a chilling **AIDS commercial** in 1989, wherein she walks through a crowded school and dramatically announces that everyone in the scene has AIDS.

She also recorded a "Nikki Finn"–esque anti–drunk-driving message for radio play the year before.

Her funniest announcement was with crooner Seal (1992) to raise awareness of global warming, in which she cooed to him, "I have some globes you can warm."

pussy: Ever the unconventional **feminist**, Madonna's definition circa 1991, was "wimp."

QSound: Useless 3-D sound effect which was introduced on *The Immaculate Collection* and never took off. Mike Ovitz, chairman of **Creative Artists Agency,** helped license worldwide QSound TV/advertising rights to Coca-Cola from Archer Communications, QSound's developers.

Queerdonna: They laughed at El Vez, the Mexican Elvis **impersonator,** but they didn't know quite *what* to do at Queerdonna, a ·300-pound Madonna-impersonator with an attitude to match his appetite. This Baby Divine has made **shock**ing appearances at **New York clubs** and across the country, and is known to have followed Madonna for years.

"*T*here are usually
three types of **sexuality:**
straight, gay, or bi.
I'm *tri*—
I'm very open-minded.
Safe sex is a must!"

—Queerdonna, 1994

race: Before her face became as familiar as the family cat's, Madonna's early disco **music** led DJs and **fans** to believe she was a black singer. This unusual confusion was an effective (if unintentional) bait-and-switch that earned Madonna a large black following, especially for her first two albums, which charted high on the traditionally all-black R&B charts.

Madonna has always been attracted to black culture, possibly pining for the racially-mixed neighborhood of her first home in Pontiac, or rebelling against the staid, repressed culture of all-white **Rochester Hills**. Some of Madonna's early **videos** ("**Borderline**," "**Lucky Star**") have a distinctly urban feel absent from ensuing clips until the racially-charged "**Like a Prayer**" **video**.

Her next comment on race was the song "**Vogue**," which managed to deify the pristine images of white movie stars while celebrating the age-old black tradition of voguing. That video featured several beautifully-photographed black or mixed-race men who accompanied her on tour and in *Truth or Dare*.

Madonna's incorporation of black sensibilities into her work is unmistakable—just ask **Steve Bray** or Babyface, with whom she has collaborated. Her infrequent artistic comments on race are all the more gripping for her whiteness and for the lack of racial commentary by other artists except for some of the most politically charged black performers (**Me'Shell NdegéOcello,** Neneh Cherry, **Ice-T,** etc.).

"Rain" song: Idyllic, Wilson Phillips-y ballad on *Erotica* that became the album's fourth and final U.S. single release. A favorite among **fans**, the song received Top Ten—status airplay but failed to rise above a respectable number 14 when sales during a peak period of Madonna overload failed to catch up. "R" is a simple **love** song with elegantly layered vocals

"*Some* of these new white producers are just scientists in a laboratory, making something they know all the little kids in the ghetto will want to buy. I'm at least sincere. I don't feel guilty about not being black. I think ultimately I will be able to cross over bigger because I'm not."

—Madonna, 1983

·

"*A* white Deniece Williams we don't need."

—Dave Marsh on Madonna, 1985

·

"*Made* to serve as supportive backdrop for Madonna's drama, black characters in 'Like a Prayer' remind me of those early Hollywood depictions of singing black slaves in the great plantation movies or those Shirley Temple films where Bojangles was trotted out to dance with Miss Shirley and spice up her act. . . . Madonna is a modern-day Shirley Temple."

—bell hooks, 1992

and, on the LP version, an inventive, overlapping vocal rap that makes it a standout production by **Shep Pettibone**.

"Rain" video: Elaborate, futuristic video shot on **black-and-white** stock and hand-colored, including memorable close-ups of Madonna (in a short black wig) singing into an old-fashioned mike, her **eyes** a brilliant blue. The setting of the video is a sweeping, antiseptic, Asian-seeming studio, full of **Japan**ese technicians and enormous blowups of Madonna's face on curved screens.

It's a **looks**-only video masterpiece, directed by **Mark Romanek,** that took a much-deserved **MTV award** for **art** direction.

Rancho la Puerta: Mexican fatfarm where Madonna allegedly shed a few success-induced pounds in December 1984, just as *Like a Virgin* and "**Like a Virgin**" exploded on the pop charts.

rape: In the eighties, rape came out of the closet as the most common crime against women. One of the most explosive complicating factors of rape became the issue of "willingness," sometimes judged by the victim's apparel.

Sexual availability, as first read from her provocative outfits, is a cornerstone of the Madonna myth. She popularized the street-urchin **look**—featuring visible bras, lace, and heavy hooker makeup—in 1984 and '85. From then, Madonna has regularly appeared in sexually suggestive outfits and costumes: see-through negligees, form-fitting bodysuits, **cone bras**, the works.

Primarily for her **fashion** choices, Madonna has been perceived as a slut, and her influence on popular fashion often has been attacked for encouraging sexual promiscuity . . . the undertone being that Madonna's sexy gear provokes the male sexual beast. (Overlooking the fact that the male sexual beast goes ape for anything with a heartbeat, regardless of something as superficial as *clothing*.) A reader's letter in the *New York Post* in 1992 accused Madonna of "bringing out the worst in men." Madonna's response to such criticism has always been a defiant reminder that everyone is free to dress as he or she pleases, although this is less a statement against "blaming the victim" than a steadfast urge for individual rights.

Rape has popped up only rarely in Madonna's **work**, maybe because she senses that the issue is one hotbed she may be incapable of tweaking successfully. There is a stunning **Herb Ritts** photograph of Madonna and **Tony Ward** in a 1991 issue of **Italian** *Moda* that portrays Madonna turning her head angrily away from Ward's firm sexual embrace in a scene that definitely suggests rape, possibly of the *Gone with the Wind* "Don't! . . . Stop! . . . *Don't stop!"* variety.

More **shock**ingly, Madonna includes one rape fantasy photo in *Sex*, appearing as a **Catholic** schoolgirl who grins broadly as two skinheads hold her down and reach up her skirt. The photo was one of the most controversial in the book.

In *Truth or Dare*, where life and **art** were forcibly mixed, Madonna's chief makeup artist tells the backup singers that after a drunken night at a disco the night before, she woke up to find her anus bleeding, worried that some men she'd met the night before had drugged and sodomized her. When one of the dancers informs Madonna, the camera is there to capture her instant response: a guilty snicker, followed by fear that the makeup artist was singled out by the men because she worked for Madonna. Even Madonna is leery of the potentially negative **power** of her sexual persona. At least she didn't ask the woman what she was wearing.

On film, Madonna's character in *A Certain Sacrifice* is savagely raped in the bathroom of a diner; temptress "Rebecca Carlson" is sodomized against her will (at first) in *Body of Evidence*; and she was also raped in *Dangerous Game*, scenes that Madonna plays with frightening realism.

SEE ALSO: FEMINISM

Reagan, Ronald: Didja ever see *Being There*? RR was the president who was there for the first six years of Madonna's career, one of the stubborn, conservative "papas" Madonna urged not to preach, and whose image was one of several projected on a massive screen to great effect during her **Who's That Girl tour** performance of **"Papa Don't Preach."**

As early as 1984, she was making her ill will toward RR (and Republicans in general) known to the press, growling that "I don't think about him very much, but I think he's a pretty good actor. I think he's a puppet for all the people in his cabinet. I think everybody else makes the decisions and he's the guy that gets up there and hopefully doesn't get shot."

As for RR's charming, **Frank Sinatra**-lovin' wife Nancy, Madonna could only sneer, "Give me a break." Madonna survived through RR and his successor George Bush, and shows every sign of outlasting **Bill Clinton** as well.

Reebok: After **Pepsi** dumped the too-controversial Madonna, Nike briefly flirted with and then decided against the idea of employing her services. Finally, immediately before the premiere of her hitherto sponsorless **Blond Ambition tour**, it was widely reported that Madonna would endorse Reebok shoes, and vice versa. Talks never panned out, reportedly because of Madonna's refusal to actually *wear* the tennis shoes.

This stance was similar to her agreement with Pepsi that she would never be shown in any ads actually *drinking* the stuff.

reincarnation: "I believe that some people have really old souls. In my next life, I don't know, I'd like to be something immortal, but you never know. Maybe I'll be back to something crawling on the ground like a lizard." —Madonna, 1985

Reiner, Rob: When the director of *This is Spinal Tap* and *A Few Good Men* and former costar of TV's "All in the Family" was introduced to Madonna by **Warren Beatty** in 1991, he beamed, "I never thought I'd meet Madonna!"—to which she replied, "I never thought I'd meet Meathead."

religion: SEE CATHOLICISM, CRUCIFIXES, GOD, NUNS; POPE, THE

"Rescue Me" song: One of Madonna's most lyrically daring songs was a number 8 single, the second new song released from her greatest hits package *The Immaculate Collection*.

In "RM," Madonna sings that she feels she is a freak and that she wants to conquer the world despite her contempt for it. She also rasps (during the course of a lengthy whisper-chant) that she still believes there's hope in her search for a true soulmate.

By and large, the **lyrics** were ignored and "RM" became a **dance** smash, catching minor flack for its coincidental similarity to Dee-Lite's "Power of **Love**."

Reservoir Dogs: Revered 1992 Quentin Tarantino film noted for its ultraviolence and gut-wrenching portrayal of the dishonor among a band of six thieves (including Harvey Keitel; SEE ALSO *Dangerous Game; Goose and Tom-Tom*). At the opening of the film, the men are engaged in a heated debate over the true meaning of the song **"Like a Virgin."** One man believes that the song is about first **love** whereas another thinks it's about a woman who loves big dicks, so that each new experience hurts like the loss of **virginity.**

resourcefulness: "People would say, 'you don't have a job, how do you live? How are you paying your rent? Where'd you get what you're wearing?' People couldn't understand how I could get away with those things. But I did. . . . I thought I shared a lot with "Susan" [of *Desperately Seeking Susan*]. . . . She charms her way into every situation, gets guys to take her out to dinner and girl-friends to let her stay at their apartments, and she borrows their clothes, and trades, swaps, and barters. She's a clever con artist and she doesn't let you know when you're being conned." — Madonna, 1985

restaurants: Madonna loves eating out, and her second-favorite place to do it is in a really good restaurant. In a 1990 *Egg* story, nineteen of Madonna's most frequently visited eateries in Los Angeles were listed. Of those, if you're looking for good food and the off chance of sharing it in the presence of Madonna, your best bets are Muse (7360 Beverly Blvd.), Morton's (8800 Melrose Ave.), Columbia Bar & Grill (1448 N. Gower St.), and City Restaurant (180 S. La Brea Ave.).

Retail SLUT: Trendy, accessory-excessive shop on Melrose Avenue in Los Angeles where Madonna purchased the rubber bracelets (three for fifty cents) that started a fad.

Rice Krispies treats: White-trash snack that happens to be one of the only dishes Madonna can make. She is famous for whipping up a batch on the spur of the moment, and surprised everyone by passing some around at her 35th **birthday** party at **Castillo del Lago**.

rich: She certainly is. *Very.*

In 1993, her estimated worth was $100 million (only about half of Oprah Winfrey's fortune), and she routinely makes $30 million–plus a year before taxes, overhead, and 10 percent for personal manager **Freddy DeMann**. Madonna's enormous wealth has actually become a bone of contention among many of her critics, who have argued that her riches have come between her and her street sensibility. Other critics simply use her wealth as a reason to resent her, and that sturdy **"Material Girl" nickname** doesn't help matters.

Because Madonna has been an enormous success financially, because she rose to popularity in the "me" decade of the eighties, and because her **control**ling nature has branded her a manipulator, Madonna's **art**istic ventures—though undeniably commercially-oriented—are frequently attributed only to her lust for more, more, more.

The criticism isn't valid; if Madonna only wanted to make big bucks, she could easily curtail some of her less commercial impulses (her abrasive humor, profane sensibility, affinity with gay culture, fascination with extreme **sex**uality) and churn out kinder, gentler, **Janet Jackson**-ier pop for far greater returns.

More true is that in light of her middle-class background and her impoverished years in **New York** before making it big, Madonna feels that wealth grants her the freedom to do whatever she wants artistically, and to devote all her time to working without worrying about silly little things like homelessness and Dumpster diving.

"*D*o you think *I'm* a material girl? Well, you're wrong. I don't need money, I need **love**!"
—Madonna on her "Virgin" Tour, 1985

·

"*I* always said I wanted to be famous.
I never said I wanted to be rich."
—Madonna, 1985

·

"*S*he still looks like a whore and thinks like a pimp—which as everybody knows is the very best sort of material girl."
—Julie Burchill, 1992

·

"*H*aving money is just the best thing in the world."
—Madonna, 1992

·

*W*ith her first **Sire** advance, Madonna bought a TV set and a 10-speed bike and stopped taking the subway.

Richards, Keith: The Rolling Stone who had a full-page ad in *Billboard* the same week Madonna's *Erotica* was advertised on the inside cover. KR's copy read, "Not Madonna. **God**."

Ritts, Herb: Madonna's most inspired photographer is behind most of the indelible images that helped etch Madonna into our consciousness: He shot the smoldering *Desperately Seeking Susan* poster, the starkly submissive *True Blue* **album** cover, and her **"Breathless Mahoney"** incarnations, along with directing the **"Cherish" video**.

HR's photography is characterized by a smoothly stylized sensuality and, especially in his non-celebrity work, homoeroticism.

Herb Ritts on how to take a Ritts-y photo:

(1)
"*G*o for the image, the idea, or what you see through the camera.
Don't get caught up in worrying about technical things."

(2)
"*M*istakes are healthy."

(3)
"*S*tart with **black-and-white** film. It has a fine **art** quality."

(4)
"*U*se anything decent for a camera. It's not the camera, or having a ton of equipment.
It's what you do with it that's important." —1989

His rise to fame as *the* premier celebrity photographer is a legendary success story: He took a series of spontaneous shots of acquaintance Richard Gere in a desert gas station which Gere sent to his publicist, gaining HR his first wide exposure when the photos appeared in *Esquire*, *Vogue*, and *Mademoiselle*.

Ritts and **Ciccone** are great friends, and Madonna always shows up to his star-studded **birthday** bashes in **Malibu**.

"*D*on't let the Beaver Cleaver facade fool you.
He's a barracuda with a sweet countenance."

—Madonna, 1985

·

"*W*e're on the same wavelength.
She trusts me. And I try to come up with
the best for her. She changes, I change.
It's a true image that evolves."

—Herb Ritts on Madonna, 1989

*Ritts captures
Madonna's sensuality,
as on this 1987
Italian* Rockstar.

Rivera, Geraldo: Shockmeister TV talk show host famous for occasionally inciting his guests to violence.

Rivera hosted a segment on Madonna in 1991 that featured, among others, **Erica Bell** and **Christopher Andersen**. Bell denied implying that her infamous limo rides with Madonna ended with them picking up Puerto Rican boys for **sex**, and Madonna herself called in to dare **Kurt Loder** and GR to **kiss** full on the mouth. In exchange, she promised to "come on any show, anytime you want!", but the macho men demurred.

In 1994, GR did a show titled "Has the Goddess of Pop Fizzled?" stacked with pro-Madonna panelists.

Rivers, Joan: Raspy-voiced talk-show veteran who delighted in razzing Madonna on her various TV ventures. For one all-Madonna segment, JR dressed in full "Susan" **drag**, and she decried Madonna's decision to sleep with a dog in **Sex**, adding to the chorus of voices against the bestiality that never actually occurs in the book.

JR's other Madonna connection is via her daughter, Melissa, who signed with **Maverick** in late 1993 to helm a teen-oriented cable chatshow called "Hangin' Out with Melissa Rivers."

robbery: In 1981, a few weeks after she moved into her Gotham-subsidized digs on 30th Street, Madonna was robbed. The thieves took only her personal photo collection, everyone's worst nightmare. Be on the lookout at flea markets, though—can you imagine the shots she must have had?

Another act of thievery relieved Madonna of her prized eighteenth-century French diamond drop earrings, which went missing on the set of her **Pepsi commercial**.

Though the earrings were set in platinum, we'd rather happen upon those missing photos.

Robbins, Jill S.: Judge who granted **Sean** and Madonna **Penn** their final **divorce** in September 1989, nine months after Madonna first filed.

Robinson, Leon: Sensitive actor who played the dual role of a black man wrongly accused of murder, and a black saint in the **"Like a Prayer" video**.

Rochester Hills, Michigan: Affluent, auto-exec–heavy 'hood where Madonna was raised after moving at age two from her first **home** in Pontiac.

Rochester School of Ballet, The: Located on the second floor of 404 Main Street in **Rochester Hills, Michigan**, this is the site of teenaged Madonna's **dance** instruction under the tutelage of **Christopher Flynn**, who owned and operated the school.

Rock the Vote: L.A.-based organization devoted to raising political awareness among America's youth, and especially concerned with getting young adults eighteen year old–plus to exercise their right to vote. Rock the Vote employs the free services of rock stars and celebrities to make voter-awareness clips for TV distribution.

Madonna lent a saucy **"Vogue"** send-up called "Vote" to the 1990 campaign, appearing in a red bra and panties and wrapped in the U.S. **flag**. Framed by **José & Luis** in denim cutoffs and too-tight Ts, Madonna changed the **lyrics** of her song to get across the point that freedom of speech is "as good as **sex**." The clip was timely, coming after intense debates on the sacredness of the flag, and on **censorship** in the aftermath of obscenity charges against 2 Live Crew.

After all the hubbub, Madonna was caught red-handed *not* voting—she wasn't even registered, and apparently, hadn't ever voted in her life.

Madonna's next run-in with Rock the Vote was just as effective. By 1992, she'd registered to vote, and her **black-and-white** announcement featured Madonna in a dressing room, blithely trying to decide which fabulous gown to wear while voting. Pooh-poohing one flashy frock, she sneered, "That looks like something *Cher* would wear to vote in." One snippy remark that got snipped from the final cut was a priceless jab at down-and-out **Michael Jackson**'s silly **video**, "Jam," with basketballer Michael Jordan. "Michael," she exclaimed, "white men can't jump!"

Rockford Peaches: The all-girl hardball team on which Madonna's "Mae Mordabito" plays, in *A League of Their Own*.

Rocky: Studly **New York City** male stripper Rocky Santiago, who was featured prominently in *Sex*. In fact, Rocky's is the only penis seen in the book (and it's flaccid!), in a scene full of naked men being ogled by a glammed-up Madonna at the **Gaiety**.

The story goes that Madonna saw Rocky working at the **club** Tatou and recruited him for her book. She might just as easily have seen him in the pages of *People*—they voted him one of the 50 Most Beautiful People in the World.

Rocky also performed at a small party Madonna threw in her apartment in 1992 around the time of the **Clinton**-Gore win, and Madonna bragged to reporters nosy about Rocky's finer points that he was a "registered Democrat." But does he stuff the ballot box?

Rodgers, Nile: Mastermind behind seventies disco group, Chic, his bombastic production helped make *Like a Virgin* one of the top-selling albums of the eighties.

He met Madonna in the Downtown **clubs** both frequented, before the platinum success of her first album. She could have selected almost any producer for her second effort, but went with NR, who has a reputation for crafting brilliant **dance music** for acts as diverse as Sister Sledge and David Bowie.

"*H*e is a very passionate man. He lives life to the hilt. When you deal with people who are that way, you get good stuff and bad stuff, but it was really great working with him."

—Madonna, on Nile Rodgers, 1984

·

"*M*adonna is blatantly sexual and sensual, but not sleazy, not even a little bit. In my opinion, she's an excellent natural singer, a natural musician, a serious artist."

—Nile Rodgers, 1985

·

"*J*'m always amazed at Madonna's incredible judgment when it comes to making pop records. She has the ability to try new things and always be right."

—Nile Rodgers, 1993

Rodman, Dennis: Gargantuan San Antonio Spurs basketballer known for his rebellious ways and perpetually-changing **hair** color, who heated up with Madonna in 1994. The odd couple (with an almost two-foot height difference) made spectacles of themselves exchanging signals and knowing glances at games and dodging "Hard Copy" cameras on Rodeo Drive.

Madonna dragged DR to the premiere of *With Honors*, and they interviewed each other for a *Vibe* cover story that was pulled at the insistence of founder Quincy Jones. The interview is legendary for its **rumor**ed frankness and vulgarity.

role model: Whether or not Madonna is a good role model for kids has been a subject of debate since her earliest incarnation as a bubbly **Boy Toy**, with layers of bright clothes and junk jewelry. Missing from the debate has been the idea that perhaps Madonna doesn't owe role-model status to the world.

Madonna never set out to be anyone's lily-white heroine, has never presented herself as perfect. And yet, whenever a person becomes a star, his or her life is expected to reflect society's rules of normalcy and morality, or the star is branded a "bad role model."

Madonna is an *excellent* role model if your priorities are self-

actualization, ambition, **creativity**, hard **work**, frankness, and individuality; she is a bad role model if your priorities are the status quo, religion, chastity, decorum, and altruism.

In the nineties, the debate of Madonna's influence on kids seems dated (though *Good Housekeeping* published an article on "How to Protect Your Children from Madonna"). She's made it clear that she has no problem allowing her products to be labeled with ADULT MATERIAL stickers, and that she is not in **business** just to tickle the fancies of wee ones.

The funniest example of Madonna the Role Model is a paperback book for kids published in 1986 by Turman Publishing in Seattle. The book narrates Madonna's life story in a version as sanitized as possible for elementary kids, but it can't help offering vocab phrases like "ratholes" ("dark and dirty bars and **clubs**"), "amazingly attractive," "hung," "fishnet stockings," "completely alone," "ancient looking," and "miles of buckwheat pancakes." The book also offers enrichment activities for kids which include writing a poem about Madonna and describing what they'd do if they could spend a whole day with her.

"*J* am positive about life and promote the ideas of happiness and honesty. I know that a lot of people look up to me and copy me, so I'd certainly hate to be doing anything that might be harmful to anyone."

—Madonna, 1988

·

"*J*'m not a child and all the things I do may not necessarily be for a child's consumption."

—Madonna, 1992

Romanek, Mark: Director of the **Japan**ese-flavored **"Rain" video** who envisioned and executed its "clean, Zenned-out minimalism."

Rose, Axl: Skanky rock 'n' roll singer of Guns N' Roses, whom Madonna assessed succinctly in 1991: "He doesn't have any muscle tone."

Rosenberg (-Citron), Liz (Beth): How would you like to deal with pushy reporters who are disappointed that Madonna is not HIV-positive? Or chat with **Pepsi** right after they screened the **video** for **"Like A Prayer"**? Or explain to a sobbing boy that yes, it's true, Madonna is so sick she's canceling the concert for which he's got *eighth-row seats*? Being Madonna's press agent entails such ugly little scenes on a daily basis.

LR has been Madonna's publicist from the beginning, when Madonna was in rags and rubber bracelets and worried that something as trivial as a nude-photo scandal would destroy her career. LR is the force behind all those hundreds of magazine covers and interviews, press blitzes and parties, and hand-selected most of the famous interviewers with whom Madonna's gone head-to-head.

Her responses to the press are legendarily witty (asked if Madonna smokes, Liz replied, "She doesn't smoke; she *sizzles*."), making one wonder if some of Madonna's own glibness is a trickle-down from her publicist. Only once has LR made the mistake of saying something unflattering about her most famous charge. In a 1992 *Vanity Fair* Madonna cover story, she is quoted as saying that there is a "lot of hate" in *Sex*.

LR is very well known to Madonna's **fans**, even contributing answers to a column called "The Validator" in Madonna's official **fanzine.**

"*Y*es, I'll marry you, but I have to go on Madonna's tour."

—Liz Rosenberg to future hubby Phil Citron, 1990

She's a vice president at **Warner Bros.** Records, where she has also worked with **k.d. lang**, Seal, Fleetwood Mac, Van Halen, Ricki Lee Jones, and Van Morrison. Her **office**, on the twentieth floor of the Time-Warner Building in midtown Manhattan, was pictured in *The New York Times* in 1992. It looks like a fan's room just before Mom and Dad say, "Aren't you getting a little carried away?": wall-to-wall **magazines**, memorabilia, and photos.

Only nine years younger than LR, Madonna nonetheless sometimes calls her publicist "Mom," and there are other personal effects of LR's unique position as the mouthpiece for one of the most outspoken women of the age. LR claims that her aunt Pauline in 1988, on her deathbed, asked, "How's Madonna? Is the marriage gonna last?"

"Liz Rosenberg" is also the name of a middle-aged Jewish kvetcher Madonna impersonated on the **"Saturday Night Live"** sketch "Coffee Talk," and there can be no doubt that the Yiddish mannerisms and inflection—portrayed superbly—were lifted from LR. LR hyphenated her surname and added "Citron" upon her marriage to booking agent Phil Citron in 1990. By all accounts, she is a nice lady; to do what she does for a living, she must also be a masochist.

Rosenblatt, Michael: Member of the **Warner Bros.** "kiddie corps" (young movers and shakers) who urged **Seymour Stein** to sign Madonna after receiving her **demo** from **Mark Kamins**. MR

later married and divorced Janice Galloway, one of Madonna's best friends, and an early-years roommate.

Ross, Diana: The Supreme diva visited Madonna in the studio while the latter was slaving away at *Like a Virgin*. DR brought Madonna a bottle of champagne and raved that her *children* just *loved* Madonna's **music.**

rumors: Celebrity breeds rumors, notoriety feeds them, and the public nurtures them. Madonna told *Life* magazine in 1986 that her three favorite **tabloid** rumors about herself were that she had a shrine to **Marilyn Monroe** in her bedroom, that she believed the spirit of Elvis inhabited her soul, and that she had lost fourteen pounds on a **popcorn** diet.

But the most resilient rumor is one that has made the rounds for years: that she is losing her **hair** due to constant color treatments.

Russo, James: Elemental, cut-the-b.s. actor who played a **Sean Penn** type in *Dangerous Game*. In the film, his character **rapes** Madonna's, relieves himself on her immaculate carpeting, hacks off hunks of her **hair**, and screams at her retreat to the bathroom, "There's nothing in there but Tampax and aspirin, and that's the closest you're going to get to comfort in *this* life, baby!"

Co-conspirators Madonna and Liz Rosenberg, 1992.

sampling: Besides the famous accidental appropriation of a **Public Enemy** bass line into **"Justify My Love,"** Madonna officially sampled from Kool and the Gang's "Jungle Boogie" for **"Erotica."**

SEE ALSO: *BEDTIME STORIES*

San Remo: New York co-op that dealt Madonna a stinging rejection in July 1985, when its members voted to disallow her from buying a $1.8 million apartment at their 11-15 East 70th Street location.

The members of the San Remo were mostly older conservatives, but included future *Dick Tracy* costar Dustin Hoffman and singer Paul Simon. The only prospective neighbor to back her up was **Diane Keaton**.

"Saturday Night Live": Madonna called it the hardest thing she ever did when she hosted this weekly late-night satirical show in 1985. Fresh from her circuslike **wedding** to **Sean Penn**, she appeared in a blue parka, movie-star sunglasses, and a ridiculous fur-tail stole, introducing hilarious send-ups of the wedding, complete with scenes of the descending choppers and scaggy members of the bride's family.

Madonna performed in all the major skits, imitating **Joan Collins** in a risky **AIDS** piece; a scared young woman who receives threatening calls on her **car** phone only to learn they're coming from the trunk; **Diana, Princess of Wales**; and a bizarre Latina singer/dancer called "Marika" (before Martika burst onto the scene), who performs a strangled version of a-ha's "Take On Me."

The experience was good for Madonna, a welcome chance to try her hand at comedy (she excelled) and laugh off the annoying press-siege of her personal life. In the audience were **Cher**, Jennifer Beals, and Christopher Reeve.

Madonna has since returned to "SNL" several times. In 1991, she showed up in a "Wayne's World" segment, spoofing her **"Justify My Love"** video in a dream sequence wherein she seduces "Wayne" (real-life pal Mike Myers). "Wayne's World" had shown clips of the "Justify My Love" video in an earlier segment.

"Check out the unit on THAT guy!"
— Madonna on "SNL," 1992

In early 1992, Madonna came on in an unannounced "Coffee Talk" sketch as **"Liz Rosenberg,"** mimicking an overbearing Jewish woman so convincingly many viewers couldn't tell it was M under the curly wig and rose-tinted glasses. Host Roseanne played a doddering Jewish grandmother, but more surprising was **Barbra Streisand**'s appearance when she streaked in at the end of the skit.

Madonna returned to the show as a musical guest in January 1993 to perform **"Fever"** and **"Bad Girl,"** which she did in a simple black halter top and flared pants. She wore the extra-long blonde **hair** she'd been growing for her role in *Dangerous Game*, which she was about to start lensing with that week's host, Harvey Keitel. After singing, Madonna mock-defiantly raised a photo of Long Island cradle-robber Joey Buttafuoco and, lampooning **Sinéad O'Connor**'s previous dissing of **the Pope**, exclaimed, "Fight the *real* enemy!" and tore it apart.

She had opened that show in a hilarious skit as **Marilyn Monroe singing** "Happy **Birthday"** to the Clintons, ending by suggestively summoning not Bill but *Chelsea* to join her. That saucy bit with Chelsea was excised from re-runs. She stumbled over the show's traditional intro—shouting, "Live from Sat—Live from **New York**, it's 'Saturday Night'!". She laughed good-naturedly at her goof. Like all her TV appearances, that stint on "SNL" was a ratings blockbuster—its highest showing in a dozen years—with over 29 million viewers.

"If you slip me the tongue, I'll kill you."

—Madonna to Mike Myers,
showing him how to kiss her for their "Wayne's World" skit.

Scavullo, Francesco: Renowned **fashion** photographer who first shot Madonna in 1983, when he was so impressed with her **look** that he could only exclaim, "Baby **Dietrich**!" FS has photographed Madonna for layouts in and covers of *Harper's Bazaar* and *Cosmopolitan*.

Schiano, Marina: A stylist is in charge of every aspect of the subject's **look**, interpreting the photographer's wishes and adjusting them to reality, with a dash of personal **creativity**. MS's work on the *Vanity Fair* 1991 and 1992 cover shoots helped make them among the most celebrated and infamous, respectively, of Madonna's posing career.

SEE ALSO: APPENDIX 5 (BIBLIOGRAPHY)

Scotti, Nick (a.k.a "Nick Neal"): Sexy **Italian**-American male-model-turned-singer whom Madonna took under her wing in 1991. He had met her as a fourteen-year-old sneaking into the Funhouse, but was formally introduced at **Herb Ritts**'s 1989 **birthday** party.

When NS tired of modeling he took voice lessons from producer **Shep Pettibone**'s **mother,** Marie, hooked up with Madonna, and sang a duet called "Get Over" with her for the soundtrack of the Demi Moore flop *Nothing But Trouble.* The song was later included on his self-titled debut album and released as a 12" single with Madonna's backing vocals engineered forward.

"Secret" song: The October 1994 kick-off song for the *Bedtime Stories* album, "S" became Madonna's third-highest debuting single on *Billboard*'s Hot 100 chart, appearing at number 30 before leap-frogging into the Top 10.

"S" was a departure for Madonna, a laid back, mid-tempo tune about an enigmatic secret kept from the singer by her **lover**. More haunting than **"Who's That Girl"** and **music**ally more akin to **"Justify My Love,"** "S" blazed new trails for Madonna, obsessing as it did over romance rather than **sex**. Its jacket **art** was not such a departure: Madonna, in **black-and-white**, slouching on a sofa, her dress pulled down to reveal an opalescent brassiere. Yes,

"*I*t was magic. I mean, the camera **loved** her. I mean, the camera just wanted to keep taking pictures. Madonna just had a wonderful, beautiful **look**: She was fresh, she was young, she had a very independent way of dressing. . . . She knows what's good."

—Francesco Scavullo, 1993

"*E*veryone was staring at her, and that's just something I could never do: gawk at celebrities. But we kind of caught each other's eye and started playing mind games with each other. . . . She asked for my tape. . . . It just so happened that the next day I was talking to her on the telephone, and she said, `Oh, I just got a Federal Express.' So she put my tape on and had it blasting as we sat there on the telephone together. Two weeks later, we were recording a song. . . ."

—Nick Scotti, 1991

folks, she *did* make sure a hint of nipple was visible!

A dozen years into her career, it was one of her most arresting poses (by Patrick Demarchelier), a testament to the durability of her star appeal.

"Secret" video: MTV world-premiered this **video** to the first song from *Bedtime Stories* on October 4, 1994. The video develops the song's unspecified secret into a very subtly orchestrated story of a singer's addiction to—and almost spiritual deliverance from—heroin.

Madonna's character is white-blonde (including blonde brows) and wears heavy mascara. She mixes that hyper-**glamor** with urban hipness: a pierced nose and navel, a shimmering, clingy blouse (with cleavage out to *there*), and vintage high heels so clunky you're never sure that Madonna will actually make it up the stairs she's seen climbing. The urban feel is accentuated by a supporting cast that includes a transvestite prostitute, a pimp, and a black gang member who shows off his battle scar with pride.

The video was filmed in Harlem, and Madonna's character is a Billie Holiday-esque singer in a small jazz club, simply sitting around and **singing** to entertain a small, mostly black and Latino audience. Her addiction is conquered as Madonna writhes in the lap of an older, maternal woman, who symbolically baptizes her, splashing water on her forehead.

At video's end, the Madonna character finally *does* make it up those stairs (see Madonna's deliberate strut in both the **"Papa Don't Preach"** and **"Like a Virgin"** videos), and to a joyous re-union with her family, a young Latin man and their son, who **director** Melodie McDaniel really should have forced to look happier! ("S" could almost serve as Part II of the **"Borderline" video**, taking place ten years after the events of that first scenario—it even has pool-playing!)

Madonna grins exuberantly into the camera when it's all over, recalling the impulsive giggle in the "**Justify My Love**" clip.

Coming as it did on the heels of her widely-publicized interview with the British **magazine** *The Face*, in which Madonna reemphasized her desire for an old-fashioned family, the video seemed to indicate her interest in a partner and a child—and in happy endings—more strongly than ever.

Seidelman, Susan: Imaginative **director** of *Desperately Seeking Susan*, her first Hollywood film after the critically-acclaimed, underground *Smithereens*, the first U.S. independent ever to compete at the **Cannes** Film Festival.

"She was nervous and vulnerable and not at all arrogant—sweet, but intelligent and verbal, with a sense of humor."

—Susan Seidelman, on Madonna, 1986

self-expression: A staple of Madonna's agenda, she has long been an outspoken advocate of outspokenness. She made her credo explicit with 1989's **"Express Yourself"**; practiced what she preached with the risky but self-expressive **"Justify My Love" video** and *Sex* book; and explained that her "**fuck**"-littered appearance on **David Letterman**'s talk show was actually a planned protest against **censorship** of speech on TV.

"When you're independent, when you do your own thing, when you're your own person, you do whatever you want to do, when you pull away and you're not so concerned with impressing, then the other person is very impressed."

—Madonna, 1991

sell lines: Madonna is considered the Queen of Hype, and for every Madonna product, be it film, tour, record, or **book**, there is a single line that sums up the work and entices buyers to splurge on it. For many of Madonna's works, sell lines are double *entendres*, for some, they are generic tag lines.

Some choice samples:
- **Blond Ambition, HBO** concert: "It's August. . . . It's hot. . . . And it's only going to get hotter!"

- ***Body of Evidence***, U.S. film: "An act of **love**, or an act of murder?" U.K., full, uncut film: "When is an act of love an act of murder?"
- ***Desperately Seeking Susan***, home video: "The Madonna movie!" (The last time that one worked.)
- ***Erotica***, album, print: (1) "Aural **sex**." (2) "Oh yeah, there's music, too." (3) "Assume the (price and) position."
- **The Girlie Show**, HBO concert: "You never know what she's going to do. . . . You just want to be there when she does it." Home video: "This program may contain scenes and language that is not suitable for all audiences. Viewer discretion is advised. Oh, you're soooo surprised."
- ***The Immaculate Collection***, U.S. album: "What a body of **work**!" Ireland, album (slogan later banned): "Your prayers are answered. Coming soon."
- ***A League of Their Own***, novelization: "A woman's place is at **home** . . . first, second, and third!"
- ***Like a Prayer***, album, print: "Lead us into temptation."
- *Madonna Unauthorized*, by **Christopher Andersen**, U.S. mass-market book: "The book that Madonna would give anything to keep unpublished!"
- ***Sex***, book: (1) "Don't you want it now?" (2) "Where passions rule desires dared to be dreamt."
- ***Shanghai Surprise***, film: (1) "A romantic adventure for the dangerous at heart." (2) "The Crime. The Clues. The Catch. The Couple."
- ***Truth or Dare***, film: (1) "Like you've never seen her before." (2) "The ultimate dare is to tell the truth." (3) "She does it this May."
- ***Who's That Girl***, film: "A funny thing happened on the way to the bus station."

Setrakian, Whitley: College roommate who revealed that Madonna "embarked on a campaign" to befriend her, eventually becoming physically affectionate and seducing her . . . into **shoplifting**. WS made public a letter from Madonna in which Madonna expressed delight at having been verbally accused of lesbianism several times while dancing with a galpal at **The Blue Frogge.**

sex: Madonna's image has always been sexual. The climax of Madonna's exploration of sex was even called *Sex*, a massive blueprint of the kinds of sex society considers "out there."

Madonna's own sex life has been the subject of considerable speculation. While she never had a shot at marrying Prince Charles, she probably has not been as active as biographies

"*P*rurience is in the eye of the beholder."

—Madonna, 1985

•

"`*C*ome on baby, let's get *down* to it—let's get in the bed and go right through it.'"

—Madonna spoofing the kind of explicitly sexual **lyric** her critics believed she wrote, 1985

•

"*O*nly when you don't take a bath."

—Madonna, on whether or not sex is "dirty," 1987

•

"*I* think sexuality is at the core of everyone's being. Everybody's in a different state of denying it."

—Madonna, 1991

•

"*T*hirty-three. Less than Madonna and more than **Princess Diana**."

—"Carrie" (Andie MacDowell) in *Four Weddings and a Funeral*, on the number of men she's bedded, 1994

•

"*I* would say I probably very rarely in my life had sex with someone that I didn't have real feelings of **love** for. Because ultimately I can only allow myself to be really intimate with someone if I really care for them."

—Madonna, 1992

•

"*I*'ve been called a tramp, a harlot, a slut, and the kind of girl that always ends up in the backseat of a car. If people can't get past that superficial level of what I'm about, fine."

—Madonna, 1985

•

"*H*eart and soul. With a little dick thrown in every once in a while."

—Madonna, on her priorities, 1987

•

"*T*he truth is, Madonna may already by too sexy for the nineties."

—Deb Verhoeven, 1993

hint or as public impressions presume. Madonna champions sexual exploration, but pulls back from suggesting wild, unrestrained, multi-partner sex, and in fact has strongly implied that she has had only a handful of one-night stands in her life.

As a child, she witnessed a couple making **love** standing up in a church. She lost her **virginity** at fifteen, but joked that her true sexual awakening didn't occur until 1988. By early 1992, soon-to-

be-ditched best friend **Sandra Bernhard** was blabbing to the press that Madonna was very down on sex at that point, and her unromantic *Sex* book seems to bear that out.

Whether or not Madonna has bounced back, there's no question that Madonna's **art**istic concerns with sex, and her **flirt**atious demeanor, have made her our reigning sex star, an icon of restless lust.

Sex: Shot at hip, seedy locales like the Chelsea Hotel, gay strip joints like The Variety and **The Gaiety**, the **sex club** The Vault, and in the streets of **Miami**, *Sex* is Madonna's magnum opus on all things erotic. *S* is a 128-page **book** (plus an eight-page comic book called *Dita in the Chelsea Girl* and an enclosed CD of an **"Erotica"** mix called "Erotic") of Madonna at her most unnervingly best *and* worst, both a mythmaker building herself to new heights of **fame** and notoriety, and an icon/iconoclast, gleefully debasing all previous notions of celebrity. It's a collection of erotic short stories, **poetry**, and song **lyrics** and of hundreds of photographs of Madonna and a host of models and friends attempting to illustrate Eros.

The book was photographed by **Steven Meisel**, designed by **Fabien Baron**, written by Madonna, and edited by **Glenn O'Brien**, but it is narrated as if written by the adopted character "**Dita Parlo**." Meisel shot over 20,000 photos for the book, narrowing the field down to 475, which in turn probably should have been hacked down to about 200, and more ingeniously arranged.

Fabien Baron's stylish lettering and cluttered layout distract the eye, but the photos are sometimes engaging enough to overcome their too-sweet trappings.

The text gets off to a good start with, "This book is about sex. Sex is not **love**. Love is not sex." If Madonna had wanted to portray romance, she would have written a tome called *Romance*. It's a thrillingly honest beginning that she never goes back on—the book is a stark, loveless portrayal of the roughest sex available over the counter. In fact, many of the bookstores that even *agreed* to sell *S* would only offer the book *under* the counter.

S was a turning point in the public's perception of Madonna. Before the book, Madonna's sexy image was acceptable, fun, maybe a little racy in parts, but generally accessible. But Madonna upped the ante here, portraying non–missionary position sexual forms: S&M, **bisexuality, homosexuality**, group sex, rough sex, a strong allusion to analingus, even a jokey hint at bestiality. For former admirers who felt the post–**"Justify My Love"** Madonna was too "dykey," *S* did nothing to appease them— Madonna cavorts with skinhead lesbians, one of whom flaunts a clit ring.

In addition to the anonymous lesbians, Madonna makes sisterly love with Isabella Rossellini, Tatiana von Furstenburg, and **Ingrid Casares**, and toys with **Naomi Campbell**. Other star performers include Clit Club impresaria Julie Tolentino, rapper Big Daddy Kane, **Vanilla Ice**, Daniel de la Falaise, and dearly-departed super-bottom gay porn star Joey Stefano, whom Madonna knew as a former amour of **David Geffen**. When recruiting them for her book, Madonna asked two questions: "Do you mind getting naked?" and "Would you mind **kiss**ing me?" They didn't and they didn't.

S was an expertly organized event, published simultaneously in the U.S., **England**, France, and Germany. Its initial print run consumed 750,000 pounds of aluminum for the shiny covers, and as much Mohawk Superfine paper, a high-quality stock used to properly reflect all the nuances of the original photographs. The book was published on a specially designed, three-story printing press capable of 25,000 impressions per hour, or five times the amount of a typical press. This allowed all one million copies of the book's initial print run to be produced in a little over two weeks.

Contrary to popular belief, the book went on to sell 1.5 million copies worldwide (750,000 U.S.), so 500,000 more were printed than had been announced after the demand became clear. Without a trace of irony over the book's anything-but-private contents, *S* was manufactured with eight armed guards at hand to prevent leaks. Though thousands of copies were stolen from the warehouse immediately prior to publication, the book's contents were, impressively, kept secret until a few days before its publication date of October 21, 1992.

Hysteria. The book that nobody was sure would sell sold 150,000 copies in the U.S. on its first *day*. It sold at the rate of 100 copies per hour in a single West Hollywood bookstore, and in fact outsold the entire Top 25–selling books at the time, *combined*. It completely sold out its U.S. print run within two months, blasting Rush Limbaugh's *The Way Things Ought To Be* out of the number 1 slot on the best-seller lists.

The book that Madonna, in her introduction, claims to have made up, was nonetheless categorized as nonfiction, much to her chagrin.

A previously announced 1993 trade paperback version of the book was scrapped, probably because expected high sales would not be worth the renewed antagonism the book would provoke, especially since the hardcover left many people cold.

S was published to considerable critical outcry, but surprisingly little public concern. The book's original **Japan**ese publisher, Kadokawa Shoten, dropped the book it had paid $1 million for, citing their government's stance against picturing genitalia and pubic hair (SEE ALSO: **censorship**), and fringe groups worked to ban the book in France, but for the most part, *S* was attacked by the very group it attempts to reach: the liberal-minded.

The right wing kept quiet, allowing left-wingers to crucify the suddenly radical pop star and her dirty book, churning out reviews that scoffed at her lack of sexual imagination.

In more than one instance, reviews refused to accept it as a "book" at all. Its stainless-steel covers seemed to shout its status as not only a book, but a BOOK. The Mylar in which the book was sealed may have thrown critics; such flashy packaging didn't make *S* any less of a book, but rather *more* than a book.

S is a book, but it's also an event. Judged on literary and artistic grounds, it is uneven in both capacities. Judged on grounds of sheer impact, there is no competition.

S received the most vicious, dismissive, damning reviews of the year. One recurring note in criticism of the book is money. Because *S* was the first in a $5.5 million book deal with Time-Warner, and its $49.95 price tag guaranteed a net profit in the neighborhood of $20 million, critics cynically cited profit as Madonna's only motive. The heavy hand of corporation *was* behind the book's rushed release date—Madonna wanted to work on it months longer than she eventually did, but **Warner Bros**. demanded a pre-Christmas release.

Warner also had a say in Madonna's subject matter. She was expressly forbidden to include any scenes of sex with animals, children, or religious objects, or any clear shots of actual penetration—a loose set of standards around which Madonna worked willingly, since she had no desire to portray anything of the sort. However, by her own admission, Warner *did* veto one image that Madonna wanted to include. Either her commitment to the image wasn't very strong in the first place, or her professionalism won out over her will.

Critics who hold Madonna's capitalism against her ignore the fact that it is possible to make **art** and money at once, clinging to some romantic ideal of the starving artist instead of embracing Madonna's comfy success.

In light of claims that greed fueled the project, it's fun to note that "Dita" in **Italian** means "**business** firm." But we're sure Madonna was more attracted to its other Italian meaning, "fingers." The latter goes so much better with the book's real theme, and with its desired effect on readers/viewers/fondlers.

The writing is one aspect of the project that many critics either overlooked or discarded out of hand, but Madonna is most proud of her literary contribution to *S*. Though her style is unpolished, some of the passages are memorable, creative, and highly erotic. The introduction is at once liberating and confused. "Love isn't sex," she writes, then uses the terms interchangeably. The book is all "pretend," and yet she poses with real-life lover Vanilla Ice and later recounts incidents from the real Madonna's life (certainly "Dita" never lived on the Lower East Side).

Sex was initially announced as *Erotica* in an early Warner Books advertisement, which later became the title of her concurrent album. Even the book's final shape doesn't reflect Madonna's original vision—she wanted it to be oval-shaped, a publishing near-impossibility.

The weakest part of the intro is Madonna's limp plug for safer sex, which has no place in sexual fantasy. The braver choice would have been to exclude safer sex altogether, arguing that the book is a wish, not grim reality.

The killer one-liners are the most powerful writing in the book: "I'll teach you how to **fuck**," is an effective promise and a threat so audacious it's daunting, so confrontational it inevitably made many readers shoot her a mental "Oh, yeah?" "My **pussy** is the temple of learning," she writes dreamily, a vastly underrated sentiment that is more feminist than a roomful of riot grrrls.

It's easy to be tough, but ridiculously brave to be sensitive, especially when you're big, bad Madonna and the critics have sharpened their pencils needle-fine.

Her most erotic story is her sand-soaked lesbian fantasy—funny, silly, sizzling—but above all, a balanced piece that communicates real desire and a charming sense of spirited sensuality that should have characterized the book.

Elsewhere, the writing stumbles badly, notably in her unimaginative faux letters to "Johnny" from "Dita," and in page-long diatribes on how to seduce someone, how tasty sex with the young can be, how fat people are "overindulgent pigs," and a shockingly juvenile defense of **pornography** that polarizes erotica and humor, which, if it were true, would negate *S* alive.

The photography was slammed for being amateurish, but since **fashion** photographer Steven Meisel's work is widely admired as fine art, much of the criticism can be attributed to his association with Madonna and with the unpopular premise of the book. In truth, a great number of the images crackle with desire, and many more are brilliantly stylized if somewhat mechanical realizations of sex.

The first image is a lovely silhouette reminiscent of Man Ray, or even of the girl-shadow one might find on a trucker's mud flap, and the disparity of these comparisons goes a long way toward explaining *S*'s merging of art and commerce, mystique and **exhibition**, elitism and solidarity.

The next photograph of Madonna is one of the book's strongest, a **mask**ed Madonna in leather bikini, sucking the middle finger of one hand while simulating digital sex on herself with the other. No viewer familiar with Madonna prior to picking up the book could gaze on this without gasping at her audacity, though many viewers would later deny **shock** over this or any other image.

The photo of a lesbian skinhead with a switchblade at Madonna's crotch was singled out as the "scariest," despite the fact that all parties involved are laughing gaily, obviously just

The 14 Smartest Things Ever Said About *SEX*:

(1)
"If your pornographic ideal is for no distracting interruptions to spoil your hand-eye coordination as you flog the duck, yes, it's pretty darn non-erotic. But look. Anyone who tells you that 100-plus pages of one of the world's best-known women cavorting in the nude with all sorts of other naked celebs and non-celebs can be *boring* is lying through his or her teeth." —Tom Carson, *L.A. Weekly*

(2)
"It's a sex cookbook." —Karl Lagerfeld

(3)
"Let's face it—this book is review-proof." —Laurence J. Kirshbaum, Warner Books

(4)
"Sexual fantasies require neither action nor guilt." —Harold Bloomfield, psychiatrist, *USA Today*

(5)
"*Sex* is like another comparably auspicious debut, *Moby Dick*. With 'My name is Dita' we at last have a worthy successor to 'Call me Ishmael.'" —Helen Eisenbach, *QW*

(6)
"It's Shakespeare in a G-string." —Andrea Peyser, *New York Post*

(7)
"One customer was really nervous. His hands were shaking when he gave me the money."
—Stacy Blease, sales clerk, Barnes & Noble, New York

(8)
"The *Times*'s belief that the only completely heterosexual scenarios are those involving Madonna and Vanilla Ice . . . is only accurate if you don't believe male-female S&M, sex with an older man, sex with a Botticellian younger man, biting a man's ass, shaving his pubic hair, sucking on his toe *[sic]*, or sex with a man wearing makeup to be heterosexual." —Mim Udovich, *The Village Voice*

(9)
"I'm a revolutionary and, yes, it's a burden." —Madonna, on *Sex*-ual pressures

(10)
"I've seen lots of pornography. This is not pornography. This book is about how sex is involved in the culture." —Kerig Pope, *Playboy*

(11)
"We're always happy when our neighborhood writers have books published."
—**New York** bookseller, on why they had both an open copy and a large window display of the book, on its publication

(12)
"By presenting the world with a range of sexual fantasies in which she poses successively as aggressor, victim, exhibitionist, housewife, gay, and straight, Madonna is suggesting there is nothing essential about gender or sexuality—and by implication, identity. As a sexual object who is also subject—a woman who controls and determines the circulation of her image and her fantasies—Madonna takes us to the heart of contemporary fears about social disintegration." —Catharine Lumby, 1993

(13)
"What other star has made herself so tantalizingly available while remaining so essentially remote?" —Vince Aletti, *The Village Voice*

(14)
Nonfiction, #1: *Sex*, by Madonna —Publishers Weekly, *The New York Times Book Review*

The 6 Dumbest Things Ever Said About *SEX*:

(1)
"Some of us actually like the opposite sex." —Caryn James, *The New York Times*

(2)
"Laughter is the enemy of lust." —Pete Hamill, *New York Daily News*

(3)
"Pornography doesn't hold up to much serious analysis." —Robert Hofler, *New York Newsday*

(4)
"Of the 20,000 photos shot for the book and the 475 printed, the knife-at-the-crotch image is the most violent." —Giselle Benatar, *Entertainment Weekly*

(5)
"The taboo against pedophilia is no mere prejudice, and flirting with it, even sending it up, is neither worldly or clever. Unless you are Nabokov." —Vicki Goldberg, *The New York Times*

(6)
"That book's not art. I have to defend her right to do it, but I just thought it was embarrassing, tacky, and unnecessary." —Sir Mix-A-Lot, *artiste* behind the single "Baby Got Back," the video of which featured the singer walking among a landscape of gigantic buttocks

playing around. More impressive is a two-page spread in which Madonna and two women embrace tenderly. It makes excellent use of the book's spiral binding, splitting the photo at the metal seam, a reflection of the S&M flavor of the women and of the book.

An image of Madonna, bathed in white light, tugging on **Tony Ward**'s nipple ring with her teeth is another transcendent image, a supple composition that reflects their real-life intimacy. Other shots—Madonna giggling as she's gang-**rape**d, pouring wax on a leatherman, lying prone under a cross, sucking a toe—are too self-consciously "naughty" to evoke the longing this image evokes, or the fresh lust evoked by a shot of Madonna chewing a man's ass.

Many of the photos are soft and tender, but simply don't read as such because they are relegated to **Andy Warhol**—like repetitious background collages, robbed of any chance they might have had were they splayed across two pages or arranged more carefully.

The most effective images of all are of Madonna alone, and they stand as a testament to Madonna's talent for losing herself in the character of a given photograph more thoroughly than she has usually lost herself in a character on moving film. At thirty-four,

she makes an utterly convincing adolescent in one photo, frankly exploring what appear to be newly sprouted breasts, and later, fingering herself over a mirror.

Meisel appropriates Helmut Newton in a series featuring Madonna as a glamorous socialite at a gay strip club, and also in an image taken in Miami, of Madonna arched over a ceramic fish—the sky, pool, ocean, fish, and Madonna's flesh each a different and stimulating texture. It's so beautiful you forget to laugh at the joke that the fish is spurting water out between Madonna's thighs.

The one image that lingers and that most perfectly captures Madonna's mission on earth is one of the last: Madonna is nude, her hair whipped up into a semi-bouffant, a cigarette clamped between her lips, an Azzedine Alaia purse firmly in her grip, hitchhiking on the streets of Miami. The shot was impromptu, leaving motorists to fend for themselves, the most honest representation of the exhibitionism and **voyeurism** in **stardom** you'll ever see.

Ever allusive, one shot of Madonna hanging from a lift over the ocean suggests **Leonardo da Vinci**; Madonna's slippery beach persona could be Brigitte Bardot; and together, she and Vanilla Ice look more like Charlene Tilton and Brian Austin Green.

Madonna's interracial scenes with Naomi Campbell and Big Daddy Kane are the least successful images in the book. Both Kane and Campbell are DOA.

Who *is* Madonna for thinking anyone would want to see her in all these poses?

Who are we to deny we don't?

In the end, *Sex* is like sex: sometimes brilliant, sometimes boring, but always worth fifty bucks.

Sex launch party: *Publishers Weekly* called it the "party of the century," but some of the attendees said the **book**-launching party for *Sex* failed to live up to their expectations. What did they expect? To get laid?

The Final Word On *SEX*(?):

"I never meant [*Sex*] to be the definitive statement on the most erotic fantasies ever made, and it's not meant to be taken so seriously. On the other hand, it is."

—Madonna, 1992

Eight hundred of Madonna's nearest and dearest, all required to bear a photo ID, showed up at Industria Superstudio on Washington Street in Manhattan on October 15, 1992. Space-designer Anthony Ferraz offered five thousand black roses intertwined in barbed wire as cheery party decorations.

The bash featured a single copy of the then still-top-secret *Sex* displayed in a sealed glass case at the entrance; Warner Books staffers dressed as priests to greet participants; blow-up **sex** dolls; a **bisexual kiss**ing booth; a Cleopatra impersonator dominating two submissive men; a guy in black leather hanging from the ceiling; live-action scenes of bondage

The 5 Bitchiest Things Ever Said About *SEX*:

(1)

"Artistic integrity? I'll believe it when she can spell it." —Ellen Goodman, *New York Newsday*

(2)

"*Sex* reveals the erotic imagination as daring as that of a middle-aged Westchester housewife out to shock the girls on Bingo night. . . . The images we find truly erotic are usually more mundane than sensational; it's our emotional and psychosexual history that invests them with allure. . . . And how sad that the delightfully playful **material girl** should have been reduced to the obtuse strategies of an aging hooker—whispering the word 'erotic' over and over, as if from a shadowy doorway, not even bothering to hide the motives for her unimaginative come-on. The only decent response is to avert your eyes in embarrassment, and quickly move on."

—Daniel Mendelsohn, *QW*

(3)

"I wanted to see the dick *actually* going *in*." —unidentified old man, a disgruntled customer

(4)

"*Sex* reminds me of a high-school yearbook for the School of the Performing Sex."

—Barbara Lippert, *Adweek*

(5)

"Apparently, no one among Madonna's advisers ever realized they were producing a *book*."

—Camille Paglia

and S&M involving cat-o'-nine-tails; and a naked lady in a tub full of **popcorn**, who concealed any resentment she may have had over Madonna's **love** of caramel.

At a tattoo booth, a man who was having Madonna's face etched permanently on his buttocks mused, "You could get stuck with worse"; but when Madonna said she was flattered, he sassed, "You should be."

It was an election year, so presidential debates were broadcast on one TV amid a bank of screens flashing X-rated films and life-sized blowups of photos from the book.

All parties serve munchies, and Madonna dictated the menu, which included, "Anything you can lick or suck." Ice cream and **lollipops** *galore*. The music was provided by star DJ Junior Vasquez.

Most memorable was Madonna's hands-down, all-time *least* flattering look, which nonetheless worked magnificently in context. As her guests arrived in sleazy sex gear, Madonna appeared at ten P.M. in a Bavarian dress that was a gift from a female German record-company executive. She sported Princess Leia dual buns, invisible eyebrows, about three miles of cleavage, and a white stuffed lamb: Heidi 'Ho. Though she did not strip as had been **rumor**ed she would, she did take off, at midnight.

No party is complete without a guest list, and some of the notables were **Rosie O'Donnell**, Grace Jones, Billy Idol, **Lenny Kravitz, Willem Dafoe**, Griffin Dunne, Virginia Madsen, Christian Slater, **Naomi Campbell, Debi Mazar, Francesco Scavullo**, Penny Marshall, Kevin Spacey, Pete Hamill, Mary McFadden, Robert Evans, **Alek Keshishian, Spike Lee** (who arrived early only to be told to come back later), Eric Nies, Sharon Stone, Tim Burton, Joel Schumacher, Black Sabbath, Jeanne Tripplehorn, Gregory Hines, the late Irving "Swifty" Lazar, Rae Dawn Chong, **Robin Leach**, Tatum O'Neal, Ashford and Simpson, David Lee Roth, Udo Kier, **José & Luis, Niki Haris, Donna DeLory**, Amanda Donohoe, and Jon Lovitz.

sexism: Madonna rightly believes that much of her sexually-oriented work has drawn double the criticism that it would draw were she a man, because people—including many women—are not into the idea of a sexually aggressive woman, and are even less enamored of a sexually *frivolous* woman.

In 1992, Madonna herself was accused of sexism by, of all people, a group of construction workers. When the British Safety Council distributed safe-**sex** posters depicting Madonna in leather to 26,000 job sites, leaders of the Ucatt construction union protested on the grounds that such male-oriented material was just as off-putting to female construction workers as **Playboy** centerfolds. This despite the fact that Madonna never met a female construction worker she didn't like.

Shabba Doo: Talented breakdancer of *Breakin'* **fame** who backed Madonna on her **Who's That Girl tour**, performing in a sequined, form-fitting top.

An example of how Madonna takes care to surround herself with talented co-workers: Madonna does Malkovich.

Shadows and Fog: Surreal 1991 film directed by **Woody Allen**, starring a dizzying ensemble cast—John Malkovich, John Cusack, Lily Tomlin, Donald Pleasance, Julie Kavner, Jodie Foster, Wallace Shawn, Kathy Bates, Mia Farrow, David Ogden Stiers, Kate Nelligan, and Madonna. The film is strangely pointless, yet cerebrally entertaining as far as light Fritz Lang—German expressionist pastiches go.

The story is a Kafka-esque tale set in the 1920s somewhere in Europe, featuring the struggle between a wimp (Allen) and various townfolk who want him to help them nab a local serial killer. Madonna **looks** exquisite as a high-wire artist, in a curly brunette wig and circus gear. As the moll of the strongman, she has only a few minutes' screen time—a frothy exchange with Malkovich.

The photography is a **black-and-white** lather that renders all the pedestrian goings-on **art** in motion.

If ever a Madonna film could've been livened up by some of her songs on the soundtrack, this is it, and since the film features the **music** of Kurt Weill, that's saying a lot.

Before the film's release, **New York** *Newsday* started the juicy **rumor** that Madonna's performance, in what she described as "a stupid little part," was so inept Allen had cut her out of the film. Not so, said Allen, gallantly defending her in the press. "Not a frame of hers has been cut nor has that ever been contemplated. She's first-rate in the film." She is, and though her part wasn't cut, it wasn't big to begin with.

"*J*t was like going to the psychiatrist—
not necessarily fun, but certainly educational
and enlightening."

—Madonna, on filming *Shadows and Fog*, 1991

The movie is based on Allen's never-produced, 1975 stage play *Death*. It was ready for release in the fall of 1991, but held back until early 1992 due to the Chapter Eleven bankruptcy of its studio, Orion.

Shanghai Surprise: Surprise! This 1986 vehicle is one of the worst movies ever made. Madonna starred in the romantic comedy with her husband **Sean Penn**, and a week after its premiere, *Rolling Stone* called it "Madonna's first flop." The $15.5 million film ended up earning an anemic $1,110,062, garnered some of the worst reviews Madonna has ever gotten, and lives on in the Hollywood pantheon as an atrocity of almost unspeakable proportions.

The filming of the movie could not have been more of a disaster. Widely publicized differences between the Penns, producer George Harrison (for his Handmade Films), and **director** Jim Goddard, and Sean Penn's brawling with nosy photographers on the Hong Kong, Macao, and London sets led to an almost unprecedented outpouring of antipathy for the Penns from the world press.

"*T*he nicest thing about *Shanghai Surprise*
is that you can watch it in near-total **privacy**.
Just because something takes up two
hours' worth of screen time and offers
well-known people the chance to dress
cleverly and talk about stolen opium
and jewels and secrets of the Orient,
it isn't necessarily a movie.
We'd all be better off if that were
more widely known."

—Janet Maslin, *The New York Times*

At one point, Penn held up filming for five hours when someone stole Polaroids of the couple taken for production purposes. He also threw his weight around to get well-liked publicist Chris Nixon fired when Nixon suggested that the Penns pose for photos to get the press off their backs.

Madonna gave a rare **press conference** before seventy-five reporters at London's ritzy Roof Gardens to lay to rest all the ugly **rumors**, and appeared in control of herself and on good terms with George Harrison, whom most of the reporters forgot was doing *his* first press conference in a dozen years. Sean Penn skipped the event.

The plot of *SS* has Madonna playing "Gloria Tatlock," an idealistic, repressed missionary working in Shanghai in the thirties, helping to soothe the injured in the war between China and **Japan**. She is in search of a large cache of opium, which she hopes to use as an anesthetic, and is forced to enlist the aid of a brassy American tie salesman (Penn). Enter the bad guys.

Madonna's **look** for the film was a drastic departure from her previous **club**kid wardrobe: a classic thirties 'do, figure-obscuring missionary suits, and refined **glamor** makeup. Her performance is mechanical, deserving of all manner of mockery. Looking like a million bucks and with star presence to spare, Madonna seems all dressed up with no place to go and no way of getting there.

Shangri-La: Malibu hotel where the Penns spent several days "reconciling," after Madonna dropped her first petition for **divorce** in December 1987. Their suite? Number 607.

Shelter, The: New York disco at 157 Hudson Street where the *Truth or Dare* post-premiere party was held.

Shimizu, Jenny: Japanese-American supermodel, called a "lezbopunk bike-dyke" by the *Los Angeles Times* for her open lesbianism and fondness for tattoos, Harleys, and working as a mechanic. She rose to **fame** in 1993 after being discovered riding on her **motorcycle**. This unconventional model is good buds with Madonna ("galpal" seems too *girlie-girl* to adequately describe their **friendship**), and sees her about once a month. Her attitudes toward **sex** sound vaguely familiar: "I'm all for sexual freedom: S&M, bondage, dancing half-naked. I just think it's great."

Sho-Bar: Evansville, Indiana, gay bar on East Franklin Street, where Madonna partied to alleviate the stultifying **boredom** of small-town life while filming *A League of Their Own*. Though she refused to sign individual **autographs** (can you imagine how many hours it would take Madonna to pass out John Hancocks to all the patrons of a gay bar?), she did impulsively spray-paint an autograph across the outside wall.

shock: Because she is unpredictable and so many of her **projects** push the envelope of what's considered permissible, Madonna has been unfairly branded a shock artist. True, Madonna suddenly saying "**fuck**" thirteen times at a **David Letterman** taping, French-**kiss**ing a woman in a **music video**, peddling a book of naked pictures of herself, and baring her breasts at a **fashion** show are all done for shock value, but Madonna never does anything *just* to shock. Rather, she uses shock to rouse people who need it (What's so wrong with "fuck"? Don't we all say it? Doesn't Dave?), and to invigorate those who are not shocked but who identify with her actions.

The point is that Madonna is not attempting to shock everyone, just those whose shock threshold is dangerously anemic. The rest of us she'd much prefer to amaze.

"*T*he problem is that, thanks to herself, Madonna can't really shock us anymore, short of taking a dump onstage or receiving an **abortion**. ['Papa Don't Preach' could take on new overtones if the baby were dead]."

—Michael Musto, *The Village Voice*, 1993

·

"*N*ow let's suppose that Madonna . . . made caca onstage. That would be truly shocking. But—while it's not something Joey Heatherton would do (and this is probably why Madonna won't be doing Serta mattress **commercials** in two years)—admitting you pee in the shower is barely a three on the risqué meter. After all, Bono said 'fuck' on the Grammys, **Sinéad O'Connor** tore up a picture of **the Pope**. The fact that Madonna may have contracted Tourette's syndrome is hardly an occasion for a moral meltdown."

—Guy Trebay, *The Village Voice*, 1994

·

*I*nterviewer: "What shocks you?"
*M*adonna: "Ignorance shocks me."

—1991

shoplifting: Not just grapes. Madonna frequently shoplifted **candy**, **magazines**, and other small sundries as a teenager from **Rochester Hills** establishments like **Mitzelfeld's** and the D&C dime store. She introduced her college roommate **Whitley Setrakian** to the fine **art** of sticky fingers.

shopping: What else are you going to do with all that money? Madonna loves to shop and has frequently been spotted out on her own, scouting for outfits at Agnes B. and Maxfield in L.A., and Comme des Garçons, Parachute, and Charivari in **New York**. In **Truth or Dare**, she takes her entire **dance** troupe on a wild spree at Chanel in Paris, gaily trying on outfit after outfit and, off-camera, indulging them all in *couture* the likes of which they'd never seen before.

shove: The day after **Speed-the-Plow** opened, Madonna shoved and cursed ten-year-old Keith Sorrentino, the younger brother of an obsessed **fan** named Darlene. Darlene was a regular nuisance, staking out Madonna's apartment and snapping photos even after being told not to. Madonna snapped on this particular occasion, attacking Keith and trying to snatch his camera away.

Meanwhile, another fan at the scene, Michael Lupinacci, took two damning photos of Madonna struggling with her pursuers.

So distraught was Lupinacci that he could barely pull himself together to call the *National Enquirer*, meet with **Liz Rosenberg**, then sell his photos for big bucks. "I'll never feel the same about Madonna again," he said wistfully at the time, though it's hard to imagine how he expected one to behave when one's **home** is being staked out by meddlesome glommers-on.

shrimping: Erotic toe-sucking. "The feet are very sensitive—as long as they are clean," she chirped in 1992. "All your nerve endings are in your feet, I found out from a reflexologist."

Madonna shrimps in a photo from **Sex** that was also used as the back cover for her **Erotica** album. That same photo was used on a picture disc (a collectible album with an image directly on the vinyl) in **England**, but was recalled when Princess Fergie was embroiled in the Great Shrimping Scandal of 1992, caught by **paparazzi** being shrimped by a man not her husband. Only 40 copies of the disc were issued, and they now sell for anywhere from $650 to $1,000.

siblings: In **"Keep It Together,"** Madonna sings of the importance of **family**, but the song is an argument for family in response to her own internal pulling away from hers. Madonna has always had a tumultuous relationship with her seven brothers and sisters, and her desire to be special couldn't have helped. When asked in 1983 what her siblings did, she said impishly, "Envy me!"

Her sister Paula was reported to have thrown a fit at Madonna's **wedding**, sobbing at the injustice of Madonna's success and her marriage (take heart, Paula), and brother Martin has done every talk show on wheels (and such lowbrow productions as the discount video *Madonna: The Name of the Game*) to dish his sister, all the while attempting to jump-start his own career as a DJ/rapper.

Mario has had run-ins with the law more than once, even doing time in jail. Jennifer helps mom Joan run a day-care business. Madonna is closest to her brother Christopher, who works with her, and her sister Melanie, who is married to her childhood sweetheart.

'I am girlie, hear me roar!'

Jennifer and problem-child Mario are half-siblings of Madonna's, the progeny of Madonna's natural **father** and his second wife, **Joan** (née **Gustafson**).

Anthony, nicknamed "T.C." for "top cat," is the oldest, born in 1956. After him, it's: Martin "Mard," 1957; Madonna "Squeeze," "Little Nonni," "Mouth," 1958; Paula "P," 1959; Christopher "Mr. Cynic," 1960; Melanie "Smell," 1962; Jennifer "Bunny," 1968; and Mario "Mar," 1969.

SEE ALSO: CICCONE, CHRISTOPHER; CICCONE, MADONNA LOUISE FORTIN; CICCONE, MARTIN; CICCONE, PAULA

"Sidewalk Talk" song: An infectious ditty about the propensity of street urchins to gossip, this number 16 single from 1986 was written by Madonna for her ex-beau, **Jellybean**. The song is mixed by Jellybean and contains almost duet-level vocals by Madonna herself.

Sinatra, Frank: Madonna met "the Chairman of the Board" September 18, 1992, backstage at his dual concert with Shirley MacLaine. Madonna reportedly cowered behind the curtains at the concert, trying to avoid seeing ex-beau and MacLaine sibling **Warren Beatty**. When she met FS, Madonna posed for a photo that shows both grinning exuberantly, tangled in a bear hug.

singing: Madonna's true claim to **fame** is her singing career, despite having a voice that is not as technically strong as the voices of peers like Mariah Carey and Whitney Houston. That her voice is fragile and wears out easily (compare her vocals at the first and last stops on any given tour) is certain.

That she is, as some critics allege, a lousy singer, is *not*. Madonna may not have the range or output of some singers, but her voice makes up in sincerity and personality for what it lacks in note-by-note perfection. Madonna-haters can't understand how her admirers can find her voice appealing.

Regardless of any other trappings, Madonna's voice is always laced with immediacy and unimpeachable emotion. She imbues even her most pedestrian **lyrics** with a sense of purpose, as she does with the simple romantic ballad, **"La Isla Bonita,"** which was one of her biggest international hits, partially because she emotes the longing that the straightforward lyrics specify.

"*M*adonna has a voice that takes some getting used to. At first, it doesn't sound like much at all. Then you notice its one distinguishing feature, a girlish hiccup that the singer uses over and over until it's irritating as hell. Finally, you get hooked. . . ."

—Don Shewey, *Rolling Stone*, 1983

•

"*I*'ve heard the talk about how Madonna can't sing, and I can tell you that's bull. She's a natural, intuitive singer with great intonation, and she puts across a vulnerable quality that you can't copy, and I know because I've heard people try."

—**Patrick Leonard**, 1987

•

"*M*adonna does at least prove the existence of A Voice. Like Evelyn King, or early **Diana Ross**, it has a frailty and girlie sweetness to compensate for what it lacks in guts: crossover potential to the max."

—James Truman, *The Face*, 1983

•

"*H*er sound is her own; her voluptuous voice, sometimes sugary and high, sometimes steamy and low, delivers a vitality, a *humanness*, that's more bewitching than any of her glamour-girl poses and more luminous than her **fame**. Many of her original lyrics may be little more than romantic clichés, but like girl-group divas Ronnie Spector, Darlene Love, and Mary Weiss (the Shangri-Las), Madonna uses her wholehearted singing to enrich her words."

—Joyce Millman, *Boston Phoenix*, 1986

•

"*I*n truth, she is an indifferent singer, but her voice has the whispered assurance of one of those phone-for-**sex** girls."

—*Time*, 1985

•

"*I* think she has the perfect pop voice."

—Joan Armatrading, 1985

•

"*H*ers is one of the most compelling voices of the eighties."

—*Rolling Stone*, 1989

Madonna's singing is also appealing for its natural-sounding voice, *sans* improvisation that only dogs can hear à la Carey. This earthiness makes Madonna's music more accessible, and is an example of her **"Dreams Come True"** credo in action. If Madonna can become the most famous singer in the world with only a reasonably strong voice, anything's possible.

Sire Records: Owned by **Warner Bros.**, this is the very first record label to sign Madonna.

She's still associated with them (in conjunction with her own **Maverick** label), and why not? They've served her well. In the process, they earned an estimated *low* figure of a half billion dollars on Madonna recordings from just the first ten years of her career, and have helped peddle over 90 million copies of her albums.

Siren Films: Before **Maverick**, Madonna formed this film development company in January 1987. Though Siren never produced a single film, it landed a five-picture deal with Columbia Pictures.

"Do you know what a siren is? It's a woman who lures men to their deaths."

—Madonna, 1989

Sister Norma: Her first-grade teacher at St. Frederick's, from 1964–65.

SEE ALSO: NUNS

size: Contrary to popular belief, Madonna has gone on record saying that penis size "doesn't matter" to her, casting doubt on **rumors** that she once led a cartoonishly well-endowed man around by his schlong at size-queen–infested Club Nine.

Slam: Real name Salim Gauwloos—the strapping, darkly handsome dancer featured in the **"Vogue" video**, on **Blond Ambition**, in *Truth or Dare*, and as the most prominent boob-squeezer in Madonna's **MTV Music Video Awards** performance of **"Vogue."**

Slam French-**kiss**ed Gabriel Trupin in *Truth or Dare* at Madonna's dare, a smooch that Trupin later sued Madonna over, claiming it had outed him to his **grandparents**.

"She's a very sensitive, sweet person and she's actually also very insecure, especially with other women around, because, I mean, we would have parties and there would never be beautiful women around."

—Slam on Madonna's insecurities, 1993

Though Slam didn't sue Madonna as some of her other dancers did, he held a grudge because she didn't remain close with him after Blond Ambition was over, and said so on **Robin Leach**'s "Madonna Exposed," where he also debuted his still-unreleased song, "Bring It," in which he likens feelings of **love** to the designer drug Ecstasy.

slump: After the bad reaction to *Sex* (despite its financial success) and the flop that was *Body of Evidence*, the press officially proclaimed Madonna to be in a slump. Never mind that her singles were still high-charters, never mind that *Erotica* went triple-platinum, or that **The Girlie Show** sold out all over the globe. Because Madonna's likability had nose-dived with her foray into hard **sex**, and because Madonna's **power** provides an irresistible target, an array of publications pronounced her "over."

WHAT SLUMP?

Us magazine, which itself has been "over" ever since *Entertainment Weekly* hit town, published the most damning piece, "Immaterial Girl" by Jamie Malanowski. The article provided the results of a phone poll, in which 54 percent of respondents denied they would walk across the street to look at Madonna. That 70 percent of men polled denied they'd enter an **MTV** contest to win a date with Madonna is more interesting for the result that 30 percent of 400 under-40 men would enter *any* MTV contest. The result that got the least attention is that 61.7 percent either loved Madonna or liked some of her **work**, and another 20.8 percent were open to having their socks knocked off by her next **project**.

New York wit **Michael Musto** reported that Madonna cried over the article, but if so, she must've passed out over an article Ken Tucker wrote in *Entertainment Weekly* after her disastrous

"What babies did she murder to warrant such press pleasure from her temporary popularity dip?"

—Liz Smith, 1993

David Letterman appearance. But by then it had become self-evident that Madonna was not washed-up. When a "celebrity" segues into a "has-been," it's a foregone conclusion—no articles are written arguing her unimportance, she simply dries up and scabs off.

Slutco: Ingenious name of Madonna's inactive **video** production company, which was dissolved into **Maverick** in 1992.

Smith, Liz: Madonna's guardian angel and her most vehement public defender in the world of gossip. Smith is the legendary, nationally-syndicated tattletale for *New York* Newsday, who has grown to **love** Madonna over the years, probably because Madonna plays the celebrity game in such a refreshingly original, ballsy **fashion**.

Smith's defense of Madonna can border on blind loyalty, but her unaffected, clever writing always raises valid points toward a favorable reading of Madonna and often attacks other members of the press when their condemnation reaches ridiculous heights.

"*Y*ou're fed up with her? Nonsense. Millions of **fans** are still panting."

—Liz Smith, on 1991 Woman of the Year co-honoree Madonna, 1992

"*S*even, count 'em, seven days without one mention of Madonna! And we're fine, yes we are. OK, OK, I *do* keep seeing bats, snakes, and spiders—wrapped in Mylar— all over the walls, but other than that, it's been a fairly uneventful withdrawal."

—Liz Smith, 1992

smoking: Though **Liz Rosenberg** denies it, Madonna is a social smoker who favors Marlboro Lights. Cigarettes have been used to effect **glamor** in many of her **projects**, including *Desperately Seeking Susan*, the **"Express Yourself"** video, and *Dangerous*

Game. Madonna puffed on a cigarette with mock hauteur at the 1989 **MTV Music Video Awards**, and chomped on a stogie on "The Late Show" with **David Letterman** in 1994. She contemplated the empty habit in her single **"Bad Girl,"** in which the burned-out singer (in the song) laments her vices: drinking, sleeping around, and smoking way too many cigarettes.

"*W*hen I'm recording and people light up I say, 'Put that cigarette out RIGHT THIS MINUTE!' It's so rude!"

—Madonna, 1985

Snatch Batch: A takeoff on the "Rat Pack" moniker from the sixties used for **Frank Sinatra** and his cronies, the "Snatch Batch" is the off-color name devised for Madonna, **Sandra Bernhard**, Jennifer Grey, and their female comrades.

The Batch was born in 1988, while Madonna was on Broadway, and gradually dissolved as Grey drifted from the group and Madonna and Bernhard fell in loathe.

"*I*'m a brat for sure, but I don't travel in a pack."

—Madonna, 1990

spectator: Since she's the biggest spectacle of the twentieth century, it's difficult to imagine Madonna as a spectator herself.

Certainly she's watched all her own movies and those of her ex-husband, as well as all the movies and performances that have inspired her in her own **work**, but she has also viewed many contemporary films and performances, perhaps all the while itching to hijack them and do them better herself. An abridged list follows on the next page.

Speed-the-Plow: Tense, abrasive, anti-Hollywood **play** written by **David Mamet** that became Madonna's Broadway debut from May to September 1988. Film **director** Mike Nichols told Madonna about the role, and she immediately "pursued it like a

Madonna has referred to seeing or has viewed:

Entre Nous, The Marriage of Maria Braun (and all other Fassbinder films),
A Place in the Sun, Spike of Bensonhurst, Grey Gardens (1976 documentary of the eccentric Bouviers, Edith
and Edie Beale), *Lair of the White Worm, House of Games, Ms. 45, Far and Away* ("hated it!"),
Frankie and Johnny, Sleepless in Seattle, State of Grace (**Sean Penn**'s sophomore directorial effort),
The Piano Lesson, Goodfellas, The Bad Seed, and *Sunset Boulevard* (on the plane en route to London
to kick off **The Girlie Show**), *Farewell, My Concubine,* and *The Nasty Girl.*

Madonna has attended:

Robin Williams live at the **New York** Metropolitan Opera House (she was particularly amused by Williams's
impersonation of Sylvester Stallone as Hamlet: "To be, or *what?*"); *A Streetcar Named Desire* on Broadway,
with Alec Baldwin and Jessica Lange; Mike Tyson–Michael Spinks title fight; Chicago White Sox–Cleveland
Indians baseball game at Comiskey Park in Chicago; Mike Tyson–Razor Ruddock title fight,
on TV at Ditka's Restaurant in Chicago; Knicks, Lakers, Suns, and Spurs **basketball** games.

motherfucker," calling up playwright Mamet to request an audition. Mamet recalled being "blown away" by her reading, and when Elizabeth Perkins removed herself from consideration for the part, Mamet and director **Gregory Mosher** confidently chose Madonna.

Madonna originated the role of "Karen," a seemingly naïve, principled young office temp who attempts to convince a conniving producer of the validity of her pet **project**: a film adaptation of a brainy book called *The Bridge, or Radiation and the Half-Life of Society—A Study of Decay.* The movie mogul "Bobby Gould," played by **Joseph Mantegna**, already made a bet with his producer colleague "Charlie Fox" (Ron Silver) that he would be able to bed "Karen," which he did.

The play actually implies that "Karen" is no better than the sleazy producers, and perhaps was manipulating the events the entire time. Still, Mamet referred to "Karen" as a "latter-day Joan of Arc." Interpretations aside, Madonna hated the role but was toughened by the rigorous experience, both in playing a character so unlike herself, and in receiving malicious reviews for her efforts.

The play was a phenomenal success all the same, Tony-nominated for Best Dramatic Play and Best Lead Actor in a Play,

the latter of which Silver won. The show was originally slated to play at the Mitzi Newhouse Theater at Lincoln Center, but explosive ticket sales bumped it over to the Royale at 242 West 45th Street. It sold out six months in advance, translating to over a million dollars in ticket sales, on the strength of Madonna's appearance, sales that dropped 60 percent when she left the show at the end of her contract.

Only two unscripted incidents marred the run of the play, not bad, considering how unprotected the world's biggest star was from some of her most eager **fans**. Once, a crazed **wanna-be** leapt onstage to meet her, only to be escorted off by Mantegna. The other incident was of Madonna's doing, though still beyond her **control**. While reading from *The Bridge*, she suddenly developed a case of the giggles, which she nearly fooled the audience into accepting as part of the play.

Opening night was attended by the likes of the late Jackie Onassis (whose son **JFK Jr.**, had supposedly already trysted with Madonna), Brooke Shields, Cathy Lee Crosby, Jennifer Grey, Jennifer Beals, Anthony and **Christopher Ciccone**, Tatum O'Neal and John McEnroe, and Christie Brinkley and Billy Joel.

It was during her time on Broadway that Madonna met and bonded with **Sandra Bernhard**.

One non-star who saw the show and loved it was a Vietnam veteran who sent Madonna a medal praising her courage in tackling Broadway. Some critics awarded her medals, too, and some reviewed her so aggressively she was an instant candidate for the Purple Heart.

"Speed-the-plow . . . So our lives, in acts exemplary, not only win ourselves good names, but doth to others give matter for virtuous deeds, by which we live."
—George Chapman. The quote from which *Speed-the-Plow* sarcastically takes its name

•

"She's a sympathetic, misunderstood heroine who speaks the truth at any risk."
—Madonna, on her character, "Karen"

•

"I've been bad—I know what it means to be bad. . . . I just wanna be good."
—"Karen," in *Speed-the-Plow*

"It's a relief to report that this rock star's performance is safely removed from her Hollywood persona. Madonna serves Mr. Mamet's play much as she did . . . ***Desperately Seeking Susan***, with intelligent, scrupulously disciplined comic **acting**. She delivers the shocking transitions essential to the action and needs only more confidence to relax a bit and fully command her speaking voice."
—Frank Rich, *The New York Times*

•

"NO, SHE CAN'T ACT."
—headline, *New York Daily News*

•

"Madonna, not yet an accomplished actress but a steady performer in the Mamet style, convincingly shows the steely conviction beneath her protestations of being 'only a temporary.'"
—Richard Christiansen, *Chicago Sun-Times*

•

"She really challenged herself and I think she should be proud."
—Brooke Shields

•

"Her ineptitude is scandalously thorough. She moves as if operated by a remote control unit several cities away."
—Dennis Cunningham, WCBS-TV

•

"Though she looks terrific, she recites her lines prosaically and without much character. She attempts to stretch a talent she doesn't seem to have developed. Worse, she brings the production down with her."
—David Patrick Stearns, *USA Today*

•

"It was like great sex!"
—Madonna after opening night

Spy: Smart-assed **magazine** known for airbrushing famous faces into satirical situations on their covers. Madonna had two brushes with *Spy* immortality, once as a **cheerleader** perched on the shoulder of General Norman Schwarzkopf in 1990, and again in 1991, when her face was tacked to the nude, whitewashed body of *Spy*'s voluptuous photo research editor, Nicki Gostin.

The latter stunt was a send-up of Demi Moore's appearance on **Vanity Fair** wearing nothing but a painted-on suit. "Madonna"'s suit was of the paint-by-numbers variety.

stamps: In 1989, Grenada became the first country in the world to slap Madonna on a stamp, featuring her in a live pose from her **Who's That Girl tour**. The tiny Caribbean island of St. Vincent issued a set of nine $1 Madonna stamps in 1991, paintings of mostly early poses with one then-current **Blond Ambition** pose thrown in for good measure. Since then, other countries have also "honored" Madonna with a stamp, including a series from the African nation of Gambia in 1992.

Don't look for the United States to follow suit. For one thing, Madonna's image is probably too over-the-top for the stodgy U.S. Post Office. For another, in order to be pictured on a stamp, you have to be seven years in the grave.

The stamps that BEG to be licked.

Stanton, Harry Dean: Grizzled character actor and close pal of **Sean Penn**'s, who interviewed Madonna for her first *Interview* cover story in December 1985.

stardom: "You have to have a very large, um, ego, and a good tolerance for pain, and you have to be addicted to **work** and keep going and going and going." —Madonna on maintaining stardom, 1987

statue: In 1987, a bronze, thirteen-foot-tall likeness of Madonna in her **Who's That Girl** bustier was commissioned to stand in the hometown of her **grandparents, Pacentro**, Italy. The statue was designed by an artist named Walter Pugni, and included a suitcase in Madonna's grasp, meant to represent the 20,000 emigrants who had made their way from Pacentro to the United States. It cost over $400,000, not counting the fees for an elaborate unveiling, but was removed after parish priest Don Giuseppe Lepore denounced it as a sacrilege. That's all it takes sometimes.

The statue's whereabouts today are unknown.

Stearns, Jeff: The good-natured "world's fastest grocery bag-boy" from Shenandoah, Iowa, who in 1994 lost his big chance to perform on "The Late Show" with **David Letterman** when Madonna commandeered his scheduled segment.

He didn't mind, though, because in the greenroom she pulled him into a corner to keep warm in the freezing studio. It was all a **flirt**ation—had to be since his pregnant wife Connie was tapping her foot nearby—but JS did find Madonna to be exceptionally charming. "She was great backstage," he beamed. "She was terrific. Very nice."

Steel, Dawn: The first female studio head and driving force behind films like *Fatal Attraction*, *The Accused*, and *Cool Runnings*, she was president of Columbia Pictures at the time of that studio's production deal with Madonna's **Siren Films**.

In her unfortunately-titled, poorly-received memoir, *They Can Kill You . . . But They Can't Eat You: Lessons from the Front*, DS says of Madonna, "She's a real girl's girl. Usually women are their own worst enemies. She's not threatened by other women. She's completely open and honest."

Stein, Seymour: Sire Records executive responsible for signing Madonna, after she was paraded before him by **Michael Rosenblatt** while recuperating at Lenox Hill Hospital. He was among the first with the vision that Madonna could become "the next **Marilyn Monroe**," or even, he mused cautiously, another **Barbra Streisand**.

Steinberg, Ed: Founder of Rock America, **video** supplier who produced the 1981 **Konk** video in which Madonna and **Martin Burgoyne** danced overenthusiastically in an attempt to scene-steal. He was later asked to produce Madonna's first **video,** **"Everybody,"** and claims to have been the man who introduced Madonna to tragic **graffiti** artist **Jean-Michel Basquiat.**

"*S*he's a nice-looking person, but she's no model, I think. But once you get to know her, she's extremely **sexual,** very alluring, very strong, yet you want to be close to her, you want to touch her."

—Ed Steinberg, 1993

stepmother: SEE: GUSTAFSON (CICCONE), JOAN; SIBLINGS

"Steve McQueen": Cropped, boyish **hair**cut that Madonna sported on the **Girlie Show tour,** named for the seventies film actor.

Stewart, Marlene: Talented designer and **stylist** responsible for the imaginative costumes that were the hallmark of Madonna's second world tour, the **Marilyn Monroe** knockoff in the **"Material Girl" video,** the deliciously vulgar baby-vixen **look** of the **Virgin tour,** and even Madonna's **wedding** gown, which featured a black bowler cap as the "something old."

"*I* hate this costume, Marlene!"

—Madonna complaining to Marlene Stewart of her Pop Art charm-bracelet jacket from the Who's That Girl tour, 1987

Most famously, she designed the **Fellini**-esque blue-black corset with gold nipple tassels worn by Madonna in her role as a stripper at a peep show in the **"Open Your Heart" video.** That bustier has since been inextricably linked with Madonna, and toured the world on Madonna's back for her **Who's That Girl** concerts. Madonna wore many of MS's designs offstage, including the blue floral summer dress she preened in before the press opening night of ***Speed-the-Plow.***

MS was to have designed the costumes for the **Blond Ambition tour** in 1990, but was bumped from the assignment by **Jean-Paul Gaultier** with his expressionistic fantasy gear. Madonna's move from Stewart to Gaultier marked her move into the world of brand-name designers, evidenced by her preoccupation with high **fashion** and the seasonal shows in Paris and Milan.

Stewart, Michael: Graffiti artist Madonna hung out with, especially in 1982 when he appeared briefly in her rarely seen **"Everybody" video.** He was later beaten while resisting the **New York City** Transit Police, and died as a result of his injuries.

stick: Sean Penn taught Madonna how to drive a stick shift in anticipation of purchasing a Porsche, but they went with the Mercedes 560SL, so Madonna has never had to test her skill.

Streisand, Barbra: The voice! "Like *buttah.*" Madonna's first encounter with The Other Diva was in 1983, when they met over Chinese for Madonna and BS's then beau Jon Peters to discuss her **singing** role in his film ***Vision Quest.***

Much later, BS made a surprise cameo during Madonna's own unpublicized stint on **"Saturday Night Live"'**s "Coffee Talk," floating in to grace the cast with her magnificence. Madonna was pleasantly shocked to see Babs—her **eyes** lit up and her jaw dropped in a delighted grin—and she immediately bowed and prostrated herself, exhorting, "We're not worthy!"

"*A*s for ambition, she makes Streisand look squishy."

—**Liz Smith** on Madonna, 1988

In 1993, a disaster was averted when secret plans for a **Ciccone**-Streisand duet of "Anything You Can Do, I Can Do Better" were exposed and then fell through. Barbra Joan has pulled off some inspired duets in the past, but sometimes enough is enough.

suicide: Marilyn Monroe committed suicide (or did she?). She was blonde. She was famous. Madonna is blonde. She's pretty famous, too. Gee, that must mean she'll commit suicide! Media analysts and other crackpots have consistently implied or stated that Madonna's very public life and what they interpret to be her overriding lust for attention will result in suicide. That they would speculate such an un-Madonna outcome underscores their misreading of her character, and, consequently, of her appeal.

Madonna is only human, and is probably a good deal more vulnerable than she sometimes appears, but she is about as likely to commit suicide as Rush Limbaugh is. It just isn't going to happen. The main reason writers speculate that Madonna will off herself—aside from the superficial parallels to Marilyn—is that it would fit very romantically with the whole package: "Willful star cuts wide swath through international culture, flashes skin, loses favor, slashes wrists, broken and alone."

Rather than a "KEVORKIAN GIRL!" headline, a more likely scenario involves Willard Scott III wishing a happy 106th birthday to a pretty little lady named Madonna **Ciccone.**

If she made it through her **mother'**s **death,** homelessness, being called a slut by *Rolling Stone,* a nude-photo scandal, ***Shanghai Surprise,*** the death of her best friend to **AIDS,** an abusive marriage and heartbreaking **divorce**, papal condemnation, the betrayal of her best galpal, possible **miscarriages** or **abortions**, the trashing of *Sex, Body of Evidence*, **David Letterman**, and being declared "over" by *Us* and *Entertainment Weekly*, what could possibly drive Madonna over the edge at this point? Having a single not go Top Ten?

Supercuts: National **hair**styling chain that in 1990 introduced a 'do inspired by Madonna's **look** in *Dick Tracy*, the "**Breathless** Bob."

Hint: Not everybody looks good with chin-length platinum ringlets.

Superior Court of California, County of Los Angeles: Court where the Madonna–**Sean Penn divorce** was decided, located at 1725 Main Street.

"Supernatural": This ghostly **love** song originally appeared as the B-side

"*T*ime may be running out for Madonna . . . unless she can admit to herself that what she does onstage in her thirties might seem grotesquely inappropriate for a woman in her fifties."
—(Don't tell Tina Turner that!)

—**Christopher Andersen**, a man in his forties, 1991

.

"*A* story published in America said she had bought a crypt so she could be buried near Marilyn Monroe at Westwood Memorial Park. She hasn't done that. Yet."

—Douglas Thompson, 1991

.

"*S*omewhere along the line, I wouldn't be surprised if we see a suicide gesture."
—(Like a pirouette off a cliff?)

—Stuart Fischoff, media psychologist, 1992

of the **"Cherish"** single in 1989. Almost three years later, it was remixed and donated to *Red, Hot + Dance*, a compilation whose proceeds benefited the **AIDS** group AmFAR.

Sylbert, Richard: *Dick Tracy*'s set designer, he also created an entire fantasy bedroom for Madonna, full of **Herb Ritts** and **Steven Meisel** portraits and *Dick*-inspired primary colors. The masterpiece was one room at the Metropolitan Home Showhouse at 115 East 79th Street in **New York City** in a 1991 benefit for Design Industries Foundation for **AIDS** (DIFFA).

RS's bedroom was the most popular room, competing against a kitchen by Alice Waters, a Tom Wolfe writer's room, and others by similarly gifted artists/designers. RS also handled the production design for the **"Open Your Heart" video**.

tabloids: Typical tabloid news item: "MADONNA SONG WAKES TEEN FROM COMA! . . . Relatives, friends, and nurses took turns playing Millie's favorite Madonna tapes on her Walkman. 'A couple of times I thought I saw Millie's lips move to the beat of **"Vogue,"'** Regina says. . . . She thought she saw a blonde woman sitting on Millie's bed talking to her. ' I swear, it looked like Madonna. But when I looked again, there was no one there.' On the thirty-first day, Millie suddenly sat up, vigorously belting out **"Material Girl"** . . . Millie told Regina and Patty that Madonna's music kept her from drifting toward a bright, white circle of light. . . . 'It's **God**'s work.'" —May Turner, *The Sun*, 1994

taxes: France sued Madonna in 1987 for back taxes due from her **Who's That Girl tour**. And after her regal welcome by **Jacques Chirac!**

SEE ALSO: LAWSUITS

Taylor, Elizabeth: Sweet-smelling **glamor**puss of the fifties who called Madonna a "heroine and a symbol of our times" in a written statement sent to AmFAR's Award of Courage benefit. ET had sent regrets when she was bitten by the flu bug, and she bagged plans to cohost **Truth or Dare**'s **New York** premiere in May 1991 due to unspecified illness. The women share a passion for **AIDS** awareness.

teeth: According to a dentist contacted by *Allure* magazine, Madonna's "central incisors are mismatched in length." Buyer beware.

television: If you've ever wondered why Madonna hasn't incorporated "Mrs. Brady" or "Laverne" or "Mary Tyler Moore" into her work, it's because as a kid she was not allowed to watch TV. She

*"*T*V is mesmerizing, you know? It's very* **powerful**, *television—very, very powerful—and it's kind of scary to me. I probably could get very addicted to TV."*

—Madonna, 1991

had to sneak to her friends' houses to watch shows like "Dark Shadows," "The Monkees," and "The Partridge Family." Once she had the freedom to watch TV, she had no interest or felt it too absorbing, preferring classic films.

Tenuta, Judy: "I admire her so much. She's like a breast with a boombox." —Judy Tenuta, on Madonna, 1990

"This Used to be My Playground" song: Timeless, mournful ballad that served as the theme song for **A League of Their Own**, though it did not appear on the soundtrack, but only on an Olympics collection called *Barcelona Gold*.

Madonna herself tends to view her movie **music** as "assignment **work**" that she rattles off quickly and with minimum emotional investment, but the ballad—however marred by a few clichés on the shortness of life and the importance of living and learning—became a number 1 hit for its honest delivery and aching sense of loneliness, regret, and nostalgia for **friendship** lost. Cowritten by **Shep Pettibone**, the song was the last completed from their *Erotica* sessions, but preceded that album's release by several months.

*"*C*halk up another hit with no errors for Madonna. 'This Used to be My Playground' is a desperately sad ballad that oozes vulnerability and exhibits none of the singer's legendary toughness. It's the last thing you'd expect. In other words, it's* very *Madonna."*

—Edna Gundersen, *USA Today*

"This Used to be My Playground" video: Most **videos** of movie theme songs are straight performance pieces featuring haphazard clips from the film in question. "TUTBMP" avoids that trap. It's a stylish rendering featuring masculine hands slowly flipping pages in an old-fashioned photo album. The photos are moving images of Madonna: in a black beret on a pewlike seat, roaming in hand-colored shots of grassy fields, lying in bed with a criss-crossing shadow on her face, writing on pages in a café.

The video makes use of the image of a mirror, as when Madonna sees herself in one and removes a photo of herself that is stuck to its corner, and when her **singing** lips are shown in reflection. Though simple, the imagery cleverly depicts the act of introspection. At the end, the man who has been looking back at his scrapbook of Madonna lays his head down longingly on the album, sealing the video with the perfect bit of sadness to resonate with Madonna's *ennui*.

three wishes: If Barbara Eden were a Madonna fan, Madonna would probably ask her to grant the three wishes she's said are her dearest: (1) peace on earth, (2) a cure for **AIDS**, and (3) eight hours of sleep every night.

Tiffany's: Madonna registered here for her **wedding**, choosing Monet's Giverny ($260 per setting) and Coeur de Fleur ($660 per setting) China patterns.

***Time*:** When the serious news**magazine** featured Madonna on their cover in 1985, the interview they published with her was one of the longest in the magazine's history.

toilet: Though she **shock**ed **David Letterman** by spontaneously confessing that she pees in the shower, Madonna's "most contemplative moments" are when she holds it until she's sitting on the toilet.

Tony Awards: The year of her Broadway debut in ***Speed-the-Plow***, Madonna made her debut as a Tony presenter before an audience of 28 million viewers. She appeared in a **Rachel London** form-fitting black gown studded with enormous pink roses, her **hair** dark brown and pulled back.

In peak form, she read clumsily from cue cards but saved herself by joking that she was being punished for skipping rehearsals. Her crack brought down the house and the approval emboldened the academy's littlest presenter—she then joked that she just *knew* her badly positioned mike was going to ruin her posture, and beamed while she handed a regional theater award to the two founders of the South Coast Repertory Company in Costa Mesa, California.

"*T*wenty-four years ago, two men—two *young* men—set out to . . . now they're *old* men . . . two *young* men set out to start a new theater in Costa Mesa, California."

—Madonna, cracking wise to cover a cue-card crisis at the 1988 Tonys

Her *STP* costar Ron Silver walked away with a Best Featured Actor Tony that evening, thanking Madonna profusely.

toy: Madonna told *Interviewer* Mike Myers that her favorite toy is her answering machine.

True Blue **album:** Internationally, Madonna's biggest album, and without a doubt the first solid proof that she had **music**al legs. The album sold over 5 million copies in the U.S. and another 12 million worldwide, hitting number 1 in 28 countries (an achievement that *The Guiness Book of World Records* called "totally unprecedented") as diverse as Austria, Brazil, Ireland, Israel, the Netherlands, New Zealand, and, of course, the good old U.S. of A. It produced five Top Five hits, three of which went to number 1 in America.

Critically, it is not Madonna's best-reviewed album, but it will probably survive as her most fondly remembered for its vibrant, carefully crafted pop magic and its summer (June 30, 1986) launch; summer has a way of burning music into your consciousness.

For her third album, Madonna wrote or cowrote every one of its nine songs, working mainly with **Steve Bray** and **Patrick Leonard**. She also coproduced herself, the first step on the way to total musical **control**. In stark contrast to her behind-the-scenes control is the submissive jacket, a colorized **Herb Ritts** portrait of Madonna's profile, her jugular exposed. It's her most famous album **art**, and ranks as one of the most instantly recognizable of all time.

The leadoff song was the second single, the much-misunderstood **"Papa Don't Preach."** Instead of tapping their feet to it, the National Organization of Women and Planned Parenthood shook their fists. It shot to number 1 anyway. The song was written by Brian Elliot, though Madonna scored an "additional **lyrics**" credit. **"Open Your Heart"** follows, another number 1 hit as the album's fourth single. It was cowritten by Madonna with Gardner Cole and Peter Rafelson, though that credit doesn't accurately reflect the fact that an early Cole-and-Rafelson version was recorded in **demo** form by **Donna DeLory**, and that Madonna stepped in to rewrite parts of it to make it her own.

Her love for the Golden Age of Hollywood comes to the fore with an embarrassing Jimmy Cagney tribute—a snippet from his famous *Public Enemy* speech—that prefaces her scorching rendition of "White Heat," a sort of warm-up to **"Express Yourself"** that never received the attention it deserved as a steel-willed ode to self-esteem.

Side one ends with an unbeatable wallop, the powerfully undulating ballad **"Live to Tell,"** which was a number 1 hit before the album's release and doubled as the theme of **Sean Penn**'s vehicle ***At Close Range***. It's arguably Madonna and Pat Leonard's best collaboration, though Leonard prefers **"Oh Father."**

Side two begins with one of Madonna's most beloved album tracks, the frothy good-time anthem "Where's the Party," which took Bray, Leonard, *and* **Ciccone** to pound it into shape. "Party" was performed on tour during **Who's That Girl** and **Blond Ambition,** despite never being released as a single. **"True Blue,"** Madonna's irresistible girl-group *hommage*, follows, a number 3 single.

"La Isla Bonita" would become one of Madonna's biggest international hits, "only" hitting number 4 in the U.S., but going number 1 most everywhere else, especially in Latin America, where her performance of it on her **Girlie Show tour** was ecstatically received.

The album's closing songs are the weakest, one reason some reviewers walked away lukewarm. "Jimmy Jimmy" is an obnoxious, up-tempo, bad-boy song beneath Bray-Ciccone, and "Love Makes the World Go Round" is a pseudo-calypso number so saccharine it was only successful at its worldwide debut, at the equally feel-too-good **Live Aid** event in July 1985.

The album is dedicated to Sean Penn, "my husband, the coolest guy in the universe."

"True Blue" song: Sweet girl-group tune that features Madonna at her chirpiest and most **flirt**atious, beginning with a pert call to attention (echoed in the later **"Express Yourself"**), which goes from coy *rejoinder* to bossy command. "TB" is the song that best illustrates *True Blue*'s—and Madonna's—dedication to **Sean Penn**. The singer's **lyric**al vow of chastity is utterly convincing, espe-

"Catchy."

—John Updike, 1987

cially in light of her admission to having had other **lovers**, an odd note in such an unabashed valentine.

"True Blue" video: MTV sponsored a "Make My **Video**" competition for Madonna's third release off *True Blue*, which culminated with a daylong airing of some of the best—and weirdest—entries, and the unveiling of the winner, a well-crafted, **black-and-white**, poodle-skirted affair by Angel Gracia and Cliff Guest that went into heavy rotation.

For non-U.S. release, Madonna filmed a **Jamie Foley**—directed quickie video, featuring her with dead white **hair**, jet black

*"**M**aking a record can be very difficult, but this one wasn't at all. It was fun and easy because Madonna is such a pleasant person to be around."*

—collaborator **Pat Leonard**

·

*"**T**rue Blue is a less lustrous achievement than Madonna's two prior albums, but that may have been inevitable. If the past is any indication, she'll continue to shed images—and critical assessments—in the future. She seems, more than ever, unstoppable."*

—*Rolling Stone*

·

*"**T**he songs are shrewdly crafted teenage and preteenage ditties that reveal Madonna's unfailing commercial instincts. And her singing, which has been harshly criticized as a thin imitation of the sixties girl-group sound, has strengthened."*

—Stephen Holden, *The New York Times*

·

*"**T**rue Blue is Madonna's Rubber Soul, as a critical moment when she drops the veil of somnambulism and reveals trade tricks and secret fantasies."*

—*L.A. Weekly*, 1989

brows, and bloodred lips, cavorting in royal blue splendor on an all-blue set. In the non-U.S. version, Madonna sits astride, and even campily pretends to steer her Thunderbird, while girl-group extras dance behind her (one of them is **Debi Mazar**).

Much is made of a hanky **dance**, after which Madonna drops hers, a cute visual trick that leaves the viewer wanting to pick it up, either to chivalrously return it to Madonna, or to stash the **artifact** in a safety-deposit box. Though this version of the video was obviously a chore for Madonna (she looks bothered at having to do it), it looks snazzy and is preferable to the American one, if only because Madonna is actually *in* it.

Trump, Donald: Smug wheeler-dealer with a penchant for dumb blondes who don't mind fighting over him. Madonna had comp tickets to the Tyson title fight in 1988 at the invitation of The Donald, but blew any favor she had with him by telling an interviewer, "He's a wimp. Oh, don't print that. I want tickets to the next Tyson fight."

Reasserting his manhood (two years later), DT said of *Sex*, "Not great. I don't think you'll be impressed. If Madonna were in this room, she'd be the least attractive woman here." Since he was in a crowd of old biddies at the time, flattery got him everywhere.

Truth or Dare: Madonna's critical acclaim and popularity merged and—so far—peaked, with the release in May 1991 of this inventive, engaging combination of all the best elements of a tour movie with the voyeuristic thrill of a convenience store surveillance tape.

Madonna's first concept for the film was a straight documentary of what she knew would be her most extravagant and important tour, **Blond Ambition.** She'd lined up **David Fincher** to direct, but when he pulled out at the last minute, she indulged in one of those eccentric decisions that superstars sometimes make: She called a small-time **video director** whose college thesis she'd admired, and offered him the job. **Alek Keshishian**, a self-professed Madonna **fan**, flew to **Japan** to start shooting within a week.

Over the course of the shoot, Keshishian realized from his

dailies that this was no mere *Rattle and Hum*, but a unique peek inside the truly private moments of a star's existence. Keshishian had footage of Madonna without makeup, behaving like a spoiled brat, flashing her breasts, calling her brother crazy, calling her **lover Warren Beatty** "**pussy** man" before a roomful of people, fellating a water bottle . . . the works.

He also had the quiet moments: Madonna at rest, chatting tiredly with her best girlfriend **Sandra Bernhard**, worrying over Beatty's lack of attention to her, succumbing to a throat ailment, mothering her troupe of mostly gay dancers.

When Madonna got a load of Keshishian's work and realized how deliciously iconoclastic it was, she bit, giving him *carte blanche* to continue, despite the fact that the icon in question was herself. Or maybe *because* of it. At one point, Madonna remarks that her screaming fans want her no matter what. Perhaps *TOD* was meant to test that desire.

TOD, in its stylish frankness, is unprecedented. Forget about comparisons to Dylan concert movies— that's not what this film's about anyway. This film is about Madonna, about the life of the world's most famous and controversial woman. It's not about the road, or about **music**. It's about **fame** and its corrupting influence on public perception. Its existence proves why Madonna is a bigger, or at least greater, star than any of her peers.

The rarely-seen teaser ad for Truth or Dare.

Try substituting Mariah Carey or Whitney Houston and you'll come up with two hours of dead air. They have no personality, and their popularity begins and ends with their latest saccharine hit or Grammy-laden thanks to **God**. **Michael Jackson** and **Prince**, the two other stars audiences would be most interested in peeping in on have too much to hide to do such a film. Don't even *talk* to me about **Paula Abdul**.

Parts of the film leave some viewers cold. Madonna visiting her **mother**'s grave in Michigan for the first time since she was a child is a stagey-seeming scene that Keshishian maintains was completely unrehearsed. She famously disses Kevin Costner, who stops backstage after a show to proclaim it "neat," saying he's bought some programs for his *kids*, then sends her a comically phony air-**kiss**. Madonna's reaction, and the only sane response, is to stick her fingers down her throat and mock vomiting.

Her crass rejection of Costner is a juicy metaphor for her self-fueled outcast status in Hollywood, a status she reiterates toward

the end of the film, when she and her dancers sneer to the camera that they don't want to be accepted by Hollywood. It's a winning moment, but is the very sort of behavior that alienates mainstream audiences.

Does the film stop at nothing? Well, even Madonna has limits. She refused Keshishian access to any **business** meetings, and also refused to allow her frail grandmother to be photographed. "You just can't," she decreed, afraid the cameras would startle the elderly **Ciccone**.

Shot alternately in grainy **black-and-white** (for the behind-the-scenes moments) and super-vivid color (the concert sequences), the film ingeniously juxtaposes the flawless choreography and nonstop fun of the performance with less-than-perfect reality. In real life on the tour, Madonna's makeup person was sexually assaulted, a random event that left most of the players indifferent or confused. The gay dancers and the lone straight dancer clashed angrily behind the scenes, and **sex** siren Madonna couldn't win the affections of Spain's handsomest leading man (**Antonio Banderas**) simply because he's married.

Through all this fascinating chaos, the tour remains perfect and immutable, so uniform that the performance sequences are sneakily interchanged throughout: When Madonna is threatened with arrest for indecency in Toronto, and manager **Freddy DeMann** bets a cop that she'll go out of her way to make her performance of **"Like a Virgin"** all the raunchier, the audience can't help but feel that the ensuing performance *does* seem really out there. But the performance was not taped in Toronto; she sports the curly **hair** she only reverted to later, when the tour swept through Europe.

Madonna's most emotional outbursts, in fact, occur in direct relation to technical snafus that threaten to mar the concert's perfection. When testing a sound system early in the film, her demeanor is all business, take no prisoners. The most **shock**ing moment in the film isn't the ballyhooed male-male kiss, but the clip of **"Keep It Together"** being performed with chunks of Madonna's vocals lost to electrical malfunctioning. Confronted with disaster, some divas' impulse would be, "The face! Not the face!" But Madonna's far more concerned with the visage of her **work**, of which her face, her breasts, and her voice are all important parts.

"*I*t's kind of like **Fellini** meets *The Boys in the Band*. It's also a political film.
It brings out all the family secrets that everybody wants to keep in the closet."

—Madonna

•

"*I*t's like being in psychoanalysis and letting the whole world watch."

—Alek Keshishian

•

"*T*he organizing subject of the whole film is **work**. We learn a lot about how hard Madonna works,
about her methods for working with her dancers and her backstage support team, about how
brutally hard it is to do a world concert tour. Unlike most rock documentaries, the real heart
of this film is backstage, and the onstage musical segments, while effectively produced,
seem obligatory—they're not the reason she wanted to make this film."

—Roger Ebert, *Chicago Sun-Times*

•

A one-and-a-half-minute trailer for the film was slapped with an R rating for its excessive
use of the dreaded *M* word . . . ***masturbation***

•

"*I* love that people will go home and talk of it. I live for things like that."

—Madonna on the gay kiss

•

Truth or Dare's original working title was *Truth or Dare: On the Road, Behind the Scenes, and In Bed With Madonna*.

A gay porn video send-up surfaced six months after its release, called *Truth, Dare, or Damian*.
"Damian" is like the Madonna of gay porn: He changes his hairstyle, attitude, and sexual position with each of his videos.

Miramax hosted a screening of *Truth or Dare* at Manhattan's TriBeca Film Center for an audience entirely composed of 150 self-
proclaimed Madonna-**hate**rs in order to gauge the film's appeal to a broad audience. They knew they had a hit when 65 percent of
the haters had to admit they liked it, and liked Madonna more after seeing it.

In the film, Madonna addresses a **Japan**ese audience with, "Hello, Japan-ites!"
Japanese viewers of the film, however, were presented with the baffling translation "Japan-itis!"

•

"*A*s she disembowels herself in desperate and spectacular splatter, we cannot even muster,
much less justify, our love to put an end to this suicidal psychosis."

—Fenton Bailey, *Paper*

•

"*F*or the first time on film, the bitch goddess descends from her pedestal to laugh at her narcissism. She
bares her nipples and her soul. She wants to be liked. Is this vulnerable Madonna the real thing or a ploy
to ingratiate herself with film audiences who've found her chilly and strident? You be the judge. But there's
no denying that *Truth or Dare* is at its raunchy best when Madonna is kicking ass instead of **kissing** it."

—Peter Travers, *Rolling Stone*

Much was made of the gay content of *TOD*. Madonna herself expressed pride at riling America with her depiction of gay sexuality, a good example of how Madonna doesn't often **shock** only for the sake of shocking, but does so in order to scare out some prejudices that she feels shouldn't be allowed to comfortably exist.

Her attempt is praiseworthy, but the **gay men** in the film are allotted so little screen time that they're almost indiscernible from each other. Their lack of personality (due to time constraints) renders them all as one familiar type: the queeny dancer with attitude. They are flamboyant without joy, and we never get to see the kind of personal awakening that we see happening with **Oliver Crumes**—in a scene where he visits with his **father** after years of estrangement.

The gay kiss—Madonna's favorite scene—is supposed to be liberating, but the way it emerges—as a *dare*—colors it as a freakish act. The kiss is a cool idea, but in execution is too scary for homophobes to warm up to, and too straight-directed (literally, since Madonna dared Gabriel and **Slam** to do it) to be a proud moment for gay audiences.

Much more effective are the later scenes of Madonna in bed with her dancers (hence the film's non-U.S. title, *In Bed With Madonna*), in which her charm and her sympatico with them goes a long way toward humanizing a star as well as gay men.

Despite its flaws, *TOD* is a masterfully-executed piece of film that lives up to its name as half truth, half dare. The fun is in trying to figure out the *"or"*: Which is which? It's hilarious, can't-take-your-eyes-off-it reportage that preserves Madonna for all time, warts and all.

Critics were won over by Madonna's candor, giving the pic near-universal raves, though retrospective analyses have grown more pointed, pleading the case that the film's "reality" is itself constructed for the camera. But Madonna has the last word: "Even a lie is telling."

Madonna launched the film triumphantly at **Cannes**, and for its U.S. premiere, Madonna went all out. She appeared first at an L.A. screening at the Hollywood Cinerama Dome wearing her brunette hair long and straight, with almost ghoulish eyeliner, then danced the night away at the after-party at Arena. That event was so overheated that guest Marlee Matlin's signer read Madonna's lips for the press: "It's so fucking hot!"

Besides Matlin, other celeb guests included **Rosanna Arquette**, Alan Thicke, **Sandra Bernhard, k.d. lang**, lover **Vanilla Ice**, Wendy and Lisa, Steven Seagal, **Barry Manilow**, Valerie Bertinelli and Eddie Van Halen, **David Geffen**, Matthew Modine, Gerardo, Kid 'n' Play, **Herb Ritts**, and Madonna's sisters Paula and Melanie, with all profits going to **AIDS** Project Los Angeles.

Two days later, she showed up for the film's **New York** premiere wearing a sparkling minisuit and sporting glamorous, *Evita*-like coiffed hair. The celebrities at that launch included Keenan Ivory Wayans, **Deborah Harry**, Susan Sarandon, and **Naomi Campbell**, with all monies going both to APLA and the Washington-based AIDS Action Foundation.

Fans and a significant portion of the general public flocked to see the movie, making it the most financially successful documentary of all time, bringing in $15,012,935 at the box office domestically (the film was made on a $4 million budget). A bootlegged version was reported to be available in New York with a $10,000 price tag. This version was said to contain Madonna's private phone calls to Warren Beatty and a reference to **Sean Penn** as an ex-husband who sucks. This significantly different version actually exists as an early promotional video made before final edits were decided.

The film was distributed by **Miramax**, marking Madonna's first collaboration with the Brothers Weinstein.

Tuck, James: Toronto stuntman to whom Madonna was briefly romantically linked in 1989, before her **divorce** from **Sean Penn** was final. Did they? Didn't they? Who knows? But it's fun to imagine Madonna's expression when she realized that her latest romantic conquest was a *stuntman*.

Turnberry Isle: Florida town where Madonna and **Sean Penn** rekindled the romance after a brief separation in 1987, immediately before he left to serve prison time and Madonna was about to appear at Madison Square Garden in **New York** to perform a **Who's That Girl** show for **AIDS**.

turn-ons: Like any good *Playboy* bunny, Madonna wouldn't be caught dead without some. In a man, she's turned on by intelligence, confidence, humor, **art**istic passion; she also expects him to like antiques, write her lots of letters, and smell good. She also prefers a man who can pay his own rent.

underwear: Madonna has reinvented the term, routinely donning men's boxer shorts, bras, girdles, garter belts, and bustiers as *outer*wear, making unmentionables eminently mentionable.

In concert, **fans** often throw their undergear at Madonna, which usually annoys her (though more-aerodynamic **condoms** are welcome). "Stop throwing your underpants up here," she told London at a **Who's That Girl** performance. "First of all, they're not my size."

In 1984, she incorrectly predicted, "I wouldn't wear *just* sexy underpants in public."

U.S. Blues: Long Island biker bar variously known as Uncle Sam's and Spit, where Madonna debuted her act as shaped by then manager **Camille Barbone** in 1981. She performed early versions of **"Sidewalk Talk," "Holiday,"** and **"Burning Up,"** and was even persuaded to record a "Merry Christmas" **commercial** for the bar.

vacations: By her own estimation, the hardest working girl in showbiz has had about three in the last dozen years. But don't press her to define the three, because she's very likely referring to weeklong jaunts en route to movie locations or while writing entire albums.

Vanilla Ice: Everyone was shocked to see the has-been white rapper featured so prominently in cooler-than-cool Madonna's *Sex*. **Rumors** that VI and Madonna were having an affair had been swirling since they went to see *Frankie and Johnny* while on location in **Evansville** shooting *Cool as Ice* and *A League of Their Own*, respectively. He looks terrific in the book, and Madonna has said he reminds her of, gulp, *Elvis*.

VI later 'fessed up to the relationship, detailing their "eight-month" fling. "She would freak out, do weird, crazy things out of the blue. She would call me at strange hours, 'Are you in bed with another girl?' At six in the morning, I'm like, 'I'm **fuck**ing sleeping. All alone!'" He says

Madonna is "ten different people in one," and that he split when the relationship got too serious.

Vanity Fair: High-gloss, self-consciously classy mag that nonetheless affords the same sort of juicy dish that **tabloids** provide, except *VF* manages to do it with their celebrity cover-baby's cooperation. Madonna has been thoroughly documented in its pages via four complete cover stories. She made the cover in 1986 ("Lady Madonna: A Change of Face," by Michael Gross), showing off her new pale, trim **look** with photos by **Herb Ritts**; in 1990 ("White Heat: Madonna Expresses Herself to Kevin Sessums and Undresses Herself for Helmut Newton"), publicly baring a breast for the first time since her rise to **fame**; 1991 ("The Misfit: Who Can Justify Her **Love**?" by Lynn Hirschberg), with **Marilyn Monroe**—like photos by **Steven Meisel**; and 1992 ("Hot Madonna! The **Material Girl**'s Sexual (R)evolution," by Maureen Orth) with "Madonna in Wonderland" photos, also by Meisel.

"*M*adonna's like every normal girl, man. She's very **sexy**, she's hot, she's romantic. She's got a great body for her age."

—Vanilla Ice, 1994

"*I* don't eat flesh. Vegetarians are paler."

—Madonna, 1986

vegetarianism: Madonna doesn't eat flesh, period. (SEE ALSO: **blow jobs**) Even during her darkest days in **New York**, when she claims to have rummaged in trash cans for sustenance, she would discard half-eaten Big Macs in favor of stray french fries.

Though her vegetarianism is well known, gossips sometimes forget that when making up outlandish tales of Madonna and **Warren Beatty** devouring Whoppers or Madonna scarfing down a hot dog while her **bodyguards** roughhouse **paparazzi**.

Veronica: Madonna chose her **Catholic** confirmation name to honor the woman who wiped the face of Jesus Christ on his way to Cavalry.

VH-1: **MTV**'s sister network that plays more pop, as opposed to MTV's favoring of heavy metal and rap. Madonna is a VH-1 favorite.

Interestingly, she managed to provoke controversy in 1993, via VH-1, without even trying. The network bought space on **New York City** buses and at bus stops for ads featuring an image of Madonna from the **"Like a Prayer" video** juxtaposed with an image of Mary, Mother of **God**, and the tag line: "VH-1: the difference between you and your parents."

Catholic groups denounced the ad as blasphemous and seemed to blame Madonna (the newer, sexier one), as if she'd been behind it herself. This has more than a little to do with the **power** of her **"control freak"** image.

videos: Madonna is recognized as one of the pioneer artists in the field of **music** videos. She was awarded MTV's first Video Vanguard **Award** in 1986 for her maverick accomplishments, and also received their Video Artist of the Decade Award, which she accepted by **kiss**ing and licking the prize with gratitude.

Madonna's first video was the extremely low-budget **"Everybody."** She has followed it with videos for most of her major single releases, including several compilation clips thrown

"*To* me, it was like making little movies, and I've always been excited about that. It was like filming it to the three minutes of a song."

—Madonna on making videos, 1985

"*Video* has made it possible to reach the masses without touring."

—Madonna, 1986

"*Video* is an incredibly efficient form, so where do you go after the ultimate in entertainment technology? Will everybody go back to playing acoustic guitars and watching **plays**?"

—Madonna, 1988

together for movie songs and for songs that were only released abroad.

SEE ALSO: **Appendix 2**

Virgin tour, The: Her aptly-named first full-scale tour was such a smashing success, manager **Freddy DeMann** had to hustle to bump up all the bookings from the small venues he'd originally scheduled. Madonnamania was in full swing as 17,672 tickets sold out for her show at Radio City Music Hall in 34 minutes flat, quickly following suit in the 27 other cities she invaded. In San Francisco, tour shirts were selling at a clocked rate of one every six seconds.

Madonna tore through her shows with the zeal of a new kid on the block, exuberantly proposing to her audiences—"Will you marry me?"—and seducing them with her enthusiasm, and with what by then had already become a long list of solid-gold hits: **"Dress You Up," "Holiday," "Into the Groove," "Everybody,"** "Gambler," **"Lucky Star," "Crazy for You,"** "Over and Over," and the bombastic encores **"Like a Virgin"** (during which she broke into a brief passage from **Michael Jackson**'s "Billie Jean") and **"Material Girl."**

The **look** was Vegas Urchin, with an array of changes in and out of brocade jackets, a faux **wedding** gown with "fun fur", and **crucifixes** and peace symbols at every turn. Most prominent was her bare midriff, exposing the famous **belly button** that was getting so much press, and the tendency for her lacy bra to peek out from beneath a lavender halter with each shake and shimmy.

The concert endeared Madonna to all her **fans**, many of whom arrived in full **Boy Toy** regalia, threatening to make her a walking, talking *Rocky Horror Picture Show*. Her performance was scrutinized cynically by rock critics, many of whom openly admitted in the text of their lukewarm reviews their inability to accept **sex**uality as part of artistic entertainment.

"What Madonna is really about is sex. . . ." Michael Goldberg stated in his *Rolling Stone* recap of her Seattle debut, polarizing that aspect from the loftier aspects of **music** and **dance**, but missing the point that personality—often sexually charged—is on an equal par when it comes to any live performance.

TVT was considered a guilty pleasure at best for the critics who praised it, but has since attained a mythic status as

"*I*'ve had fights with people right before I've gone onstage, and then gone onstage with tears in my eyes. I would always go onstage unless something truly horrible happened."

—Madonna, 1986

•

"*M*adonna . . . simply didn't sing very well. Her intonation was atrocious; she sang sharp and she sang flat, and the combination of her unsure pitch and thin, quavery vocal timbre made the held notes at the end of her phrases sound like they were crawling off somewhere to die."

—Robert Palmer, *The New York Times*

•

"*I* ignored the critics because I knew deep down in my heart that it was good and . . . I always will meet up with a certain amount of controversy, a certain amount of opposition to what I'm doing."

—Madonna

•

"*C*yndi Lauper will be around for a long time. Madonna will be out of **business** in six months. Her image has completely overshadowed her music."

—Paul Grein, *Billboard*

•

"*P*erhaps every generation needs reminding that rock and **sex** are sometimes indistinguishable. At the moment, Madonna's the apostle of the body gospel, and, as her show makes apparent, it's hard to recall a more fetching zealot."

—Paul Evans, *Record*

Madonna's most accessible image. She's become a much stronger performer since then, improving her voice, her dancing skills, and her stage presence, even if she's never been so huggable. It was packaged for home video as *Madonna: The Virgin Tour Live.*

virginity: Madonna is very interested in extremes. Most obvious is her interest in the "whore," but she has also explored the "virgin" from the beginning of her career. Her breakthrough song, the one that established her as a force of nature, was **"Like a Virgin,"** which riled radio stations and parents by flaunting the hitherto taboo word "virgin" for all to hear and sing. Madonna did not write the song, but by choosing it, she embraces the idea of a rebirth of **sex**ual newness even in the face of experience. The singer has been around, but her new **love** has made her feel virginal, a theme exactly duplicated by **"True Blue."**

Her **"Like a Virgin" video** expresses the song's theme vividly, juxtaposing the sexuality of a lion's mask with Madonna's virgin white **wedding** gown.

In her video for **"Open Your Heart,"** the virgin-whore dichotomy is sketched by Madonna's performance as a stripper and the innocent adoration awarded her by a teenaged boy. In the end, Madonna chooses to **dance** off with the boy, forsaking carnality for innocence. A video like **"Cherish,"** with Madonna cavorting in the tide, showcases her childlike qualities, enhanced by another **friendship** with a child, this time a little merboy. Even in these heady days of sexual evolution she has time to flash a bit of innocence, as in a (literally) touching photo from *Sex* where she is pictured—almost unrecognizably—as an adolescent girl examining her breasts.

More famously, and to greater outrage, Madonna appeared on the cover of and inside *Vanity Fair* in 1992 in a spread that portrays her in preteen poses, floating on a water toy, having fun on a playground, and standing unself-consciously nude. The *Vanity Fair* images, like the **"Open Your Heart" video**, proved that Madonna's own image is so powerfully that of a sexual predator that presenting her as an innocent, as a virgin, is threatening to a large part of the American public.

Offstage, Madonna lost her virginity at fifteen, to her only serious high-school boyfriend, **Russell Long**.

virtual sex: The concept of using computer images and interactive technology to simulate **sex**.

In 1990, a British service called Computer Information Exchange (CIX) offered to subscribers a package that included renegade virtual-sex programs with scenes of bestiality, incest, **masturbation, rape,** and group sex, as well as photos of famous women, doctored to make them appear nude and engaged in all of the preceding.

"*I* didn't lose my virginity until I knew what I was doing."

—Madonna, 1985

The women featured included **Princess Diana of Wales**, Glenda Jackson *(???)*, Samantha Fox, Brooke Shields, and Madonna. Completely unauthorized cyber-spunk, but does it foreshadow a "Virtual Madonna"?

Vision Quest: Madonna's first post-**fame** film appearance was in this appealing juvenile romance starring Matthew Modine as a young athlete who falls in **love** with sultry Linda Fiorentino. This is one film role in which Madonna *was* playing herself, a sexy singer who performs two songs in a **club**. In *V*, Madonna debuted her first hit ballad, **"Crazy for You,"** and one of her most beloved album tracks, **"Gambler."** Originally, she was to have sung another song (both "Lies In Your Eyes" and "Warning Signs" are two titles listed on early promo material for the film), but it was dropped at the last minute.

Her part was small, but she made the most of it, making a strong impression with magnetic confidence, helping land her the part of "Susan" in ***Desperately Seeking Susan***. Madonna shot *V* in November 1983 on location in Spokane, Washington. The film was a disappointment for producer Jon Peters, but it did manage $12,993,175 at the box office. In deference to Madonnamania, it was released as *Crazy for You* in parts of Europe.

visitations: Or "Madonna sightings," when witnesses, reliable or not, report having actually *seen* Madonna, and are able to report specific details that they swear will be imprinted in their memories forever.

In the late summer of 1991, when Madonna was in Chicago filming *A League of Their Own*, the town went ape, every paper bearing multiple Madonna sightings on a daily basis. Some of the sources were so dubious they were only able to assure columnists that Madonna did indeed have the reddest lipstick in town . . . but they all made the paper.

During this time, Madonna was **rumor**ed to be showing up at a **club** called Cairo. The entire club ended up gawking at an admittedly convincing young **wanna-be** who, upon closer inspection, was actually ten years younger, and Mexican. Nevertheless, the papers reported that Madonna had been spotted at Cairo that evening. Sometimes, having faith that you've just experienced a visitation is enough to make it real. . . .

In August 1993, Madonna was spotted walking out of the Sound Factory in **New York**. There was no mistaking it—there were the Pippi Longstocking-red pigtails and the jumper with leather straps peeking out. She was with friends, very much in **control** of them, and as she crossed the street was heard to muse, "You could catch a *disease* in that place." Or was it, "You could catch a few Z's in that place."?

The night after her shaky **David Letterman** appearance in 1994, Madonna was spotted at the World Room Restaurant with a gaggle that included **Debi Mazar** and **Ingrid Casares**. The girls had just stopped in on Annabella Sciorra's **birthday** festivities, and were nonchalantly blocking a bank of pay phones. According to some, a model on crutches screamed that she didn't care who Madonna was, she and her friends better get their asses out of her way. They did, and the model made her call. As she hobbled away, she was treated to a chorus of obscenities by everyone except Madonna. . . .

Sightings like these are notable not for the information they hold, but for the fact that they prove Madonna's every move to be of interest to us, like watching a gerbil in a Habitrail. The problem with sightings is that people tend to let their excitement blur the moment, making it easy to fabricate entire scenarios and conversations. Or, they convince themselves they are seeing *the*

Madonna, when in reality they are seeing a cute club-girl with the most fleeting of resemblances, or perhaps they're seeing Lori Petty. Still, there is nothing quite like seeing . . . not a poster, not a **magazine cover**, not a photo . . . but Madonna *herself.*

"*M*adonna and Tom Hanks were spotted at a Chicago Cubs game. She wore a baseball cap. She had a hot dog *[sic]* and fries but she only ate four fries! No wonder she keeps her figure!"

—Chicago evening news item, 1991

·

"*I*'m very happy today because yesterday *I saw Madonna.* I'm not jocking *[sic]*, it's true, it's true! She's wonderful. I can't believe that it's reality."

—anonymous **Italian** Madonna **fan**, 1992

·

"*M*adonna's been spotted in Roy Rogers. . . ."

—Guy Trebay, *The Village Voice*, 1994

"Vogue" song: It's only fitting that Madonna would popularize a **dance** craze, and "V" became Madonna's most popular song and biggest-selling number 1 single. Originally, this **Shep Pettibone–Ciccone** collaboration was written and recorded as a killer B-side for the final release off *Like a Prayer,* **"Keep It Together"**—to help ensure that the single wouldn't sag on the charts as its predecessor, **"Oh Father"** had. When **Sire** execs heard the tune, however, they pushed to release it as a single, and "Keep It Together" was left to perform on its own merits.

"V" came a year after Malcolm MacLaren's "Deep in Vogue" dance single and decades after **gay** black **men** held the first voguing "**balls**" in Harlem. The song describes a dance that co-opts the attitude of models and movie stars and suggests modern dance done to a disco beat.

To vogue is to mimic to a ridiculous degree, snapping your body into mechanical poses, your face never deviating from a sternly haughty stare. Though most voguing is a **glamor**ous event and voguers often don chic **club**wear, some voguing is actually concerned with mimicking everyday "types" like corporate CEOs and high-school kids.

Madonna's **lyrics** baptize the dance floor as a place where no boundaries exist, where rebirth is possible, where a new life based on gesticulation can replace motionless and emotionless reality and anyone can become, if only for the duration of a song—or of

one's stamina—a "superstar." Because of this and because it is so concerned with appearances, voguing holds special appeal to its gay black and Latino pioneers, who know from experience that how you look sometimes defines who you are perceived to be.

Madonna's read on voguing is as an ***hommage*** to the Golden Age of Hollywood, stressing our—and her—affection for movie icons as she encourages us to strike the unforgettable poses they struck. It's an irresistible dance song that went multi-platinum, introducing voguing to the mainstream and helping (along with Jennie Livingston's film *Paris is Burning*) to make stars of its most prominent Harlem practitioners, especially King Voguer Willi Ninja.

Celebrities mentioned in "Vogue": Fred Astaire, Lauren Bacall, Marlon Brando, Bette Davis, James "Jimmy" Dean, **Marlene Dietrich,** Joe DiMaggio, Greta Garbo, Jean Harlow, Rita Hayworth, **Katharine Hepburn**, **Gene Kelly**, Grace Kelly, **Marilyn Monroe,** Ginger Rogers, Lana Turner.

"Vogue" video: Madonna's most popular **video**, a **glamor**ous workout shot in **black-and-white** that presents Madonna posing convincingly as the celebrities she sings about (plus an extended Mae West impersonation), and, most effectively, as herself.

The video is directed by **David Fincher**, and contains Madonna's most vigorous video **dancing** since **"Lucky Star."** She cuts a rug amid mirrors, feathers, and her beautiful gay dancers, who are photographed as reverently as if they were stars in their

own right, all of whom joined Madonna on her **Blond Ambition tour**.

Madonna herself has never looked more gorgeous, nor has her form been better utilized. It's exhilarating to see her voguing in **Marlene Dietrich drag**, forcing icon Dietrich into the nineties, and her re-creation of legendary portraitist Horst P. Horst's famous photograph of a woman in a corset is explosive, her sensual wiggling revitalizing a stock image and adding new mystery to it.

"*Y*ou can't fault her for taste. But the video should have been called '*Hommage* to Horst.' We just wish we could have worked something out beforehand—like doing an original photograph of her in the nude."

—Richard Tardiff, Horst's manager

von Unwerth, Ellen: Acclaimed **fashion** photographer who dominates *Vogue* and created the successful Guess? Jeans ads that launched Eva, Claudia, and Anna Nicole. She was slated to direct the **"Bad Girl" video** after Tim Burton backed out, but her schedule didn't permit, and bad boy **David Fincher** took over. EVU shot Madonna exclusively for *Paris Vogue* in 1993, rendering her in stark **black-and-white** with heavily-kohled eyes.

von Wernherr, Otto: Mysterious German avant-garde singer/actor, star of the cult film *Liquid Sky*, veteran of episodes of the daytime soap "The Edge of Night," and—most famously—the alien-sounding voice on a series of records featuring prominent vocals by Madonna. Madonna sold her backing vocals in 1981, and they were later remixed into oddball punk **dance** songs and licensed all over the world by **Mia Mind Music** as Madonna singles.

OVW, who also performed the **parody** song "Madonna Don't Preach" and appeared in the video, disappeared with his wife and child into Europe in the late eighties after suffering from a serious illness.

"*Of* course I tried to pick her up—she would stand against a telephone pole and smile at me—but it was only out of animal habit."

—Otto von Wernherr on Madonna, 1986

voyeurism: The usually secret act of "looking in on." Madonna wisely views all audiences as potential voyeurs (as did Alfred Hitchcock), performing as if it were for only one earnest viewer. The connection is particularly apt for Madonna because voyeurism connotes a **sex**ual thrill for the watcher, and Madonna's **art** is frequently sexual in nature.

Videos like **"Open Your Heart,"** in which Madonna performs as a stripper, and **"Justify My Love,"** in which she makes **love** in the seeming **privacy** of a hotel room, encourage viewers to watch as if from a peep-show booth or through a keyhole, respectively. When the object of a voyeur's gaze is performing knowingly, the object is known as an **"exhibitionist."**

"*Do* I like to watch? Yeah, I suppose I do. But I'd rather, um, I don't want to *watch* a **basketball** game, I want to *play* it."

—Madonna, 1992

Wailing Wall: Place of holy pilgrimage in Jerusalem that Madonna tried to visit while in Israel with her **Girlie Show.** It was a Jewish holiday, so she was denied access.

wanna-be: In 1985, when **"Like a Virgin"** went nuclear, a spate of teenaged girls (and, at home in the **privacy** of their rooms, not a few teenaged boys) began dressing and acting like their idol, copying her revealing clothes, mesh gloves, sunglasses, and streaked, tousled **hair.** These were the Madonna wanna-bes.

Though their numbers and fervor have diminished through the years along with Madonna's growing movement toward adult themes, wanna-bes persist to this day. In 1990, the word "wanna-be" was added to *Webster's Dictionary.*

NOW you've seen everything.

"*I* get huge bags of mail. Many letters are from teenage girls. They write about wanting to meet me, or be my friend, or even *be* me. They send pictures of themselves dressed up like me. I think it's great. I'd like to see every teenage girl in America dressed up like me. Why not?"

—Madonna, 1985

·

"*I'*m flattered by it. On the other hand, my message is to be your own person, to be an individual. So it's a little bit strange. They'll get over it, though. I'd like to think of it as a bad phase they're going through."

—Madonna, 1991

wanted: A wanted poster was printed in the *Hong Kong Evening Standard* while Madonna and **Sean Penn** were in the city quietly trying to film scenes for ***Shanghai Surprise***, offering $500 for any information on the couple's movements in the city. No citizens stepped forward to claim the reward, but the paper's editor staked out their hotel room and got the scoop himself.

Ward, Tony (Anthony Borden Ward, a.k.a. Tony Troy, modeling name): Madonna's boyfriend for the '90–'91 season, to many **fans** TW was Madonna's perfect mate. His unorthodox, edgy looks were an admittedly fine complement to Madonna's own, and his sexual proclivities—purported to include transvestism and S&M—were leagues ahead of ex-hubby **Sean Penn**'s stick-in-the-mud attitudes. He was even a manageable size for tiny Madonna: 5'7 and 170 lean pounds.

TW had been an up-and-coming model, working (clothed and unclothed) for such photographers as Greg Gorman, Bruce Weber, **Herb Ritts**, and **Steven Meisel** before working with Madonna on the **video**s for both **"Like a Prayer"** and **"Cherish"** (in which he played one of several too-hot mermen). Supposedly, he did not make a lasting impression until her 32nd **birthday** party, where, the story goes, Madonna's brother Mario re-introduced TW to her as "your birthday present." The story also has Madonna putting out her cigarette on TW's arm, and commenting that she could balance her drink on his buoyant ass.

Their torrid affair came to an end amid **tabloid** reports that TW had engaged in a marriage of convenience to Greek national Amalia Papadimos in Las Vegas shortly *after* liaising with Madonna, and that he was engaged at the same time to designer Jayme Harris, who had **miscarried** his baby. Since their breakup, TW has continued to pop up close to Madonna, whether accompanying her to parties (Love Ball II, etc.), hanging out on the Chicago set of ***A League of Their Own***, or slithering shaven-headed through ***Sex***, posing as, among other things, a foot worshiper to Madonna's dominatrix and a rapist to Madonna's delighted **Catholic** schoolgirl.

Though he also sometimes works in construction, the most memorable item on Tony's résumé is experience as a nude model for at least one gay softcore porn magazine, *In Touch For Men* (issue no. 101, March/April 1985). At the height of the Madonna-TW relationship, the tabloids tried to hype the discovery of TW's nude poses as a scandal, but since Madonna's image makes allowances for **nudity** and **homosexuality**, the scandal was a little anemic. The credits for the shoot were: "Photographed by Blue Leader. Camera by Canon, sweatpants by Big 5, socks by Calvin Klein,

Like BUTT-ah.

linens by Vera, carpet by Dynasty, scent by Old Spice, body by **God**, financial partner? New England Life, of course."

So who supplied the saucy ankle bracelet? Some of the photos, along with different early shots, were reprinted in *In Touch For Men* (no. 168, February 1991). The title of that layout? "**Boy Toy**." Madonna's response to the whole affair was a resounding "So what?"—echoing her response to her own nude-photo scandal of 1985.

And yes, one could feasibly balance a drink on his ass.

Warhol, Andy: Pioneer of Pop **Art**, famous for his confoundingly plotless, absorbing/banal films and literal interpretations of ordinary objects like Campbell's soup cans as high art. AW was also the reigning spirit of the **New York club** scene from the late sixties until his untimely **death** in February 1987.

Madonna was acquainted with AW, who was close friends and a collaborator with **Keith Haring** and **Jean-Michel Basquiat**, and who also served as a celebrity judge at the first Macy's Madonna look-alike contest.

In his infamous, posthumously published diaries, AW has high praises for Madonna's stage debut in *Goose and Tom-Tom* and for her **Virgin tour**. Had he lived, it's impossible to believe that AW wouldn't have eventually immortalized Madonna as he did **Marilyn Monroe**. *The Andy Warhol Diaries*, edited by Pat Hackett (Warner Books, 1989), is chock-full of Madonna references, but there's no index. Take note of pages: 574, 599, 613, 616, 632, 637, 648, 649, 655, 665, 667, 669, 670, 671, 674, 675, 687, 693, 698, 706, 718, 728, 750, 754, 755, 756, 762, 765, 772, 773, 778, 779.

Warner Bros.: Mega-corporation that is the parent company of **Sire Records** and **Maverick Entertainment**. Since Madonna's rise in the eighties, Warner's fortunes have become increasingly dependent on the girl's material. As Madonna goes, so goes Warner Bros.

Washington Square Park: Landmark Greenwich Village park, full of doe-eyed young **lovers**, skate punks, drunken chess players, skanky drifters, and charming certifiables. It was the site of Madonna's first face-to-face with *A Certain Sacrifice* director **Stephen Jon Lewicki**, and also the setting for several of the film's scenes, most notably where Madonna's character, "Bruna," is discovered dancing wildly in streams of water.

Wazoo: Clothing line based on Madonna's first **look**, featuring all the **Boy Toy** rags that the **wanna-bes** craved. It burned brightly and fizzled quickly, lasting only a little over a year starting in 1985. It was operated by French designer **Maripol**, and was sold in the Merry Go Round chain nationwide, at Bullock's in California, and at Macy's in **New York City**. Macy's really went all out to launch the line, creating for the summer an entire "Madonna Department" and holding one of the first Madonna look-alike contests.

SEE ALSO: **WARHOL, ANDY**

wax: Lifelike figures of Madonna are must-haves for wax museums worldwide. The most celebrated and realistic wax girl is housed at London's Rock Circus Museum, of Madonna in her **Blond Ambition** corset and ponytail.

SEE ALSO: **DEPILATION**

webo: Madonna's **music** publishing company Webo Girl takes its name from the Spanish slang for "**ball**-shaker," accurately bestowed upon Madonna by then **lover Jellybean**.

WED 51050: Case number of the Madonna–**Sean Penn divorce**.

wedding: Madonna's was from hell. When she decided to wed **Sean Penn** in 1985, the couple tried to keep the ceremony shrouded in secrecy, thereby making it all the more attractive to **paparazzi**. The invitations alerted guests to the date and time of the nuptials, but warned that the exact location would not be given out until the last minute.

When guests were finally guided to Penn family friend Dan Unger's $6 million **Malibu** mansion at 6970 Wildlife Road, they told waiting press that there was no wedding going on, just a party. The exceptions, **Andy Warhol** and **Keith Haring**, paused to flaunt their joint gift, a painting of the *New York* Post cover blaring Madonna's nude-photo scandal. Madonna was most displeased with the disloyalty, but she got over it.

Or it was drowned out, like her wedding vows, by fiercely beating helicopters whose occupants snapped distant photo after distant photo. Leave it to the **paparazzi** to find a way to crash a wedding discreetly, and leave it to Sean to find a way to welcome them warmly: with a giant **FUCK** YOU spelled out in footprints on the beach.

Photog Kip Rano had actually donned camouflage and secreted himself in the shrubbery from 1:30 A.M. the evening before, only to be booted out by Sean Penn personally.

Madonna was resplendent in an off-white gown with a ten-foot formal train, a pink sash studded with rosebuds and jewels, and a jaunty black bowler cap. **Herb Ritts** was the official wedding photographer, and a portrait of the bride-to-be in his 1992 book, *Notorious,* shows a face of Madonna we've never seen: She's radiant with **nerves**, excitement, and **love**. Sean wore a $700 double-breasted Versace tux.

*"A*lthough there will be times that your moods may falter, and you'll question each other's actions, the faith and love that you share will help to show that your inconsistency is only for the moment."

—Judge John Merrick at the ceremony, 1985 [Yeah, but what if he ties you to a chair?]

There were 220 guests at the wedding, including **Cher** with escort Josh Donen, Martin Sheen, Rob Lowe, **Carrie Fisher**, Christopher Walken, **Diane Keaton, David Letterman**, Steve "Studio 54" Rubell, **Debi Mazar**, Candy Clark, **David Geffen**, producer John Daly, **Rosanna Arquette**, Emilio Estevez, **Timothy Hutton,** Eric Stoltz, **Martin Burgoyne**, and skater Tai Babilonia.

Madonna's sister **Paula Ciccone** was her maid of honor, and fought tooth and nail to catch the bridal bouquet, while Sean's actor brother Chris caught the garter. His best man was not a brother, but his best friend, **director Jamie Foley**.

The reception afterward featured mostly swing and jazz records, including Bing Crosby, Ella Fitzgerald, and Cole Porter. Vangelis's "Chariots of Fire" boomed when the couple kissed, and Sarah Vaughan's "I'm Crazy About the Boy" played over the bride and groom's first **dance**.

The menu was fit for a king, including lots of Madonna's beloved **caviar**, curried oysters, lobster ravioli, rack of lamb, swordfish, and Pinot Noir wine from the Madonna Vineyards.

Madonna was ecstatic over Sean's gift of a coral pink convertible '57 Thunderbird.

weight: When she made cinematic history in *A Certain Sacrifice* she was a gaunt 102 pounds. By the time **The Virgin tour** rolled around, so did Madonna, at a voluptuous 120. Now, Madonna tips the scales at 110 rock-hard pounds.

Wembley Stadium: Famous London arena at which Madonna first performed on her **Who's That Girl tour**. She was the first woman in history to top the bill at the 70,000-seater.

"Whole Lotta Love": Madonna preferred to blast rock tunes like this Led Zeppelin standard while the **sex** scenes were being filmed for *Body of Evidence*.

***Who's That Girl* album:** For her third major film, Madonna had the pleasure of putting together the soundtrack. The fruit of her labor is this so-so collection whose highlights are Madonna's own songs, including the title ballad, the electric **dance** tune **"Causing a Commotion,"** sweeping ballad "The Look of **Love**," and throwaway ditty "Can't Stop." In between are a lot of unlistenable songs by acts that never went anywhere (Duncan Faure, Club Nouveau, Michael Davidson, Scritti Politti, and Coati Mundi).

The album jacket is her worst, a garish close-up of Madonna sporting bleached, super-teased **hair**, harsh makeup, thick brows, with her neck badly touched up and unnaturally extra-wide.

Nonetheless, on the strength of its two hit singles, the album sold a million copies domestically and 5 million worldwide. It didn't have much of a shelf-life, though, becoming Madonna's first cutout.

***Who's That Girl* film:** Madonna's third major movie was her second bomb in a row, a misguided attempt at a modern screwball comedy that sank without a trace at the box office, dying a quiet **death** amid the hype and critical raves for her world tour and song of the same name. Though it only grossed $6,910,761 in the U.S., *WTG* did well overseas, recouping its investment and gaining Madonna the favorable notices she lacked in America.

The movie is a souped-up take on the Melanie Griffith dud *Something Wild*. Madonna plays convict "Nikki Finn" (a play on the phrase "Mickey Finn"—meaning powerful knock-out pills often slipped into drinks), who is freed after spending time in jail for a crime she didn't commit. Uptight "Loudon Trott" (Griffin Dunne) is forced by his boss and future **father**-in-law "Mr. Worthington" to escort "Finn" to the bus station to be sure she returns to Philadelphia, so she won't cause trouble that'll expose his wrongdoing. It wouldn't be a screwball comedy without complications, and this film's got 'em in spades, including an antsy cougar (shades of *Bringing Up Baby*) and a disastrous **wedding** party made worse by "Nikki's" demeanor.

Madonna is quite good in the film, except she affects an unlistenable **accent** that is a cross between Brooklyn and a bullhorn that all but destroys her obvious screen presence. She's only really great in scenes where she's relaxed or even silent (as on the bus, where "Nikki" reflects quietly).

Madonna—and many of her **fans**—always liked this movie and couldn't understand why it was so badly received in America. Her guess was that it was lost in the shuffle of her tour, but it is also pedestrian, if harmless, fare.

The film was launched at the National Theater in Times Square, where Madonna's appearance drew an unruly crowd of 10,000. In contrast, the opening-day audience at the 1,151-seat Ziegfeld Theater a few blocks away boasted only 60 takers.

WTG broke the land speed record, showing up on **video**

"'Who's that girl?' isn't really the question. 'What the hell happened?' is."

—Mike Clark, *USA Today*

·

"Who's That Girl is a good deal better than its own distributors thought it was when they refused to screen it in advance to the press. It's an eighties comedy that qualifies as screwball, with a promisingly nutty screenplay. . . . In the second half of the film, when she's allowed to play at her own insinuating pace, Madonna at last emerges and is a delight. . . . In Madonna, Hollywood has a potent, pocket-sized **sex** bomb. So far, though, all it does is tick."

—Vincent Canby, *The New York Times*

·

"Madonna turns in a cunningly dizzying, often affecting portrayal."

—*Rolling Stone*

·

"She's sweet and she's smart and she's street-smart. . . . She's resourceful and she's funny, and I think I'm funny."

—Madonna, on similarities between herself and "Nikki Finn"

·

"I could have done others, but I liked my character in this one."

—Madonna after it bombed

·

"Desperately Seeking An Audience."

—*Us*

·

"Remember the old days when you used to have sex without a condom on a Sunday morning? That's how great it was."

—singer/actor Coati Mundi, on working with Madonna, 1993

within three months of its theatrical release. It stands as Sir John Mills's last film.

"Who's That Girl" song: Madonna was unstoppable in the summer of '87, and she racked up another number 1 smash with this laid-back, effortlessly haunting song. The title was seized by the media as a good excuse to psychoanalyze Madonna and to remark on her enigmatic presence in light of her **overexposure**.

Who's That Girl tour: The tour responsible for Madonna's reputation as the world's premier live entertainer. For her sec-

ond tour, Madonna incorporated multimedia components to go along with her already heavy choreography and her maturing **music**. She featured gigantic **video** screens against which stark images were projected to comment on the words she sang, most effectively with images of **the Pope** and **Ronald Reagan** during **"Papa Don't Preach."** Her opening was gripping, a series of silhouettes of herself from behind a screen, finally emerging in the bustier from her **"Open Your Heart" video**. She had literally reinvented herself from her first outing: She'd altered her body through strenuous training, bleached her **hair**, and sported a new, supreme stage confidence that she'd previously lacked.

The show included flashy, glitzy costumes by **Marlene Stewart**. Besides the bustier, Stewart gave Madonna seven costume changes, including the **Andy Warhol**–inspired Pop **Art** jacket, **Cyndi Lauper drag**, pointy sunglasses with a black feather boa, frilly underpants with **KISS** embroidered on the bottom, and a baby blue fifties prom dress. Madonna filled them all, skipping from song to song with an appropriate personality for each tune. Madonna's voice was noticeably stronger on the tour, and her performance of **"Live to Tell,"** with its prolonged pauses, ranks as one of her most memorable live moments.

In **Japan**, a thousand troops had to restrain a crowd of 25,000 fans seeking to greet Madonna at the airport. When severe storms forced the **cancellation** of her first shows, despondent **fans** nearly rioted, and Madonna was confronted with out-of-control teenagers soaking themselves in the rain outside the stadium. Promoters had no choice but to refund $7 million to ticket-buyers.

When the U.S. portion of the tour kicked off in **Miami**, one of her dancers slipped and fell on the moving platform at the **back** of the stage. With all eyes on her, Madonna good-naturedly covered, chuckling aloud that "It's slippery up here."

Madonna had triumphs on the tour, including her Madison Square Garden performance, which was an **AIDS** benefit for AmFAR. She dedicated "Live to Tell" to her late friend **Martin Burgoyne**. And there's no denying the commercial success of the tour. She sold 150,000 tickets for her Japanese shows at $45 each,

The Set for the Who's That Girl tour:

"Open Your Heart," "Lucky Star," "True Blue," "Papa Don't Preach," "White Heat," "Causing a Commotion," "Look of Love," "Dress You Up," "Material Girl," "Like a Virgin," "Where's the Party," "Live to Tell," "Into the Groove," "La Isla Bonita," "Who's That Girl," "Holiday."

and her first two shows at **Wembley Stadium** in London (144,000 tickets) sold out in eighteen hours nine minutes. She grossed over a half million dollars for every date she played.

Joining her on the tour was sixteen-year-old **Christopher Finch**, taking over from Brit **Felix Howard** as her waifish backing dancer.

"Who's That Girl" video: A creative effort to make a movie-plugging video that stands alone, "WTG" shows us a Madonna dressed like a little boy in a porkpie hat and spiky brown **hair**. She possesses a **Michael Jackson**-like Pied Piper quality, attracting several small children, who **dance** with her adoringly while she watches or triggers scenes from the *Who's That Girl* film. A cute video from 1987 that was rarely played thereafter.

"*It* was an endurance test, and Madonna came through it with aplomb. . . . As shallow, kitschy, pop entertainment—no big messages, no revelations, familiar sounds and images, plenty of catchy tunes—the show was easy to enjoy."

—Jon Pareles, *The New York Times*, 1987

Wilborn, Carlton: Backup dancer from **Blond Ambition** (as the priest Madonna seduces) and **The Girlie Show,** and also the guy whose penis is flashed (too fast to glimpse) in *Truth or Dare*. Madonna glimpses it, however, and immediately informs viewers that it's blue. CW went on to star in the critically-acclaimed **art** film *Grief* (1994).

William Morris Agency, Inc.: Madonna was represented by this prestigious firm for all her movie work until she bounced them in March 1985.

Williams, Freedom: The original lead rapper for the group C + C Music Factory. Madonna, when asked to evaluate his appeal, said, "He's OK from the neck down."

Willis, Bruce: Rascally leading man given to bossiness and bloat, married to Madonna **wanna-be** Demi Moore. Before he struck it big as one half of the TV show "Moonlighting," and later as an action-adventure star on the big screen, he tended bar under the moniker "Bruno." In fact, he did the honors at the wrap party for *Desperately Seeking Susan* at the Kamikaze Club in December 1984.

BW was signed as the male lead in the film *Blind Date* when Madonna signed on, but she later bailed.

Wilson, Mary: The Motown songbird and former Supreme had first dibs at recording **Jellybean**'s song **"Holiday,"** but passed, only to grit her teeth when Madonna made it into a Top 20 hit and timeless anthem.

Winger, Debra: The Academy **Award**–nominated tomboy actress and star of films like *Terms of Endearment* and *Shadowlands* (and an early stint as "Wonderwoman"'s kid sister "Drusilla"), Winger was originally signed as the lead in *A League of Their Own*, but noisily backed out when Madonna signed on. DW was probably just annoyed—Madonna had recently scoffed her presence in the film adaptation of *The Sheltering Sky*, calling her "all wrong" for the part.

Their bad relationship had previously started as terms of infringement: Madonna was considered for a Libby Holman biopic that producer Ray Stark had previously "promised" to DW.

Winters, Shelley: The *zaftig* method actress, known for her wild youth and faulty memory, bragged to *Vanity Fair* in 1988 that she had coached Madonna for *Speed-the-Plow* and that Madonna wanted to play her in a TV movie of her life. Madonna wrote an officious rebuttal to the **magazine**, politely asserting that she'd never even met SW, and that "I must have been out of the room when she was preparing me for my role in *Speed-the-Plow*."

wiretapping: Madonna bugged her **phone calls** with **Warren Beatty** for inclusion in *Truth or Dare*, but had to edit them out of the final cut when Warren asked her to. "There were some phone conversations I thought were really moving and touching and revealing. . . ." But, in the end, ". . . it wasn't fair, plus it's a federal offense."

Wolf, Naomi: Postmodern diva of **feminism** who has praised Madonna for her **power**.

In a 1994 *Esquire* poll of 1,000 women aged 18–24, 58.9 percent said they'd rather be Madonna than NW, but those results should reflect that 74.1 percent of the women polled weren't familiar with **Camille Paglia**, Phyllis Schlafley, Susan Powter, Susan Faludi, or Clarissa Pinola Estes, so "Naomi Wolf" as an answer probably translates into "anyone but Madonna."

women, favorite: In a Brazilian interview with *Veja* magazine in 1993, Madonna decided her favorite women of all time were Grace Kelly, **Marlene Dietrich, Marilyn Monroe,** Billie Holiday, and patron of the arts Betsy Guggenheim.

words, big: Madonna is bright, but her vocabulary isn't stellar. In taped interviews, she often appears to be struggling to articulate her thoughts. Therefore, when she finds a "big word" that makes an impressive soundbite, she sticks with it. The problem is that she usually enunciates these words with an audible, visible sense of pride.

Some big words to look for in the typical probing interview are "cathartic" (especially re: **Blond Ambition**), "*hommage*"

(Francophonically correct), and "oxymoron" (which she frequently confuses with "redundancy," as to **David Letterman**: "False **rumors**? Isn't that an oxymoron?"). Madonna also tends to bolster the weight of her remarks, and to stall for time, by peppering her speech with "ultimately."

words she mispronounces: Like much of the rest of the free world, Madonna consistently mispronounces mischievous as "mis-CHEE-vee-us" and tacks a final *s* on "anyway." She has embarrassed herself by calling legendary French erotic writer Anaïs Nin "A-*NY*-is" in her best **Midwest** twang, instead of "Ah-nah-*EES*," and, in a 1984 British telephone interview, referred to **director** Francis Ford Coppola as "Co-*POH*-la."

According to interviewer Andrew Neil, Madonna struggled to pronounce "totalitarian" and asked if she were using "iconoclastic" correctly during the course of their talk about *Sex* in 1992. She confused job descriptions in *Vanity Fair* that same year, responding to the question, "Do you enjoy having **sex**?" with "That's like saying to a gynecologist, ` Do you enjoy having children?'"

Ultimately, nobody's perfect.

work: Even her detractors admit that Madonna is a hard worker. She has had only three **vacations** in the last decade, and has been in the public eye almost nonstop the entire time. Even between albums she has films, single releases, a Broadway **play**, a **book**—always something to fill the gap. She credits her "Protestant work ethic," and her middle-class upbringing for her feelings of guilt if she is idle even briefly.

In a 1994 sidebar, *Us* magazine used a pie chart to represent what portion of Madonna's **fame** was due to her work (as opposed to scandal, just being famous, **sex**/romance, charity work, or hanging with other celebs). She scored an impressive 41 percent in the work category, as opposed to **Michael Jackson**'s puny 10, and Julia Roberts's anemic, 19 percent.

Wright, Robin: Actress who got Madonna's sloppy seconds by hooking up with **Sean Penn** and bearing him a child in 1991, two years after Madonna dropped Penn. RW said in print that she pitied SP for having to put up with Madonna, and Madonna "responded" with a song called "Thief of Hearts" on her *Erotica* LP that could also apply to ex-lover **Warren Beatty**'s wife Annette Bening. In the song, Madonna seethes about a man-stealer who thinks bearing a man's child is something special when, evidently, *anybody* can do it.

"*E*veryone's going to see me going into the movie—is this pathetic?"

—Madonna on her embarrassment at going to see ex, Sean, and Robin Wright in *State of Grace*, 1991

X: The original **work**ing title of *Sex* before **Spike Lee**'s epic *Malcolm X* laid unofficial claim to the twenty-fourth letter of the alphabet for 1992. The book was also called *Erotica* before its final title was selected.

You Can Dance album: Rather than releasing a greatest-hits album, Madonna's first compilation was a groundbreaking remix album of some of her best **dance** hits segued into one long grind, made available just in time for Christmas 1987. The concept caught on, and soon artists like **Paula Abdul** and Jody Watley were following suit.

YCD bore remixes by **Jellybean**, Bruce Forest and Frank Heller, Steve Thompson and Michael Barbiero, and **Shep Pettibone**.

The only original song on the album is the spritely "Spotlight." That song was to have been a single release, but fears that it wouldn't be a major hit (it had previously

failed to pass muster to make it onto *True Blue*) scrapped those plans.

It didn't hurt the energetic, innovative album, which sold a million copies in the U.S. (5 million worldwide).

The orgiastic liner notes by Brian Chin make an excellent connection between Madonna and dancing, from club DJs to dancers to the **music** itself.

On the jacket (by **Herb Ritts**), Madonna appears in a bolero outfit against a flaming red backdrop. The photos were done simultaneously with her taping of a **Mitsubishi commercial** for the Japanese market in 1987.

Zhero by Madonna: **Italian**-made perfume for men that has no connection to Madonna's own plans for a fragrance line. But the bottles are self-consciously phallic, so we can't blame you for asking.

Ziegfeld, The: Legendary movie theatre at 141 West 54th Street in **New York City** where several Madonna films have had their New York premieres. *Who's That Girl* bombed here, but *Truth or Dare* fared much better. That film's official premiere here, an AmFAR benefit, raised hundreds of thousands of dollars.

When *A League of Their Own* world-premiered at the Ziegfeld, it attracted the entire cast (minus Geena Davis), plus Cindy Crawford, Sonia Braga, John McLaughlin, Robert DeNiro, David Lee Roth, Charles Grodin, James Brooks, Nicole Miller, and Lauren Hutton.

For *Body of Evidence*, Madonna spoke before the screening, saying "I don't think I have to introduce myself, unless some of you don't recognize me with my clothes on," thanked the crowd for coming, then took off ahead of the widely-reported jeers that followed.

zits: Madonna breaks out easily, one reason to be grateful for **black-and-white** film—it hides zits better than concealer. When asked why he shot so much black-and-white footage for *Truth or Dare*, **Alek Keshishian** explained, "Because it covered her zits better than color—no kidding."

THE MADONNA U.S. DISCOGRAPHY

NOTES

* The primary format listed is vinyl, with cassette and CD notations.
* All titles are LP versions, unless otherwise noted.
* All releases are on Sire Records, unless otherwise noted.
* Catalog numbers are listed where available.
* This discography does not contain references to promotional releases; DJ-only remix issues (i.e., Disconet, Razormaid, Ultimix, etc.); bootlegged/illegal recordings (of which there is an abundance); Westwood One Radio recordings; Back to Back Hits, Backtrax or other re-issues; or "in-house" (i.e., unreleased commercially) mixes of songs like "Fever" and "Now I'm Following You" that are known to exist and are routinely sold through collectors' services. Compilations, Madonna-related materials, and soundtracks are listed selectively.
* Please address all corrections/queries/correspondence to the address given at the back of this book.

* **Abbreviations used: album = "LP"; alternate = "alt"; cassette single = "cs"; compact disc = "CD"; CD 3" single (deleted format; no longer produced in the U.S.) = "CD-3"; CD 5" maxi-single = "CD maxi"; edit = "ed"; extended = "ext"; instrumental = "instr"; picture sleeve = "ps"; remix = "re"; version = "ver"; vinyl single = "vs"**

SINGLES CHRONOLOGICALLY:

Title, A-side/B-side:	Catalog #:	Year:
Holiday/Holiday[1]	29478	1983
Borderline/Think of Me[2]	29354	1984
Lucky Star/I Know It[1]	29177	1984
Like a Virgin/Stay	29210	1984
Material Girl/Pretender	29083	1985
Crazy for You/No More Words[3]	29051	1985
Angel/Angel (Re Ed)	29008	1985
Dress You Up/Shoo-Bee-Doo	28919	1985
Live to Tell/Live to Tell (Instr)	28717	1986
Papa Don't Preach/Pretender[4]	28660	1986
True Blue/Ain't No Big Deal[5]	28591	1986
Open Your Heart/White Heat	28508	1986
La Isla Bonita/La Isla Bonita (Instr Re)	28425	1987
Who's That Girl/White Heat[6]	28341	1987
Causing a Commotion/Jimmy, Jimmy	28224	1987
Like a Prayer/Act of Contrition[7]	27539	1989
Express Yourself/The Look of Love[7,8]	22948	1989
Cherish/Supernatural	22883	1989
Oh Father/Pray for Spanish Eyes[9,10]	22723	1989
Keep It Together/Keep It Together (Instr)	19986	1990
Vogue/Vogue (Dub Ver)	19863	1990
Hanky Panky/More	19789	1990
Justify My Love/Express Yourself 1990 (Ed)	19485	1990
Rescue Me/Rescue Me (Alt Ver)	19490	1991
This Used to be My Playground (Single Mix)/This Used to be My Playground (Long Ver)	18822	1992
Erotica/Erotica (Instr)[11]	18782	1992
Deeper and Deeper (Ed)/Deeper and Deeper (Instr)	18639	1993
Bad Girl (Ed)/Fever	18650	1993
Rain (Radio Re)/Waiting	18505	1993
I'll Remember/Secret Garden	18247	1994
Secret/(Instr)	18035	1994
Take a Bow/(In Da Soul Mix)	18000	1994

NOTE: The 7" singles Everybody, Physical Attraction, and Burning Up were only released promotionally. They *were* released commercially in various forms on the 12" vinyl format.

[1] Originally issued without ps.
[2] Some issued with fold-out poster sleeve, same catalog number.
[3] On Geffen label; B-side performed by Berlin.
[4] Also issued on CD/laser disc single format with bonus track Papa Don't Preach (Ext Ver).
[5] Some issued on blue vinyl, same catalog number.
[6] Starting here, all singles also issued on cs format.
[7] Also issued on CD-3 format.
[8] Cs issued with two different ps, one a title design, and one a portrait.
[9] B-side is same as Spanish Eyes on Like a Prayer LP.
[10] Starting here, all vs issued without ps.
[11] Starting here, all singles on Maverick/Sire label.

MADONNA-RELATED SONGS CHRONOLOGICALLY (SINGLES, UNLESS OTHERWISE NOTED):

Title, A-side/B-side:	Artist:	Label:	Year:
Like a Surgeon/Slime	"Weird Al" Yankovic	Rock 'N' Roll	1985

NOTES: A-side is an authorized parody of Like a Virgin.

| Sidewalk Talk/The Mexican | Jellybean | EMI | 1986 |

NOTES: A-side written by Madonna; primary vocals by Catherine Buchanan, vocal refrain by Madonna. LP: Wotupski!?!

| Each Time You Break My Heart/Each Time You Break My Heart (Instr) | Nick Kamen | Sire | 1986 |

NOTES: Written/produced by Madonna and Steve Bray, backing vocals by Madonna. LP: Nick Kamen. Madonna sings back-up on Tell Me, a song from Kamen's follow-up LP, Us (1988).

| Tuff Titty Rap;Into the Groovey/Burnin' Up | Ciccone Youth | New Alliance | 1986 |

NOTES: Remakes/reworkings of Burning Up and Into the Groove by Sonic Youth featuring samples of Madonna vocals. LP: The Whitey Album.

| Santa Baby (non-single) | Various | A&M | 1987 |

NOTES: Remake of Eartha Kitt tune appears on the benefit LP A Very Special Christmas.

| Possessive Love/Homeless | Marilyn Martin | Atlantic | 1988 |

NOTES: A-side co-written by Madonna. LP: This Is Serious.

| Scheherazade (non-single) | Peter Cetera | Warner Bros. | 1988 |

NOTES: Madonna sings back-up on this LP track, under the alias "Lulu Smith." LP: One More Story.

| Just a Dream (non-single) | Donna Delory | MCA | 1992 |

NOTES: Written and produced by Madonna and Patrick Leonard. LP: Donna Delory.

| Get Over/Alone With You | Nick Scotti | Reprise | 1993 |

NOTES: A-side written by Madonna and Steve Bray, produced by Madonna and Shep Pettibone, Madonna sings back-up. LP: first version appeared on soundtrack for Nothing But Trouble (Warner Bros., 1991), reappears on LP Nick Scotti.

| Queen's English (non-single) | José & Luis | Sire | 1993 |

NOTES: Madonna sings back-up. Song originally mixed/recorded in 1992, played at Dolce & Gabbana fashion show, remained unreleased for over a year. Six mixes are included on a maxi single, including the Mo Mo's In the House version, chock-full of Madonna's vocals. LP: New Faces (compilation).

NOTE: Madonna's backing vocals on Otto von Wernherr songs have been remixed into dance singles and distributed variously by Mindfield (U.S.), Trojan (U.K.), and other labels since 1986. Titles of these pastiches include: Cosmic Climb, The Da-Da-Da-Dance, Get Down, Oh My!, On the Street, Shake, Time and Time Again, Time To Dance, We Are the Gods, and Wild Dancing. Songs recorded by Madonna (written by Daniel Giorlando) and released later by Mia Mind Music include Little Boy, On the Ground, and Shine a Light. SEE: **Mia Mind Music.**

MAXI-SINGLES CHRONOLOGICALLY:

Title: A-side/B-side:	Catalog #:	Year:
Everybody[1]/Everybody (Dub Ver)	29899	1982
Burning Up[2]/Physical Attraction	29715	1983
Borderline (New Mix)/Lucky Star (New Mix)	20212	1984
Like a Virgin (Ext Dance Re)/Stay	20239	1984
Material Girl (Ext Dance Re)/Pretender	20304	1985
Angel (Ext Dance Mix)/Into the Groove	20335	1985
Dress You Up (The 12″ Formal Mix)/Dress You Up (The Casual Instr Mix); Shoo-Bee-Doo	20369	1985
Live to Tell/Live to Tell (Ed); Live To Tell (Instr)	20461	1986
Papa Don't Preach (Ext Re)/Pretender	20492	1986
True Blue (The Color Mix); True Blue (Instr)/Ain't No Big Deal; True Blue (Re/Ed)	20533	1986
Open Your Heart (Ext Ver)/Open Your Heart (Dub); White Heat	20597	1986
La Isla Bonita (Ext Re)/La Isla Bonita (Instr)	20633	1987
Who's That Girl (Ext Ver)/White Heat[3]	20212	1987
Causing a Commotion (Silver Screen Mix); Causing a Commotion (Dub)/Causing a Commotion (Movie House Mix); Jimmy, Jimmy[3]	20762	1987
Like a Prayer (12″ Dance Mix); Like a Prayer (12″ Ext Re); Like a Prayer (Churchapella)/Like a Prayer (12″ Club Ver); Like a Prayer (7″ Re/Ed); Act of Contrition	21170	1989
Express Yourself (Non-Stop Express Mix); Express Yourself (Stop & Go Dubs)/Express Yourself (Local Mix); The Look of Love	21225	1989
Keep It Together (12″ Re); Keep It Together (Dub); Keep It Together (12″ Ext Mix)/Keep It Together (12″ Mix); Keep It Together (Bonus Beats); Keep It Together (Instr)[4]	21427	1989
Vogue (12″ Ver)/Vogue (Bette Davis Dub); Vogue (Strike-a-Pose Dub)[5]	21513	1990
Hanky Panky (Bare Bottom 12″ Mix)/Hanky Panky (Bare Bones Single Mix); More	21577	1990
Justify My Love (Orbit 12″ Mix); Justify My Love (Hip Hop Mix)/Justify My Love (The Beast Within Mix); Express Yourself (1990) (Shep's 'Spressin' Himself Re-Remix)[6]	21820	1990
Rescue Me (Titanic Vocal); Rescue Me (Lifeboat Vocal)/Rescue Me (Houseboat Vocal); Rescue Me (SOS Mix)[7]	21813	1991
Erotica (Kenlou B-Boy Mix); Erotica (Jeep Beats); Erotica (Madonna's In MyJeep Mix)/Erotica (Wf 12″); Erotica (Underground Club Mix); Erotica (Bass Hit Dub)[8]	40585	1992
Deeper and Deeper (Shep's Classic 12″); Deeper and Deeper (Shep's Deep Makeover Mix); Deeper and Deeper (Shep's Deep Beats)/Deeper and Deeper (David's Klub Mix); Deeper and Deeper (David's Deeper Dub);	40722	1993

Deeper and Deeper (Shep's Deeper Dub)[9]

Bad Girl (Ext Mix); Fever (Ext 12"); Fever (Shep's Remedy Dub)/ Fever (Murk Boys Miami Mix); Fever (Murk Boys Deep South Mix); Fever (Oscar G's Dope Mix)[10]	40793	1993
Rain (Radio Re), Rain/Up Down Suite (Non-Album Track); Waiting (Re)	40988	1993
I'll Remember (Guerilla Beach Mix), I'll Remember/I'll Remember (Guerilla Groove Mix); I'll Remember (Orbit Alternative Mix)	41355	1994
Secret (Junior's Sound Factory Mix); Secret (Junior's Sound Factory Dub)/Secret (Junior's Luscious Club Mix); Secret (Junior's Luscious Club Dub); Secret (Allstar Mix)[11]	45767	1994
Take a Bow (In Da Soul Mix); Take a Bow (In Da Soul Instr)/Take a Bow; Take a Bow (Instr); Take a Bow (Silky Soul Mix)	41887	1994

[1] This 5:56 ver is different from the 4:57 ver later released on the LP Madonna.

[2] This 5:56 ver is different from the 3:41 ver later released on the LP Madonna.

[3] Also available as cassette maxi.

[4] Starting here, all maxis also available on CD; CD maxi includes Keep It Together (Single Re), but excludes Keep It Together (Dub) and Keep It Together (Bonus Beats).

[5] Starting here, all maxis also available on cassette; cassette and CD maxis include Vogue (Single Ver).

[6] CD and cassette maxis also include Justify My Love (QSound Mix).

[7] CD maxi also includes Rescue Me (Single Mix).

[8] Starting here, all maxis on Maverick/Sire label; CD maxi includes Erotica (Album Ed) and Erotica (Masters At Work Dub), and excludes Erotica (Bass Hit Dub). There was also a CD included with purchase of the Sex book, containing versions of Erotica under the title Erotic.

[9] CD maxi includes Deeper and Deeper (Album Ed), Deeper and Deeper (Shep's Fierce Dub), and Deeper and Deeper (David's Love Dub), but excludes Deeper and Deeper (David's Deeper Dub) and Deeper and Deeper (Shep's Deeper Dub).

[10] CD maxi includes Bad Girl (Ed) and Fever (Hot Sweat 12"), but excludes Fever (Shep's Remedy Dub) and Fever (Oscar G's Dope Dub).

[11] CD maxi includes Secret (Ed) and Secret (Luscious Single Mix), but excludes Secret (Junior's Sound Factory Dub) and Secret (Junior's Luscious Club Dub).

Albums Chronologically:

Title (track list):	Catalog #:	Year:
Madonna: Lucky Star, Borderline, Burning Up, I Know It, Holiday, Think of Me, Physical Attraction, Everybody.	23867	1983
Like a Virgin: Material Girl, Angel, Like a Virgin, Over and Over, Love Don't Live Here Anymore, Dress You Up, Shoo-Bee-Doo, Pretender, Stay.	25157	1984
True Blue: Papa Don't Preach, Open Your Heart, White Heat, Live to Tell, Where's the Party, True Blue, La Isla Bonita, Jimmy, Jimmy, Love Makes the World Go Round.	25442	1986
Who's That Girl Soundtrack[1]: Who's That Girl, Causing a Commotion, The Look of Love, 24 Hours (Duncan Faure), Step By Step (Club Nouveau), Turn It Up (Michael Davidson), Best Thing Ever (Scritti Politti), Can't Stop, El Coco Loco (Coati Mundi).	25611	1987
You Can Dance[2]: Spotlight, Holiday, Everybody, Physical Attraction, Over and Over, Into the Groove, Where's the Party.	25535	1987

Like a Prayer[3]: Like a Prayer, Express Yourself, Love Song, Till Death Do Us Part, Promise To Try, Cherish, Dear Jessie, Oh Father, Keep It Together, Spanish Eyes, Act of Contrition.	25844	1989
I'm Breathless: Songs From and Inspired By the Film *Dick Tracy*: He's a Man, Sooner Or Later, Hanky Panky, I'm Going Bananas, Cry Baby, Something to Remember, Back in Business, More, What Can You Lose, Now I'm Following You, Part 1, Now I'm Following You, Part 2, Vogue.	26209	1990
The Immaculate Collection[4]: Holiday, Lucky Star, Borderline, Like a Virgin, Material Girl, Crazy For You, Into the Groove, Live To Tell, Papa Don't Preach, Open Your Heart, La Isla Bonita, Like a Prayer, Express Yourself, Cherish, Vogue, Justify My Love, Rescue Me.	26440	1990
Erotica[5]: Erotica, Fever, Bye Bye Baby, Deeper and Deeper, Where Life Begins, Bad Girl, Waiting, Thief of Hearts, Words, Rain, Why's It So Hard, Secret Garden, Did You Do It?	45154[6] 45031	1992

NOTE: All LPs are currently in print on CD and cassette. All LPs through *The Immaculate Collection* also originally available on vinyl. All LPs through *You Can Dance* also originally available on 8-track tape. Note that Ain't No Big Deal appears on *Revenge of the Killer B's* (Warner Bros., 1984), Crazy For You and Gambler appear on the *Vision Quest* Soundtrack (Geffen, 1985), Santa Baby appears on *A Very Special Christmas* (A&M, 1987), This Used to be My Playground appears on *Barcelona Gold* (1992), I'll Remember appears on *With Honors* Soundtrack (Maverick, 1994), and Goodbye to Innocence appears on *Just Say Roe* (Sire, 1994).

[1] This soundtrack was selected by Madonna, but only four of the songs are performed by her; the other songs are attributed accordingly. While this is often considered a "Madonna LP," it's important to distinguish the *Who's That Girl* Soundtrack from Madonna's other full-length studio efforts.

[2] Re LP of previously released material, with one previously unreleased song (Spotlight), segued. Cassette includes bonus dubs of Spotlight, Holiday, Over and Over, and Into the Groove; CD includes same bonus Holiday, Over and Over, and Into the Groove dubs, excludes Spotlight bonus dub, includes Where's the Party bonus dub. As with the *Who's That Girl* Soundtrack, You Can Dance is not a Madonna LP proper.

[3] All original vinyl copies scented with patchouli oil and stuffed with small AIDS Fact Sheet printed on glossy stock.

[4] Greatest hits collection, featuring QSound; not a Madonna LP proper. *The Immaculate Collection* was also packaged as *The Royal Box*, a specially-designed box set containing either a cassette or CD of the LP, eight postcards, a copy of The Immaculate Collection video, and a folded poster (26464).

[5] Starting here, all LPs on Maverick/Sire label, and no LPs available on vinyl.

[6] First catalog number refers to "Clean Ver," which contains all tracks listed except for Did You Do It?, which is only available on the "Nasty Ver," represented by the second catalog number.

VIDEOGRAPHY

"Everybody"—1982
"Burning Up"—1983
"Holiday"—1983 (unreleased)
"Borderline"—1984
"Lucky Star"—1984
"Like a Virgin"—1984
"Material Girl"—1985
"Crazy for You"—1985
"Into the Groove"—1985 (movie clips only)
"Dress You Up"—1985
"Gambler"—1985 (movie clips only)
"Like a Virgin"—1985 (*Madonna: The Virgin Tour Live* version)
"Live to Tell"—1986
"Papa Don't Preach"—1986
"True Blue"—1986   (Two versions—U.S. and non-U.S. Note: In U.S. version, Madonna not in video.)
"Open Your Heart"—1986
"La Isla Bonita"—1987
"Who's That Girl"—1987
"Like a Prayer"—1989
"Express Yourself"—1989
"Cherish"—1989
"Oh Father"—1989
"Dear Jessie"—1989 (non-U.S.)
"Vogue"—1990
"Justify My Love"—1990
"Like a Virgin"—1991 (*Truth or Dare* version) 1991
"This Used to be My Playground"—1992
"Erotica"—1992
"Deeper and Deeper"—1992
"Bad Girl"—1993
"Fever"—1993
"Rain"—1993
"I'll Remember"—1994
"Secret"—1994
"Take a Bow"—1994

FILMOGRAPHY

untitled, 1972. Director unknown, running time unknown, unrated. (Super-8 film project in which an egg is fried on Madonna's stomach.)

A Certain Sacrifice, 1980. Stephen Jon Lewicki, 60 minutes, unrated.

Vision Quest, 1983. Harold Becker, 107 minutes, R.

Desperately Seeking Susan, 1985. Susan Seidelman, 104 minutes, PG-13.

Shanghai Surprise, 1986. Jim Goddard, 90 minutes, PG-13.

Who's That Girl, 1987. James Foley, 94 minutes, PG.

Bloodhounds of Broadway, 1988. Howard Brookner, 90 minutes, PG.

Dick Tracy, 1990. Warren Beatty, 105 minutes, PG.

Truth or Dare, 1991. Alek Keshishian, 118 minutes, R.

Shadows and Fog, 1992. Woody Allen, 85 minutes, PG-13.

Blast 'Em, 1992. Joseph Blasioli, approx. 90 minutes, PG. (Note: Paparazzi documentary includes footage of Madonna being pursued by, and reacting viscerally to, pushy shutterbugs.)

A League of Their Own, 1992. Penny Marshall, 124 minutes, PG.

Body of Evidence, 1993. Uli Edel, 99 minutes, R. (Unrated version also released on video.)

Dangerous Game, 1993. Abel Ferrara, 108 minutes, R.

Four Rooms, 1995. various directors, cameo, R.

Blue in the Face, 1995. Wayne Wang, cameo, R.

DIRECTOROGRAPHY

A selective listing of some men and women who have directed Madonna:

Woody Allen: *Shadows and Fog*
Fabien Baron: "Erotica"
Steve Baron: "Burning Up"
Warren Beatty: *Dick Tracy*
Howard Brookner: *Bloodhounds of Broadway*
Uli Edel: *Body of Evidence*
Abel Ferrara: *Dangerous Game*
David Fincher: "Express Yourself," "Oh Father," "Vogue", "Bad Girl"
James Foley: "Live to Tell," "Papa Don't Preach," "True Blue" (European version), *Who's That Girl* film
Jim Goddard: *Shanghai Surprise*
Michael Haussman: "Take a Bow"
Alek Keshishian: *Truth Or Dare*, "I'll Remember"
Mary Lambert: "Borderline," "Like a Virgin," "Material Girl," "La Isla Bonita," "Like a Prayer"
Stephen Jon Lewicki: *A Certain Sacrifice*
Penny Marshall: *A League of Their Own*
Melodie McDaniel: "Secret"
Jean-Baptiste Mondino: "Open Your Heart," "Justify My Love"
Gregory Mosher: *Speed-the-Plow*
Arthur Pierson: "Lucky Star"
Joe Pytka: "Make a Wish" Pepsi commercial
David Rabe: *Goose and Tom-Tom*
Herb Ritts: "Cherish"
Mark Romanek: "Rain"
Stephane Sednaoui: "Fever"
Susan Seidelman: *Desperately Seeking Susan*
Ed Steinberg: "Everybody"
Wayne Wang: *Blue in the Face*

A SELECTIVE U.S. BIBLIOGRAPHY

Desperately Seeking Madonna, edited by Adam Sexton. Delta, trade paper, 1993. (0-385-30688-1)

Holiday With Madonna, Gordon Matthews, Julian Messner. Simon & Schuster cloth and trade paper, 1985. (cloth: 0-671-60375-2; paper:0-685-10385-4)

I Dream of Madonna: Women's Dreams of the Goddess of Pop, edited by Kay Turner. HarperCollins San Francisco cloth, 1993. (0-00-255257-4)

The I Hate Madonna Handbook, Ilene Rosenzweig. St. Martin's Press, trade paper, 1994. (0-312-10481-2)

The I Hate Madonna Jokebook, Joey West. Pinnacle, mass paper, 1993. (1-55817-798-1)

Madonna, Marie Cahill. Gallery Books, cloth, 1991. (0-8317-5705-1)

Madonna, Nicole Claro. Chelsea House Publishers, 1994. (0-7910-2355-9)

Madonna, Keith Elliot Greenberg. Lerner, cloth, 1986. (0-8225-1606-3)

Madonna!, Mark Bego. Pinnacle, mass paper, 1985. (0-523-42576-7)

Madonna: Blonde Ambition, Mark Bego. Harmony Press, trade paper, 1992. (0-517-58242-2)

Madonna: The Book, Norman King. William Morrow, cloth, 1991. (0-688-10389-8)

The Madonna Connection: Representational Politics, Subcultural Identities, & Cultural Theory, edited by Cathy Schwichtenberg. Westview, cloth and trade paper, 1992. (cloth: 0-8133-1396-1; paper: 0-8133-1397-X)

Madonna: The Girlie Show, preface by Madonna. Callaway Editions/Boy Toy, cloth, 1994. (0-935112-22-7)

Madonna: Her Complete Story, David James. Signet, trade paper, 1991. (0-451-82240-4)

Madonna Illustrated, Tim Riley. Hyperion, trade paper, 1992. (1-56282-983-1)

Madonna: Lucky Star, Michael McKenzie, Contemporary, trade paper, 1985. (0-8902-5233-3)

Madonna: Portrait of a Material Girl, Courage Books, cloth, 1993. (1-56138-236-1)

Madonna Revealed: The Uncut Biography, Douglas Thompson. Birch Lane Press, trade paper, 1991. (1-55972-099-9) Leisure, mass paper, 1992. (0-8439-3319-4)

The Madonna Scrapbook, Lee Randall. Citadel, trade paper, 1992. (0-8065-1297-0)

Madonna Speaks, A Bruce Nash and Allan Zullo Book compiled by Mike Fleiss. Expression Press, 1993. (0-941263-83-5)

Madonna: The Spirit and the Flesh, Signet, trade paper, 1985.

Madonna: Superstar, Karl Lagerfeld. W.W. Norton, trade paper, 1991. (0-393-30766-2)

Madonna Unauthorized, Christopher Andersen. Simon & Schuster, cloth, 1991. (0-671-73532-2) Dell, mass paper, 1992. (0-440-21318-5)

Madonnarama: Essays on Sex and Popular Culture, edited by Lisa Frank and Paul Smith. Cleis, trade paper, 1993. (9-39416-719)

Sex, Madonna. Warner Books cloth, 1992. (0-446-51732-1)

The Sexiest Jokes about Madonna, "Cardinal Syn." Shapolsky Publishers, mass paper, 1994. (1-56171-074-1)

The Good-bye Girlie: Madonna salutes her audience at

The End

of a performance of "Holiday."

CREDITS

All memorabilia/ephemera and publicity photos pictured are from the author's personal, exclusive, highly-guarded (BEWARE OF DOG, CAT, and MADONNA QUEEN) collection.

All still photography of collages and memorabilia/ephemera, unless otherwise noted, is by **Lori DeVito**, Mahwah, NJ, USA.

All collages were designed by the author and Lori DeVito.

If you have any questions, comments, or (God forbid) corrections regarding *Encyclopedia Madonnica*, or if you are interested in buying, selling, or trading "Madonnabilia," please write (enclose self-addressed, stamped envelope): Matthew Rettenmund, P.O.B. 149, New York, NY 10113-0149, USA. Vulgar letters will receive priority handling.

Hundreds of Madonna magazines are available from Keith A. Davies, P.O.B. 456, Hove, Sussex, BN3 1DY, ENGLAND. Catalog available on receipt of $1 (U.S. currency).

Magazine covers courtesy: The Advocate; Australian Rolling Stone, Issue No. 488, October 1993; Autograph Collector, 510 Suite-A, South Corona Mall, Corona, CA 91720, USA; Bravo; Cosmopolitan Spain magazine, G Y J Publicaciones Internationales & Hearst Corporation. Cover photo by Alberto Tolot; Elle (American and French); Everybody; Esquire; Express Yourself; The Face; French Penthouse; German Max; Harper's Bazaar; I-D magazine. Design and art direction: Terry Jones/Photography: Mark Lebon; In Dublin; In Touch, Inc. (In Touch For Men); Interview; Italian Max; KAIK; Like a Faggot!; Like a Virgin; Madonna; MLC; New Flix, Victor Entertainment, Inc., 3F Parabo Bild. 6-23-2 Jingumae Shibuya-Ku, Tokyo, JAPAN; New Woman; Photo; Playbill® cover printed by permission of Playbill Incorporated. Playbill® is a registered Trademark of Playbill Incorporated, New York, NY; Playboy España; Rockstar; Satellite TV Europe; Sette; Shueisha, Inc. (Japanese Playboy), copyright Shueisha, Inc.; Sky; Spin; Switch; Time, Inc. (Picture Week); Time Out magazine, London; Virgin; Who.

Black-and-white photos/illustrations courtesy: **Archive Photos (Special thanks to Noble Works, Hoboken, NJ, USA):** page 134 card; **Nancy Barr-Brandon:** page 44 (both; these and hundreds of other Madonna photographs are available from Nancy Barr-Brandon, 506 Windemere Ave., Interlaken, NJ 07712, USA); **Nancy Burson:** page 91 (Copyright Nancy Burson & David Kramlich. Courtesy Jayne H. Baum Gallery); **The Stephen Caraco Archive:** page 47; **Antonio de Felipe:** page 140 painting; **Francesco De Vincentis:** pages 165, 204; **Karen J. Dolan:** pages 77, 97; **Eclipse Enterprises:** page 55 card (Art copyright 1993 Greg Louden from "AIDS Awareness Trading Cards"/Eclipse Cards); **Brad Elterman:** page 134; **Alex Escarano:** page 9 painting (Alex J. Escarano, 315 Navarre Ave., #5, Coral Gables, FL 33134, USA); **Gay Men's Health Crisis, New York City:** page 44 letter; **André Grossmann:** pages 20 (Erica Bell), 29, 35, 36 (both), 38, 84; **JEF-FOTO:** page 89; **Joseph A. Lawrence:** pages 55, 83; **LFI/UMAZ:** page 39; **LFI/URO:** page 152; **Luca Mautone:** pages 73, 80 illustrations; **Steve Meyers:** title illustrations, pages 61, 78; **Photofest:** pages 17, 23, 48, 128, 136, 162; **Rhonda Piliere/Globe Photos:** page 54; **Matthew Rettenmund:** (Talk about *nepotism!*) dedication illustration, pages 18, 102, 111 (photo), 155, 167 illustrations; **Albert Sanchez:** page 145 (courtesy Queerdonna); **Oliviu Savu:** pages 6 (both), 20 (Sandra Bernhard), 64, 114, 138; **Fred Seidman:** pages viii, 124, 125 (both; Photos by Fred Seidman. Photographer lives in New York City); **United Colors of Benetton:** page 65 ad (United Colors of Benetton advertising campaign. Concept and photo by O. Toscani); **Village Voice:** page 122 ad; **Virgin:** pages 130, 153.

Color photos courtesy/by: **Arnal/Urli/Garcia/Stills/Retna:** on shoulders (copyright Arnal/Urli/Garcia/Stills/Retna); **Nancy Barr-Brandon:** dancing in sweatshirt (This and hundreds of other Madonna photographs are available from Nancy Barr-Brandon, 506 Windemere Ave., Interlaken, NJ 07712, USA); **Francesco De Vincentis:** all Girlie Show performance shots; **Express News-papers/Archive Photos:** Blond Ambition basque, gold tooth/beret, and gold tooth/boa; **Steve Granitz/Retna Ltd.:** with Patric, Foley, & Ritts and in blue sari (copyright Steve Granitz/Retna Ltd.); **LFI/URO:** with Lee; **Photofest:** 1983 publicity photo, brunette bangs period look; **Monica Rebosio:** Blond Ambition polka dots; **Oliviu Savu:** limo, leopard-print coat, and smiling brunette portrait; **Shueisha, Inc.:** Japanese Playboy cover and Mitsubishi ad, copyright Shueisha, Inc.